WESTON-SUPER-MARE
AND THE
AEROPLANE
1910–2010

WESTON-SUPER-MARE
AND THE
AEROPLANE
1910–2010

ROGER DUDLEY & TED JOHNSON

AMBERLEY

First published 2010

Amberley Publishing Plc
Cirencester Road, Chalford,
Stroud, Gloucestershire, GL6 8PE

www.amberley-books.com

© Roger Dudley & Ted Johnson, 2010

The right of Roger Dudley & Ted Johnson to be identified as the
Authors of this work has been asserted in accordance with the
Copyrights, Designs and Patents Act 1988.

British Library Cataloguing in Publication Data.
A catalogue record for this book is available from the British Library.

ISBN 978 1 84868 221 4

Typesetting and Origination by Amberley Publishing.
Printed in Great Britain.

CONTENTS

*This book is dedicated to the pioneers of aviation in the West Country
and to the people and councillors of Weston-super-Mare who gave their
whole-hearted support to the development of aviation in the town.*

Reproduced with the authority of Weston-super-Mare Town Council.

FOREWORD

by

Richard T. Riding

Richard T. Riding is the son of Eddie J. Riding, the well known aeromodeller, aviation journalist and photographer who was killed in a light aircraft crash in April 1950. After many years as an aerial photographer, in 1971 Richard joined the editorial staff of *Flight International*, and in 1973 founded *Aeroplane Monthly* where he remained until early retirement in 1998. He has published several books including, in 2008, *British Seaside Piers*, and is editor of the journal of the British Piers Society.

Weston-super-Mare is best known as a popular seaside resort and was once described as the largest between Blackpool and Cornwall. Like so many seaside resorts during the nineteenth century, Weston's fortunes changed for the better with the arrival of the railway. During the next century visitors began arriving via buses, charabancs and private car, mostly from the Midlands and South Wales. Early flying machines were not uncommon over the town but Weston had to wait until the early 1930s before coming face to face with aeroplanes in any number when Sir Alan Cobham's National Aviation Day Displays gave many Weston people their first taste of flying.

In the early days Sir Alan Cobham, together with Claude Grahame-White, probably did more than anyone else to encourage air-mindedness in Britain. In addition to getting people into the air Cobham was instrumental in setting up many municipal airports all over the British Isles. After he had spread the word almost every town worth its salt wanted an airport and it was probably Cobham who inspired Norman Wallace George Edgar to set up a passenger service (Western Airways) between Bristol (Whitchurch) and Cardiff (Splott). Although only separated by twenty-two miles, the road and rail route between the two cities is much longer, both in distance and in time. Edgar realised that where time means money, flying beats surface travel hands down, particularly routes over water. Good at PR, Edgar's catchy slogan 'Save Time, Save Money — Fly Western Airways' attracted customers. The company quickly expanded and Edgar decided to shift his headquarters to Weston, managing to sweet-talk local councillors and others that such a venture would be a great benefit to the town. Work on construction of the grass airport, built on shifting sands and peat, began two miles to the south-east of the town in February 1936. Later that year Western commenced operation, joining Railway Air Services who were already operating a service from Plymouth to Bristol via Weston. Western Airways' 8-minute services across to Cardiff took off and in no time Weston was declared one of the busiest out of the thirty or so municipal airports then in existence.

In October 1938, twenty-five-year-old American millionaire Whitney Willard Straight took over Western Airways and operation of the airport. With war clouds on the horizon RAF aircraft began to outnumber the civilian occupants. The sound of Gipsy engines gave way to Cheetahs of the Ansons rebuilt by Western Airways and the unmistakeable sound of the Bristol Hercules engines of the 'Whispering Death' once shadow production of the Bristol Beaufighter eventually got moving at adjacent Oldmixon. With war production underway Weston soon attracted the attention of the Luftwaffe and these raids, occurring throughout 1941-44, are well documented. Production of the Beau continued until 1945, by which time a single 4,200-foot hard runway had been laid across the potentially boggy grass airport.

By 1946 Weston was being run by the Ministry of Civil Aviation, production of the Beaufighter had ended and Bristol was planning to assemble the mammoth Brabazon at Weston, though ultimately it was built at Filton. In the meantime the company was engaged at Weston upon the unglamorous task of turning out prefabricated bungalows for the bombed-out homeless at the rate of around 125 per week!

By the mid-1950s, Western Airways had settled down to the production of Bristol Freighters, and the Bristol Helicopter Division at Filton had moved to Oldmixon and was producing Sycamores, and what would eventually become the Belvedere and Weston skies were filled with the 'thwack thwack' of rotary wings. After Westland Aircraft took over the division in 1960 it bought and operated the airport for a time but moved out in 2000. This was not to be the end of rotary-winged activity at Weston. Elfan ap Rees, once employed by Westland's Bristol Division at Oldmixon, and a contributor to *Aeroplane Monthly* during my editorship, had an all-consuming passion for rotary-winged craft and in 1969 began collecting hardware. By 1974 he had amassed enough helicopters to form the British Rotorcraft Museum and in 1988 the museum was moved to a four-and-a-half-acre site on Weston Airport. A very successful affair, it is now known as The Helicopter Museum with more than eighty rotary-winged machines. Ap Rees' vision and hard work has resulted in a fitting memorial to one area of Weston's aviation past. I suppose the perfect memorial to Weston would be a Beaufighter, but these days it would have to be a plastic one!

It is often said that the best books are written by those who have a working knowledge of their subject. This certainly applies to the authors of this book. Being on the clerical side at Oldmixon during the time the Beaufighter was produced, co-author Ted Johnson is well placed to document that type's production at the shadow factory and his account is detailed and well told.

Similarly, co-author Roger Dudley did his apprenticeship with the Bristol Aeroplane Company at Oldmixon and was immersed in helicopter production. His record of Weston's rotary-winged activity is exhaustive.

Although I never managed to visit Weston's airport, my late father, Eddie Riding, did so on several occasions. Some of the photographs he took there in the late 1940s appear in this book. One visit was made on 4 July 1948, when he flew from Weston to Cardiff return in the Cambrian Air Services DH89A Dragon Rapide G-AKUC, piloted by a chap called Everest. As the outward journey took twenty minutes and the return trip took half the time one must assume the outward flight was made into a strong headwind! The experience cost my dad 22 shillings and 6 pence!

This book will doubtless be of particular interest to helicopter enthusiasts, the many fans of the Beaufighter, the thousands of RAF servicemen who went through their technical training at RAF Locking in addition to aviation enthusiasts countrywide and to those interested in the development of Weston Airport. This readable record of Weston's contribution to aviation is highly recommended.

ABOUT THE AUTHORS

Roger Dudley. Born in Weston-super-Mare during 1940, Roger with his father working at Western Airways at nearby Weston Airport repairing Avro Ansons, soon became accustomed to hearing about what was happening at the airport and to seeing aeroplanes constantly flying over. Spruce off-cuts from the repairs brought home for kindling were used by Roger in early attempts at making model aeroplanes and this was to develop into a life-long hobby. In 1945, Western Airways had its VE-Day party, and much to the lad's delight, for the first time he had the opportunity to climb into an aircraft, sit in the pilot's seat, handle the controls and take in that special aeroplane smell of dope, varnish, oil and aviation spirit. He was now hooked on aeroplanes! His education commenced at the kindergarten in Weston's Boulevard, but with the return of evacuees to the cities, closer-at-hand schools became less crowded and a move was made to Milton Junior School. In its elevated position there was a reasonable view of the airport, and it was easy during lapses in attentiveness to watch aeroplanes flying around rather than listen to the teacher.

However, in 1951 the whole school was allowed an official glimpse of an aeroplane when all were ushered out into the playground to see the Bristol Brabazon, the world's largest aeroplane, fly over at low altitude. That year a move was made to Worle Secondary Modern School. Like many other budding aviators, it was in a DH Dragon Rapide at Weston Airport that Roger had his first flight, and it took him and his dad across the Bristol Channel to Cardiff's Pengam Moors Airport. Once trusted to go off on his pushbike unaccompanied, visits to the airport became possible and frequent. The sound of powerful aero-engines being run-up gave early warning of aircraft activity, and a short ride with binoculars and camera to Milton Crescent, where his partner in crime Mike lived, and from where there was an excellent view of the airport, gave visual indication of what was happening. It was then a rush down to the Borough Arms, over the two humpback bridges of Locking Moor Road to the airport. From a roadside concrete pillbox aircraft activity was observed, with sometimes the airport manager being asked if photographs could be taken of a particular aeroplane. Gliders belonging to the Air Training Corps (ATC) were also seen. After what appeared to be a frighteningly steep winch-launch, they were steered around the airport to arrive back near the take-off point. Quite often the instructor's voice could be clearly heard giving orders to the pupil as he wrestled with the controls — 'keep the wings level', 'watch the speed', 'I have control!!' Was learning to fly going to be that difficult? When sixteen years old, Roger would find out, for by now he was a member of the ATC, and after the necessary experience had been gained, he would instruct cadets in those same open-cockpit machines.

In 1955, at the start of an apprenticeship with the Bristol Aeroplane Company at Weston's Oldmixon Factory, there was basic training at Filton, after which there were periods in Oldmixon's Detail Fitting Shop and a spell in the flight sheds where new developments and airport activities could be observed. The delights of helicopters were also experienced, flying in a Sycamore and a Type 173 tandem-rotor machine. When transferred to the staff, a window position in the prototype AIROH prefab school building permitted continued observation of aircraft taking off and landing. 1960 saw the factory taken over by Westland and in early 1963 he was transferred to the company headquarters at Yeovil. Although this meant contact with Weston being reduced, other opportunities in and around Yeovil were opened up. In due course, this would mean obtaining a Private Pilots Licence and gliding and aero-towing at RN Yeovilton's Heron Gliding Club. There was also the acquisition of pre-war Tipsy 'B' Trainer G-AISC by the company's newly formed Westland Wagtail Flying Group. The person responsible for obtaining this delightful aeroplane was one Harald Penrose, who as Westland's chief test pilot, in 1952 inadvertently provided boys at Worle School with some excitement when he belly-landed a Wyvern not far away. The little red-and-white Tipsy with Roger at the controls, from its home at Compton Abbas, and later Henstridge, would also for a time be a fairly frequent visitor to Weston Airport.

Marrying Kerrie, who was also a glider pilot, and with the family's association with aeroplanes, it was probably not much of a surprise when their two sons decided to follow father into the aircraft industry. Although managing to escape to Twyford Moors Helicopters for a time, Roger returned to Westland where, until retiring to Dorset in 2000, he was responsible for the preparation of the company's aircrew publications. Until the onslaught of miniature radio-controlled model helicopters a few years ago, Roger had also been an avid designer of free-flight model helicopters, and had over the years several articles and plans published in the international model press. These days, contact with Weston Airport is still maintained through being a volunteer at The Helicopter Museum, and it was through this association with the museum that, during preparation of an exhibition celebrating the airport's seventy years of existence, he was lucky enough to meet co-author Ted Johnson. Ted, amongst other things, introduced added impetus to a book project on Weston's aviation heritage started by Roger in 1994, and provided hitherto unknown information on various military aviation activities and wartime development at the airport and its Bristol-run aircraft factories.

Ted Johnson. Born in Sydney, Australia, Ted came to Weston-super-Mare in 1932 and attended Christ Church Junior School where, in 1936, a scholarship to attend Weston County School for Boys was obtained. Here began a keen interest and association with aviation when No.159 Squadron of the Air Defence Cadet Corps was formed, later to become the Air Training Corps. In the cadets, Ted had his first air-experience flight at Lulsgate Bottom and during his cadet service progressed from cadet to flight sergeant. Leaving school in 1941, he was keen to join the Royal Air Force and volunteered for aircrew duties in 1942, but in the meantime he began working as a subcontracts clerk at the Bristol Aeroplane Company's Weston aircraft factory at Oldmixon. He was principally tasked with the paperwork related to the regular flow of modifications to the Beaufighters and this gave him opportunities to liaise with production engineers and visit some of the subcontractors involved including Standard Motors, Riley and Singer in Coventry. With some help from his manager Ted also had the occasional very exciting test flight in a Beaufighter and later a Beaufort with test pilot Ronnie Ellison.

Call-up finally came in July 1944 and, after the usual induction training in London and Torquay, Ted completed ITW at Bridgnorth as a U/T bomb aimer. There then began a wait for a posting to Bombing and Gunnery School, but with the end of the war on the horizon this never came, and in 1945 it became a question of whether to commit to signing on for further aircrew training as pilot or navigator, or re-mustering to a ground trade. Ted chose to become a flight mechanic (engines) and with a course completed at RAF Melksham he found himself to be categorised as one who knew a bit about Beaufighters and its Hercules engines. First posting was to the Radar Research Establishment aerodrome at Defford in Worcestershire and then to the RWE at Watton in Norfolk, both stations with many types of aircraft but a Weston-built Beaufighter was 'his' aeroplane. Next it was a posting overseas and, after a somewhat circuitous journey by sea and rail via Singapore and India, Ted arrived at RAF Negombo, Ceylon and 45 Squadron with its full complement of Weston-built Beaufighter Xs. In addition to the daily duties there were opportunities for some flying and this included a detachment to Trincomalee in the north-east where the squadron, flying from the China Bay airfield, took part in exercises with units of the Royal Navy.

Leaving the RAF in late 1947 Ted joined brother George in operating a small metal finishing business in the town but, on getting married to a local girl who had also worked at the Weston Aircraft Factory, deciding to obtain more experience in the trade, moved to Birmingham as a technician with R. Cruickshank Ltd, a company supplying plating equipment and processes to electroplaters and engineers. Promoted to area manager in the north of England and then London he was headhunted by Efco, another metal finishing supplier who would in due course become part of the American Occidental Group of companies engaged in chemical manufacture and North Sea oil. He became sales manager of the Oxy Metal Finishing Division but after twelve years with the group, the West Country called and Ted and his family returned to Somerset.

Taking over the management of a small electroplating company in Bath, Ted found he had a little more time on his hands and decided to complete his flying training, and in due course, with the assistance and patience of instructors of the Bristol Flying School at Lulsgate, got his Private Pilot's Licence in 1992. Ted was also actively engaged with the Bristol Aero Collection at that time, and was chairman in its early days and continues to support its efforts, whilst as a member of the Rolls-Royce Heritage Trust he has received tremendous help from them in putting together details of the Bristol Aeroplane Company's Weston aircraft factories. Following semi-retirement in 1990 Ted, now a fellow of the Institute of Metal Finishing, took on a part-time role as technical manager with RACO Ltd (now Nu-Pro Surface Treatments) at Stroud, a company specialising in the finishing of aircraft components, and this provided involvement with many of the major aviation companies including British Aerospace, Rolls-Royce, Dowty and Smiths Instruments. For a short time Ted was employed by another Metal Finishing Company, again with major customers in the Aircraft Industry, South West Metal Finishing of Exeter and its Bristol subsidiary Neptune Plating Ltd.

Now fully retired and living in Weston with his wife, his daughter and four grandsons living nearby, Ted decided that he would like to record what he knew of his time with the Bristol Aeroplane Company's Weston Aircraft Factory at Oldmixon, and this brought about a meeting with co-author Roger Dudley who was already well underway recording the various historic events associated with aviation in and around Weston.

GLOSSARY

AA	Anti Aircraft
AAC	Army Air Corps
A&AEE	Aeroplane and Armament Experimental Establishment
AFCS	Automatic Flight Control System
AI	Airborne Interception
AID	Aeronautical Inspection Directorate
AIROH	Aircraft Industries Research Organisation for Housing
AMSL	Above Mean Sea Level
AOC	Air Officer Commanding
ARP	Air Raid Precautions
ASI	Airspeed Indicator
ASR	Air Sea Rescue
AST	Air Staff Target
ASV	Air-to-Surface Vessel
ATA	Air Transport Auxiliary
ATC	Air Training Corps
AUW	All-Up Weight
BBC	British Broadcasting Corporation
BEAC	British European Airways Corporation
BOAC	British Overseas Airways Corporation
CAA	Civil Aviation Authority
CA Release	Controller Aircraft Release
Category 4/Category 5	A repair, due to the damage involved, contracted to the constructor's works for action
CFI	Chief Flying Instructor
CG	Centre of Gravity
C of A	Certificate of Airworthiness
CRO	Civilian Repair Organisation
DTD	Directorate of Technical Development
FAA	Fleet Air Arm

F/F	First flight
GWR	Great Western Railway
HT	High Tension
IPN	Iso-propyl-nitrate (AVPIN)
ITF	Interim Torpedo Fighter
ITW	Initial Training Wing
MAP	Ministry of Aircraft Production
MCA	Ministry of Civil Aviation
MoA	Ministry of Aviation
MoD	Ministry of Defence
MoS	Ministry of Supply
MU	Maintenance Unit
NCO	Non-Commissioned Officer
POW	Prisoner of War
RAE	Royal Aircraft Establishment
RAAF	Royal Australian Air Force
RAF	Royal Air Force
RAFVR(T)	Royal Air Force Volunteer Reserve (Training)
RCAF	Royal Canadian Air Force
RFC	Royal Flying Corps
Rhyne	A term used in North Somerset to denote a ditch
RLG	Relief Landing Ground
RN	Royal Navy
RNAS	Royal Naval Air Service
R/T	Radio Telephone
RWE	Radio Warfare Establishment
SAR	Search and Rescue
SoTT	School of Technical Training
TA	Territorial Army
TDU	Torpedo Development Unit
UAS	University Air Squadron
USAAF	United States Army Air Force
WAAF	Women's Auxiliary Air Force
WIPL	Westland Industrial Products Ltd

INTRODUCTION

"Probably no seaside resort affords better facilities for aviators than Weston-super-Mare, included in the advantage being the fact that it is separated by but 12 (nautical) miles of sea from the Welsh coast, thereby permitting of some very interesting cross channel flights." These were the words of Mr S. S. Jacobs, Honorary Secretary of the Weston-super-Mare Carnival Committee as reported in the *Weston Mercury & Somersetshire Herald* of 11 June 1910, and came following a flight on 7 June by 23-year-old Ernest Thompson Willows, in an airship of his own design named *Willows II*, from East Moors near Cardiff, to Cardiff City Hall. East Moors was only a stone's throw away from what in 1931 would become Cardiff's Splott (later Pengam Moors) Airport. The flight gained considerable publicity on both sides of the Bristol Channel, and caused Mr Jacobs to write to Willows endeavouring to persuade him to fly across the Channel to Weston, where a landing area would be made available to

Willows hovers his small airship alongside Cardiff City Hall in early June 1910

receive the aviator and his craft. In fact, on 13 June, Willows did visit Weston to discuss the flight and the possibility of setting up a cross-channel airship passenger service. In the event, the flight to Weston didn't happen for a number of reasons including weather, financial constraints and significantly the flyer's commitments. Subsequently, on the evening of 6 August, Willows did cross the Channel, overflying Clevedon (9 miles [14.5 km] to the north of Weston), on his way to London. Whilst there he gave demonstration flights, and having room for two passengers gave a few lucky individuals sight-seeing flights over the city. In November, in a later variant of the airship named *Willows III*, to the great pleasure of large crowds including government ministers, Willows set out from London to Paris where the Eiffel Tower was circled. These events gave support to the views of Weston's dignitaries that aviation could be employed to attract greater numbers of visitors to the town, and much thought was to be given in the following years as to how this might be achieved. As time would tell, Weston-super-Mare, as Mr Jacobs had predicted, would become increasingly associated with aviators, their machines and the Principality of Wales.

1

THE ADVENTURING YEARS

In the Beginning

Before the coming of the railway, Weston-super-Mare was little more than a fishing village on the Somerset coast. Although its seaside location and stretch of golden sand attracted visitors, because of the lack of transport most were only from the nearby towns and villages. However, this position of semi-isolation started to change in 1841 when Brunel completed the railway line between Bristol and Bridgwater, and provided a branch from the line into Weston that used three 4-wheel horse-drawn passenger carriages. A terminus for passengers was opened in 1866 but it and the branch line closed in 1884 when a loop line and a station were brought into the town's centre. Rail facilities were further improved in 1914 when a passenger terminus was provided alongside Locking Road that was intended to exclusively handle excursion trains. By this time the town and beach areas were also served by an electric tramway which had been up and running since 1902, and the Locking Road railway terminus was conveniently on its route. Also, since 1897 a standard gauge railway known as The Weston, Clevedon & Portishead Light Railway had existed between Weston and Clevedon, and by 1907 would be extended northwards to Portishead. By then visitors were also coming to Weston by bus and charabanc and from the late 1920s, arrived at an impressive covered Bristol Tramways & Carriage Company's Beach Garage and Bus Station on the seafront.

The new railway systems now provided prospective visitors to Weston with low-cost and convenient access to the town and they arrived in their thousands on cheap day excursions from Bristol, the Midlands and even further afield. But the railway found less favour with South Wales residents since they had good beaches nearer home and to reach Weston the Severn Estuary had to be crossed well up-river. A more attractive alternative, however, especially on Sundays when alcohol was not freely available in Wales, was the crossing on board the splendid paddle steamers of the P & A Campbell White Funnel Fleet. The many visitors and their activities boosted the town's finances and provided good job opportunities for the locals. The seafront area was developed, new hotels, cafés and shops were built as were houses to meet the needs of the growing population. But on the downside, although during the summer months there was no shortage of work for Westonians, out of season many found themselves jobless as there was little industry nearer than Bristol where some did manage to find full employment.

One with similar insight to Messrs Jacobs and Willows, mentioned in the introduction, was Mr E. Baker, secretary of the Grand Pier Company Ltd. In January 1909, he had distributed an Air Ship Company prospectus to eminent entrepreneurs, its aim to form a board of directors to operate passenger-carrying airships from the 1,500-foot-long (457 metres) extension to the Grand Pier. The structure, known locally as the New Pier, went far out into Weston Bay so that paddle steamers plying in the Bristol Channel could berth in deep water. Built to take trade away from Birnbeck Pier, a mile (1.6 km) to the north and known locally as the Old Pier, the extension became redundant after having received only four ships. Its demise had been brought about by the strong tides and currents that made it extremely difficult and dangerous to bring vessels alongside its jetties. One can well imagine, had the Air Ship Company plan progressed, the difficulties and hazards of handling a lighter-than-air machine in the gusty conditions experienced offshore.

The *Weston Mercury & Somersetshire Herald*, later commenting on the Willows flight, gave its views and stated, 'There can be no disputing the fact that the selection of the town for aerial flights constitutes an incomparably more potent advertisement than any other form, with a deal of foresight and ready apprehension many towns and watering places have appropriated the airship as a most fruitful source of advertisement, several such towns were little known or not known at all until the flying men made their appearance in them'. The scene was now set for Weston to welcome the Aviator and his Machine.

Visits by Pioneering Aviators

With Jacobs having failed to attract Willows and his airship to Weston, in 1910, Mr J. H. Stevenson, manager of the Grand Pier Company, had success in inviting another aviator, Colonel Samuel Franklin Cody (his real surname was Cowdery!), to the town to give a lecture on the new science of aviation. Recognised as having made the first powered flight in Britain, Cody was one of the most famous people of the time and, following his lecture in the Grand Pier Pavilion, he received a tremendous reception. His lecture included a dissertation on the benefits of aviation and how events might be set up to attract the crowds with the sands providing a ready-made landing and spectator area.

In the following year, Cody, a competitor in the *Daily Mail* Circuit of Britain air race, took off on Saturday 22 July from Brooklands in his mighty but slow 'Cody Cathedral' biplane. This was a very testing course of 1,010 miles (1,625 km). The route ranged from Edinburgh in the north to Exeter in the south-west and the newspaper had offered £10,000 to the first aviator to complete the

An excited crowd marvels at Cody's 'Cathedral' biplane on Weston Sands 3 August 1911 (From the collection of North Somerset Museum)

flight in an airborne time of under twenty-four hours. Towards the end of the course, on Thursday 3 August, Cody left Filton with Exeter the next official stop. Due to poor weather and an alternative motive, he was about to become the first to land an aeroplane at Weston. Flying at an airspeed of 56 mph (90 kph), he battled doggedly through the very strong and turbulent westerly wind, taking 1 hour 5 minutes to cover the 25 miles (40 km). Approaching from over Worle, he swept the machine in low over Weston Gasworks before flying carefully through a multitude of kites flown by children on the beach. Touching down at 8.15 p.m. on the sands opposite the Grand Atlantic Hotel, he was greeted, not unexpectedly, by an enthusiastic crowd of holidaymakers and residents.

Although Cody was still continuing, the race had already been completed nine days before by Frenchmen Jules Vedrines in a Morane-Borel monoplane and Andre Beaumont in a Bleriot XI monoplane, who had arrived back at Brooklands on Wednesday 26 July. These two machines could have been seen by early risers at about 6 a.m. on that day, chasing each other as they followed the GWR line down from Bristol to Exeter, the next official stop for rest and refuelling. This was the first time that a Westonian would have seen an aeroplane flying locally. If this exciting event had been missed, there was a chance to see the third of the remaining competitors a week later on Wednesday 2 August at 7.15 a.m. when a Briton, James Valentine, in a French Duperdussin Type B passed low over Uphill Church, also on his way to Exeter.

Just off the Grand Pier, the *Daily Mail's* Henri Farman 'Waterplane' in August 1912 being supported in its operation by Weston's pleasure boats (*Weston Mercury* via J. Bailey)

Because of pilot fatigue, crashes, structural failures and engine problems, Cody was now fourth and last of the thirty entrants that had started the race at Brooklands. Although he was still determined to complete the course, he had elected to take advantage of an overnight stay in Weston to further the cause of aviation in the town. Although arriving unannounced, Cody had taken the precaution of phoning the local police to see if they could receive him and possibly provide a guard for his aeroplane. With an eye on publicity, Mr Stevenson had also been phoned by Cody who was now giving him another opportunity to further his reputation and standing in the community. Before leaving his machine a short appreciative speech was given to the crowd, and then Mr Stevenson escorted Cody to the nearby Queens Hotel where he was wined and dined and would stay the night. It was then onto the Grand Pier Pavilion where, as with his previous visit, an address was given to an excited crowd on his latest thoughts on how to further aviation in Britain. Meanwhile, the biplane was being refuelled with petrol and oil obtained from Mr C. M. House of Messrs Warrilow & Co. of Oxford Street and an airscrew, damaged in a forced landing several days before, was receiving the attention of Mr E. A. Beisley, a local carpenter and joiner.

Early next morning, at just before 3 a.m., the machine was wheeled down to firm sand, and at first light its engine was started and warmed. There were well over 7,000 people on the beach to see him on his way with many having stayed there all night. Cody's first attempt at taking off had to be aborted when people got in the way, but at the second attempt he managed to lift off and, in just over two minutes, was out of sight. Arriving at Exeter shortly after 5 a.m., it was then on to Salisbury Plain (Larkhill), although due to compass problems, he landed first at Hanham (Bristol). After Larkhill, it was Brighton (Shoreham) and finally Brooklands which was reached on the evening of Saturday 5 August. Cody received much acclaim for his determination in completing the race as his was the only British machine to finish, it having been designed, built, financed and supported by Cody alone, whereas most of the other entrants were supported by a factory team.

Later that month, another noted aviator Benny C. Hucks, a pilot employed by Blackburn to test its aeroplanes and also a competitor in the *Daily Mail* Circuit of Britain and the first British aviator to loop-the-loop, flew into Weston, landing in Mayled's Field in a Blackburn Mercury monoplane. Between the end of Hughenden Road and the tram terminus on Locking Road, and about a mile (1.6 km) from the town centre, the field had been named for the occasion the 'Aviation Ground'. The visit lasted for over a week, during which time Hucks made history on 1 September by making the first crossing of the Bristol Channel by aeroplane. With a borrowed cork lifejacket stowed in the cockpit and a motorboat stationed in mid-channel, he set off at 5.10 a.m. in calm conditions and had soon disappeared over Worlebury Hill, to return forty minutes later having demonstrated the huge advantage in time saved by using the aeroplane for cross-channel excursions. This trip also fulfilled a long-held desire of Hucks to see his home town of Cardiff from the air. During the week, Hucks made further demonstration flights from the Aviation Ground, with the public, on payment of 1s (5p), being admitted to see the aeroplane at close quarters and talk to the pilot.

26 June 1912 saw the next arrival, when Monsieur Henri Salmet, a noted French aviator, came in from Taunton and landed his Bleriot monoplane on Clarence School playing field, only weeks after becoming the first to fly from London to Paris and back in one day. Subsequently, he also flew across the channel to Cardiff. On Monday 4 May 1914, Salmet was due to visit Weston again, but after setting out from Minehead, his engine failed when passing Daws Castle and the aircraft had to be ditched about a mile (1.6 km) from shore. A boat launched from Watchet rescued the pilot and his passenger, Mr Van Trump of Taunton, and the machine was salvaged by the Norwegian steamer *Drafn*.

For August 1912, an event had been organised by the Weston Town Advertising and Entertainments Committee in conjunction with the *Daily Mail*. It was hoped that this would really bring in the crowds on the many special excursion trains laid on in the Midlands and several southern counties. It was to be staged on the sands between Saturday 10 and Tuesday 13 August, and a Henri Farman 3-seat floatplane, known for the occasion as the *Daily Mail Waterplane*, was to be brought in to give passenger flights from an extension on the south side of the Grand Pier. At night, the frail machine was to be housed in the *Daily Mail* hangar, a temporary structure on the sands protected by the wall of the Sanatorium. Although many took advantage of the railway excursions, difficulties created mainly by adverse weather conditions allowed pilots Messieurs Fisher and Hubert to make only a few flights. One on Tuesday ended prematurely, when the failure of the aircraft's Gnome rotary engine over the town required a hasty about turn with a resulting heavy landing on the water. On other days, the waves were often high and caution had to be exercised when attempting to take off, as spray whipped up by the floats slicing through the choppy water on occasions stopped the machine's engine.

Captain E. R. Prestridge also arrived by floatplane at the end of the month and, after landing, had the machine pulled across the sands up to the wall of the Sanatorium, covered, then weighed down with sandbags. The captain was making a circuit of Britain and stopping off at different watering places where the beaches were suitable and he could rely on bathers and paddlers for assistance. He also made other flights to Weston where there were always eager helpers ready to move his floatplane to and from the water's edge.

Civil flying ceased at the outbreak of the Great War and, for its duration, people living in and around Weston seldom saw an aeroplane. Those that were observed were from the nearby British and Colonial Aeroplane Company at Filton and Parnalls of Yate where aircraft were being built for the Royal Flying Corps. They were also being built at Yeovil where, from 1915, Petters, with its oil-engine manufacturing business at its new Westland Aircraft Works, diversified and started the construction of mainly floatplanes for the Admiralty. Other than the normal war-work, probably the greatest contribution Weston made to the aviation industry in the war years was the supply of ash for airframes, obtained from Weston Woods.

Visits by Joy-riding Outfits

When official clearance was given at Easter 1919 to restart civil flying, many slightly modified wartime training aeroplanes started to appear in the hands of joy-riding outfits. On hearing of this new form of entertainment that would obviously be a big draw in attracting more visitors to the town, Weston Urban District Town Council eager to participate opened up for tender a licence for passenger-carrying aeroplanes to operate from the sands. Two organisations responded: Avro Joy-riders under the direction of Lieutenant-Colonel G. L. Henderson MC, AFC ex-RAF, a part of the aircraft manufactures A. V. Roe & Co. Ltd of Hamble; and a Mr C. H. Sturley who ran the Warwick Aeroplane Company of Birmingham.

The highest tender came from the Avro outfit which was also holding negotiations with several other town councils to fly its small fleet of Avros during the summer months from their beaches. In addition to giving joy-rides around Weston, the company also intended to operate excursions to Bristol

One of the Avros on 'The Sands Aerodrome' with Weston Golf Club's clubhouse in the background, 18 September 1919 (From the collection of Weston Library)

The Warwick Aeroplane Company's Airco DH6 that was operated from Brean Down Farm during the summer of 1919 (From the collection of Weston Library)

and, on the other side of the Bristol Channel, to Barry and Cardiff. The licence fee of £50 duly changed hands, allowing A. V. Roe's aircraft to be operated from 300 sq. yards (274 sq. metres) of sand near the Sanatorium. From then on, this became officially known as The Sands Aerodrome. With its lower tender, a less desirable flying area had to be accepted by the Warwick Aeroplane Company and, although within sight of the Sands Aerodrome, it was on the far side of the River Axe on a part of Brean Down Farm, reached from Weston by foot via the River Axe ferry crossing at Uphill. Smaller than the A. V. Roe set-up, it only had two machines; the one at Weston being Airco DH6 G-EAHI (ex-C6889) powered by an American Curtiss OX-5 and it offered flights for 10s 6d (52.5p).

Having secured the licence to operate, Flight Lieutenant Nelson Appleford DSO, an ex-RFC pilot, was hired by A. V. Roe and made manager of the Weston Station with its headquarters in the town at 17 St Pauls Road. Machines allocated to the station were a 5-seat Avro 536 G-EAGM, still wearing its wartime markings K-161, and G-EAKB (ex-H2588) a 4-seat Avro 504K. Appleford was to be assisted by another ex-RFC pilot Captain Denis G. Westgarth Haslam and a couple of young volunteer ground crew. Adverts were placed in the local newspapers offering 'popular flights' daily at £1 1s (£1.05) per head, the intention being to start operations during the forthcoming August bank holiday. In fact, flying started during the last week in July and, despite the high price of a ride, the Avros were kept very busy. This was especially so during the holiday period when there were long queues of people, the majority often being women waiting to experience the thrill and excitement of becoming airborne.

Most take-offs were towards the River Axe with Brean Down being overflown, and it was during the evening of Thursday 28 August that Westgarth Haslam, in another Avro G-EAAN (ex-E4225) with a naval officer and his wife as passengers, experienced an engine failure over the Down. Selecting Brean Down Meadows for the forced landing, the aircraft, at the end of its landing run nosed-over into a rhyne, leaving its tail high in the air. Luckily nobody was injured. The field chosen for the landing happened to be close to the strip used by the Warwick Aeroplane Company's operation and Mr Sturley wasted no time in announcing to the public via the press that it wasn't one of its machines that had been involved in the incident. Meanwhile, the London office of A. V. Roe, seeing how popular joy-riding was becoming, formed the Avro Transport Company at Southport and engaged as its Air Transport Manager (Civilian Flying Section) 32-year-old ex-RFC pilot Brigadier-General Charles F. Lee. He lived at Stoke Court, Taunton, and a part of his duties was to visit the various southern stations.

It was whilst at the Weston Station on Monday 1 September that the brigadier-general in his position of authority insisted on taking up G-EAGM for a test flight. Its rotary engine had just been refitted after overhaul and although ground-run for an hour, it had not been test-flown. With the two ground crew volunteers on board acting as ballast, the aircraft took off at 7 p.m. heading towards the River Axe. After completing a left turn to take it over the golf links, the engine spluttered and backfired three times, indicating to the two pilots watching from below that an over-rich mixture was being used. The machine, now at some 200 feet (61 metres), appeared to lose flying speed. It then dropped a wing, entered a spin and disappeared from view behind the sand dunes. The Avro had come down near the second green approximately 150 feet (46 metres) from the clubhouse, narrowly missing two golfers, and was badly smashed, with the nose and port wing having taken most of the impact. The pilot, thrown clear, was unfortunately dead, and both crewmen still in the wreckage were injured, one seriously. Luckily for the company, although this was witnessed by hundreds of visitors, as it was the end of the season and with no fare-paying passengers onboard, the accident was given minimal publicity. A. V. Roe again came to Weston in 1920 for the summer season, this time operating its 504Ks from Brean Down Farm. It is believed that G-EAAN was used initially, but following an accident was withdrawn and replaced by a similar type of aircraft.

In the early 1920s, the Essex Aviation Company, operated by owner-pilot Frank T. Neale, also gave joy-rides from Brean Down Farm using Avro 504K G-AEBCK. In the late 1920s, Avro 504Ks continued to be used for joy-riding from the Weston area by owner-pilot Captain W. Jordan of Western Aviation of Cheltenham. Another similar one-man-band joy-riding organisation was Taxiplanes Ltd of Clevedon. It had a DH51 G-EBIQ with a specially enlarged cockpit to carry two passengers, and, from August 1928 to 1931, it was flown in the summer from a designated area on Brean Down, taking up passengers from 5s (25p) per head for a loop over Weston. As with previous operations this one was not without incidents, for, during the evening of 27 August 1929, the machine, with two young ladies on board, went into a rhyne whilst being taxied across the field by owner-pilot Sidney Clarke. In this case the large 4-bladed airscrew and the undercarriage were damaged and one of the passengers unfortunately ended up in hospital. The flying site was reached from Weston by charabanc, bus, or on foot via the River Axe ferry crossing at Uphill.

By May 1929, the number of aircraft on the British register was 130, many being the treasured possessions of the landed gentry. One such owner was Edward Matthias Tiarks, the elder son of Frank C. Tiarks, a director of the Bank of England, who lived with his family at Webbington House, Loxton, near Weston. Edward, a member of the Wessex Aero Club which, at that time, operated from the Bristol Aeroplane Company's Filton Aerodrome, had purchased a DH60M Moth G-AAHB and kept it at Priddy Kennels on the Mendips. He was also a keen motorist and had recently gained publicity by driving an old car to the summit of Crook Peak, one of the prominent points on the Mendip Hills. Having had the Moth for just four months, on Monday 23 September 1929, Edward was to fly a weekend guest, Edward Somerset, a well-known sportsman and relative of the Duke of Beaufort, to Filton to catch a train. This was a regular trip with a few miles of the route following the railway line near Hambrook. Leaving Priddy at 3.30 p.m., the attraction of seeing a passenger train on the line seemed to have been an opportunity too good to be missed. Eyewitnesses said they had seen the Moth 'beat-up' the train, then stall and crash. Wreckage was scattered over a wide area and, regrettably, the two occupants, hurled some 60 yards (55 metres), were fatally injured. There was an added pathos to the crash in that it had occurred within 100 yards (91 metres) of the spot where the famous Kings Cup airman Captain Frank Barnard had lost his life on 28 July 1927 when testing the Bristol Badminton racer G-EBMK. Around that time other machines were also being test flown in the locality. On 27 January 1930 the 709-foot-long (216.1metre), 130-foot-diameter (39.6-metre) Vickers airship R100 droned slowly over Weston at about 1,000 feet (305 metres), part-way through its manufacturer's 54-hour acceptance trial. And it was seen again on the 29th near the end of its flight as it headed up the Channel towards Bristol and thence Cardington.

On Tuesday 24 June 1930, Cornwall Aviation Co. Ltd, based at St Austell and notable in that during its previous seven years it had safely carried 75,000 passengers, opened for the summer season at Weston. The field selected for the operation was next to the second bridge on Hutton Moor Lane, and only a 5-minute walk from the Locking Road tram terminus. Preparing the field, which was to become known as Locking Road Aerodrome, had started two months previously and some 1,000 tons (1,016 tonnes) of soil had been used to level it. The company had wanted to operate from the Sands Aerodrome but complaints of engine noise from previous operations interfering with Sunday church services had stopped permission being given. The season opened at 5 p.m. when several thousand people jammed the narrow lane to pay 6d (2.5p) to see the company's pilot, Captain H. Lawson DFC, in a scarlet Avro 504K give a display of 'crazy flying' which included wing-walking and inverted flying. Following the display, and until the end of the season, joy-riding flights could be had every day from 9 a.m. until dusk for 5s (25p) upwards. Looping flights were 15s (75p) and full stunts were by special arrangement. To ensure prospective customers could easily get to the field for a flight, the company offered a motor car to pick up from anywhere in town. The following year, at the end of June, the company returned, again operating from Locking Road Aerodrome, but this time the pilot was Captain Edward Duncan Crundall, a Great War double-ace fighter pilot.

Over the previous two years, business had been brisk at Weston, and in 1931, the company again requested permission to return. With the Locking Road Aerodrome being some distance from the town's centre and beach, another attempt was made to gain access to the Sands Aerodrome, but again to no avail, so it was back to the old venue. As in the previous year, Crundall was pilot and, ironically, just before 7 p.m. on Sunday 6 September, whilst flying over the town with two young passengers on a 10s (50p) trip, the Avro's engine spluttered, emitted black smoke and stopped, luckily within gliding distance of the beach.

Crundall touched down opposite Clarence Road North but some 200 yards (185 metres) below the high-water mark and the machine's wheels sank through the thin crust of sand into the mud below. The rapid deceleration caused the tail to rise until the fuselage was vertical where it remained for a moment, when the passengers, not being secured to the cockpit, were catapulted into the mud as the aeroplane flipped over onto its back. None of the occupants were hurt, but with the tide on its way in there was a frantic rush to de-rig the machine and move it to a safe position. There was much adverse publicity following the event which had been witnessed by many holidaymakers. In the company's defence, it was stated that it had been the first such occurrence with passengers at Weston, where in the two seasons there had been up to fifty flights a day.

The 'Circus' Comes to Town

It was in 1931 that Weston began to see the type of aerial entertainment long desired by the town's dignitaries to attract visitors, when the 'Circus came to Town'. Lasting for a period of only seven years, a collection of highly colourful aeroplanes and pilots belonging to various new 'Circus' organisations toured the length and breadth of the British Isles bringing aviation to the general public. Like the conventional travelling circus, such as Bertram Mills, its members led a largely nomadic life living in tents and vans and having to move the circus' equipment some 60 miles (97 km) a day on narrow winding roads to the next venue. This included a petrol bowser, the public-address system and the non-flying personnel that looked after catering, laundry, stores, site cleaning, private policing, publicity and ticket/programme sales.

The first circus to come to Weston was C. D. Barnard Air Tours Ltd. Described as 'The World's First Air Circus' it arrived early Friday 26 June from Redruth, approximately half way round a tour of some 118 towns in the British Isles. Operating from the Sands Aerodrome, admission was free and flying commenced at 11 a.m. when for 5s (25p) joy-rides could be had with Captain Charles Douglas Barnard in his famous Fokker F.VIIA G-EBTS 12-seat, the *Spider*, in which he, with the Duchess of Bedford, had recently carried out several record-breaking long-distance flights. Interestingly, in July this aircraft, flown by Captain Barnard, would be used on an experimental Bristol (Whitchurch) Airport — Cardiff (Splott) Airport passenger service. In the company's advertising, prominence was given to its work in encouraging development of aviation in the youth of Britain, and, with this in mind, for one lucky boy in each town who visited a show, there was a chance to win a flying scholarship and be taught to fly free of charge.

Flying displays watched by thousands were given at 2 p.m. and 6 p.m. and included demonstrations by Cierva C19 Autogiro G-AAYP, the 'Windmill Plane', flown by Captain Reggie Brie, while Leonard H. Stace flew the scarlet Red Herring Sports Avian G-AAXH. There were also aerobatic displays by

Captains Edward D. Ayre and F. S. Crossley in two 3-seat Spartans, one of which had wireless telephony and was used to give the trainee pilot flying lessons with instructions and responses broadcast to the crowd via a massive loudspeaker. There was also 'An Amusing Interlude' when famous comedians Clapham and Dwyer, know to everyone from their BBC wireless broadcasts, were taken aloft for 'A Stunt Trip' and their reactions were described to the crowd below via the wireless telephony.

Thursday 25 August 1932 saw the first visit to the town of the National Aviation Day Ltd Display. More commonly known as Cobham's Flying Circus, it had been formed earlier in the year by Sir Alan Cobham, a greatly respected aviator. For some unexplained reason the venue chosen was a large field just to the north of the town at Woodspring Priory, Sand Bay, rather than the more central Sands Aerodrome. Two air displays, one at 2.30 p.m. and the other at 5.30 p.m., consisting of twenty events, were watched by thousands who paid 1s 3d (6.2p) per adult and 6d (2.5p) per child to enter the field. Many others watched for free from along Sand Bay Beach and on top of Worlebury Hill. The fleet comprised fifteen aircraft, amongst them two new 10-seat Airspeed Ferrys G-ABSI and G-ABSJ designed especially for Cobham, Cierva C19 Autogiro G-ABGB, a DH Gipsy Moth, a DH Tiger Moth fitted with a fuel system for inverted flying, an all-red Avro 2-seater, a silver Avro 3-seater, a three-seat Desoutter G-AANE, a Spartan 2-seater and a BAC glider. There was also a DH Fox Moth flown by Captain H. Lawson and an Avro 504K flown by Captain Crundall, both of whom had previously done summer joy-riding seasons at Weston with the Cornwall Aviation Co. Ltd.

This impressive line-up of aircraft began the show with all in the air together. Then there were aerobatics by Flight Lieutenant Turner-Hughes, wing-walking by Martin Hearn, balloon-bursting by Charles Bebb firing a revolver from the cockpit of the Gipsy Moth, aerobatics by Lowe Wylde in the glider that had been auto-towed up to height, a parachute descent from 2,000 feet (610 metres) by Ivor Price, flour-bag bombing and a triangular-course air race. There was also joy-riding in most display aircraft starting at 4s (20p), and trial lessons. That evening, Sir Alan addressed a meeting of the local rotary club when he took the opportunity to press home to those present the importance of every large town such as Weston having its own municipal airport that would help boost British trade both internally and internationally, provide jobs, and make the British people, especially the youngsters, air-minded. Next day the circus left for Taunton. In that year, the circus would visit 170 towns.

Early in 1933, Jimmy McEwan King and Henry A. C. G. Barker announced their intention of organising a new display team using expertise gained when employed the previous year by Cobham National Aviation Day Ltd. The new outfit, named 'British Hospitals Air Pageant Ltd' was set up in direct opposition to Cobham, supposedly to provide funds for hospitals in the towns to be visited on their proposed tour of the British Isles. As a means of countering this new competition Cobham decided to split his 1933 tour into two.

Number 1 tour was to be managed by Sir Alan and visit venues on the country's easterly side, and Number 2 tour, run by his general manager Major Dallas L. Eskell, would look after the country's westerly side. On Friday 19 May, Number 2 tour, with twelve aircraft, arrived in Weston at the Sands Aerodrome and set about publicising itself with formation flights over the town. This time entrance was free with displays at 2.15 p.m. and at 5.30 p.m. In a break at 3 p.m., during the first display, there was the unfurling of the company's new civil air ensign carrying the slogan 'Hands Off British Aviation'. This was a message to the decidedly non-civil-air-minded government of the day, delivered by Major Eskell accompanied by the chairman and vice chairman of the very air-minded Weston Town Council. As had been said previously, there was mention of the importance of Weston having its own airport with the possibility of the recently established Great Western Railway airline's Westland Wessex G-AAGW, then operating a Cardiff (Splott) Airport — Plymouth (Roborough) Airport service, calling at Weston on its extended route to Birmingham (Castle Bromwich), should the aerodrome be built.

In the late afternoon, so great was the demand for the 4s (20p) joy-rides, that flying carried on until it became almost dark. A consequence of this was that the blue DH Fox Moth, whilst landing at about 9.15 p.m., with a full complement of four passengers, struck an unseen boundary-marker post. Although the aircraft was badly damaged, luckily neither the pilot nor passengers were injured. After camping overnight on the Sands, Eskell and his team left for the circus' next venue, Hereford. By the season's end, the two tours had visited 306 towns with approximately a quarter of the 800,000 visitors having experienced a joy-ride.

After a display at Devizes on Thursday 6 July 1933, the touring British Hospitals Air Pageant Ltd arrived in Weston. The town's Queen Alexandra Memorial Hospital was said to be the beneficiary on this occasion. However, there is little evidence of any direct benefit to Weston's hospital or indeed to any hospital of the towns visited on the tour. Held in the field at Woodspring Priory previously used by National Aviation Day Ltd, there were two displays, one at 2.30 p.m. and the other at 6.30 p.m; at other times joy-rides could be had for 4s (20p). The fifteen aircraft taking part in the twenty events were flown by many famous pilots, some of whom, like the organisers, had also changed sides. Amongst them were C. W. A. Scott (chief pilot and winner to be of the great air race from England to Australia), Victor Bruce, Miss Pauline Gower, Miss Dorothy Spicer, Captain R. H. 'All Weather' McIntosh, Captain E. B. Fielden, Captain P. Phillips, Captain Rollason and Flight Lieutenants J. R. W. Pugh and A. G. Hill.

On Wednesday 18 April 1934, Sir Alan Cobham's Circus, now renamed 'National Aviation Displays Ltd', came to Weston close to the start of its 1934 tour. Again the venue was the Sands Aerodrome and the display was to be similar to that of the previous year. As Sir Alan was deeply involved in planning a forthcoming attempt to fly non-stop to India using his recently invented in-flight refuelling system, the show was again led by general manager Major

Cobham's Handley Page HP33 on 'The Sands Aerodrome' 11 June 1935, being loaded with the next batch of joy-riders (From the collection of Weston Library)

Eskell. During the opening ceremony in which that year's slogan 'Make the Skyways Britain's Highways' was unfurled, the chairman of Weston's Town Council, Frank Young, was told publicly in no uncertain terms by Eskell that it was essential that Weston should have an aerodrome, and hoped the council would soon move on the matter. As it happened, matters were already moving. Progress had been made in acquiring a suitable site and, subject to agreement, it would be leased to a company from Bristol.

Prior to the show's opening, members of Weston Town Council were to be given a flight in the largest machine at the event, but, as its engines were being warmed up, one of the aircraft's wheels started to sink into the wet sand and, when power was increased, the tail swung round and hit a parked van and the VIPs embarrassingly had to be transferred to another aircraft. Although the weather was not ideal, causing cancellation of the glider display and parachute descent, the crowd was kept entertained by the Three Aces Avro Cadet formation team in their red, white and blue colour scheme, led by Cecil Bebb which carried out inverted flying, triple loops and many more exciting manoeuvres, and there was a pylon-racing event with three aircraft carrying thrill-seeking joy-riders.

Cobham's last visit to the town was on Whit Tuesday 11 June 1935 when flying was again from the Sands Aerodrome. Pilots for this display were C. W. A. Scott, Flight Lieutenant Geoffrey Tyson, famous for picking up a handkerchief with a spike on his DH Tiger Moth's wing-tip, Flight Lieutenant H. C. Johnson who was said to have taken more people up for a joy-ride than anyone else, and Flight Lieutenant Louis Rowley known as 'The Wizard of

Crazy Flying'. Then there were the ladies, Miss Joan Meakin, 'The Glider Girl', who flew a German 'Wolf' and Miss Naomi Heron-Maxwell, 'The Society Girl Parachutist'. On this visit, the circus' pending arrival was heralded by an advance guard which carried out some low-level passes to raise a crowd and then the rest of the team arrived flying a variety of machines led by Cobham's Handley Page HP 33 Clive 22-seat airliner G-ABYX. By the end of the season when this machine was scrapped, it was estimated that during its life it had carried a remarkable 120,000 passengers. As with earlier visits there were two displays, each lasting three hours, and, at 5.30 p.m., there was a 'Children's Hour' when parties of youngsters were escorted around. Admission was free with joy-riding at 4s (20p) a head. During each show there was a display of aerobatics, inverted flying, wing-walking, parachuting and height and speed judging. A glider performed aerobatics and a pilot took instructions from the ground via wireless telephony as to the manoeuvres he should fly.

It was Cobham who did more than any other to bring aviation to the masses and encourage councils to open up municipal airports on the edge of their towns and cities. Resulting from this policy, a 1929 grand tour of the British Isles and visits by his touring circus had ensured that, by early 1935, there were in the country twenty-three cities or towns with licensed aerodromes, five with sites purchased, four with sites reserved in planning schemes and 108, with Weston amongst them, with sites already inspected by the Air Ministry.

In front of Norman Edgar's first Dragon G-ACJT at Whitchurch are left to right: Norman Edgar and his Chief Pilot David Cubitt, Flying Officer G. W. Monk and Lieutenant-Colonel Grey. By the time this machine and the others had arrived at Weston Airport, their wheel-spats had been removed to prevent them clogging with mud (W. K. Kilsby via K. Wakefield)

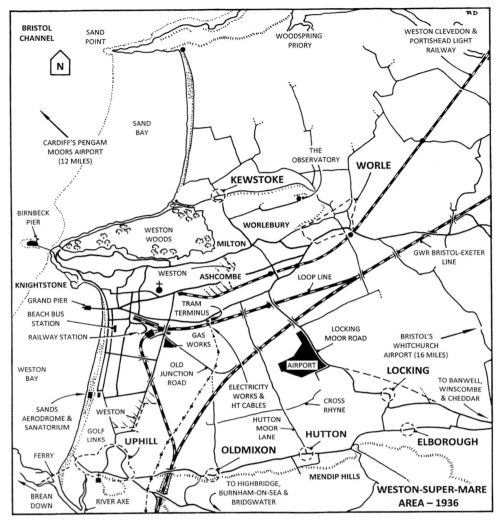

Some of the notable features/buildings in and around Weston that are relevant to this chapter are highlighted on this map. The extent of Weston's development in 1936 was mainly to the north and west of the loop line (R. Dudley)

Norman Edgar (Western Airways) Ltd

One such individual that Cobham may well have influenced was Norman Wallace George Edgar, an Army captain in the Great War, who on 26 September 1932, as Norman Edgar & Co., with a DH Fox Moth G-ABYO had started a twice-daily 20-minute passenger service between Bristol's (Whitchurch) Airport and Cardiff's (Splott) Airport, which was to the north-east of the city on 60 acres (24 hectares) of land reclaimed from the sea. The service proved to be very popular and, anticipating an increase in business, the following year, Norman Edgar (Western Airways) Ltd was incorporated as Aircraft Dealers and Air

Transport Contractors with its headquarters at Whitchurch. Norman Edgar was managing director, the chairman was the Lord Apsley DSO, MC, TD, who was also a local MP and President of the Bristol and Wessex Aero Club; the other directors were the Lady Viola Apsley and Kenneth Machonochie. Initially operating with DH Dragon G-ACJT, the fleet was soon to be increased in size as additional routes were established between Whitchurch, Le Touquet and Paris, and between Whitchurch, Splott and Bournemouth (Christchurch). Later in 1932, Edgar, looking to further extend his activities, saw that Weston might provide such an opportunity for the location of a new base with the short 12-mile (19-km) Weston — Splott crossing by air probably being much preferred by customers to the 60-mile (97-km) road and rail journeys then available.

Edgar considered that Hutton Moor, an area of flat moorland 17 feet (5 metres) above Mean Sea Level (AMSL) on the southern edge of Weston, lying between Laney's Drove to the south and the GWR main line to the north, and between Locking Moor Road (A371) to the east and Hutton Moor Lane to the west, would be ideal, and in consequence in January 1933 he flew a group of Weston councillors from the Sands Aerodrome to view the extent of his proposal. The council was very enthusiastic and didn't want to miss out on the opportunity and benefits to be enjoyed by the town as a result of the development. Following an initial review, the town council's engineer and surveyor Harold Brown and Councillor Mr E. Macfarlane, who was elected chairman of an airport committee, were tasked to report back on the way they considered it best to proceed. Investigation went ahead, not just in Britain but in Europe and America, and from the subsequent report, the town council agreed on 27 May 1935 to negotiate purchase of 52 acres (21 hectares) of land from Somerset County Council, and local landowner Mr A. E. Lance who owned 26 acres (10.5 hectares) of land. The resulting airport would be roughly 2,250 feet (686 metres) east — west and 1,200 feet (366 metres) north — south.

To finance its activities in the venture, two new companies, Western Air Transport and Airways Union, were set up and financed by Western Airways. The first company was registered 12 December 1935 and its purpose was 'To purchase such of the present or future debts due and owing, or to become owing by Norman Edgar (Western Airways) Ltd' and 'To operate airlines'. Its directors were those of the existing company together with Harry Crook (director of the Kleen-e-zee Brush Co. Ltd), Leonard Guy (director of Weston-super-Mare Grand Pier Co. Ltd) and Leslie Ivor Arnott (director of Tintern Quarries Ltd). The second company, on the other hand, was registered on 6 February 1936, and its stated purpose was 'To establish lines of aerial connection', and its directors were Norman Edgar and the Lord Apsley. In the same month a 10-year leasing arrangement was drawn up between the town council, which had now bought the land, and Norman Edgar, and it provided that the cost of airport construction, some £56,000, was to be carried by the council, funded from the rates. This was an expensive undertaking for a town with just 30,000 residents; however, recovery was planned by applying a levy of 1s (5p) on each landing and 3d (1.2p) on each passenger carried. For the first couple of years, this levy was expected to amount to not less than £300 per year, increasing pro rata so that, for the tenth year, the figure would be at least £1,000, this to be offset somewhat by a payment to Western Airways of an airport management fee.

With plans and legal matters finalised, the construction of Weston Airport began in February 1936 with removal of hedges and the installation of drains and the filling in of low-lying areas. In the south-east corner of the field a hangar of 14,000 sq. feet (3,900 sq. metres) with a 200-foot (61-metres) frontage was erected by John Lysaght of Bristol and, adjacent to it, a timber passenger terminal, that in an earlier life had served as an American Great War hospital block, was erected. Three free car parks and a spectator viewing area were also provided around the terminal and a large shed for airport ground equipment built some 400 yards (366 metres) away to the north alongside Locking Moor Road. It is interesting to note that as early as 1935, when plans were being drawn up, it had been agreed with the Air Ministry that the airport could be enlarged when required to an area of just over 170 acres (69 hectares) to allow for the establishment of an RAF Reserve Training School and an aircraft factory. Norman Edgar was now able to set about informing the public of the services and routes that would soon be available from the new airport. Included would be flying from Weston to Australia by means of the countrywide network of air routes that interlinked with international traffic operating from London's (Croydon) Aerodrome, frequent ferry flights to and from Splott starting in May, and the introduction of other routes and destinations as the airport and its facilities became established. During this time the citizens of Weston were very supportive of the development and it became, for its size, one of the most air-minded towns in the country.

Edgar was ever keen to move the project along and, on Thursday 9 April 1936, whilst the airport was still under construction, he had his chief pilot Flying Officer David C. R. Cubitt, bring down from Whitchurch Airport the company's DH Gipsy Moth G-AAVR to try out the grass runway. With the test successfully completed, it was intended to carry out some joy-riding on Sunday 19 April at 5s (25p) a flight, but the day was cold and windy and, with no customers, it became a non-event. In May, Weston Airport was licensed for passenger carrying in DH Dragons, but there was a proviso that they could be flown only by pilots already familiar with the airport since work to bury overhead telephone lines along Locking Moor Road was still to be carried out. However, when the task was completed it would mean that any operator could use the airport, with first off the mark Railway Air Services (RAS); owned equally by the four railway companies and Imperial Airways. At the end of April it announced that from Monday 25 May, Weston Airport would be used on two of its 1936 summer services. This was not well received by Western Airways since these services would encroach on those that Western Airways was about to start and, more importantly, RAS had already stated that its intention was to monopolise the country's internal air routes and drive others like Western Airways, which was unlicensed and unsubsidised, out of business.

As promised, RAS duly commenced flights into Weston Airport on the 25th when one of its silver, green and red Dragons flew in having departed Splott at 10.25 a.m. on a daily return Splott — Weston — Whitchurch service that on weekdays linked with its Shoreham — Whitchurch — Birmingham (Castle Bromwich) Airport — Stoke on Trent (Meir) Airport — Liverpool (Speke) Airport service. From Liverpool it was possible to fly on to Manchester, Leeds, Blackpool, the Isle of Man and Glasgow. The same day, another RAS Dragon, having set out from the north, also flew into Weston from Whitchurch on its way south to Plymouth (Roborough) Airport via Splott and Teignmouth (Haldon) Airport. This service to Plymouth had replaced the previous year's Nottingham (Tollerton) Airport — Plymouth service that, with two new DH Dragon IIs G-ADDI and G-ADDJ, from May, went via Castle Bromwich, Splott and Torquay (Denbury) Airport with the aircraft being seen from Weston, weather permitting four times daily (except Sundays), flying over Flat Holm heading for either Denbury or Splott.

Western Airways responded to the competition with Norman Edgar, ever aware of the value of advertising, inviting the local newspapers to experience at close hand his newly announced ferry service. For their benefit, on Wednesday 27 May, a Dragon flown by Flying Officer A. L. 'Dick' Mortimer was diverted from the 15-minute Whitchurch — Splott run. The event went right to plan and the local newspapers carried glowing reports about the new service which started the next day, Sunday 31 May, when DH Dragon G-ACJT flew in from Splott, which had recently been enlarged to an area of about 90 acres (36 hectares) and renamed 'Pengam Moors'. Having initiated the service, the aeroplane was kept busy during the rest of the day flying passengers back and forth between the two airports.

Norman Edgar continued to make good use of the newspapers to gain further publicity for his company and had published in the following week's editions a tongue-in-cheek apology. In it he expressed regret to those who, because of the great popularity of the new service, had been unable to obtain seats on the Western Airways Express and promised additional aeroplanes. He also advised those intending to travel to book early to avoid future disappointment. When the airport was officially opened less than a month later on Thursday 25 June by the Deputy Lord Mayor of Cardiff, who had arrived with other civic representatives in three Dragons flying in formation, some 1,700 passengers had already used the airport.

With most of his customers not having flown before and probably somewhat apprehensive about the prospect, the Dragon was advertised as having armchair comfort where one could enjoy a smoke, have hot and cold ventilation, and, most of all, the aircraft was promised as being sturdy and absolutely reliable and safe to fly in. To book a flight from Weston, one could call the terminal's

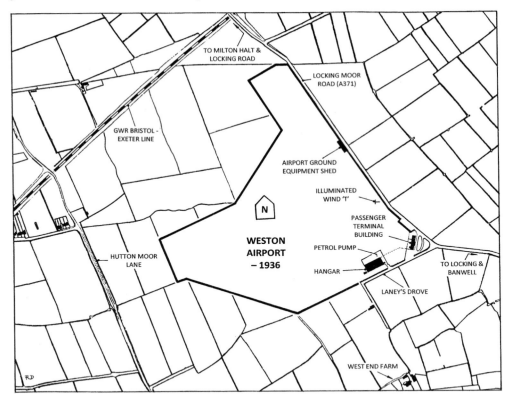

The layout of Weston Airport, May 1936 (R. Dudley)

booking office on Weston 2002, a number easy to remember, or any travel or motor-coach agent, the Beach Bus Station or any branch of the Bristol Tramways & Carriage Company. Whereas, to book a flight from Pengam Moors, one could call the booking office and waiting room just outside the airport's main gate on Cardiff 3688, or any travel or motor-coach agent, or Red and White Services, which had many offices around Wales. This development in Wales had been considerably assisted by the local airline Cambrian Air Services who had badly wanted to take an active role in running the earlier Whitchurch — Splott ferry service, but Western Airways had declined, the resulting hostility soon causing the association to fold.

To run the new ferry service, the Whitchurch — Pengam Moors service, the service between Weston and Whitchurch and a new twice-daily Weston — Birmingham service that commenced in July, Western Airways obtained another DH Dragon. Thus, by the end of July when relocated at Weston, the fleet comprised four Dragons G-ACJT, G-ACPX, G-ACAO and G-ACMJ all finished in the company's blue and silver colour scheme. The Dragon was an excellent aeroplane for the ferry service; it carried six passengers and had the advantage of wing-folding that allowed the fleet to be hangared side by side at night. Another benefit was that the aircraft was easy to service and initially this

May 1936, Norman Edgar's two Puss Moths and his Gipsy Moth in front of the Passenger Terminal, which was about to have added the 'Verandah Café'. One of the telephone poles with its lines, which delayed a Full Public Use Licence from being granted, can be seen in the background (Via E. ap Rees)

Press photographer Pete Warrilow and colleague with an unknown party, large enough to fill four Dragons, celebrates a trip across the Channel with a group photograph (Via S. Terrell)

was performed by Airwork engineers called in as required from Whitchurch.

Norman Edgar's slogan was 'Save Time, Save Money – Fly Western Airways' and this was readily accepted by the public on both sides of the channel, who responded by going on shopping expeditions to Cardiff where a baggage allowance of 20 lb (9 kg) came in handy, or in the other direction, a day on Weston Beach could be very attractive. Another possibility was to just go along and enjoy the thrill of flying for the first time. The crossing, available every day of the year, took eight minutes or so and could be had for as little as *6s 6d* (32.5p) single or *9s 6d* (47.5p) return, this being only just above that of the third-class rail fare. Departures, with the first at 9 a.m., were from both sides every hour on the hour, but in busy periods the Dragons were flown in convoys of two, three or even four. To reach the airport from Cardiff city centre a bus service was available that ran every twelve minutes, and, from Weston Airport, a No.43 bus operated by the Bristol Tramways Company for *6d* return (2.5p) or *4d* (1.6p) single took arrivals to the Beach Bus Station. This improvement in services also led to the urgent need for the airport's manually operated petrol pump to be replaced by an electrically driven one to allow each Dragon to be refuelled at high speed.

In 1936 the skies over Weston were becoming extremely busy, not just with traffic from the airport but from near and far. Just after 6.30 p.m. on Sunday 5 July the ill-fated 813-foot (248-metre) German Zeppelin *Hindenburg* droned slowly by on its way back to Frankfurt. Setting out from Lakehurst New Jersey at 9.44 p.m. Eastern Standard Time on Friday, the airship, unannounced, had coasted up the Bristol Channel and turned south-east just before reaching Weston. At the airport there was a rush to get three machines airborne so that it could be seen at close quarters, but as was to be expected, its sheer size had given a false impression of low altitude and speed, for when they caught up airspeed was found to be 80 mph (129 kph) and altitude 4,000 feet (1,220 metres). It was generally thought that as the airship overflew the south of England some of the passengers seen waving to the aeroplanes were also taking photographs of locations that might be of use should there be future hostilities. *Hindenburg* arrived back at Frankfurt at 1.20 a.m. BST Monday 6 July. Going the other way, Beryl Markham, daughter of a Kenyan farmer had taken off from Abingdon at 6.50 p.m. Friday 4 September 1936 in Vega Gull VP-*KCC The Messenger*, circled Weston Airport in the gathering dusk then, after waving to those below, set course for New York, and 21 hours 35 minutes and 2,612 miles (4,200 km) later she had become the first woman to fly the Atlantic from England to North America solo. However, due to fuel shortage the flight ended up slightly short of target in a peat bog at Baleine on Cape Breton Island.

Even with the airport established, Edgar continued to arrange events to publicise Western Airways and also attract the continued support and interest of the people of Weston. To this end he wanted a 'Big Show' in which the public could participate and that would attract coverage by the all-important

BBC. But this was not to be, as on his chosen day the BBC was otherwise engaged. However, the public would not be deprived of a show, for although it was getting late in the year, he managed to arrange for C. W. A. Scott's Flying Display Ltd, at the end of its 1936 touring season, to give a 2-day display on Friday 14 and Saturday 15 August. Similar in content to the shows provided by the Cobham Circus, tickets available from several shops in the town were priced 1s 3d (6.2p) adults, 6d (2.5p) children, 1s (5p) cars, 6d (2.5p) motorcycles and 2d (0.8p) cycles. In each of the two daily displays, a Cierva Autogiro, three Avro Cadets, a DH Tiger Moth, a Mongoose Avro, a Lynx Avro, a BAC Drone and a Wolf glider performed, and two Airspeed Ferries took up eleven passengers at a time on joy-rides at 5s (25p) a head. For the budding aviator, flying lessons could also be arranged in the 2-seaters. As a prelude to the event Jack Pruens of Oxford Street displayed in its car showroom Pou-du-Ciel *Flying Flea* G-AEFK. It was Scott who, with a partner, had purchased at the end of 1935 much of Cobham's Circus, with which he had flown earlier in the year when Weston was last visited.

Weston Airport received its eagerly awaited 'Full Public Use Licence' in mid-August on completion of the work to bury the telephone cables that had been hanging along Locking Moor Road. This coincided with Railway Air Services on Sunday 16 August starting a daily Weston — Brighton service in which the Dragon, exchanged for a DH Dragon Rapide at Whitchurch, then went on its way to Brighton (Shoreham) via Southampton and Ryde on the Isle of Wight. Western Airways didn't have the monopoly on the Weston — Pengam Moors route either, for on Saturday 22 August, after obtaining Air Ministry approval, RAS started an hourly service to Pengam Moors, that, with the one provided by Western Airways, gave the travelling public a departure every half-hour. But at the end of the summer service, much to the relief of Western Airways, RAS services to and from Weston finished 12 September and were not to be restarted.

In addition to the Dragons, Western Airways also had in its fleet two DH Puss Moths G-ABWZ and G-ABFV. Used primarily for taxi and charter work at the rate of 6d (2.5p) a mile they were also used occasionally for joy-rides when a flight could be had for 5s (25p). Under previous ownership both machines had been involved in much travelling with G-ABWZ, flying to India to take part in the 1933 Mount Everest Expedition, and G-ABFV, whilst owned by the Prince of Wales, being shipped to Brazil on board HMS *Eagle* for his tour of 1931.

With the coming of winter 1936, there was a reduction in the frequency of the Western Airways ferry service to five flights a day from each side. At this time of the year the majority of passengers were business people but, in true Norman Edgar fashion, in September he announced that a contract had been negotiated to fly workmen employed by a Weston electrical company from Weston to Cardiff where they would be working on the city's Ministry of Health building. To last twelve months, the contract involved the men being flown over with tools Monday mornings and returning Friday evenings. The ferry service had been chosen as it was considered to be the most reliable and cost-effective way of getting the men there and back. During the Christmas holidays, so keen was the public to travel on the ferry that the service was tripled and operated at half-hourly intervals, and by the year's end, the company was proudly able to announce that 14,289 passengers had been carried on the service.

Weston Airport amongst the Busiest

There was even better news after the first twelve months of operation when it was announced that 25,158 passengers had been carried, 23,837 of them in the company's machines, the numbers being far in excess of those expected when the move to Weston was contemplated. With these figures, Weston Airport, which by now was one of thirty-one municipal airports in the country, was hailed as being amongst the busiest, a remarkable achievement in such a short space of time. This success was due in part to visitors being attracted back to the airport. Many remarked that they liked its ambience, it being more continental in conception and operation than others and the public was actually encouraged to visit and watch the aeroplanes in action. This could be from the car parks or from the viewing area, whilst having lunch in the fully-licensed restaurant run by Mr G. M. Hutton on behalf of Ushers, or tea in the Verandah Café. Even though there were excellent facilities for viewing at the airport's Locking Moor Road main entrance, so keen was the public to see the aeroplanes that their cars frequently blocked the road and, after complaints to the police, two extra car parks were provided. In addition to the usual passenger aeroplanes, visitors in March/April 1937 might have observed Mayor Elect Henry Butt boarding a DH Dragon to leave on the first stage of a continental tour, a DH Hornet Moth on its way to Manchester, a BA Swallow taking off for Castle Bromwich and two Hawker Harts flying-in from RAF Worthy Down.

During this period, in addition to its own aeroplanes, 565 others had also visited the airport. Of those 362 were from other British airports and 203 from abroad. The number of passengers carried by Western Airways would have been greater but for flooding which closed Pengam Moors in the winter of 1937/38. At that time, flooding of airports in southern England had caused much inconvenience to air travellers, but Weston Airport remained open, principally due to the excellent work done by Weston Town Council's Engineer and Surveyor Harold Brown, who had managed to get the airport open in record time and had also installed a first-class drainage system. This was demonstrated very effectively in February when the airport was the only one remaining open in the west of England able to take an airliner of Imperial Airways.

From 1937 a newly formed Western Airways Aero Club offered visitors the opportunity to learn to fly, with dual instruction given in the DH Puss Moths for £2 5s (£2.25) per hour. With early club members obtaining licences, the more well-off were tempted into buying their own aeroplanes when two

The Western Airways Hangar and Passenger Terminal together with car parks and spectator viewing area in the corner between Locking Moor Road and Laney's Drove, mid 1936. At this time mud was to feature prominently! (Via E. ap Rees)

Aeronca 100s, advertised as being the world's smallest 2-seat cabin aeroplane, arrived at the airport Wednesday 21 April part-way through a demonstration tour of the country. Robert Kronfeld, the internationally known Austrian gliding expert and owner of the British Aircraft Company at Maidstone, was also after the same market, as he paid the airport two visits, the last in early July when his incredibly noisy 30 hp Carden Ford-powered BAC Drone was superbly demonstrated.

As well as carrying on with its normal civil work, Western Airways, like many other similar organisations, was looking to make the most of the 1930s military expansion programme. This was where many of the large numbers of RAF training aircraft coming into service were being operated by civilian organisations under contract to the Air Ministry, and some, mainly twin-engined civil aircraft were being leased to the military. In this connection, Western Airways since 1935 had been leasing some of its aircraft for Army co-operation flying over Pembrokeshire, and since 1936 a similar service had been provided for the Royal Navy at Devonport.

In early 1937 Norman Edgar managed to secure what was considered to be the largest Army Co-operation contract in the country, involving about 1,500 hours of night-flying in connection with anti-aircraft practice. To fulfil this contract, the town council agreed to fund the purchase of basic night-flying

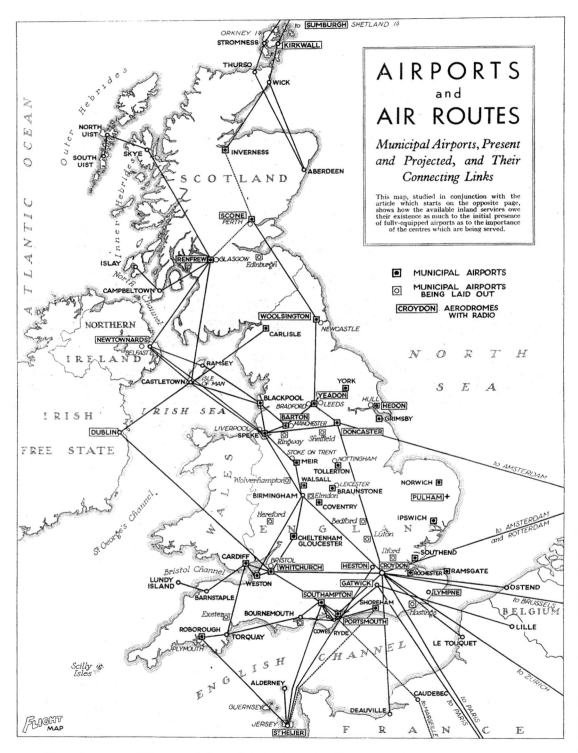

The Airports and Routes of Great Britain from the *Flight* magazine for 21 January 1937 graphically shows how Weston Airport integrated with the existing aerial network (*Flight* via R. Dudley)

equipment for the airport. Costing a total of £4,500, it comprised a Chance Brothers 3-lamp, 1¼ million candle power aerodrome landing floodlight, a control tower, orange boundary lights, red warning-lights for the tall buildings and an illuminated wind-direction 'T'. Meanwhile, Western Airways urgently bought and fitted its aircraft with wireless sets allowing for limited Army co-operation flying to start in April, with the aircraft having to be landed with ground illumination provided only by their landing lights. The floodlight unit was installed by the end of April and after successful test flights were carried out by Knowles Breakell in Dragon G-ACPX at the beginning of May, the Army co-operation flying was able to begin in real earnest on the 16th. The other lighting equipment was delivered and installed a short time later.

Edgar, ever on the lookout for further opportunities to get publicity for his activities and increase company revenue, and at the same time reward the citizens of the town for their interest and support, included the airport in the list of civil and military aerodromes to hold a 1937 Empire Air Day. Organised by the Air League of the British Empire and actively encouraged by the King, the financial benefits went to the RAF Benevolent Fund. The Air Day held on Saturday 29 May provided a chance for visitors to experience the thrill of seeing at close quarters some of the RAF's latest aeroplanes, most having done a considerable amount of cross-country flying to bring variety to the display. One could also see the almost completed control tower that had been located next to the northern corner of the roadside viewing car park. The previous week, the tower's concrete foundation had been laid and the pilots had lost no time in building its timber sides, and it had been capped-out using the roof of a redundant Weston seafront cab-shelter complete with its ornate cast-iron guttering. On completion, the floodlight was installed directly in front so that its beams shone out in a westerly direction. The tower's location was several yards to the left of today's entrance to The Helicopter Museum.

Visitors to the Air Day were able to see the local airline's two new DH Dragon Rapides G-ACTU and G-ADDD, the latter obtained primarily for the Birmingham route since it had a toilet and a wireless-operator's position. G-ADDD, with only 194 flying-hours, had been bought by Norman Edgar for £3,345 after negotiations with the captain of the Kings Flight Wing Commander Edward 'Mouse' Fielden AFC in London 15 March. This was a very well-known aeroplane, as it had been personally owned by Edward, Prince of Wales who, on becoming Edward VIII, flew in it from RAF Bircham Newton to RAF Hendon making G-ADDD the first aeroplane to carry a reigning British monarch. To make the most of its arrival, a large advert was placed in the local newspapers inviting people to visit the airport Saturday 15 May (Whit weekend), watch it land at 4 p.m. and then for 5s (25p) have a flight in it. As promised, witnessed by an enormous crowd, the Rapide duly turned up on time, and by the end of the holiday weekend a record 1,100 passengers had been carried by G-ADDD and the other machines on the Weston — Pengam Moors ferry service alone, and 604 on Whit Monday.

On these two pages is shown some of the new equipment and aircraft seen by the massive crowd that attended the 1937 'Empire Air Day'.
Above: The control tower with floodlights (Via E. ap Rees). Below: The partly burnt-out skeleton of RAF Heyford bomber K6880 (Via E. ap Rees)

Above: The newly arrived ex Kings Flight Dragon Rapide G-ADDD (Via M. Mansbridge)

Below: RAF Anson K6278 (Via E. ap Rees)

However, it would appear that there had been a certain amount of economy with the truth over the arrival of G-ADDD. It had, in fact, been flown in the previous Saturday by Fielden and, in accordance with the conditions of sale, its colour scheme had been changed from the red, blue and silver of the Brigade of Guards to an overall purple. The Rapide was then worked on in the shops of Western Airways with, amongst other things, the four royal blue Connolly leather armchairs and an occasional seat for an attendant being replaced by standard passenger seats. It was then flown to another airport where it awaited take-off time for its return at 4 p.m. Another Rapide to join the fleet a day or two later was G-ADBV. Prior to being registered to Western Airways it had been owned by John Dade, a pilot with Olley Air Service and, although having 'Western Airways' on its nose, was to remain in the silver and black livery of its previous owner for some time.

Also at the air day was one of the RAF's last biplane bombers, Handley Page Heyford III K6880 *T for Toc* from 166 Squadron RAF Leconfield. Hangared overnight, the machine would end up being the highlight of the show with the emphasis on 'light', for when the mechanics were starting its port Rolls-Royce Kestrel engine it backfired and flames set alight the fabric covering. Squadron Leader Wake, in the open cockpit, rapidly closed the throttle, shut off the fuel, and beat a hasty retreat down the steeply sloping rear fuselage, closely followed by the flames! In less than five minutes, the entire fabric covering had disappeared leaving just the metal skeleton. Weston's fire brigade had been called but was delayed in getting to the airport by slow-moving air day traffic on Locking Moor Road. Inspection showed that, surprisingly, the aeroplane could be temporarily repaired on site as its main structure was virtually undamaged, and in due course the flying surfaces were recovered and the machine was last seen some days later heading north-east, still minus fabric covering on its fuselage. K6880 was finally struck-off charge on 5 November, perhaps a relevant date considering the incident at Weston.

The arrival of three gleaming RAF Hawker Furies soon took the spectator's minds off the morning's excitement; they climbed, rolled and formed themselves into the Prince of Wales feathers then one peeled off and landed. Meanwhile, five Hawker Harts circled high above and Hawker Demons with gunners in their rear cockpits came out of the sun diving at full speed in a mock attack on the airport; three of these were also to land. Various military aircraft were already in front of the control tower including an FAA Fairey Swordfish and two silver-doped Avro Ansons from Boscombe Down, one of which had a glistening dorsal turret. Civil aircraft were also present including a BA Swallow from the Cardiff Aero Club.

For 1937 the ferry service carried on much as before, although from the beginning of July there was an increase of 2s 6d (12.5p) on the return fare and 1s 6d (7.5p) on the single fare due to the price of fuel and the salary of pilots being increased. The summer Weston — Birmingham service, which the previous year had been twice-daily, due to lack of demand was now twice-weekly and so arranged to give 'Brummies' a long weekend in Weston. This service commenced Friday 16 July when G-ADDD, now commonly known as the Three Ds, piloted by Knowles Breakell, took off at 5.55 a.m. with a full load of passengers on the 46-minute flight to Castle Bromwich. On reaching 2,000 feet (610 metres), the aircraft's trailing aerial was extended so that contact could be made with those on the ground. Being only one of eighteen civil airports in Britain with the necessary equipment to use this new technology, Western Airways was again showing its forward thinking. A ticket for a weekend return was £2 9s 6d (247.5p), single £1 9s 6d (147.5p) and a day-return £1 19s 6d (197.5p).

Friday 23 July saw another service introduced, this time one linking Weston with Le Bourget and Le Touquet. Leaving Weston at 5.10 a.m., David Cubitt, flying DH Dragon Rapide G-ACTU, after calling at Lympne arrived Le Bourget at 8.20 a.m. Coming back a call was made at Le Touquet as well as Lympne, arriving Weston at 9.40 p.m. The return fare was £9 or £10 depending on destination. In hindsight, it was found that G-ACTU was not the best machine for this flight, as just prior to purchase by Western Airways it had been earmarked for delivery to Spain to join the Civil War and put on the government's blacklist. As a result, a number of urgent phone calls had to be made to the authorities before the aircraft was cleared to leave Britain outward bound and France homeward bound. It later transpired that DDD had been allocated for the flight, but in the event was found to be unavailable on the day. These internal and European services were in addition to the ferry service which, by the end of 1937, was in full swing with 14,923 passengers having been carried.

Since the mid-1930s Richard Cadman, who was a director of the Cardiff Aero Club and a pilot in 614 (County of Glamorgan) Auxiliary Air Force Squadron at Pengam Moors, had entered a Western Airways machine in the annual London (Heston) to Cardiff (Pengam Moors) Air Race. In 1937, Cadman, now squadron leader and commanding officer of the squadron and chairman of the aero club, decided to enter one of the company's new Rapides in that year's event which was to take place Saturday 10 July. Flown proxy by David Cubitt, the machine came sixth at an average speed of 127 mph (204 kph) with first over the line Geoffrey De Havilland in the TK2 and second Alex Henshaw in his Mew Gull. Most competitors stayed on at Pengam Moors until Sunday, and some on their way home decided to divert to Weston when weather conditions to the east deteriorated rapidly. One was Lieutenant-Colonel Louis Arbon Strange DSO, MC, and DFC in his Spartan Arrow. A director of the Straight Corporation which operated a string of aerodromes across the country, Strange, during his enforced stay at Weston Airport, would be able to witness from close quarters Norman Edgar's ferry service and aero club activities. As future events would show, his stay had a marked effect on the future of Weston Airport.

Around that time there was an amusing event at Weston that could have warranted its perpetrator a position in one of the early aerial circuses. The

Reverend Cecil Dudley Claire Boulton of London, well known as the 'Flying Parson', had an elder brother the Reverend H. P. Boulton who was vicar of Winscombe, a village just a few miles away to the east of Weston. Early in 1937 Cecil had acquired 3-seat Simmonds Spartan G-AAHV, the two front seats of which were in tandem in their own cockpit, making an ideal pulpit for the parson. In the lead up to the Whitsun bank holiday, an advert in the local newspapers announced that on Whit Monday he would land on Weston Sands and give an address from the cockpit pulpit. Although being warned off by the local constabulary, he flew into Weston Airport to refuel and, had he not inadvertently taxied into the fuel pumps and damaged the Spartan, he would have gone ahead with his illegal plan.

Still determined to carry on with the scheme, August bank holiday saw Cecil staying with his brother with the aeroplane parked in Hawkhurst Field at Bridgwater. According to the court case brought some weeks later, for 'flying the Spartan in such a manner to cause unnecessary danger to persons on Weston foreshore', he had taken off from the field with only just enough fuel to get to Weston Airport. Due, it was said, to a 'leaking on/off fuel cock' a precautionary landing was made on the beach near the Sanatorium, after first making three low-level runs to clear the area of holidaymakers. Leaving the machine tended by a bystander, he disappeared returning later in a van with 'The Flying Parson' posters on its sides. Two 2-gallon fuel cans were then unloaded for the aircraft which was now under 'protection of the law' in the person of PC Stacey, and the van then proceeded to go up and down the seafront rallying holidaymakers by loudspeaker to the aircraft. Before take-off, a short sermon was delivered from the pulpit and broadcast via the van's loudspeakers, and mission badges were sold. However, the aircraft was known to have experienced a fuel leak some weeks before, and because of this the reverend was given the benefit of doubt and the case dismissed.

To the outsider, Western Airways with its impressive growth, would appear to be doing very well financially, but the truth was otherwise. In fact, since moving to Weston Airport, the company had failed to make anything like a profit, and such was the state of affairs that in early 1938, when it came to increasing its chief pilot's salary, David Cubitt had to make do with the issue of 250 of the company's ordinary £1 shares.

The Straight Corporation

During 1937 Whitney Willard Straight, a 25-year-old millionaire entrepreneur, expressed interest in the takeover of Norman Edgar (Western Airways) Ltd and the operation of Weston Airport.

Whitney Straight, born in 1912, was the son of New York banker Willard Straight and the heiress Dorothy Whitney, members of America's super-rich establishment. In 1926, with his younger brother Michael, he was brought to

England by his mother and stepfather Leonard Elmhirst where, at Dartington Hall, Totnes, Devon, they founded a progressive school and artistic and agricultural community. Aged sixteen, whilst out on his motor-cycle, Whitney visited nearby Haldon Aerodrome (just above Teignmouth), presented the owner Mr Parkhouse with a £1 note and asked if he would take him flying for as long as it lasted. With no further ado an Avian was wheeled out of the hangar and off they went, and the lad was able to experience for the first time the thrill of flying. Whitney's first cousin C. V. Whitney, at one time chairman of Pan American Airways, no doubt had an influence on Whitney who rapidly developed a passion for aviation. With Parkhouse's tuition, only a few days after his seventeenth birthday he gained his Pilot's 'A' Licence and bought Parkhouse's machine, which was followed a bit later by the purchase, from the same source, of a DH Gipsy Moth, and later still a DH Moth Major. Whitney's other passion was motor racing, and in the early 1930s he took on the directorship of several automobile companies and also became a well-known competitive racing driver, one of his cars being the 8 C 2500 black and silver Maserati straight-eight, bought in 1932 from Dean Butler.

In October 1931 Whitney moved to Trinity College, Cambridge, only to find that first-year undergraduates were not permitted motor cars, but there didn't appear to be any restrictions on the keeping of aeroplanes. Straight therefore kept his Moth Major at nearby Marshalls Fen Dillon Aerodrome, easily reached on a pushbike, allowing him to fly to Brooklands to race the Maserati. In 1933, he left Cambridge to establish a professional racing-car stable, but soon it was to suffer a severe loss when one of the team was killed at Berne. Meanwhile, aviation was still a serious interest and he had Westland at Yeovil build in its Woodmill the prototype of a 2-seat low-wing cabin racing monoplane named the Hendy Heck. Among its unique features were slats, slotted flaps and a retractable undercarriage that gave it a remarkable speed range with a top speed of 170 mph (273 kph). Meanwhile, concerned about the dangers of motor racing, Whitney's parents had consulted Parkhouse regarding what to do about their son's ambitions, and this was to result in Whitney giving up motor racing and moving into aviation full time. On 17 April 1935, with funding from his personal trust, Whitney formed Straight Corporation Ltd, its policy: 'To obtain operational-control of various municipal airports (up to fifteen) across the length and breadth of the country and at each provide first-class passenger-terminals, restaurants and flight-training centres.' Longer term, it was also intended to expand the number of internal air routes within Great Britain.

Straight's Men

All of the company's related interests for tax and liability purposes would be limited companies registered to Whitney Willard Straight of Brettenham House, Strand WC2. Straight's Dartington Hall trustee and solicitor Frederick

A. S. Gwatkin, the so-called 'Hard Man' of McKenna & Co., would handle the various acquisitions. Gwatkin was also to subscribe to some of the purchases, and together with Straight's wealthy friend Richard Seaman, also of racing-car fame, were the Straight Corporation's Board of Directors. Three months after forming his new company Whitney married the Lady Daphne Finch-Hatton, daughter of the 14th Earl and Countess of Winchilsea and Nottingham.

Run by a young and enthusiastic team from its office at Manchester Square, London, the company set about acquiring suitable aerodromes for the business, the first being Ramsgate's (Thanet) aerodrome, leased June 1935 and others followed rapidly. Exeter's (Clyst Honiton) was next in January 1936, Ipswich in February and Plymouth's (Roborough) in March, Teignmouth's (Haldon) and Inverness in 1937 and Clacton in May 1938, where the company also licensed Pouts Field at Swalecliffe, Herne Bay. Also leased was a large field at Bury St Edmunds for a future municipal airport, Newquay's (Trebelzue) airport and a large field known as Jersey Marine that would in due course become a municipal airport for Swansea. Straight also attempted to lease Norwich Airport, Stoke on Trent's (Meir) and Cardiff's (Pengam Moors) but his overtures in each case were rejected.

With his aero clubs in mind, F. G. Miles, the well-known aircraft designer, produced from Straight's conception a fast, general-purpose, low-wing monoplane. The prototype of this 2-seater, named the Miles MIIA Whitney Straight had its first flight in the Spring of 1936. Even at his young age Straight was already becoming well known in aviation circles for his charm and integrity, and, being like his mother, a public benefactor giving much-needed employment at this difficult time. Whilst Miles was having the new machine constructed, with all his financial interests now in Britain, Straight decided to become a British citizen and, early in 1936, this was granted by the Home Secretary. Amongst other benefits, he would be allowed to enter the famous Kings Cup Air Race from which, as an American, he had been barred. In the new organisation Straight was well aware of the need to have the support of well-qualified managers and engineers, and several individuals were significant: company secretary was Stanley John Cox and T. F. 'Frank' Allen was to look after the financial side, and both would remain with the concern until their retirement. There was also Miss Mary de Bunsen, who, as the public-relations representative, was to look after the house magazine *Straightaway* which would keep all employees and aero club members up to date with the latest developments. During the forthcoming war Mary would join the Air Transport Auxiliary as a ferry pilot. Other early members of the team were his mentor William Richard 'Parky' Parkhouse and Louis Strange.

Parkhouse, a former apprentice with a Bath engineering firm, in 1915 had joined the RNAS and eventually trained as a pilot, in due course becoming an instructor at Gosport. Returning to civil life in May 1919, he formed the Agra Engineering Company in Teignmouth. In 1923, as a pilot officer, he started to instruct at the Bristol Aeroplane Company-run RAF Reserve School at Filton, then in 1928 he acquired the lease of moorland at Little Haldon where a flying school was established. Initially with an Avian, which provided his introduction to Whitney Straight, the following year he was awarded the De Havilland agency for the West Country when he bought Gipsy Moth G-AAJG which was to remain at Haldon until 13 May 1937, when its ownership was transferred to Straight's Plymouth & District Aero Club at Roborough. Meanwhile, in 1937-38 for a period he was at Exeter Airport as Manager, and it was this position that he was to takeover full time in 1939.

Louis Strange, a Dorset man, after leaving St Edwards School, Oxford, farmed 600 acres (243 hectares) at Spetisbury, approximately 3 miles (5 km) south of Blandford Forum, and, for a weekend interest, joined the Dorsetshire Yeomanry as a part-time soldier. During the Yeomanry's 1913 annual summer training manoeuvres, Strange, who in 1910 had been privileged to fly over London in the Willows airship, mentioned to his colleagues that as soon as possible he intended to become a pilot and made a wager that during the following year's manoeuvres he would fly over the Yeomanry Camp. True to his word, he enrolled with the Ewen School at Hendon and learnt to fly in its 35 hp (Anzani) Caudron, and as promised he did fly over the 1914 summer camp, but due to events the bets were never collected. Obtaining a commission in the RFC Reserve, whilst waiting for a course at the Central Flying School (CFS), Upavon, he occupied himself instructing and taking part in the many flying meetings at Hendon. On leaving the CFS, and with the declaration of war, whilst fighting in France and later Belgium he gained note for the arming of Henri Farmans, Avro 2-seaters and BE2Cs. In England, during September 1915 as a newly promoted Major, at Fort Grange, Gosport, he formed 23 Squadron. Then promoted Lieutenant-Colonel to look after a number of Schools of Aerial Gunnery, he was soon back in France getting up-to-date in the latest art of aerial flying, but in April 1917 he was back at the CFS taking up the post of Assistant Commandant only recently vacated by Major Trenchard, later Marshal of the Royal Air Force. Early in 1918, in France again, he took command of the 23rd Wing, then the 80th Wing in the Tenth Brigade and latterly the 51st Wing. With his many wartime exploits he had been awarded the DSO, MC and DFC and remained in the service until 1921, when due to ill-health, he retired to again take up farming. Missing flying, he then founded the Isle of Purbeck Flying Club and had close association with Simmonds Aircraft and later Spartan Aircraft and Spartan Airlines. Then in 1935 Strange resigned from the Board of Directors of both Spartan companies and to much acclaim from the British aeronautical press, joined the board of Straight Corporation.

The Takeover of Norman Edgar (Western Airways) Ltd

Following negotiations between Norman Edgar and his other directors, Weston Town Council and high-ranking officials from the Air Ministry, who arrived

Friday 10 December, speculation was fuelled that big changes were afoot at Weston Airport. Since September 1937 Weston had been a Borough with a mayor and 'Ever Forward' on its new coat of arms. The speculation was proved well-founded when £15,000 was injected into the capital funds of Norman Edgar (Western Airways) Ltd by Whitney Straight thus giving him a controlling interest, and in January 1938 he effectively took over the organisation.

Discussions with the council had won for Straight a relaxation in the airport lease, whereby aeroplanes belonging to Western Airways would no longer be charged a landing fee, and it was also agreed provisionally that from 1 January 1938 the lease would be extended for a further twenty-one years. Removal of the landing fee allowed for fares on the ferry service to be reduced to the original 6s 6d (32.5p) single and 9s 6d (47.5p) return, while a book of twelve return tickets could be obtained for £5. At this juncture operating times were also adjusted so that an aircraft left Weston at every ten minutes to the hour and an aircraft left Pengam Moors on the hour. Another benefit for the company was the commencement in 1938 of a government subsidy based on the payload of the aircraft and mileage flown on regular routes. Under the new management, Flight Lieutenant William E. Knowlden, who had joined the Straight Corporation in 1936, was brought in from Plymouth Airport and on 1 February appointed Air Superintendant. He had learned to fly in 1916 with the RFC and after the war became well known as a pilot with Imperial Airways, Jersey Airways and other companies. Amongst his early responsibilities at Weston was the equipping of ground staff and the pilots, who by now were Messrs Cubitt, Knowles Breakell, Dick Mortimer, R. J. T. Barrett, C. F. Almond and G. G. McLannahan with new uniforms. Another task was to oversee the installation of a teleprinter so that contact could be made with the Bristol Radio Station and Whitchurch and Pengam Moors Airports.

The takeover didn't officially come into effect until 18 October 1938 with members of Weston Town Council being informed of this sometime later at its monthly meeting on Monday 28 November. Straight didn't intend the corporation to become an airline-operating firm and was keen to keep the name Western Airways in being for this purpose and, as a result, what had been Norman Edgar (Western Airways) Ltd became Western Airways Ltd with directors Whitney Straight, the Lord Apsley, Owen G. E. Roberts and Leslie Arnott. Owen Roberts had been brought in recently and was concerned with the flying side of operations; he owned a Monospar ST 12 and his Pilot's Licence had an instructor's endorsement. The original fleet of Western Airways aircraft was now registered to its new owner and in due course repainted in the Straight Corporation's house colours. This was a dark metallic blue/grey with crimson lettering outlined in white and a rudder with crimson and white horizontal stripes, and although 'WESTERN AIRWAYS' was retained on each side of the nose it was accompanied by the Straight 'S' logo. The man in charge of the paint shop that carried out this work was Freddy Froome, brought in recently from Phillips & Powis.

Following the Straight takeover other changes soon took effect. Western Air Transport was renamed 'Straightways Ltd', and the aero club was reformed 10 March 1938 as Weston Aero Club Ltd with Dick Mortimer Chief Flying Instructor. He was also chief pilot of Western Airways and a flying officer in the RAF Reserve. When Mortimer left the organisation 3 June 1939 to take up a position with Air Service Training Ltd at Hamble on flying boats, he had made some 5,000 crossings of the Bristol Channel and was amongst the last of Norman Edgar's former employees.

At this time Straight Corporation, which was advertising Western Airways as being 'The Flying Centre of the West', would have preferred to equip Weston's and the other aero clubs with mainly De Havilland and Miles training aircraft, but because the military had first option on these types in the massive RAF expansion programme, it had to make do with a miscellany of machines. For the same reason, obtaining spares and materials for the repair and maintenance of these aircraft was also causing serious problems. In previous years an annual overhaul that would have taken three to four weeks was now taking from seven to eight and one had even taken three months!

During the first half of 1938 flight training at Weston was in a single DH Hornet Moth, but in May another was obtained, although one was unfortunately away in August on Army co-operation work. Disappearance of the Hornet Moth on military work was associated with a further large Army Co-operation contract obtained by Louis Strange. Totalling some 1,514 flying hours, although this did include a certain amount of ferrying aircraft to the areas of operation, it occurred mainly in the two months leading up to September and involved pilots under Mr Banting in the company's single- and twin-engined machines flying accurate courses in hilly districts under the most adverse of British weather conditions. The largest of the contracts provided 800 hours of flying in support of the 27th (BC) AA Group, TA, and over the most active 24-hour period of this operation, nine machines flew a total of ninety hours.

A New Fleet of Aircraft and Improved Services

In early 1938, the company received the first four of its long-awaited new training aeroplanes. These were Miles Hawk Trainer Mk IIIs G-AFET, G-AFEU, G-AFEV and G-AFEW, that were to be used for aerobatics and blind-flying at Ipswich, Ramsgate, Exeter/Weston and Plymouth Aero Clubs respectively, where they were to be flown dual for £2 5s (£2.25) and solo for £1 15s (£1.75) per hour. Delivered to Western Airways in primer with registration letters chalked on, the last two, G-AFEV and G-AFEW, were not to emerge from the paint shop until May and, when they did get to their allotted clubs, were soon destroyed in crashes. The last was lost Wednesday 30 August 1939 when Henry Foulds of Exmouth, a member of Exeter's Civil Air Guard and

One of the three Hawk Trainer Mk IIIs, in this case Weston Aero Club's G-AFET (E. J. Riding Collection)

well known at Weston, was taking G-AFEV on a cross-country flight. Knowles Breakell, who was now CFI of the RAFVR School at Exeter, had taken Foulds up on an offer of a ride to Weston where Breakell was to attend a meeting at Western Airways, but half an hour after dropping off his passenger, and on the way back to Exeter, Foulds became lost in low cloud and crashed into high ground just above Lyme Regis.

1938 also saw a small number of lower-powered, less expensive aircraft join the Straight organisation. Five were new Czechoslovakian-designed Praga ultra-light side-by-side 2-seaters with fully enclosed cockpits built under licence in Manchester by F. Hills & Sons. Together with the 40 hp twin-cylinder American Aeronca E-113C engine specified by Straight and licence-built as the JAP J-99 by J. A. Prestwich & Co. Ltd of Tottenham, this allowed Straight to obtain a government subsidy as the entire machine had been built in Britain. The aircraft were distributed to the aero clubs at Ipswich, Ramsgate and Weston, and the one allocated to Weston was G-AEUU, arriving in the late afternoon of Wednesday 16 March already painted in the company colours. With this aircraft, an 'A' Pilot's Licence course could be obtained for as little as £12 10s (£12.50), dual-training £1 10s (£1.50) per hour and solo flying for £1 per hour, or a trial lesson for 15s (75p). Joy-rides could be had in any of the club's aeroplanes from 5s (25p).

Very soon pilots of the DH Dragons and Dragon Rapides, who frequently had to put up with the Praga crawling slowly along in the circuit, nicknamed it *The Bug* because of its looks. The irritation would, however, soon be over, for on Saturday 7 May during take-off *The Bug's* engine failed, and Knowles Breakell who was giving Mr F. S. Fry a short instructional flight had to put down in a small field on Locking Moor that was unfortunately littered with drainage

Weston Aero Club's Hillson Praga G-AEUU *The Bug* (E. J. Riding Collection)

pipes. In the ensuing forced landing from which both escaped uninjured, the Praga ran into a tree which damaged its nose and undercarriage and ripped off a wing-tip. Having extricated himself and his pupil from the aircraft, Breakell remembered that he was due to take over as ferry pilot on the Pengam Moors run and had to borrow a pushbike from a farmhand to dash back to the airport. Breakell at this time was CFI of the Exeter Aero Club and was well known for his ample proportions, and it was often said at his expense that, once installed in the small side-by-side cockpit of the Praga, 'when Breakell breathed in, his Pupil breathed out'. Engine problems were to be a persistent problem on the Praga until late 1938 when modifications developed by the company's engineers were embodied across the Straight fleet, and these, in addition to improving reliability, increased power by a useful 8 hp.

Following the unfortunate accident, because there was no other light training aircraft at Weston, BA Swallow G-ADPS was borrowed and, a little later, British Klemm Swallow G-ACRD was sent across from Ipswich. Remaining until the Praga was repaired, the Swallow was found to be a more effective trainer than the Praga and several were to be used by the company. On Monday, only two days before the Praga incident, shortly before 6 p.m. a single-seater from Pengam Moors undershot whilst landing at Weston and ended up in the rhyne bordering Locking Moor Road, but although one wing was badly damaged the pilot was luckily unhurt. So concerned was Christ Church Parochial Council with low-flying aircraft and accidents, that it decided to insure the church, which had a tall spire and was on the hillside just to the east of the town centre, against any possible damage. The monthly meeting at which it was decided to take out the insurance coincidentally happened to be held during the week in which both accidents occurred. A month after the Praga accident, there was another when the

Cardiff Aero Club's all-red Hawk Trainer nosed-over on landing and its engine was damaged. Grass cutting was in progress at the time with horse and tractor-hauled gang-mowers moving about in the long grass, each with a little red flag hoisted, and it was thought that this activity could have distracted the pilot.

Although the company's Pragas were in constant use, their replacement was being considered, with a Taylor Cub demonstrator being put through its paces at Weston on Sunday 31 July 1938 and a Tipsy Trainer on Wednesday 31 August. Despite the club aircraft being a bit thin on the ground, in August Weston had fifteen pilots go solo and eleven obtain their 'A' Licence. On the lighter

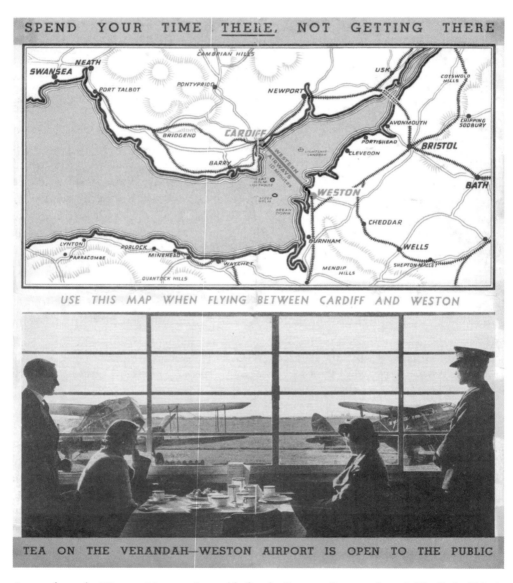

A page from the Western Airways time-table for the Summer Season of 1938 (Via D. Stabbins)

side, permission was given to the Weston Model Aero Club for its members to fly from the large areas of long grass that surrounded the mown runways. This activity continued until Sunday 8 May 1938, when a 7-foot (2.1-metre) wingspan, petrol-engined, free-flight model belonging to the club secretary and well-known local manufacturer of model aircraft, Lewis Green, caused a certain amount of concern to the airport authorities. After being launched it spiralled up through the cloud and after twenty-five minutes landed to the north of the airport in a garden at Milton Brow, just below Worlebury Hill. This incident caused the club to be banned from flying at the airport but it soon restarted from a field not far away near the village of Locking.

Meanwhile, the winter ferry service of 1937 continued until 1 June when the summer service started. Departures from Weston were now at ten minutes to every hour from 8.50 a.m., and from Pengam Moors every hour on the hour, with the first at 9 a.m. This was except for Mondays, when the first departures were at 8.20 a.m. and 8.30 a.m. respectively. Until 6 June, the last flight from Weston departed at 8.50 p.m. and that from Pengam Moors at 9 p.m., but from then until 18 September, when the summer service merged with the winter service, evening departure times had come down progressively to 6.50 p.m. and 7 p.m. respectively. The winter service then began again with flights from Weston at 8.50 a.m., 10.50 a.m., 2.20 p.m. and 3.50 p.m., and from Pengam Moors at 9 a.m., 11 a.m., 3 p.m. and 4 p.m. This hectic schedule ran like clockwork, with locals being able to set their watches by the regularity of take offs and, at the year's end Western Airways was again able to announce a record twelve months with 25,309 passengers carried on the ferry service. Fares for these services had been:

Single adult 6s 6d (32.5p), single child 4s 6d (22.5p).

Return adult 9s 6d (47.5p), return child 6s 6d (32.5p).

Series tickets for twelve return journeys: £5 adult, £3 10s (£3. 50) child.

Group tickets with a party of not less than eight adults: return 8s 4d (42p), child 5s 10d (29p).

The Birmingham summer service that had commenced Friday 24 June continued once-daily in both directions from Friday to Monday inclusive until Monday 29 August, the fares being:

Single adult £1 9s 6d (£1.48), single child £1 1s (£1.05).

Return adult £2 9s 6d (£2.48), return child £1 15s (£1.75).

A new passenger route had also been introduced in 1938, this being a twice-daily return summer service inaugurated on Wednesday 27 July that connected Swansea's new seashore Jersey Marine aerodrome with Pengam Moors and Weston. This was replaced 19 September by a twice-weekly Monday and Friday winter service that on each day provided two through-connections in each direction. Jersey Marine was owned by the Lord Jersey and leased to the Straight Corporation; Whitney Straight and the Lord Jersey being long-standing friends. At this time the Pengam Moors — Weston — Le Touquet — Paris service was still available but arranged on request.

Lew Lisle in white overalls supervises maintenance work on Western Airways Dragon Rapide G-ADBV (Via D. Stabbins)

The ex royal Dragon Rapide G-ADDD in its new Straight Corporation colours (E. J. Riding Collection)

In spite of the considerable changes at Western Airways, Norman Edgar stayed on in the newly-created position of commercial supervisor but it was not a happy arrangement, and his departure from the company came more quickly than planned. On 10 August he was dismissed, due, it was thought, to his accusations that, after-hours, some Weston Town Council dignitaries were often seen drinking on the premises with company pilots, and then the pilots would go flying whilst under the influence. A court case brought by him for unfair dismissal was to have front-page coverage in the local newspapers for several weeks in 1939, and led to much acrimony between him and some of the directors and staff, with it being aired publicly on pages of *Flight* magazine until well into 1940. Norman Edgar's position was filled in June 1939 by 'Watty' Watson, a well-known pilot with over 2,000 flying hours to his credit.

The New Maintenance Organisation at Weston

Until the takeover, aircraft maintenance at Weston had been carried out initially by Airwork staff from Whitchurch and later by Portsmouth, Southsea & Isle of Wight Aviation Ltd, which was contracted to run a repair, maintenance and service department in the Western Airways hangar. This arrangement ran well, but with the extra work that was now coming its way, the company was in need of its own maintenance organisation. As a consequence, in October 1937, Straight took on Frederick 'Freddy' George Jeans, former chief maintenance engineer of British Airways Ltd as chief engineer to look after all engineering work in the Straight Corporation, and early in 1938 Llewellyn Adolphus Lisle, a likeable but rather dour Lancastrian known as Lew, was brought in from Jersey Airways as chief ground engineer. Lew was to look after all aircraft overhaul and maintenance work in the Straight Corporation, although most engine work would continue to be done at the rapidly-growing facility at Ipswich Airport, which until recently had also provided airframe overhaul and paint-shop work. In addition to his engineering skills attained at Vickers and in the RAF, Lew also held a Pilot's 'A' Licence which would stand him in good stead in later years, but also sadly lead to his demise.

To guarantee a steady supply of engineers for this facility, Western Airways in February announced the formation of an Air Training School with school-leavers invited to apply to the Air Superintendent for an interview. On offer was a 3-year course in aircraft engineering and, at the end of it, 'A' and 'C' Ground Engineer's Licence examinations could be taken. Allowed to start when eighteen years old, the trainee or, more likely, his father had to pay Western Airways £50 a year for the course, of which £13 would be paid back at 5s (25p) a week pocket-money. The company would also pay the trainee's National Health and unemployment contributions, and, if taken on by the company on completion of the technical training, he or she would be eligible for free training to obtain a Pilot's 'A' Licence. The course was run with the assistance of various specialists with apprentices spending three days a week under instruction and the rest of the time in the workshops. As well as looking after its own machines that now totalled forty, by September 1938 Western Airways was also providing maintenance and hangarage for private owners such as Colonel Hamilton Gault, the former MP for Taunton who, from October 1937 had Vega Gull G-AEIF; Max Moore who had BA Swallow G-ADPS and, from May 1939, Mr G. Harben who had Monospar G-ADLL.

Extending the Ferry Service into the Night

During the first winter of operation from Weston, Norman Edgar had considered that much business was being lost due to the ferry service having to stop operating at 3.35 p.m. because of deteriorating light conditions. This put off business people from using the service if they were to return late afternoon, as, in addition to the single air-ticket, there was the added cost and inconvenience of having to buy a return rail ticket. The answer was to extend the service by several hours, but at that time there were no internal night time air routes in Britain, and discussions would have to be held with the Air Ministry to ascertain its requirements.

   Although the lighting system installed at Weston Airport during the first half of 1937 for an Army Co-operation contract had been approved by the Air Ministry, to obtain a full licence for passenger-carrying, Western Airways was informed that it would have to provide illumination by direct lighting of the eleven national grid pylons, some 2 miles (5 km) from touchdown, that stretched across the approach from the west. Estimated to cost £3,000, Weston Town Council rebelled at the price and refused funding to illuminate any more than the four pylons directly adjacent to the airport. Following protracted discussions, the Air Ministry eventually relented, issued a temporary licence to cover the four pylons and also allowed for an ingenious form of cheaper lighting to be used. Already in operation at Daventry in the Midlands, for the cost of only £980, neon tubes were fixed to the HT cables between the pylons and the radiated electrical field utilised to illuminate the tubes. With the installation completed, an Air Ministry representative approved the lighting during a proving flight on the night of 2 September. In addition to the lighting improvements, the grass runways had also been lengthened so that the runs were now: north – south 840 yards (768 metres), north-east – south-west 725 yards (663 metres), east – west 870 yards (796 metres) and south-east – north-west 700 yards (640 metres). With the Pengam Moors Airport lighting system also having to be approved, it was Sunday 2 October 1938 before Western Airways was able to start what was the country's first scheduled night service, the inaugural crossing to Pengam Moors being made by DDD piloted by William Knowlden accompanied by the company's other DH Dragon Rapide. Such was the importance of this event that it was broadcast live by the BBC with commentators Patrick Beech at Weston Airport, Leslie Bridgmont accompanied by author Jack Jones airborne in DDD and Wynford Vaughan-Thomas at Pengam Moors, with a reception committee including famous aviators Sir Arthur Whitten-Brown and Jim Mollison. However, due to torrential rain during the crossing, radio contact with the aeroplane was lost and Vaughan-Thomas had to improvise until the Rapides were heard approaching.

The Future Looks Bright

Things looked bright for the start of the 1939 ferry service, as towards the end of the previous year it had been announced that from 5 February, making use of the newly-approved airport lighting system, there would be a further departure from Weston at 4.50 p.m. However, as it happened, the service didn't get off with the expected swing, as on 13 January Pengam Moors was closed down by the Air Ministry as it had become flooded for the third successive year. It had been particularly difficult during the previous year when it had been closed for thirty-three days in March/April, and again days were lost in December. As to be expected, members of Weston Town Council were annoyed having spent so much money to transform Hutton Moor from a near swamp into a first-class airport (although in truth some parts did tend to suffer after prolonged rain), but it was felt that Cardiff City Council appeared to have done little to improve its facility on which Weston's operations so heavily relied.

So exasperated had Western Airways become in December 1938, that a temporary one month operating licence had been obtained from the Air Ministry to use a small aerodrome on a farm at Wenvoe, 4 miles (6 km) from Cardiff that was owned by Mr J. H. A. Wells, and it was this licence that was renewed in January and yet again sometime later. On each occasion when Wenvoe was used some Western Airways staff had to be inconveniently sent there to look after arrivals and departures until Pengam Moors dried out. Wenvoe Aerodrome, some 425 feet (130 metres) AMSL, had two grass runways, one of 1,500 feet (460 metres) running roughly north — south and the other of 1,350 feet (410 metres) running roughly east — west. Where the runways intersected there was a slight mound and it was on this in the 1950s that the TV transmitter was erected. It is said this aerial can easily be seen from Weston on a clear day when rain is due.

On the other hand, at the beginning of the year the future of the airport began to look assured when the Straight Corporation and Weston Town Council finally reached agreement on the airport's long-term future. The 21-year lease, provisionally agreed in January, now allowed for plans to be drawn up for the improvement and development of facilities at Weston Airport, including the construction of a new terminal/engineering building that was considered by Straight essential for his future operations as there had been a progressive expansion of Western Airways charter work, the ferry service, scheduled passenger services and there was the probability of a Straight-operated RAF Reserve Flying School being established. However, due to disagreements with the council on several points the matter was unable to be finalised for the time being.

The new terminal/engineering building was to be based on those already erected for Straight at Ipswich and Exeter, and again they were to be designed by his architects, Anthony M. Chitty and Robert Henning. Henning had made his first contact with Straight at Dartington Hall where he was engaged as its resident architect. In 1937, Henning entered into a partnership with Chitty, who, in the early 1930s with colleagues, had been responsible for the modern techniques used in the design of many of the country's well-known buildings, and from September 1938 both were made responsible for architectural design at Dartington Hall. In 1937 Chitty took his Pilot's 'A' Licence to help with learning the practical side of airport siting, layout, zoning, construction and operation, and this expertise from late 1938 was to be utilised by the Straight Corporation who offered an Aerodrome Consultancy Service, led by Chitty, to municipal authorities.

Following a number of months of delaying tactics by the Straight Corporation, early in 1939 it asked Weston Town Council to fund construction of the 2-storey terminal/engineering building to the tune of £23,000. This would house two squash courts, a public lounge, a dining room, kitchen, bar, club rooms and sleeping accommodation for members of the RAF Reserve Flying School; also there would be the usual waiting rooms and booking offices for the airline. Although £5,000 would be available from the Air Ministry to cover administration of the school, the council was not happy, considering it to be an 'amazing request' for what was seen as a palatial building. After eighteen months of attempts to arrive at satisfactory terms, the Straight Corporation capitulated and announced that it was now itself prepared to fund the building and was requesting from the town's planning department permission to erect the complex. Following inspection of Exeter's buildings by the airport committee which was flown there 4 May, a special council meeting held 23 May agreed Straight's proposal. This was now for a 42-year lease with an annual rental of £1,750 to be reviewed every five years, but by now the requirement for the building was close to being overtaken by events and no construction work was ever undertaken.

As a part of the Straight Corporation's strategy in providing flight-training, on 1 January 1939 a new subsidiary, Straight Aviation Training, was formed to look after the introduction of large-scale commercial flying training, and it was registered as a private company on 30 March, with directors Whitney Straight and Owen Roberts who had invested a nominal capital of £5,000 in the project. Captain William Neville Cumming DFC, with some 7,000 flying hours, was then brought in as director of training. Having flown with the RNAS and RAF, he later achieved a most distinguished civil flying record pioneering air routes in Canada and then across the Empire and Atlantic with Imperial Airways, and had also carried out the first long-range tests of the Empire Flying Boat *Caledonia*. One of his first tasks with the company would be to supervise establishment at Weston Airport of the No.5 Civil Air Navigation School on behalf of the Air Ministry.

On the strength of another Ministry contract, the establishment of No.39 Elementary and Reserve Flying Training School at the airport, the Straight Corporation began in February 1939 with the erection of a new 60,000-sq. foot (5,574-sq. metres) hangar to the west of the original one. Attached was a range of workshops and, alongside, a garage for an ambulance and fire-tender. There was also a small powerhouse that contained a stand-by generator driven by an engine taken from an old Army tank. Accommodation for the staff and pupils was built on open fields behind the hangars alongside Laney's Drove and the existing grass runways were extended to conform to Air Ministry requirements, the extra land, some of which extended to Hutton Moor Lane, being acquired by compulsory purchase which pleased Weston Town Council and the townspeople as there was no charge on the rates.

A World Record

Once Pengam Moors had dried out, the remaining weeks of the 1938 winter ferry service continued uninterrupted and merged with the summer service that commenced 1 May. Departures to and from Pengam Moors were now at half-hourly intervals with the first leaving Weston at 8.20 a.m. and the last from Pengam Moors at 10.30 p.m. With this new timetable the Weston — Pengam Moors ferry operations with fifty-eight services a day became recognised as the most frequent in the world! In fact, during the five days of the August bank holiday, Western Airways was to carry a remarkable 4,872 passengers. This was almost double the numbers carried over the five-day Whitsun bank holiday which in itself may have been a world record. The majority of the passengers carried, of course, flew on the ferry service. Although the distance to Pengam Moors was short and on a clear day from Weston seafront an aircraft could be followed with binoculars to the airport, a lot could happen over the stretch of water in poor visibility. One such instance occurred on the evening of 17 May.

During that evening, Tommy Farr was to fight Larry Gains at Cardiff and five aircraft had been flown from Weston with a full complement of passengers for the entertainment. As the evening wore on the weather rapidly deteriorated, such that just before take off for the return trip, cloud base was down to about 300 feet (91 metres), visibility was about half a mile (0.8 km) and in squalls there was torrential rain. Led by Chief Pilot Brian Oakley, the plan was to climb through the cloud to around 800 feet (244 metres) then turn on to a heading of 200 degrees, hold this for seven or eight minutes until

The Express G-AETM finally emerged from overhaul mid 1939, just in time for a short summer season (Via Bob Cooke)

G-AEDH, one of the Straight Corporation's two Dragonflies (W. K. Kilsby via K. Wakefield)

Straight Corporation's first Q6 G-AFIX on the Manchester service picking-up passengers at Birmingham's new Elmdon Airport (*Aeroplane*/www.aeroplanemonthly.com)

Dragon Rapide G-AFSO was also used initially on the Manchester Service (Via M. Mansbridge)

One of the two Scions operated by the Straight Corporation, in this case G-ADDX that was initially based at Roborough (E. J. Riding Collection)

picking up a bearing of 50 degrees from the Bristol Radio Station when a let-down would be commenced, hopefully to bring them into clear conditions over Weston's seafront and away from the surrounding high ground. Captain T. R. 'Panda' Watson, whose DH Dragon, like the others, was full of slightly inebriated passengers, was to experience particular difficulties during the flight. He unfortunately had little experience of instrument flying and at times found his aircraft unexpectedly descending rapidly in a series of steep turns, recovering only to find the aircraft climbing rapidly up to around 1,000 feet (305 metres). The compass was no help in this situation and, being unable to pick up the Bristol beacon, considered he was lost. In desperation, the cockpit side-window was lowered in the hope of seeing some recognisable feature and, quite unexpectedly, lights on Weston's Grand Pier appeared faintly through the cloud and pouring rain. Watson immediately lowered the Dragon's nose and, emerging from the clag, flew past the pier at about 150 feet (46 metres) with airspeed well above the maker's top limit! William Knowlden had been made fully aware of the situation and, with some machines still overdue, organised a display of lights and pyrotechnics that would not have looked amiss on 5 November. This had the desired result, with the remaining aircraft eventually homing onto the lights from varying directions, some having been airborne for over thirty minutes and, like Watson, the other pilots had alarming tales to tell. There appears to be no record of any comments from the passengers!

On 8 May a twice-daily Whitchurch — Penzance (Lands End/St Just) service had commenced that after calling at Pengam Moors, went by the way of Swansea (Jersey Marine) with a call at Barnstaple (North Devon) and Newquay

(Trebelzue) Airports. For safety reasons, on the Swansea — Barnstaple leg a wireless operator was carried. The Whitchurch — Pengam Moors — Jersey Marine part of the route had five return services a day, and from 27 July to make the most of Swansea's catchment area, Jersey Marine was used twice a day in an extension of the normal Weston — Pengam Moors ferry service. From 17 June, there also started a thrice-daily service from Weston to Whitchurch, Birmingham (Elmdon) and Manchester (Ringway) where Straight had recently opened a booking office, and the service was extended to the north once a day to connect with Liverpool (Speke) Airport. Prior to the allocation of licences to fly these 1939 routes, there had been conflict between Western Airways and Great Western & Southern Airlines that had been formed 5 December 1938 by the Great Western and Southern Railway companies. With both airlines applying for permission to operate the same services, the new Air Licensing Authority, in an enquiry in which Whitney Straight put a strong case, considered that Western Airways offered the public a better deal and granted it the licence.

To provide extra capacity for the summer ferry service, Western Airways obtained in April DH 86b Express G-AETM, a 4-engined machine with seats for seventeen passengers. This aircraft, already well-known as the *Norseman*, had two years previously inaugurated, and since then operated, the Newcastle — Stavanger, Norway, route of Allied Airways. Maximum publicity was achieved with it flying into Weston Airport accompanied by several of the Western Airways fleet, but unfortunately the machine would turn out to be a bit of a white elephant, for due to non-availability of spares, in early June it was still in the hangar in Allied Airways colours with its engines in a dismantled state and for some reason referred to as the *Condor*.

In 1939 Elmdon had replaced Castle Bromwich as Birmingham's airport, and the first aircraft to land there on 30 March in advance of the official opening was DH Dragonfly G-AEDH bringing in Whitney Straight to announce his new service from Weston. Western Airways was also closely associated with the airport's opening, for the company sent up seven aircraft to give joy-rides, but unfortunately cloud base was around 300 feet (91 metres) and little flying was done. This new service to the north broke with the Western Airways tradition of using only De Havilland airliners, as two Percival Q6 6-seat low-wing monoplanes powered by two 200 hp DH Gipsy Six engines were to be used. Norman Edgar had considered obtaining a Q6 in 1937 for a Paris service, and a demonstrator visited Weston at the beginning of March, but the service was not started and it was to be a further two years before the type joined the company.

The first of these machines, G-AFIX, arrived at Weston during the afternoon of Saturday 3 June already finished in the company colours. It was the twelfth off the production line and the first of the type to have a retractable undercarriage, giving a cruising speed of 183 mph (295 kph). Delivery of this machine brought the number of Straight Corporation aircraft at Weston to twenty. Pending arrival of the second machine G-AFVC a few weeks later, the service was operated by the single Q6 and DH Dragon Rapides G-ACTU and G-AFSO, and occasionally DH Dragonfly G-AEDH, the Rapides making good use of the stop-overs at Elmdon to give joy-rides. G-AFVC was an earlier version of the Q6 with a fixed trousered undercarriage that gave a top speed that was 8 mph (13 kph) slower than that of G-AFIX, but it was fitted with Ratier constant-speed airscrews that gave a superior take-off performance. To give greater visibility in conditions of bright sunlight and at dusk, G-AFVC was doped experimentally overall bright yellow with white horizontal stripes on the fin, and had small black registration letters close to the tail. These two mini-airliners flew the trunk routes at a cruising speed far in excess of the aeroplanes then operated by other internal airlines, thus further enhancing the names of Western Airways and the Straight Corporation. The elapsed times and fares current from Weston in August 1939 were:

Birmingham 55 min – £1 9s (£1.45), Manchester 1 hr 30 min – £2 7s 4d (£2.37), Swansea 30 min – 17s (85p), Barnstaple 1 hr 5 min – £1 11s (£1.55), Newquay 1 hr 55 min – £2 14s (£2.70) and Penzance 2 hr 30 min – £3 5s (£3.25). The Weston — Pengam Moors service took a nominal ten minutes and cost 6s 6d (32.5p), the same price charged for the Whitchurch — Pengam Moors service although it took slightly longer.

During the summer, Western Airways machines available for airline use comprised five DH Dragons, four DH Dragon Rapides, the two Percival Q6, the DH Express and Dragonfly. There were also two Short Scions G-ADDX and G-ADDV that had been obtained by the Straight Corporation in 1936 and initially operated by Ramsgate Airport Ltd and Plymouth Airports Ltd respectively. Later, with Dragonfly G-ADNA, they were operated by Southern Airways Ltd, another subsidiary of the company, flying daily services along the Thames Estuary; alternatively, they also provided Army co-operation support and carried out joy-rides. As well as providing machines for these services, some were also sent in the summer months to Filton and Pengam Moors for their Empire Air Days. To fly and service the company's airliners and training aeroplanes, fifteen pilots and forty hangar staff were now employed, with the majority based at Weston. At this time, directors of Western Airways were chairman Whitney Straight, the Lady Apsley, Basil Watling an accountant and major shareholder, Fredrick Jeans and Stanley Cox.

Weston's Civil Air Guard and No.39 Elementary and Reserve Flying Training School

On 1 October 1938, as part of the national build-up to provide pilots for the probable forthcoming war with Germany, a unit of the Air Ministry-sponsored Civil Air Guard (CAG) had been established at Weston. Like all of the others in the country and those at the other four Straight-operated aero clubs, it was for people aged between eighteen and fifty, was to be integrated into the aero club and use its aircraft and instructors. Nationwide, the CAG had come into being 1

Members of Straight's Weston Civil Air Guard in front of Hornet Moth G-AFMP, 26 February 1939. Centre is Chief Flying Instructor Flying Officer Dick Mortimer, and on his left Norman House and at the end of the line Bill Cooke, both Western Airways Inspectors (Via B. House)

Straight's British Klemm Swallow G-ACRD that was used by the Weston Aero Club for a time in 1938 (E. J. Riding Collection)

September 1938 and gave clubs a grant of £50 for each 'A' Licence gained on a normal machine (more than 1,200 lb (544 kg) All-Up Weight (AUW), or £30 if a light aircraft (below 1,200 lb AUW) such as the Praga was used. The scheme also gave members reduced rates for their flying and, as to be expected, the Weston Aero Club, like most others, was overwhelmed with applicants with the club having too few aeroplanes and instructors. By the end of the year, so successful was the scheme proving nationwide in encouraging applicants, that some 36,000 had been received. After training, the pilot would be expected to serve in the RAF or any other branch of aviation as directed by the Air Ministry.

By February 1939, the CAG scheme was producing good results and, notwithstanding the winter conditions, Straight's five clubs were achieving a success rate of one CAG 'A' Licence every three days, and in March the number would be one a day. The Weston CAG was run by Mr Muspratt-Williams, whose brother was a flight commander with 59 Squadron at Old Sarum, operating Army co-operation Hawker Hectors, and he was talked into visiting Weston on two occasions to give an insight into service flying. The first was on Tuesday 9 May, when two of the squadron's aircraft gave a demonstration of picking up messages by hook and some CAG members were flown in the aircraft; the second visit took place a couple of weeks later.

Weston CAG members normally flew the aero club's Praga or Swallow but, for more advanced training, heavier aircraft were used, three being DH Hornet Moths G-AFDY, G-AFMP and G-AFEE. On Tuesday 9 May, Swallow G-ADPS on CAG work had engine failure on take-off and Mr Riley-Sawdon the club's new CFI instructing a Mr Whenham of Weston, luckily managed to put the machine down with only slight damage to its undercarriage in a field at the end of Mansfield Avenue in Ashcombe, a district of Weston. It was dismantled and taken back to the airport, but, although it was repaired and flying again by the following evening, only three weeks later, on the evening of Tuesday 6 June, it was involved in another accident. Mr A. Studley, who was close to obtaining his 'A' Licence, had been instructed to carry out solo a simulated engine-failure at 2,000 feet (610 metres) and then make a glide-approach and landing, but a misjudgement during the final stages of this operation unfortunately allowed the machine to clip a tree and the pilot had to extricate himself from the wreckage that ended up just inside the airport boundary. Replaced by Swallow G-AEAU, this aircraft was expected to remain at Weston until the number of machines in the club had increased to seven. A month later, club members saw how to correctly carry out a powerless approach, when Christopher 'Kit' Nicholson, a leading pre-war exponent of cross-country soaring, and incidentally Straight Corporation's Gliding Consultant, landed at the airport in his German Rhonsperber sailplane after a 4-hour cross-country flight from Oxford.

Come July, there were 186 uniformed members of Weston's CAG of which no less than fifty-two held 'A' Licences, and as war became more certain, some of the more experienced members were called upon to assist the local ARP (Air Raid Precautions) who wanted added realism in the now frequently staged

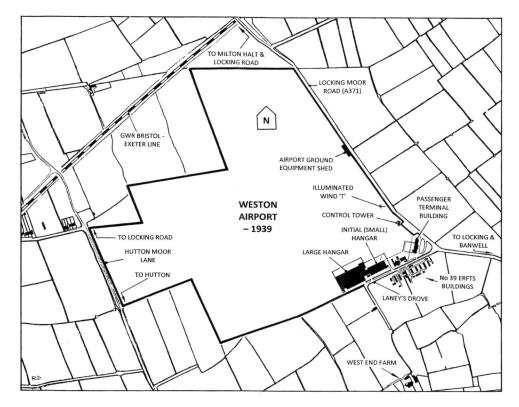

By mid 1939, the second (larger) hangar and accommodation had been built alongside Laney's Drove for No. 39 ERFTS, and the airport extended west to Hutton Moor Lane (R. Dudley)

exercises. One took place on 28 July when CAG members flew low over targets in and around Weston and small devices were set off on the ground to simulate exploding bombs.

In 1939, two further types of new training aircraft were to be received by the aero clubs to supplement the Miles Hawk Trainer IIIs obtained the previous year, the first being the DH Tiger Moth and the other the Piper Cub Coupé. Earmarked for advanced aerobatic training mainly by the CAG, Weston's Tiger Moth G-AFSP arrived towards the end of June, and a few days later three all-yellow Coupés arrived; J-4As G-AFWB and G-AFWS powered by the 50 hp Continental, and a J-4B G-AFTC powered by the 60 hp Franklin. On their way to supplement the existing fleet of training machines at the various aero clubs, G-AFWS flown into Weston early July was used until early August when it was transferred to the new aero club at Inverness by Louis Strange where it was to be used for solo flying. A further eight J-4As were brought in from America shortly afterwards, but barely had time to enter service before the outbreak of war. Weston initially had two of these machines, one of which was G-AFVF on loan from the Ipswich Club, and they proved to be so popular that during the first week of August, even though there had been two days of heavy rain, 113 hours were flown.

By early June, facilities at the airport for No.39 Elementary and Reserve Flying Training School had been completed and the establishment was officially opened 3 July. The new hangar initially housed the school's six yellow RAF Miles Magisters, N3822 , N3823, N3969, N3970, N3971 and N3972, Hawker Hind K5523 and an occasional Westland Lysander; their numbers would have increased to about twenty-five, with Hawker Harts and Avro Ansons being introduced, had not war been declared in September. Weather permitting, the school flew each day of the week between 9 a.m. and dusk, but as most of the ten or so members of the initial and only intake had jobs, much of the training was at weekends and in the evenings. The commanding officer and chief instructor was Flight Lieutenant H. P. Hudson and under his command were instructors Flight Lieutenant Drabble, Flight Sergeant Simmonds and Mr Littlejohn. The training of observers, air gunners and wireless operators, the latter to be flown in Ansons, was due to commence at a later date. Around this time the Straight Corporation also opened similar schools at Exeter (37 ERFTS) and Ipswich (45 ERFTS). The trainees, all given the rank of sergeant, were mainly from North Somerset and had applied to join the existing schools at Filton and Whitchurch, but these were already full and they had to await the opening of the one at Weston. The school was soon to put the maintenance organisation of Western Airways under pressure, for the *Flight* magazine of 17 August carried an advert for two deputy chief engineers, one for Ipswich and the other for Weston, to be rewarded with a good salary and staff pension scheme.

On completion of a 3-month ground-training course at the RAF establishment in Julian Road, Stoke Bishop, Bristol, flying at Weston commenced. Initially, normal circuit work was practised and this was followed by low-level flying in an area south of the Mendips between the sea and the Weston — Highbridge railway line; aerobatics were carried out in an area to the east of it. The destination of the mandatory cross-country destination appeared to be at the whim of the instructor who usually had a reason to be taken to a particular station, i.e. to see a girlfriend. However, the contract and school were to be short-lived, as following declaration of war on 3 September, and with most pilots having completed only around forty hours flying, its aircraft were withdrawn to swell the ranks of the rapidly expanding RAF Elementary Flying Training Schools.

The Coming of War

Until the 1930s, few aircraft of the Royal Air Force had been seen over Weston, but with the establishment in 1930 of a flying-boat base at RAF Pembroke Dock on the South Wales coast, there was a gradual increase in military air activity. Soon flying-boats were frequently seen going about their duties. There were Short Singapores, Saro Londons, Short Lerwicks and Sunderlands passing over at a fairly low level. One Singapore was even seen with a crew member out on the starboard lower mainplane fiddling with an engine cowling. There were also

Hawker Hart variants galore and an oft-seen Vickers Vildebeest I that headed south at about 1,500 feet (457 metres). As war drew nearer, from Weston Zoyland, near Bridgwater, Hawker Henleys towing drogues with gunners in Westland Lysanders popping-off at them were often over Weston Bay, and one drogue even broke adrift and fluttered down onto the sands near the Grand Pier. In fact, one of the first military aircraft to crash-land at Weston Airport was Hawker Henley L3314 belonging to 1 AACU at Weston Zoyland, that on 5 February 1940 undershot whilst landing, hit a bank and had its undercarriage collapse. No.501 Auxiliary Air Force 'County of Gloucester' Squadron from Filton with Hawker Hinds was also a frequent visitor to Weston at weekends. At that time there were also sightings of Hispano Suiza-powered Vildebeests at low level just off the beach heading for Uphill and a Fairey Fantome low down over Sand Bay. Another unusual sighting was a Vickers Virginia X dropping two parachutists whilst overflying to the west.

On Monday 23 and Tuesday 24 May in 1938, further military aircraft were seen when there was a spectacular fly-past of seventy-two RAF bombers. Mainly Bristol Blenheims, Fairey Battles, Hawker Harts and Demons, they were rehearsing for the Empire Air Day fly-past over London. The outgoing flight included towns and cities that lay in a rough line from Newbury to Cardiff and on the way back to London the aircraft overflew Weston, Taunton, Frome and Salisbury. Other Battles were also seen in the following year, as in early March 1939 it had been announced by the town council that Weston was to become affiliated with the 218(B) 'Gold Coast' Squadron stationed at Boscombe Down. As a part of the arrangements, aeroplanes from the squadron to be known as Weston's Own would pay the town a ceremonial visit later in the year, and on Saturday 19 August the promise was kept when twelve Fairey Battles flew over in formation, landed and lined up alongside Locking Moor Road for spectators to view the aircraft and meet the crews.

During 1939 Western Airways had been called upon to provide additional assistance to the military, including the participation in an exercise in February when a DH Dragon was flown around the city of Bristol to give the newly formed 66 Searchlight AA Regiment its first opportunity to locate a blacked-out aeroplane. Other similar work was carried out further afield with DH Dragon Rapide G-ADBV flown over Liverpool Bay in July from a temporary base at Manchester Airport, and both DH Dragonflies and Q6 G-AFVC in August flown by pilots Blackaller and Arnott out of Elmdon, but in September the Q6 was unfortunately damaged in a forced landing at Brierley Hill in Staffordshire. With war imminent, all the Pragas were flown to Weston where G-AEYM from the Ipswich club was damaged on landing. Although impressed into the RAF in April 1940, most were soon scrapped as they were found to be unsuitable for military service, and with their large non-folding wing, took up too much valuable storage space.

Weston Airport and the local areas would be subject to much change in the months leading up to the war and this would have a significant effect on the population of Weston and surrounding district. During the years 1937-38, the British Government had become increasingly aware of the need to rearm, and following much thought and discussion, plans were made to re-equip the armed forces. The introduction of new aircraft was high on the list and this would call for immediate steps to be taken to set up production lines in new shadow factories and training facilities established to enable the country's workforce and the Military to maintain and operate the new equipment efficiently.

One of the first inklings that Westonians had of rearmament occurred in early 1938, when it was announced in the local press that an area of land totalling some 250 acres (102 hectares), that was about a mile (1.6 km) to the east of Weston Airport and close to the village of Locking had been obtained by the Government. Rumoured to be for a munitions factory, it was flanked to the north-east by Wolvershill Rhyne, to the south by what was then the new A371 Locking Village Bypass, which joined with Locking Moor Road that ran past Weston Airport and extended eastwards to Devil's Elbow near the village of Banwell. When purchased, owners of the affected farmland, mainly Somerset County Council, were warned not to sell any further property on Locking Head, Larkhill and Manor Farms to other parties as it was probable that the establishment would in due course have to be extended, and those farming the land were informed that they would have to vacate the area at the latest by 1 January 1939. The actual reason for the land acquisition soon became clear, however, for during the RAF Expansion Debate in the House of Commons on 12 May 1938, the Air Ministry announced that a number of additional RAF Technical Training Camps were to be built and one of them was to be near Weston-super-Mare (*see chapter 3*).

Towards the end of 1938, when the camp soon to be named RAF Locking was nearing completion, there were strong rumours circulating that by Easter of the following year the building labourers working there would have moved to Sand Bay, where it looked as though an Empire Seaplane Base would be located. Further credence to this rumour was given in early January when it became known that Eric Armstrong, who owned much of the land in that area, had agreed to sell 100 acres (40.5 hectares) to a mysterious Mr C. Smith of Exeter. His address and business were unknown but he was thought to be secretly representing the Air Ministry. Extending from Kewstoke through to Woodspring Priory, the real-estate included two farms and two cottages. Whether it was really intended for a seaplane base is not known, but it was soon to become apparent that the Ministry had use for much of the land, which, together with Weston's Birnbeck Pier, Brean Down and Brean Sands, would be used extensively during the next few years for weapon ranges and secret work on weapon-delivery systems. The arrival at Weston Airport in 1941 of a special flight from the Torpedo Development Unit at Gosport, Hampshire, was to give a means of delivering some of these weapons (*see chapter 3*).

With the declaration of war on Sunday 3 September, the 257 civil transport aircraft and all aerodromes within Britain were requisitioned by the National

Air Communications (NAC) organisation. Most of the machines that were considered suitable for military use were then flown to pre-arranged airfields where they would be taken on charge by the RAF. To this end, most of the Western Airways aeroplanes were initially loaned to RAF units, two being DH Dragon G-ACJT and Dragon Rapide G-ACTU which went to 24 Squadron at Hendon, but a couple of machines were retained for use by Western Airways. Unlike the other commandeered machines, the DH Express, which for months had been parked in the back of a hangar gathering dust and bird-droppings, was overhauled and delivered to Airwork at Gatwick, where between 10 and 27 January 1940, it was converted into an air-ambulance named *Silver Star* for work on behalf of the Finnish Fund.

The requisitioning of airports had been preceded by the Air Navigation (Emergency Restriction) Order 1939 issued 31 August, prohibiting all civil flying without special permit. A further series of regulations were then issued under the Air Navigation (Restriction in Time of War) Order 1939 that concerned five airports. These regulations were mainly involved with the introduction of air corridors from the airports, along which civil landplanes under the control of the NAC when entering or leaving the United Kingdom were allowed to pass. Any departure from the corridor could result in the aircraft being fired upon. One of the airports was Whitchurch, from where aircraft had to keep to a 2-mile-wide (3.2 km) corridor extending from the airport in a westerly direction to Long Ashton Railway Station. From there they were to follow the railway line to Weston, then fly on a bearing of 265 degrees true through a 4-mile-wide (6.4 km) corridor until the limit of territorial waters was reached. This was to result in many previously unseen machines overflying Weston including Armstrong Whitworth AW 27 Ensigns and Handley Page HP 42, as within several days of the regulations being issued, fifty-nine airliners belonging to Imperial Airways Ltd and British Airways Ltd, that were about to be amalgamated into the nationalised British Overseas Airways Corporation, descended on Whitchurch, where they were to remain for the war's duration.

With no immediate signs of war in South-West England, there was a strong call for the Weston — Pengam Moors ferry service to be resumed, and on Saturday 25 November, having obtained the necessary clearance from the NAC, a limited one-hourly service commenced in both directions. Shortly after the restart of the service, Western Airways was to suffer its second fatal accident when, during the morning of 20 December, after climbing to about 200 feet (30 metres), DH Dragon G-ACJT stalled and then dived onto the airport. It was thought that the pilot, Leslie Arnott, who was the only occupant and received fatal injuries in the ensuing fire, had become incapacitated as the Dragon gained flying-speed. There had been an earlier fatal accident in 1935 when on 22 July Dragon G-ACMP, on lease from Jersey Airlines, on a normal Whitchurch — Splott run had spun onto the mudflats whilst landing. In this case, the pilot Mr M. J. Mansfield and his two passengers were killed and the aircraft submerged by the incoming tide. The ferry service, however, was soon to be forcibly shut down, the last trip to Pengam Moors being flown by Knowles Breakell on 30 March 1940 in a Dragon. During this short period there had been an increased demand for seats, passengers in December totalling 720 compared with 457 in the same period of the previous year. As a consequence, the company ran an anti-shut-down poster campaign and there were also strong representations to the Air Ministry from the Lord Apsley, still a director of Western Airways, Weston Town Council and the other town councils who had an interest in the ferry service continuing, but it was all to no avail.

So ended for the time being one of the world's most successful airlines, that in 1933, when operating from Whitchurch, carried a mere 2,558 passengers compared to the heady days of 1939 when a remarkable 44,351 were carried. In each of the pre-war years Western Airways had operated at a loss, and only in 1939 did the company come close to breaking even, no doubt assisted by the government subsidy.

Until Louis Strange was recommissioned into the RAF in early 1940 as a Pilot Officer acting on behalf of the Air Ministry he had taken control of the airports at Weston, Exeter and Plymouth, and to assist him and other NAC personnel, two DH Puss Moths G-ABKD and G-ABLB had been positioned at Weston. G-ABLB was to remain there until 5 April when it was requisitioned, and as X9400 for a few months was placed under control of RAF Locking. On 27 March, most of the Western Airways fleet that was being operated under NAC conditions was impressed into the RAF and the Straight Corporation was informed that in April eighteen of its twenty-six aeroplanes, if not already requisitioned, would be, with their inspection commencing 2 April. The NAC was soon disbanded and Strange was sent to France with 24 Squadron where during the retreat he instigated the saving of many serviceable RAF aeroplanes, and for this was awarded a bar to his DFC. In mid-1940, following orders from Winston Churchill, as a Squadron Leader he took on the responsibility of forming the Central Landing School, Britain's first parachute force, and later in the war he was closely associated with equipping merchant vessels with catapult-launched fighters.

By 1939, the aircraft factory mooted for the airport by the Ministry back in 1935, was about to come to fruition. The Bristol Aeroplane Company at Filton had been investigating various sites in the Midlands for a shadow factory where its twin-engine Beaufighter could be assembled, but when, due to various problems, these sites came to naught, the area around Weston was investigated, and a site a few fields away from the westerly edge of Weston Airport chosen (*see chapter 2*). By 1940 building construction of what was known as the Oldmixon Factory was underway and work on extending the airport out to the factory commenced. Bristol's requirement for concrete cross runways, then cancelled in favour of three grass runways, after the first winter was replaced by an urgent requirement for a single concrete runway.

Worried about the possibility of enemy attack, meanwhile, the Ministry had Bristol disperse its second Erecting Hall and Flight Shed from Oldmixon to other nearby locations (*see chapter 2*). The Flight Shed was positioned on Hutton Moor that was within the confines of the extended northerly side of the airport, but the Erecting Hall was to be built further away at the hamlet and manor of Elborough that was just off the newly completed A371 Locking Village Bypass that had already been used to locate RAF Locking. As with the RAF camp that had a requirement for some of its aircraft to be delivered by road from the airport, the Erecting Hall would also utilise the road for transportation of its aircraft to the Hutton Moor Flight Shed. However, the road running past the airport was narrow and to give it extra width for the passage of aircraft which were to enter through double gates in the airport's north-easterly corner, the old road then became a path and a new road was laid alongside and to the east of it.

Straight Joins Up

Meanwhile, in early 1939 Whitney Straight had joined the Auxiliary Air Force and was commissioned as an Acting Pilot Officer in 601 (County of London) Squadron. Called up in August 1939, with the prospect of being killed or incapacitated whilst serving in the RAF, to look after his interests Mr P. D. de Laszlo became a member of the Western Airways Board of Directors; the others being two of the original members, Fredrick Gwatkin and the Lord Apsley. By now Straight's expertise in establishing aerodromes was well known and soon put to good use when, with the temporary rank of Squadron Leader, in mid-April 1940 he was sent by sea as a part of a taskforce to central Norway. Here, as British Air Liaison Officer to the Norwegian High Command he was to reconnoitre airstrips and frozen lakes considered suitable for RAF Gloster Gladiators to operate from. This was necessary as all suitable airfields in this mountainous country were occupied by the enemy, and there was an urgent need for the RAF to provide air cover to the small force of Norwegian and British soldiers that, amongst their other duties, were attempting to disrupt the supply of Swedish high-grade iron-ore that in the winter went via Norway to Germany.

Landing on 17 April, Straight set to work immediately and selected a couple of possible landing-grounds, the one chosen for RAF use being Lake Lesjaskog which was frozen and covered in deep snow. Soon he had managed to gather around 200 people from the sparsely populated area and commandeered a passing herd of some 3,000 reindeer to prepare a runway, the latter by trampling the snow. Eighteen Gladiators of 263 Squadron from Filton, shipped to Norway aboard HMS *Glorious* were then flown off on the 24th. The lake was quickly attacked by the Luftwaffe and by the second day the landing ground and the aeroplanes had been virtually destroyed with Straight injured in one of the attacks. Evacuated to Britain to recuperate, he was awarded the Norwegian War Cross and, somewhat later, the British Military Cross, for his efforts against the odds in Norway. Whilst awaiting his return to operational flying with 601 Squadron, he was appointed ADC to the Duke of Kent and also took on supernumerary flying duties at HQ Flying Training Command. Rejoining his squadron 28 September, Straight, now a flying officer, was stationed at his pre-war Exeter Airport, where on 12 December he claimed the destruction of a Heinkel He 111. Made a flight commander in early 1941, a Messerschmitt Bf 109 was soon to fall to his guns on 2 February over the English Channel.

On 23 April, Straight joined 242 Squadron at Stapleford Tawney as its commanding officer, and on the night of 12 June, whilst on an intruder operation over Merville Airfield, destroyed a Messerschmitt Bf 110. Sharing the destruction of a 109 whilst escorting Blenheims to St Omer on the 21st, two further 109s were claimed as probables on 27 July. Whilst attacking shipping at Fecamp on the 31st he was shot down by light flak and force-landed in a field. Avoiding immediate capture he reached the American Embassy in Paris, found it shut, but with 12,000 francs provided by the caretaker started to work his way south to Vichy France where he was captured. In his absence, on 8 August, Straight was awarded a DFC. Escaping on 22 June 1942, with help from the French Resistance he reached the beach at St Pierre Plage near Narbonne where, during the night of 13 July, he was evacuated by HMS *Tarana* to Gibraltar, and on 21 July, almost a year after being shot down, was able to report to No.1 Depot, RAF Uxbridge, for further duty. Shortly after arriving back in Britain, Straight found time to fly a Spitfire into Weston Airport and gave Western Airways apprentices a pep-talk and details of his recent exciting escapades. Then selected to use another area of his expertise, that of operating airlines, Straight was posted to the Middle East on 10 September as Acting Air Commodore with 216 (Transport) Group. Several other similar RAF groups of transport aircraft were operating in other parts of the world, and these, together with Straight's group, and the civilian-staffed BOAC, were brought together in March 1943 to form RAF Transport Command. So successful had the organisation and operating techniques of Straight's group been that he received a Mention in Dispatches, and when the command was formed it was based closely on his group. Appointed Air ADC to King George VI in 1944, he was made a CBE in June and returned to Britain a year later as AOC 46 Group Transport Command attached to the British Air Forces of Occupation. Released from the RAF in November as a Group Captain, but retaining the rank of Air Commodore, it wasn't long before his experience with wartime Transport Command was utilised by the British Government in the first of a number of important peace-time positions.

Western Airways and the War

With the declaration of war, Western Airways initially carried on much as before with the onus being on keeping its existing fleet of twin-engined machines serviceable for the NAC/RAF and the ferry service. Soon, however, military contracts were to be awarded that required a fairly rapid expansion of the workforce, so that, by mid-war, some 300 were employed by the company, which was now under the control of Lord Nuffield's Civilian Repair Organisation (CRO) to carry out the repair, overhaul, modification and rebuild of various types of British and American aircraft. Administration of the company was from buildings located between the two hangars where there was also a centrally-heated parachute-packing room with long polished tables, a bag room in which fabric was stitched up to set patterns and later used to cover various airframe components, and a Link trainer facility to keep aircrew current; this was also very popular with cadets belonging to the local ATC squadrons. With the work being carried out on military aircraft, the inspection department was enlarged and a representative of the Ministry's Aeronautical Inspection Directorate (AID) was brought in. A drawing office responsible for some of the smaller modifications embodied by Western Airways was also set up, as was an armoury to look after weapons and ammunition recovered from the various aircraft.

Many employees had been seconded to the organisation, some from other parts of the country and they had to be billeted locally. One joining the inspection team was W. T. 'Bill' Dann, or 'Danny' as he became known. An ex-Westland apprentice he arrived in mid-1940 from the post of Station Manager of Jersey Airlines, Southampton, and would over a number of years become an important member of the team of Western Airways managers/directors. Other adults, skilled, but with no aircraft experience, such as carpenters and cabinet makers were also brought in to repair the many timber components, as were garage mechanics to work on metal structures and mechanical systems. Many unskilled workers were also taken on and given the necessary training to enable them to do a variety of jobs, as were a few RAF personnel that had just completed their basic engineering training. Others were school-leavers that joined the company when fourteen years old and received 14s (70p) a week; one of the many was Brian Kick employed as a boy aircraft cleaner. His first task was the removal of oil and dirt from the bottom of Fairey Battle fuselages with a tin of paraffin and a brush. After a while, like other youngsters with an aptitude for the work, he was given a screwdriver and graduated to the removal of panels from the various aeroplanes. Except for National Service, Brian stayed with Western Airways and was eventually made a director of Barber Industries, a subsidiary of the company. Another young employee was Tony Britton who had moved to Weston from Birmingham, via Stone in Gloucestershire and he became a 'Chaser'. After the war he lived in London and became a leading actor in theatre, film and television. His daughter Fern also became famous as a presenter of ITV1's *This Morning*. Many girls just out of school were also taken on. Some were employed in the fabric-covering and doping of aircraft and their assemblies, whilst others became sheet-metal workers shaping blisters for engine cowlings and manufacturing/repairing aircraft seats.

Although it was wartime, apprentices were still being taken on, one being 16-year-old Alan Wilkes who started 19 August 1940 with a commencing weekly wage of 15s 6d (77.5p). His first day was rather more eventful than he might have expected, for when being shown the gunner's position in a Fairey Battle, his guide inadvertently released the seat that was held in its low position. Lifted under the influence of a powerful coiled spring and with no one on it to slow its motion, it rose rapidly and forcibly contacted Alan on the jaw, banging his head against the cockpit canopy framework. Blood was spattered everywhere and after being pulled from the cockpit onto the wing he lost consciousness. Freddy Froome the First Aid Officer arrived, diagnosed a possible fractured jaw and sent for an ambulance from RAF Locking, and in true military fashion the medical orderly that arrived cleared Alan for twenty-four hours of rest and then to resume normal duties. Pre-war, Freddy Froome had been in charge of the paint shop and now had additional responsibilities. He still kept his hand in with the spray-gun and at the beginning of the war had painted his Ford in a fashionable dark earth and dark green and, wearing a brown trilby and whilst smoking, was often seen spraying repaired Battles. Freddy was also a sign-writer and usually added serial numbers and notices to the aircraft. There were occasions when this was a bit fraught, as some of the lads hidden under a wing would gently rock the aircraft causing a wavy line to be painted. However, he was a good-natured individual considered by most a father figure. In addition to being first aid officer, Freddy was also the company's security and employment officer, and on arrival he interviewed all new employees and presented them with a 'Green Card'.

In those days small workshops were often pretty grim places but new arrivals found those at Western Airways to have a friendly environment, to be clean, and, except in the winter with the hangar doors open, warm. Another surprise for the new employee was that once a week a small area of the parachute-packing room was set aside and, with the aid of a local barber, became a hairdressing salon, thereby allowing war-work to carry on to all hours without interruption. Many of the young trainees took courses at Weston Technical College, and passing the exams was quite important as it would mean an extra penny or two an hour on their rate of pay. Overtime rates also applied and, on reaching eighteen years, one could join the company group life and pension scheme and a company sickness benefit scheme. With all the youngsters around, lunchtime activities became more adventurous with two redundant wing fuel tanks lashed to planks used as a raft on the deep water surrounding the pumping station, and nearby in an adjacent field atop a small hillock a machine gun in a turret belonging to 10 EFTS came in for attention. Other uses were also found for the thick canvas curtains of the Blister hangars which were used as slides. Most lunchtimes there was also a knock-around by the younger members of the Western Airways hockey team, but, probably predictably, this fun ended in tears after a ball was sent through the fabric of a newly refurbished Anson.

Early on, Western Airways had a contract to service and overhaul RAF primary trainers and to fit anti-spin strakes to Miles Magisters and DH Tiger Moths, most of the Tigers belonging to 10 EFTS. Another early contract was for the conversion of a number of Avro Anson Is into navigational trainers. Following on from work on the Tiger Moths and the Anson conversion task, new contracts were placed with Western Airways for the repair and refurbishment of Fairey Battles, Curtiss Mohawks and Tomahawks and the rebuild of Ansons. With these new tasks, out of necessity the layout of the small hangar had to be reconfigured with it being given in addition to an improved Paint Shop, an aircraft Stripping Shop and an Engine Bay, and at its west end a Radio and Electrical Workshop, together with an Armoury that was in a curtained off restricted area. Dismantled or stripped in the small hangar, the aircraft's sub-assemblies or components after cleaning and repair or refurbishment were reassembled in the large hangar.

Eleven Battles at least were received during 1940, some peppered with bullet holes and others with wrinkles in the fuselage skin above the wing caused by a too-rapid recovery from a dive. Delivered between 18 June when K7705 arrived and 13 November when K7574 was received, each stayed for between one to three months for repair and maintenance. They were then test flown by Mr V. G. Wilson, late of Jersey Airways, who had been seconded by Fairey Aviation to the company as a test pilot. The following year Battles continued to trickle through the shops; one was K7683 which, whilst with 16 Polish Flying Training School, was damaged after the pilot became lost and, during a forced landing at Bunny, Nottingham, overshot the selected field and hit trees. Combat aircraft coming in straight from the scene of a crash were often still armed, and in this case, guns and ammunition were made safe by personnel from the Armoury, but if bombs were on under-wing racks, armourers with the necessary skills were called in from RAF Locking. Normally guns and ammunition were handled with great care and stored securely in the Armoury, but on 25 September 1940, the day of the heavy German raid on Filton, safety procedures failed. The workforce had turned out to watch the formations of aircraft pass over and initially most thought them to be British, but when they were correctly identified by an aeroplane spotter, people made a swift move to the adjacent trenches. In the excitement, or perhaps anxiety of the event, live rounds were accidentally fired from a machine-gun in the Armoury and bullets passed through a radiator then the hangar, fortunately without hitting anyone.

In 1941, a contract was placed that covered the assembly and modification of new Curtis Tomahawks. Brought in by Queen Mary transporters from Bristol, the wings, fuselages, undercarriage, engines, etc. were all in separate crates. Following inspection for damage, modifications required to fit these American aircraft for RAF Army Co-operation service were embodied either at Western Airway at the airport, or at Camden Garage in Camden Terrace, just off Locking Road that had been commandeered for the company. At both sites a small workforce carried out the necessary work and the aircraft were then assembled on a small production line at the airport. Camden Garage was also used for other repair work and provided wartime storage for a BA Swallow and a large amount of aircraft-grade timber, its value being such that at night during times of high enemy threat a Western Airways employee would be detailed-off to the building as a fire-watcher. As late as 1943, there were still redundant Battle wing panels in racks at Western Airways, and in 1944 Tomahawk I, II and IIBs continued to be delivered by air and road for overhaul and repair, often in desert camouflage with engine cowlings decorated with the colourful Sharks Tooth squadron insignia.

Also starting in 1940 was a contract covering what was to become the company's wartime bread-and-butter activity, the complete rebuilding of very tired Avro Ansons belonging to the Royal Air Force and Royal Navy. Arriving by road and air, the machines, after being put in an aircraft park at the westerly end of the complex were dismantled, and then on trolleys the major components were pushed, as space became available, into the Stripping Shop. The various components and sub-assemblies were then distributed to the various workshops on site, or to the commandeered workshops in Weston

In the Stripping Shop at the westerly end of the small hangar, Anson Is are being broken-down into their sub-assemblies. Behind the far wall, the hangar with a false ceiling continues into the Paint Shop. The Engine Bay is in the foreground (Via E. ap Rees)

The large hangar looking south-west; in the foreground racks of Anson wings and in the background their fuselages that have come in from the Stripping Shop await repair (Via E. ap Rees)

The Drove Road Garage Workshop with Anson flying surfaces and engine nacelles being recovered and doped, mainly by girl workers (Via E. ap Rees)

The Camden Garage Workshop with components from Ansons being refurbished (Via E. ap Rees)

The other end of the large hangar looking south-east with repaired Anson components being reassembled. In this and the previous photograph of the large hangar, a wing from a Tiger Moth against the hangar's southerly wall, brings both views together (Via E. ap Rees)

Completed Anson Is near the Western Airways compass-swinging pad await ATA delivery pilots. Note the closely hauled barrage balloon just outside the airport's southern boundary in the area of West End Farm (Via E. ap Rees)

A group of Western Airways Inspectors in front of a newly rebuilt Anson – left to right: unidentified, Jack Carey – Engines, Norman House – Airframes, Sid Holly, Bill Lancaster – Chief Inspector and Mr. Parry – Resident AID Inspector (Bob Cooke)

for refurbishment. The largest of these was at Drove Road Garage, located just below Drove Road railway bridge at the end of Bridge Road, that pre-war had been used by West of England Motors (WEMS). It was here that many of the wings, the detachable wing trailing-edges, engine nacelles, ailerons, tailplanes and elevators, rudders and flaps were dispatched. Almost all components were taken by lorry, but the wing, which was a one-piece heavy timber structure with a span of 56 feet 6 inches (17 metres) could not be moved so easily. The eventual answer lay in this component, with its centre section securely bolted to a 2-wheel trolley, being manhandled to Drove Road Garage. Pushed or pulled in a see-saw action by several men, sometimes escorted by PC Jim Davis on motorbike, the route was over the two humpback railway bridges on Locking Moor Road to Locking Road where there was a well-deserved comfort stop at the café near Mac's Garage. Then it was a further hour of pushing and pulling until Drove Road Bridge was negotiated and the garage reached. Chocks were carried and used as necessary to prevent the combination running away on the bridges. PC Davis was also landlord of the Prince of Wales pub that was just behind the Beach Bus Station. The Drove Road Garage site is now redeveloped and occupied by Weston's Mercedes Benz car showrooms. Camden Garage now tended to work on the repair of Anson wooden detachable panels and fairings, crew seats, tail wheels, aerials, windows and other small components, whilst Varley Pumps at the town end of Lower Bristol Road overhauled the aircraft's hydraulic systems. Other Western Airways premises were in George Street, Jubilee Road, Langford Road and Wooler Road. After repair/overhaul, the Anson components were brought together at the airport and reassembled in the west end of the large hangar. Finally the assembled machine was sprayed in the approved camouflage scheme in the Paint Shop at the east end of the small hangar.

This Anson work gained momentum towards the end of 1940 with K6292, operated by 48 Squadron, being typical of the several hundred of the type that passed through the workshops during the war. It arrived 23 November and after rebuild was delivered to 37 MU for further service 10 February 1941. This aircraft, like K8750 that passed through Western Airways at the same time, was unfortunately lost at sea 24 March whilst *en route* to Canada on SS *Horda,* when she was sunk by U-97. Interspersed with Anson work was the rebuilding of other machines such as DH Tiger Moth K4254 of 17 EFTS, which on 14 January 1942 had been damaged in a precautionary landing at East Langton, Leicestershire. Aircraft electrical work was carried out by Carlux Electrical Services, also of Bridge Road. An automobile company, at Western Airways it was given dedicated areas such as a battery-charging shop and an instrument shop where it carried out appointed tasks, which in due course included the conversion of Anson gun turrets from mechanical to electrical actuation.

On completion of rebuild, each aircraft had to have its compass swung, and for this complex operation a concrete pad had been laid to the west of the apron. Either by design or by accident, it was discovered that the pad had been laid so that, with an aircraft on it with its fuselage centre-line lined up with magnetic north, it would line up exactly with the prominent Observatory Tower on top of Worlebury Hill! During the various repair/overhaul operations, progress was closely monitored by the company's inspectors, and prior to flight the final inspection would be given by the AID Inspector. After AID clearance, Lew Lisle took the machine up, and if it was an Anson he was accompanied by a flight engineer whose primary task was to wind the undercarriage up or down as requested, a soul-destroying task that took around 160 turns of a crank handle located low down on the starboard side of the pilot's seat. Most of the lads in the workshops pestered Lew for a flight and this was readily given, usually when the flight engineer was otherwise engaged. The 'lucky' passenger then spent most of the short trip with head buried in the cockpit turning the crank. However, both pilot and passenger were happy with this arrangement, especially the pilot since he didn't have to raise or lower the undercarriage himself, and was given extra confidence that the repair work carried out by the lad and his or her mates was of a high standard as they were willing to risk their neck to fly in the machine. With the aircraft signed-off, it was parked with others on the grass to await delivery back to the RAF by the ATA. Until 1944, all Ansons delivered to Western Airways for rebuild had been Mk 1s, but in that year a few Mk XIs started to pass through the workshops, and they, much to the relief of the flight engineer and joy-riders, had a hydraulically-actuated undercarriage retraction and lowering system!

From 1942 onwards, in addition to his engineering responsibilities, the majority of the different types of aircraft that passed through the shops had been test flown by Lew Lisle. Lew, a brilliant and careful pilot, on occasions experienced the odd incident, one when a Tomahawk nosed-over at the start of a take-off run resulting in a bent airscrew. This, due to the soft ground, was a not uncommon occurrence with the Tomahawk for a similar incident also happened to a lady ATA ferry pilot who was about to fly out a repaired aircraft. These and other similar incidents to Western Airways aircraft, and to those of the TDU with its machines centred near the Western Airways complex towards the end of 1943, convinced the MAP that funds should be made available for this area to be redeveloped.

To cope with the higher AUW of the latest torpedo-carrying Beaufighters coming from the Oldmixon Factory, and with the high landing speed of the Hawker Tempest II fighter that was shortly to start coming from the Banwell Factory, the Ministry had agreed to Bristol's request for its runway to be extended by 400 yards (366 metres) to the east. As an add-on, a taxi-track for operators at the airport's eastern end was also agreed that would stretch from the perimeter road in the north-easterly corner of the airport to the Western Airways complex, with the end of the runway extension intersecting the new track. Between the track and Locking Moor Road, pillboxes, air-raid shelters and a group of single-storey buildings were built for the TDU. With the complex completed, to give an improved view of aircraft movements on the airport, that to a large degree had been obscured by construction of the large hangar, the original timber control tower, together with its ornate fittings, was re-erected at the northern end of the TDU complex.

One little-known wartime activity of the Straight Corporation, was that one of its subsidiaries manufactured a professional range of model aircraft. Whether in one of the services, Civil Defence, the Royal Observer Corps or a Raid Spotter, being able to recognise the type of aircraft approaching was of paramount importance. As a training aid, thousands of model aircraft were being produced in homes, clubs and factories, to be hung from the ceiling of crew rooms and workplaces and used to illustrate the subject of aircraft recognition during classroom training. One such company involved in this was Woodason Aircraft Models Ltd. Formed in 1936 by Victor Woodason it was known as Woodason Models and engaged in building professionally-made model aeroplanes at Heston Airport, and at the beginning of the war it took on government contracts for special-order scale models, usually of enemy aircraft. Some were used for photographic purposes and, with suspension wires concealed, purported to be the full-size machines in Air Publications and the *Aeroplane Spotter*, *Aeroplane* and *Flight* magazines. In the early part of the war Woodason Aircraft Models became an associate company of the Straight Corporation, and it was from a timber building that had been erected just to the south of the large Western Airways hangar that Eric Bolt, a master carpenter with a number of girls, ran a small production line to produce these models. Occasional model-making continued after the war in support of EMI, who in 1958 moved into a part of the Hutton Moor Flight Shed and formed the embryo National Radar Target Modelling Centre (*see chapter 3*).

2

THE SHADOW FACTORIES
AND THEIR LEGACY

War Clouds Gather

With war clouds gathering, the Bristol Aeroplane Company, like most other major aircraft manufacturers in 1936, was asked by the Air Ministry to provide plans to show how it could increase the numbers of aircraft and aero-engines coming from its Filton Factory. Government policy was that much of this extra production would have to be performed in new shadow factories located in areas away from centres of industry to lessen the chances of being destroyed in any future enemy action. At this time the request was rather academic to Bristol as the only modern fighting machine it had flown was a prototype of the all-metal Type 142M Blenheim light bomber. However, this machine rapidly proved to be a success, was ordered in large quantities, and gave Bristol experience in having it manufactured by other firms. The Blenheim was quickly followed by a somewhat similar design, the Type 152 named 'Beaufort'. A specialised Torpedo Bomber, the Beaufort, and the Blenheim, were both good aeroplanes but their limitations would soon be exposed in combat with the Luftwaffe. The Beaufort had, however, already played a very significant part in the conception of what would become a war-winning aeroplane, the Beaufighter.

Many specifications for new aircraft had been issued by the air staff in the mid-to late 1930s to meet the immediate and future needs of the RAF, one such calling for design of a 2-seat cannon-armed fighter. Bristol's designers, under the leadership of Leslie Frise, were determined that this specification could be satisfied very quickly, and produced a proposal whereby the Beaufort would basically be fitted with a new slimmer fuselage and its Bristol Taurus engines replaced with the more powerful Bristol Hercules. The proposal for this machine, the Type 156 named 'Beaufort Fighter', was submitted in October 1938, the month in which the Beaufort prototype made its first flight. Other manufacturers' proposals for this 2-seat cannon-armed fighter were also considered by the Ministry, but Bristol had the advantage of being an experienced volume manufacturer with the ability to get prototypes off the ground in a very short space of time. Design and planning of the Beaufort Fighter continued at Filton and the company was rewarded in February 1939 when the Air Council placed an order for 300 Beaufighters, as it was now known. The prototype first flew in July 1939, a flight which the company chief test pilot Cyril Uwins reported as being very satisfactory with only minor changes required. Reaching its maximum estimated design speed of 335 mph (539 kph) in trials, with full operational equipment duly installed, which included four 20 mm cannons and six Browning machine-guns, it became the heaviest armed fighter in the world.

The order for the Beaufighter with its Hercules engines and an increasing demand for the company's other products was overloading Bristol's existing facilities, and a search was on for other large aircraft or automotive companies that could set up and manage Beaufighter shadow assembly lines on their premises. Included in the search were Gloster Aircraft, Supermarine, Fairey Aviation, Boulton & Paul and Rootes Securities. Finally a decision was made with Fairey Aviation at Stockport, Boulton & Paul at Wolverhampton and Rootes Securities at Blythe Bridge all being selected. In addition, and very importantly, a shadow factory to produce the Beaufighter's Hercules engine that would be managed by Bristol was shortly to be commissioned at Accrington in Lancashire. The Air Ministry considered that, even with the new manufacturing facilities, more capacity was required for Beaufighter production, and Filton was asked to locate a suitable site to build an assembly shadow factory, preferably alongside an aerodrome, to be managed by the company itself on behalf of the Ministry. Bristol considered the Midlands to be the best location, as it provided good access to major subcontractors and availability of a skilled workforce that was unlikely to be a drain on its own at Filton. An added advantage was that Bristol was already in advanced discussions with the Midlands-based Austin Motor Company at Longbridge for provision of Beaufighter wings and with the Standard Motor Company at Coventry for fuselages.

In due course, Bristol, acting on behalf of the Secretary of State for Air, formed a management committee to investigate how the factory could best be set up, and in November 1939 agreement was reached that the new facility would be sited at Oakley Wood, Barford Bridge, Warwick. This was followed by a meeting in Harrogate on 29 December during which the Ministry announced that it was placing an initial contract with Bristol for 500 Beaufighters to be built at the new factory. This news was immediately followed by the first meeting at Filton of what was now the BAC Warwick Aircraft Shadow Factory Management Committee. Warwick was confirmed by early January 1940 and the company authorised to place orders with Austin and Standard for the necessary wings and fuselages. Meanwhile, in the previous December some objection to the Warwick proposal had been made and in January additional objections were raised, principally by the bursar of St Johns College, Oxford, Sir Alfred Herbert and Mr Burton of Daimlers, then finally by the Ministry of Agriculture. These objections obviously carried considerable weight for within a week or so Warwick was ruled out, the factory management committee was again looking for a suitable site and William Cowlin & Sons, who would prepare the site, lay the roads and erect the factory; John Lysaght, who would obtain and fabricate the steel structure; and quantity surveyors Gleeds and architect Mr Lee-Clarke of Herbert Ellis & Clarke were having to bide their time and await developments.

Two further Midland sites were then considered, one at Worcester which was immediately rejected by the Air Ministry and the other at Leicester where the area was considered to be too close to overhead power lines and waterlogged. After briefly considering other sites at Exeter, and at Taunton, by early March the company was endeavouring to obtain Air Ministry approval for a site near the hamlet and manor of Oldmixon which was just to the south of Weston-super-Mare and only a few fields to the south-west of its municipal airport. However, there was one problem associated with the site that, given time and money, could be solved, but initially would cause much aggravation, and that was the difficulty of reaching it by vehicles. To reach the site one first had to negotiate narrow lanes and the small villages and hamlets nestling in the lee of the Mendips that led to Oldmixon; then it was north along the fairly wide Oldmixon Drove, and the area of land was on the right straddling Cross Rhyne. If one proceeded further north towards Weston, it was along a path to the GWR Bristol — Exeter railway line with an unguarded crossing, and then one eventually came across the town's rubbish dump, known as 'The Tip'. This was fed by horse-drawn dust-carts emerging from Weston that travelled along the narrow Old Junction Road past the gasworks towards the factory site, but it terminated at what in 1841 had been the junction that provided the GWR branch into Weston's first railway station. It's possible that this site had been considered previously by the management committee but quickly dismissed due to views that there would be a lack of a skilled workforce and a possible drift of Filton employees to the seaside. Also considered would have been the difficulties associated with deliveries, especially of major components from the Midland subcontractors. Another factor may well have been Filton management's wish that the factory should be a wartime-only concern, as there was no desire to see a competitor set up with public money in its own backyard. Although trial boreholes showed subsoil in the locality of the site to comprise deep deposits of peat and areas of moist shifting sand, an order to proceed was given and a draft building contract agreed with Cowlin.

Bristol's Weston (Oldmixon) Aircraft Shadow Factory

Approval of the site brought with it a requirement for a larger airport, and by mid-May 1940 the Ministry had agreed to extend it north almost to the GWR railway line, south to Cross Rhyne and west to link up with the new factory. The total area of land covered by the airport and factory was now more than 440 acres (178 hectares). Concrete cross-runways were also agreed as were the factory's principal features that included a Quarantine Store, a No.1 and a No.2 Erecting Hall, a No.1 and a No.2 Flight Shed, a Dope Shop, an

Administration Block, a Garage, an Office Block for the Pilots, a Boiler House with an adjacent Coal Dump, a Power House, a First Aid Building (Hospital), an Ambulance and Fire-Service Station, a Canteen, two Water Towers and a GWR Railway Siding. Most principal features of the factory were considered to be of a primary nature and a few not so. These lesser buildings were the No.1 Erecting Hall and the No.2 Flight Shed, and as such would be the last erected. When completed, and until required for production, they would act as standby buildings for Filton and any of Oldmixon's primary buildings if they were disabled or destroyed by enemy action.

Come June, the company had decided concrete cross-runways were now not wanted, the need being replaced by an urgent requirement for the airport extension to be completed as soon as possible, so that new grass runways could be laid to give Beaufighters the required long take-off and landing runs in various directions. Three 400-yard-wide (366-metre) runways were proposed on the heading: 010/190 1,100 yards (1005 metres) long, 065/245 1,450 yards (1325 metres) long and 125/305 1,100 yards (1005 metres) long. The laying down of runway 125/305, however, would involve extending the airport some 350 yards (320 metres) to the south over Cross Rhyne, but early in 1941, although a certain amount of infilling and levelling had taken place, the Ministry decided to stop at the rhyne and realign the runway by approximately eighteen degrees. Cross Rhyne was being greatly enlarged with a Pumping Station to be operated by Western Airways, and this would link up with the new Main Storage Rhyne being excavated that ran from the old Hutton Moor Lane across to the south of the Oldmixon Factory, and via a sluice to the sea. The original westerly section of Cross Rhyne then continued on its former course meandering through the factory, it being later renamed The Carrier Rhyne.

With some six months taken in choosing the factory site, there was concern that a similar delay would be imparted in producing the 235 Beaufighters required by the end of 1941. But luckily by April 1940, a government licence had been granted for the steel for No.1 Flight Shed and that for most of the other primary buildings and, shortly after, Cowlin was instructed to metal the grass road that was the only access from Oldmixon Drove onto the factory site. Cowlin then had to organise its limited workforce so that maximum possible overtime could be achieved, a night shift introduced and arrangements made for government clearance for the stringent night time lighting restrictions to be relaxed. As Oldmixon was a Priority B factory and labourers were able to work more hours and get higher rates of pay at a Priority A factory, such as the Ordnance Factory being built only a short distance away at Puriton, by mid-May, Cowlin was having severe difficulty in obtaining sufficient labour and Lysaght was having to be contacted daily regarding delays in delivering steelwork for some of the primary buildings. In early August, although the men continued to work through the many local air-raid warnings, building progress was still slow due to lack of labour and materials, but it was hoped that things were about to improve, as the Ministry of Aircraft Production (MAP) Council was soon to bring A and B Priority factories into line.

The 6-month delay in finding a factory site had conveniently allowed Filton's subcontracts office additional time to train an all-important team for Weston, and arrange contracts with some thirty major subcontractors to supply the necessary components in due time for its first Beaufighters to be assembled. In addition to the already-agreed wing and fuselage subcontractors, amongst others brought in were Cornercroft Ltd of Coventry and its subsidiary Northern Aircraft Ltd & Engineering Products Co. Ltd with factories at Guide Bridge Mill, Ashton-under-Lyne, who were to manufacture some of the aircraft's control surfaces; A. P. Aircraft Ltd, who was to manufacture the rudder, fin, ailerons, engine nacelle fairings and oil tanks; Lockheed (Automotive Products Company Ltd) at Coventry, who would provide the oleo legs whilst Riley (Coventry) Ltd and the Singer Motor Company factories at Coventry, using Lockheed components, would assemble the undercarriage. Robertson Engineering Co. Ltd, together with Park Ward & Co. Ltd of Willesden, London, would manufacture the cannon's Chatelleraut feed-boxes whilst George Elt would manufacture the aircraft's seats and Hurry Heaters its fuel tanks.

Dispersal of Factory Buildings

It was on 9 September 1940, with ground for the No.1 Erecting Hall and the No.2 Flight Shed already prepared, that a Ministry announcement was made that would have far-reaching effects on the factory. Concerned with the extensive damage caused by enemy action to factories with buildings closely grouped, on that day it ordered that all work on the two buildings should immediately cease and that they should be dispersed to other areas in the locality. This resulted in Bristol suggesting that No.2 Flight Shed should be erected on Hutton Moor, which was on the airport's expanded northern side, and that No.1 Erecting Hall should be located just off the new A371 Locking Village Bypass 1¾ road miles (2.8 km) to the east of the airport near the hamlet and manor of Elborough, and only a few fields away from the recently-completed RAF Technical Training Camp. It was also conveniently alongside an existing road that wended its way from Hutton to Banwell. Weston Town Council's surveyor and West Mendip's internal drainage board were strongly critical of the Elborough site due to the effect it would have on the area's drainage and problems with connecting sewers, much preferring a site near Worle, a village to the east of Weston. However, the Ministry agreed to Bristol's proposal and, as the council had little sway, the scheme went ahead. With this reorganisation, it was agreed that the No.2 Hutton Moor Flight Shed would handle only Elborough's aircraft, although Oldmixon's Flight Shed could be used if necessary. However, all aircraft would be painted in the Dope Shop, for which Oldmixon would be paid by Elborough.

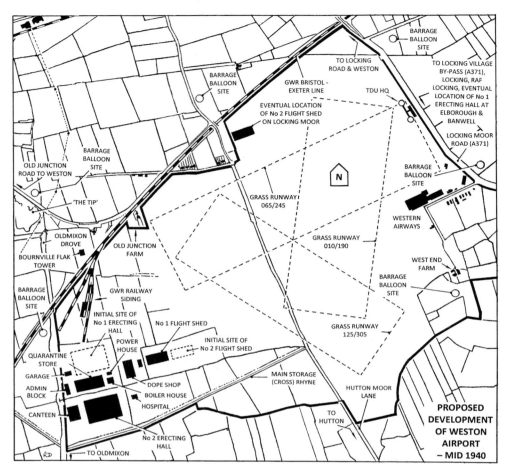

The Ministry's proposed airport development mid 1940. The Oldmixon Factory and re-location of its No. 2 Flight Shed to Hutton Moor is clearly shown. The factory's No. 1 Erecting Hall and the RAF Technical Training Camp (Locking) are to the east along the new wide Locking Village By-pass (A371). Indicated are the proposed large grass runways, and the extension south over Cross Rhyne to accommodate runway 125/305. The area of land initially commandeered by the Ministry for the enlarged airport is within the bold boundary line and extends eastwards to the road running through the village of Locking and includes West End Farm (R. Dudley)

The decision to disperse these buildings made good sense, as it was coincidently announced only a few days before 25 September when the Filton Factory suffered a major air attack. Only a few minutes after passing over the Oldmixon Factory, the fifty-eight Heinkel He 111 bombers, accompanied by many Messerschmitt Bf 110s fighters, released their load of 90 tons (91.4 tonnes) of high-explosive and oil bombs onto Filton. Inside the factory, eight aircraft were destroyed and twenty-four damaged; seventy-two workers were believed killed, many already in their shelters, and 166 were injured, nineteen of whom died later. Outside the factory many others were also killed and injured.

Once started, excavation at Elborough by Cowlin was very slow due to lack of earth scrapers and excavators and shortage of skilled men. Over Christmas 1940 things didn't improve much either as bad weather, air raids in the neighbourhood and the general influence of war conditions caused much time to be lost with estimated building completion being at the end of May 1941. With construction of No.1 Erecting Hall underway, the nucleus of what would eventually become a factory in its own right took on the hamlet's name, although before long it became known as the Banwell Factory which was the name of the nearby village.

Plans had already been drawn up to provide the Oldmixon Factory, as soon as its buildings were ready, with a core of skilled Filton personnel, together with a number of newly-trained employees, and these would include managers, shop-floor workers and office staff. By May, in advance of factory completion, certain key personnel had also been selected for transfer to Weston, including Mr H. S. Butt (Filton's Assistant Works Manager), who would be factory manager, Mr Benjamin, business manager and Mr F. Jefferies, chief production engineer. Planning was to be managed by Mr W. Yeadon whilst Mr H. V. Perman would become manager of the all-important subcontracts department. By early September, Oldmixon's buildings were coming along well, numbers of employees at the factory totalled 120, and, because of the raid on Filton, and slightly earlier than originally planned, the decision was taken to immediately transfer staff and shop-floor workers held in readiness at Filton to Oldmixon. This resulted in shop superintendents at Filton releasing around 200 of their most experienced men and thirty that had received basic training at the government training centre at Radnor Road, Bristol, that until now were receiving on-the-job training at Filton. In addition, some 150 men who had already completed the training centre course were also sent down, as were five men a week that were coming directly from the training centre. Once at Oldmixon, no doubt new staff and workers were somewhat bemused by the factory's notepaper headed 'Warwick Aircraft Shadow Factory', with 'Warwick' over-printed 'Weston'.

This earlier-than-expected influx of workers and staff was to initially cause problems as offices and other buildings were incomplete and other facilities, which included factory heating and the canteen, were not yet available. Many personnel were in fact accommodated with a field kitchen in the part-built No.2 Erecting Hall, and some office staff was to remain there until the new administration block had its roof. However, due to late delivery of the six coal-fired Davey Paxman's boilers, both staff and workers had to suffer a number of very cold weeks until the boiler house came on-line in early December. When the canteen, run by Barker (Contractors) Ltd, was ready for its first customers at the end of February 1941, it had an obligatory stage for lunchtime *Workers Playtime* performances given by ENSA and talented factory workers, and was in due course the platform used by two aircrew from a Blenheim Bomber Squadron who described to workers a recent raid over France.

Meanwhile, the Town Clerk of Weston had been assessing the availability of accommodation in the local area in anticipation of the transfer of staff and workers from Filton and advertisements had appeared in local newspapers and the cinemas. Prospects looked good as many visitors had cancelled their holidays and some had left the district, and soon there was a long list of available accommodation. But following the air raid on Filton, many of the city's inhabitants had been evacuated to Weston and were now using the accommodation, and owing to disorganisation on the railways following the raid it was difficult to get to and from Bristol. With the likelihood of raids on Weston, a secure location was also needed for the factory's drawings and master documents and the rectory in the village of Loxton was chosen for this important task. Over the following weeks and months, with efforts of the Filton and Weston management teams, other factory vacancies were progressively filled. Many individuals transferred were very experienced managers and supervisors that Filton could ill-afford to lose. One was Mr R. S. Press, and he was engaged as a charge hand in No.2 Flight Shed at a salary of £5 10s (£5.50) per week plus 15s (75p) a week cost-of-living increase. Also promised was a production bonus of 2s 6d (12.5p) per aircraft, based on an output of fifty a month, to be paid monthly until the factory was in quantity production.

The more specialist areas were difficult to fill and selected workers were, in due course, trained in electrical and hydraulic systems at Chittening, the company's salvage depot located about 2 miles (3.2 km) upstream of the Avonmouth Docks, where, under control of the Government's Civilian Repair Organistion (CRO), it also ran a training school that gave short intensive courses, mainly to RAF personnel on repairing and maintaining Bristol airframes. Blackburn Aircraft was also involved in training and provided courses on pipe-bending to men from the coppersmith department. By June 1941 many women were also being taken on, and with factory facilities having been designed mainly with men in mind there was an urgent requirement for the buildings to be modified and equipped with cloakrooms and lavatories for females. By the end of January 1942 labour input was small, one reason for this being the number of RAF fitter trainees that had been taken on. But this satisfactory state of affairs only lasted for several months, as soon the Ministry Man-Power Board requested the company release some of its deferred staff and workers that were under thirty years of age for call-up for military service and that some of the RAF fitters should be returned.

By April 1941 with roads, car park and most factory buildings almost completed, the Ministry of Home Security at Leamington advised on their camouflage, and in May specially-formulated grass seed arrived and concrete areas received bitumen paint, which unsatisfactorily dried slightly glossy and, following rain, looked like mirrors! In addition to the factory, a further camouflage problem had been noticed — that of Weston County School. Less than a mile (1.6 km) away to the west, its large white clocktower was a conspicuous landmark that lined up exactly on the newly excavated Main Storage Rhyne that ran alongside No.2

Erecting Hall. By mid-July 1941 the walls and roofs of every factory building except for the pilot's office block were camouflaged with dark green/dark earth paint but the school tower was to remain as it was.

Getting workers to Oldmixon and Banwell initially presented a problem. As far as Oldmixon was concerned, with there being no direct route from Weston and North Somerset where many of the workers lived, all transport, including buses and coaches, had to reach the factory via Oldmixon Drove. However, the Banwell Factory, although further from Weston was in fact on a more direct route and thus easier and quicker to reach. This unfortunately, was not reflected by prices charged to workers who travelled from Weston with those going to Oldmixon paying 6d for a return journey and those going to Banwell paying 9d. Bristol Tramways, who had been tasked to provide these services, was extremely unhappy with this state of affairs, complaining that they were operating the Oldmixon service at a loss due to the additional fuel used and time taken, and requested that the Banwell route be subsidised to the tune of 3d. For those workers living in the Bournville Estate, the answer lay in reaching the factory on foot. Soon paths started to appear across the fields, rhynes were bridged by planks and the safest way to cross the Bristol – Exeter railway lines was discovered. However, behind the scenes steps were being urgently taken by the company and MAP to improve accesses to the factory, the way forward revolving around Old Junction Road. Using this as a basis, by mid-July 1940 MAP had approved a new highway going from the road's end to the factory via a new railway bridge, and tenders for its construction had been accepted from George Pollard & Co. of Taunton with Lysaght supplying steelwork. Probably with post-war travel in mind, the GWR asked for the bridge to be wide enough to span four railway lines rather than the two then laid and, surprisingly, a licence for the additional steel was granted.

With the multitude of building work in the locality, great difficulty was still being experienced in obtaining sufficient building labourers and progress on the bridge was painfully slow. However, sufficient work had been completed by Sunday 19 October 1941 for the 100 feet by 40 feet (31 by 12 metres) steel structure to be swung into position. By the end of May there was good progress with the approach roads and a new target for their completion set for August/September. However, this news was countered when cracks were discovered in the bridge's reinforced concrete abutment walls. Thought to be caused by natural subsidence, it was agreed that piling should be exposed for examination and checked for any downward and outward movement twice a week. By December the total number of employees at Oldmixon had increased to 550, and with the bridge and continuing road problems Bristol Tramways was wondering how it could bus them to and from the factory in a given time and in the near future cope with handling many of the eventual full complement of 2,500. Early in 1943 buses were at last allowed to use the bridge so long as a 5 mph (8 kph) speed limit was observed, and as late as February 1945 the bridge was still moving and the Ministry had closed it to the general public, which was using it to reach their homes on the Bournville Estate. Eventually the road would be continued through to the hamlet of Oldmixon, and in the early 1950s, with potholes galore the Ministry gave permission for it, with the bridge, to become an official public highway renamed Winterstoke Road.

Protecting the Factories

The Oldmixon Factory had been provided with a works police force and it also had a detachment of the Somerset Home Guard which became known as F Company of the 8th (Weston) Battalion with Mr E. C. Lovell awarded the rank of major being made its commanding officer. Mr Lovell was also from 2 September 1940 appointed in charge of factory security which encompassed the ARP, works police, hospital and the fire department, which had formed an alliance with the Weston Brigade and the Axbridge Auxiliary Fire Service. Members of the Home Guard, the youngest sixteen years old, wore their uniform to work and kept in their possession a Lee-Enfield .303 Rifle with one clip of five rounds of ammunition. At night, to supplement the works police, sentries were posted around the factory and airport on a 2-hour on and 4-hour off basis. Off duty, the men either slept in the works canteen or, if guarding the airport, in cold and damp Nissen huts on the north side of Hutton Moor.

Tied in to some extent with factory security, was the subject of what the workforce should do following an air-raid alert. This caused some debate, and revolved around how soon the factory Tannoy broadcasting and warning system would be up and running. Ordered from Jarrett in December 1940, by August 1941, although some speakers had been delivered, twelve of the necessary sixteen valves were only 'still on their way'. This was extremely disappointing for the management, as much time was being lost due to factory personnel taking to the shelters whenever there was a general air-raid alert in the vicinity and it had been hoped that with the broadcasting system the more localised Raid Spotter System could be used. This was where factory workers with a good aptitude for aircraft recognition were made Raid Spotters and positioned on the tallest building to give warning of when a raid was about to start, and this would be transmitted to the workforce over the Tannoy when they would take up positions prearranged for their safety. Such were the delays that it wasn't until early April 1943 that the system was able to serve the complete factory.

The Oldmixon Factory was not well suited for aircraft observation with the adjacent Mendip Hills blocking views south from where the enemy would probably come. Even with this limitation, the northerly of the factory's 100-foot-high (30.5 metres), black-painted water towers was nominated for use as an observation post and when there was an air-raid alert two Raid Spotters were positioned precariously on it, one on top with a field telephone and the other mid-way up, also with a phone to give back up. Although the tower was a good vantage point, low-level attacks from the south still couldn't be observed and there was some concern that the tower was conspicuous from the air, but the arrangement worked well. In total there were to be forty-three surface air-raid shelters, and by December 1941 twenty-one had been completed giving protection to 1,050 workers. Shelters were so positioned that all workers could reach one within two minutes of an air-raid warning, although the younger element often ignored them and watched enemy bombers cross from the protection of the adjacent Main Storage Rhyne. Also, there were a number of large, open, static water tanks, their contents intended to extinguish expected fires from enemy action. By early December 1940 it was considered essential that the fire service be manned at all hours of the day and night and that fire-watchers also be available to deal with incendiary bombs. Come February 1941, on each night there were some sixty to seventy workers on the factory premises fire-watching with some 150 troops in the immediate vicinity that could be called upon for assistance. By early June, although a successful air-raid test had been carried out there was some concern that attendance for night time fire-watching was proving inadequate and a rota scheme that included all workers, staff and management, was introduced. Together with an emergency materials pool that contained roofing materials, sand, cement, glazing, piping, bricks, and asbestos sheeting, etc. for repairs following enemy action, the factory was now considered to be 'Ready for War'.

With the attack on Filton, requests were made by Weston management for the provision of a balloon barrage and a squadron of fighter aircraft to be locally based. This was to result in 341 Battery, 116 Heavy Anti-Aircraft Regiment in February 1941 being brought in to set up its 3.7 inch (94 mm) guns and searchlights at Uphill and Hutton and a number of 1.6 inch (40 mm) Bofors guns, and a range of smaller calibre weapons being set up at sites around the airport, one at its western end on the Bournville flak tower erected in a field near the GWR railway line. Subsequently, in May barrage balloons were deployed with arrival of 955 (Balloon) Squadron, a 24-unit; whilst fighter aircraft were frequently stationed at Filton and at Pembrey in South Wales. It was a closely-guarded secret that Weston's Gasworks was a major depot manufacturing hydrogen for the country's barrage balloons. In fact, it was the first in the country to have this facility, with construction started in March 1939, and eventually it went on to produce enough gas to fill no fewer than 11,400 envelopes. During the year searchlight beams from Turbinlite-equipped Douglas Havocs, probably from Colerne or Charmy Down, were also seen on a few occassions at night over the town, attempting to locate and then illuminate the enemy thus enabling their Hurricane partners to shoot the bomber down. The procedure showed some promise and short bursts of machine-gun fire were heard but not enough success was achieved for development to be continued.

To confuse enemy navigators and encourage bomb aimers to unload their stores away from the factory and airport, a decoy installation known as a Starfish Site was built on open land on Bleadon Level (South Hill Farm) near the River Axe.

Consisting of a dummy airfield and factory, it contained all sorts of inflammable materials such as rolls of roof felting, creosote, wood and coal, guaranteed to give plenty of flames and great columns of smoke, and was set alight by powder charges ignited electrically from a bunker about a mile (1.6 km) away. Lit at night as a raid started, many bombs and incendiaries meant for the Oldmixon Factory, which in fact only received three small bombs, were dropped onto this sparsely populated area, luckily without loss of human life. Those living in Weston were often able to testify to the site's efficacy by the number of craters from bombs and thousands of white patches on Brean Down and along the Mendips to Bleadon Hill caused by burnt-out incendiaries. Because of wartime security restrictions, the extreme bravery of Aircraftsman AC2 Cecil Frederick Mason Bright, who was one of a small team looking after this Starfish Site on the night of 4 January 1941 could only be made known to the public in September 1945.

On this particular night, as raiders approached Weston, the team was ordered to stand by to light fires. At about 12.20 a.m., flares were dropped followed by a stick of incendiaries. Now, sure that a raid was commencing, orders were given to ignite a decoy fire, but when the relevant switch was operated nothing happened. By now the raid was gaining momentum and other switches were tried to no avail, it appearing that the afternoon's rain had dampened the powder charges. With no time to be lost, Aircraftsman Bright with a bottle of petrol disappeared into the night to light the fires by hand and was away for 1¾ hours. Once the first of Bright's fires was burning fiercely, raiders started to drop the majority of their remaining incendiaries and bombs on the Starfish Site, but in spite of his efforts there was much death and destruction in Weston (*see chapter 3*). However, the following day the full extent of what was meant for the town and its factories became apparent, for in fields around the site there were forty-two craters made by bombs, over 1,500 incendiary fins, and eventually thousands more fins were found in the surrounding hills. For his act of gallantry on 5 April 1941 Bright was presented with the Military Medal by George VI at Buckingham Palace. Later he was also presented with a silver cigarette case by his commanding officer, and Weston's grateful mayor Alderman Henry Butt personally thanked him for services to the town. After leaving the RAF, Bright, having married a local girl, settled in Weston's Moorland Road and opened a radio and television shop.

Oldmixon's fire-watching arrangements were still being addressed at the time of the above raid, and luckily the factory wasn't attacked, but on the nights of Sunday 28 and Monday 29 June 1942 (*see chapter 3*), when Weston suffered what was to be its worst attacks of the war, Oldmixon's fire-watching arrangements were up and running and worked well, although again the factory luckily escaped serious damage. During the first raid, an attacking bomber actually managed to pass through the balloon barrage and three bombs reached the airport area, two in the factory and the other near the pumping station which damaged the Main Storage/Cross Rhyne.

Production Gets Underway

May 1940, the month in which the Ministry of Aircraft Production was established under directorship of Lord Beaverbrook, saw Standard making good progress with its fuselages but there was some concern regarding Austin and its wings. Unfortunately for Austin, its production relied totally on prompt delivery of wing-spars being manufactured by the Ratcliffe Engineering Co. Ltd at Llandudno Junction, Colwyn Bay, North Wales. This company was experiencing severe problems in obtaining equipment and a skilled workforce and, as a consequence, to get wing production underway, Austin was having to use a pooling scheme with spars manufactured by both the Fairey Company's subcontractors and Filton's Spar Shop at its Muller Road (pre-war Bristol Tramways) Factory. It was to be early April 1941 before production at Ratcliffe at last began to get going, however, and in spite of earlier promises it was mid-August before the first set of ten spars was delivered, and although they were considered by Ratcliffe to be completely satisfactory, Austin was less than delighted finding that they all required much rectification work. The pooling scheme had been introduced early on by Filton where a Beaufighter group materials committee approved, if there was good cause, the sharing or loaning of materials and components from Filton or one shadow factory to another.

Towards the end of September, Oldmixon's No.2 Erecting Hall was ready for laying the first of twenty-four Aircraft Assembly Jigs, and towards the end of October, coinciding with arrival of labour from Filton, the first Beaufighter fuselage was received from Standard together with two wing centre-sections from Austin, thus encouraging the company to predict that the first Beaufighter would now be airborne by Christmas. Tremendous efforts had been made by all concerned, especially the subcontractors in an attempt to get the first machine completed by the end of the year, but it was not to be, mainly due to component shortages.

At this time there was also pressure from the Civilian Repair Organisation for Bristol's Service Department to find extra repair capacity, and by June 1940 it had been agreed that Beauforts and Beaufighters normally assigned to Filton for Category 5 repair work would be transferred to Oldmixon as soon as the first building there had been completed. But by the end of October, the Company, having second thoughts about this scheme, had MAP agree that this specialised work would be carried out on Beaufighters only, and because Oldmixon had only Aircraft Assembly Jigs for Beaufighter production, and as yet no machining facilities, this work would have to be carried out elsewhere, with the Banwell Factory fitting in nicely with this requirement. Up until then Category 5 aircraft were returned from the RAF to Chittening where they were cleaned, stripped, and components dispatched to the relevant subcontractor for repair under a running contract with Filton. Repaired components, together with the necessary spares from RAF Maintenance Units (MUs) were then returned to Filton for aircraft assembly, flight testing and dispatch back to the service. Although repair work had been allocated to Banwell, the first aircraft for repair, R2072, was actually delivered to Oldmixon, but would only be used in courses to provide hands-on experience to shop-floor workers.

Early on much of Oldmixon's Quarantine Store was given over to the storing and fitting out of Beaufighter sub-assemblies, and off site facilities were urgently sourced for overflow storage of sub-assemblies and raw material, resulting in Banwell's No.1 Erecting Hall being used as a temporary measure. To enable swift dispatch of these raw materials to subcontractors in the Midlands and to supplement the temporary store at Banwell, premises in Bristol at Broadmead, Avon Street and Victoria Terrace were leased. Some materials moved into these premises had come from Boulton & Paul, who had recently withdrawn from the Beaufighter group of aircraft manufacturing companies. The Fairey Company took a share of these as did Filton. With raw materials having been converted into components and sub-assemblies, it was the subcontractor's responsibility to deliver them to Oldmixon, but by October, to avoid serious rail delays in the Midlands caused by enemy action, Bristol was looking for premises in that part of the country to act as a clearing house for its subcontractors' products, these to be collected by Oldmixon's vehicles several times a week.

The flow of raw materials from the stores in Bristol and Weston to subcontractors that so far had been reasonably smooth was soon to face a massive disruption, for during the evening of Sunday 24 November, in what was to be one of Bristol's worst air raids, the Avon Street premises was bombed

Oldmixon's first Beaufighter X7540 had its maiden flight 20 February 1941, and shortly after was at Boscombe Down for A&AEE trials (Via P. Jarrett)

Beaufighter IF X7583, one of Oldmixon's early machines stands ready 1 August 1941 for the demonstration flight (*Aeroplane* via E. Johnson)

and set on fire. Luckily, most alclad and other light-alloy stock was salvaged and moved as a temporary measure to Victoria Terrace which was now used as a salvage depot. As a consequence, it was decided to vacate the Bristol premises as soon as possible, and at the beginning of 1941 The Grange at Banwell and two small premises in Coronation Road at Highbridge were requisitioned and the salvaged material moved in. By April 1941, the Odeon cinema at Worcester had also been allocated to Oldmixon as a raw material store but this was soon replaced by Worcester's smaller Auto Garage. Later, a Bellman hangar on a part of the British Tyre and Rubber Co. site at Burton-on-Trent was requisitioned and by May 1943 filling up with Banwell's tube, bar and sheet metal. Early in 1942 Oldmixon was making increasing use of the railway for the dispatch of raw material to its Midlands storage facilities and subcontractors. To improve the flow of rail transport to and from the factory George Pollard & Co. was engaged to build a loading bay at Oldmixon's Railway Siding that in due course gained four Romney huts. At Banwell, completion of a Quarantine Store allowed Oldmixon's materials and components temporarily stored in No. 1 Erecting Hall to be transferred there, again as a temporary measure.

Meanwhile, the first of Oldmixon's Beaufighters, Mk IF (Fighter) X7540 with Hercules XIs installed, in a sooty black night-fighter finish flew on 20 February 1941 in the capable hands of Ronnie Ellison who had been appointed Oldmixon's Chief Test Pilot with effect from 1 January. It was to be followed by two others by the month's end and three in March. Of these, the third aircraft X7542 was the Mk VIF (Fighter) prototype and the fourth X7543 the Mk VIC (Coastal

Command) prototype. By early April thirteen aircraft were out of assembly jigs, the sixth having been embodied with the latest modifications, and it formed the subject of a DTD (Directorate of Technical Development) conference during which the factory was complimented on the aircraft's finish. It was now possible to see how the 6-month delay caused by early shadow factory sites not being available, and the factory buildings dispersal exercise was affecting the first year's MAP production programme, when it was announced that only 201 Beaufighters could now be expected from Oldmixon by the end of 1941, rather than the programmed 235. The first 200 of these would be Mk IFs with Hercules XIs and the remaining 300 of the contract would be Mk VIs with Hercules Mk VIs. On 1 August, with some forty-four new Beaufighters produced, the factory, although not specifically mentioned as being at Weston, was officially announced to the world when photographs of Mk IF X7583 being flown by Ronnie Ellison were published. Amongst the invited crowd of press and film units, one was from the *Weston Gazette & Somerset Advertiser*, which in its 9 August issue showed the factory sub-assembly and final-assembly production lines. Just over a year later, in the snow of the following winter, the 1,000th Beaufighter would have flown.

In 1940 the night blitz caused many casualties and severe damage across the country, and although Oldmixon featured on Luftwaffe target maps and production was frequently disrupted due to air-raid alerts, it fortuitously escaped damage, thus enabling production of the sorely-needed Beaufighter night-fighter to commence. Luckily, night-fighter production was already well underway at Filton with 100 having been delivered to the RAF by early December 1940. Oldmixon's and, later in the year, Banwell's aeroplanes would also be achieving similar results across the country, and to ensure that there were no delays to the flight testing programme Flight Lieutenant George Reston RAF, on 9 September 1941 was appointed assistant chief test pilot and, to meet the additional increased production from Banwell, Ernest Hugh Statham would also join Ellison's team on 1 June 1943.

The Banwell Factory

At the Elborough (Banwell) Factory site, the No.1 Erecting Hall was progressing well and by May 1941 it had been decided that, with a dividing blast wall to isolate each area, it would be used for both Beaufighter repair and production with Ernie Warner, transferred from Filton's Flight Shed, its Superintendent. As with Oldmixon, to support this mini factory a Boiler House and Coal Dump, a Power House, a First Aid building (Hospital), an Administration Block and a Canteen were also under construction. With the repair contract transferred to Banwell, the embryo Beaufighter repair section was able to move in in advance of the hall being completed and, by 11 May, three damaged aircraft had arrived from Chittening. Only Hercules-engined Beaufighters would be repaired at Banwell, the Merlin-engined variant being repaired at Rolls-Royce's Hucknall

Oldmixon's three resident wartime test-pilots. Left to right: Ronnie Ellison, Flight Lieutenant George Reston and Hugh Statham in front of a Beaufighter TF X parked on the hard-standing to the east of No. 1 Flight Shed. Statham would sadly lose his life 6 November 1957 whilst bringing Bristol Britannia G-ANCA in for a landing at Filton (*Aeroplane*/www.aeroplanemonthly.com)

plant. Soon after, Aircraft Assembly Jigs started to be bolted to the floor on the other side of the wall and by mid-July the first new Banwell Beaufighter was out of its jig, on the floor and being fitted out.

By early June the chief constable of Somerset had approved the means of aircraft transfer to Weston Airport, which was by towing tail-first with a police vehicle escort, rather than the alternative option of shutting the road whilst an aircraft was in transit. This allowed the first repaired aircraft, escorted by PC Jim Davis on motorbike, to be taken to the Hutton Moor Flight Shed from where it had its first post-restoration flight Tuesday 1 December. Until the month's end, one repaired machine was flown approximately every ten days and thereafter, spares permitting, output was to be just over one Beaufighter per week. Once inside the airport, aircraft were towed to the Hutton Moor Flight Shed parallel to the railway line, but it was over grass that soon became muddy and rutted and, in due course, a concrete perimeter road was laid. By the end of March 1942, fifty-nine aircraft had been repaired and delivered and by January 1944 the ninetieth and last machine had been repaired.

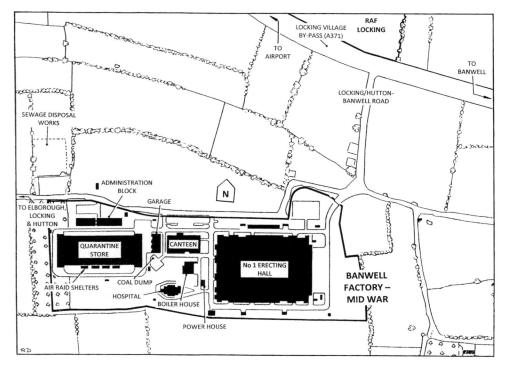

Mid-war layout of the Banwell Factory (R. Dudley)

The relocated No. 1 Erecting Hall at the Elborough site (Banwell Factory) showing the widened Locking/Hutton/Banwell road that slopes up to link with the new Locking Village By-pass (A371) (R. Dudley)

X7929, the Banwell Factory's fifth Beaufighter. A Mk VIF equipped with Mk IV AI, initially it served with 301 Ferry Training Unit, then the Overseas Aircraft Delivery Unit, 153/600 Squadrons, and is seen here serving with the USAAF in the Mediterranean area having been handed over to this operator 1 October 1943. It's difficult to imagine that not so long before the aircraft had been towed along the A371 to Weston Airport (USAAF via E. Johnson)

One of several Banwell-built Beaufort IIAs parked to the east of the Hutton Moor Flight Shed 4 November 1943. Coincidentally, it was this machine that a matter of hours before had been involved in a fatal accident when William Roberts, an airport policeman controlling Perimeter Road traffic, had been struck by one of its airscrews (Mac Hawkins Collection)

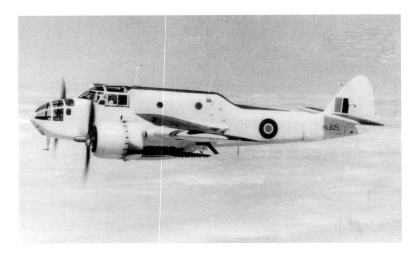

Banwell-built Beaufort IIA ML625 was completed in 1944 and left the factory as a dual-control trainer with a fairing replacing the gun-turret (Bristol via P. Jarrett)

Walter Strachan, together with other Bristol directors in No. 1 Erecting Hall show Her Majesty Queen Mary around Banwell's new Tempest II line in the summer of 1944. Rear fuselages on trestles ready for join-up, the closest for MW388, stand in front of the hall's dividing blast-wall (S. Parsons)

Banwell-built Tempest II MW422 mid-1945 on the compass-swinging pad outside the newly re-camouflaged Hutton Moor Flight Shed (P. F. Adams via E. Johnson)

As early as mid-November 1941 there was a requirement for an additional flight shed of some 17,000 square feet (1579 square metres) to be erected mainly for Banwell, where in-service machines could be flown in for repairs and retrospective modifications to be embodied. But, due to other priorities, this No.3 Flight Shed, to be located at the easterly end of the Oldmixon Factory on ground previously excavated in 1940 for No.2 Flight Shed and a running-up area wasn't to be completed until September 1943.

Meanwhile, at Banwell on the other side of the dividing blast wall by 22 October its first new Beaufighter X7925, a Mk VIC, had been completed and towed to Oldmixon's Flight Shed and was to be delivered to Filton within several days. The second machine, a Mk VIF, was also at the airport but in the Hutton Moor Flight Shed, and it would be flown to Filton shortly after. By December, six new aircraft had been taken to the airport and, come May 1942, an average of eight machines a month were following in their path. Until mid-April both repaired and new machines, because of curb-side obstructions and the narrowness of the hillside road leading up to the Locking Village Bypass

A reconnaissance photograph of Weston taken 2 October 1941 by the Luftwaffe. The Perimeter Road, stretching from the double gate on the widened Locking Moor Road to the Oldmixon Factory, is now complete, as is most of the 1,000-yard (914 metre) initial concrete runway, and the new road and railway bridge joining Oldmixon Drove with Old Junction Road are well underway. To confuse the enemy, a mixture of paint and sawdust has been applied to the grass on the original airport to give an impression of hedges (R. Dudley's Collection)

were towed without outer wing-panels resulting in valuable space being lost in the Hutton Moor Flight Shed for their storage. The increase in production of both repaired and new aircraft coincided with a request to MAP for a quarantine store similar in size to Oldmixon's and, following approval, erection was commenced to the west of No.1 Erecting Hall. Also in that year, Walter Strachan, who had joined the Bristol Aeroplane Company as an apprentice in 1925, was appointed manager of the Banwell Factory.

New Aircraft Types for Banwell

Output at Banwell continued to grow but only sixty new Beaufighters would be completed before its production was switched to Oldmixon, as the existing scheme that involved Banwell was considered to be neither economical nor efficient. The decision taken in January 1942 to offload the Beaufighter probably had a bearing on Filton taking over control of Banwell from Oldmixon on 1 February 1943.

To provide space at Filton for the new Bristol Type 163 Buckingham medium bomber, Banwell was then given the task of assembling the last 250 Beaufort IIs whose sub-assemblies were lying at Filton, the first LS129 leaving Banwell for the Hutton Moor Flight Shed on 21 June 1943 and the second on the 24th. Once Banwell had got into its stride with the Beaufort, Oldmixon's dope shop, working two shifts, was camouflaging a total of up to sixteen Beaufighters and Beauforts combined every twenty-four hours. Beaufort production in turn gave way to that of the Hawker Tempest II fighter, Bristol having obtained an order in August 1943 to assemble 300 of these machines for the RAF, the first off the line being flown from Weston on 4 October 1944 by Bristol's chief test pilot Cyril F. Uwins. Workers at Oldmixon had already become accustomed to seeing a prototype Tempest stationed at Filton for engine-development trials being flown by Uwins at below hangar height at high speed beating up the factory. However, due to the war ending, Banwell only built fifty Tempests, thirty-two of which eventually ended up with the Indian Air Force. It was said that the Dope Shop with its full-span Esavian doors at either end had a certain attraction for George Reston. His ambition was to fly a Tempest through the hangar and he would probably have carried through this daring scheme had the doors not been closed whilst airborne on his last Tempest test flight. Banwell completed its last Tempest II MW435 in August 1945. Hugh Statham performed its first flight on or about 2 August, and its last flight before delivery was by Ronnie Ellison on the 7th. Ellison test-flew all fifty machines although additional flights were made by others in his team.

The mid-war picture at Banwell, if fortunes of the torpedo-carrying Beaufighter had been slightly different would have significantly changed the factory's output. Early in the war Bristol had produced detailed design studies for the Type 158, a much modified Beaufighter for Coastal Command with a new slim fuselage, known as the Beaufighter Mk III, but due to the state of the war at the time the project had been temporarily put on hold. By September 1942 its drawings were being dusted off with the intention of it being put into production, but with the large number of modifications involved and with the need for its construction not to interfere with the ongoing conventional Beaufighter work, the directors were of the opinion that Banwell was the only factory where it could be made. Had approval been given for prototype construction and series production, the No.1 Erecting Hall's repair work would have been transferred to Bristol's Whitchurch facility thereby allowing first deliveries of the new machine to be made by Banwell to the RAF mid-1943.

Improving the Airport

As Beaufighter test flying got underway, the June 1940 decision not to proceed with concrete runways was soon regretted and MAP approved a single 1,000 yard (914 metres) by 50 yard (46 metres) concrete runway heading 250 degrees into the prevailing south-westerly wind. Completed by the end of November 1942 with a camouflage of tarred wood chippings applied a little later, the runway's westerly threshold, although in line with the end of the factory was almost 500 yards (457 metres) away to the north of No.1 Flight Shed, and for take-off aircraft had to be towed to the runway across the muddy grass. By the beginning of October, a 1,425-foot-long (434 metres), 35-foot-wide (434 metres) taxi-track that would stretch from near the flight shed to the runway threshold, and then extend further to the airport's northerly perimeter road, had been partly completed. Coinciding with this, the short stretch of road (formerly a part of Hutton Moor Lane) from the Hutton Moor Flight Shed, south to the middle of the runway was widened to 25 feet (7.5 metres) to permit taxiing, but its use was soon superseded by widening the perimeter road to 42 feet (12.5 metres) to permit aircraft taxiing from Hutton Moor Flight Shed to the runway's westerly end, via the new taxi-track. As already mentioned, through the restrictions on cost and material at that time, the runway's easterly end was unfortunately inset approximately 480 yards (439 metres) from the Locking Moor Road boundary thus denying its use to aircraft operating from that end of the airport, such as those belonging to the TDU and Western Airways.

With Beaufighters progressively becoming more powerful and heavier, greater lengths of runway were being used for landing and take-off runs and there was concern that sooner or later an aircraft would overrun onto boggy ground, and there was also the operating requirements of Banwell's new 440 mph (710 kph) Hawker Tempest to be considered. With these problems in mind the company prepared three runway improvement schemes for MAP to consider: a 400 yard (365 metres) x 50 yard (45.7 metres) concrete extension to the existing runway's easterly end; the 400 yard extension plus the addition of a new 56-yard-wide (50.4 metres) concrete taxi-track that would link Western

Airways, the easterly end of the 400 yard runway extension and the easterly end of the perimeter road and also provide the TDU with a new headquarters. The final scheme would comprise a further concrete runway reflecting the heading of an existing grass runway that would intersect and cross-over the one already laid. On 15 February 1943, Anthony Chitty, who pre-war had led Whitney Straight's Aerodrome Consultancy Department, and at its outbreak joined department APFC, a part of the Ministry of Works, visited and inspected the airport to assess the company's request. Although Chitty initially approved the runway extension with the suggestion that the 400 yards of grass runway should be temporarily reinforced with wire-netting, eventually it was the 400 yard concrete runway extension together with taxi-track that was approved by his boss the Director General of Aerodrome Planning and Organisation who on 9 September also visited to assess the situation. Due to delays in approval and winter weather, it was well into April 1944 before the Anglo-American Asphalt Company, which was subcontractor to Nuttall, completed the task.

Problems with Component Delivery

There had been delays in completing early Beaufighters due to component shortages. In some cases items had been obtained using the pooling scheme whilst one or two components had been recycled from Beaufighters under repair at Chittening. Delivery of sub-assemblies such as undercarriages, engine mountings, oil tanks and air-intakes, together with smaller components, was always a problem and certain stampings and castings had to be supplied for a time from the USA to meet demand. There was also often inadequate delivery of government-supplied embodiment loan items such as Hercules VIs and the airscrews where twenty always had to be available at any one time in the flight shed. Regarding the airscrew situation, Wednesday 26 November 1942 was a particularly bad day when stocks were down to sixteen and, to alleviate the pending problem, there was talk of clearing one aircraft and then removing its airscrews for the next aircraft and so on. Prolonged shortages of any item would cause production to slow and some workers to be put on waiting time.

With the urgency to get wing and fuselage production underway, it had been a case of subcontractors starting production of components and then Oldmixon agreeing prices at a later date. This was not an ideal situation and it was therefore not surprising when around July 1941, with the first batch of 350 fuselages almost completed, prices were only now being agreed. The effect of this was that the major manufacturers, especially Standard, had been provided a loophole for inefficiency and any incentive to save on manufacturing costs had been removed. Equally important were labour difficulties at Standard that had initially arisen through excessive rates being paid and workpeople refusing to accept any reductions as their experience grew. It was only the introduction of girl labour and married women working part-time, together with the start

Left: Wings for Oldmixon's Beaufighters being assembled in Austin's 'A Shop', Longbridge, by some of 1,060 workers allocated to the task (British Motor Heritage Trust via J. Baker)

Below: Oldmixon's Quarantine Store looking east (north-east corner) with mainly fuselage sub-assemblies in storage (Bristol via The Bristol Aero Collection)

of a night-shift, better rate fixing and the co-operation of trade unions that allowed a good production recovery with component cost reductions, thus enabling eventual high aircraft assembly rates at Oldmixon to be achieved.

Introduction of modifications also caused delays in the production programme. Around July 1942 a new tailplane with 12 degrees of dihedral started to replace the original flat tailplane. Introduced to cure a problem of low-frequency longitudinal instability, particularly in the climb, and a tendency for the aircraft to swing on take-off, the task of manufacturing the new unit had been given to George Parnall of Fishponds, Bristol. But due to production difficulties, the firm was failing to make adequate deliveries and as a result, Oldmixon's output of aircraft in August was expected to fall sharply below MAP's programme. Not only had Parnall's deliveries been inadequate, but of thirty-one units delivered to date, twenty-five had to be returned as defective and these had not yet been redelivered. The necessary materials, labour and equipment were all available at its factory and 'shock squads' had been introduced from both Filton and Oldmixon, but, despite all efforts, little improvement had been made. Therefore, as a fail-safe measure, manufacturing of the tailplane was also given to Necaco. (North East Coast Aviation Company) which had its factory a bit further afield in a quarry at Llanberis, North Wales. Meanwhile, as a desperate measure the country was scoured for old 'flat' tailplanes so that Beaufighters could be delivered. Another unwanted task at that time involved a policy decision at the Ministry that the in-service, all-black, night-fighter Beaufighters should be given a new grey and green camouflaged scheme, and this was to result in the Dope Shop being put under additional strain with many of these machines coming into Oldmixon for respray.

At the beginning of 1943 the Oldmixon Factory that up to then with the increased output from its subcontractors was just managing to produce a nominal eighty Beaufighters a month, was presented with a further challenge by MAP, and that was to increase production in the coming year to 100 machines a month. Oldmixon agreed that this could be done, preferably in two stages, providing that there was an increased quota of raw materials to the subcontractors. This happily coincided with Department DDGMP, about to allow a 7-month lead in the supply of materials to subcontractors against the present 6-month lead time. Regarding Oldmixon's labour, it had become highly trained in the specialised work and it was considered that aircraft output could be increased to 100 without the need for extra labour. An added bonus was that Banwell had now also completed Beaufighter production and its Aircraft Assembly Jigs were being laid at Oldmixon. With local issues now settled, Bristol representatives attended a meeting in London on 11 March with Sir Wilfrid Freeman, Chief Executive, and Sir Alexander Dunbar, Controller General, of MAP to decide in detail on the preferred way ahead to increase Beaufighter production.

New Aircraft Types for Oldmixon

Due to the varying demands of the war, from time to time there was the prospect of new types replacing the Beaufighters on Oldmixon's production lines. At the beginning of May 1941, when a further Beaufighter contract for 250 machines to fill the June/September 1942 production slot was about to be sought by the company, it was announced by MAP that these aircraft would be followed by the new twin-finned, twin Bristol Centaurus-powered Type 163 Buckingham medium bomber for which the factory was considered to be more suitable than Filton for its assembly. Deliveries to the RAF were due to commence in January 1943 and made construction of jigs and tools a top priority task, but due to delays in determining the aircraft's final specification, together with the success of the DH Mosquito, the Buckingham was considered obsolete, and was in fact eventually only built in limited numbers at Filton. However, prototypes of the machine were often seen on the ground at Oldmixon part-way through Filton test flights. Meanwhile, due to the success of the constantly-evolving Beaufighter, its production at Oldmixon continued with night-fighters forming only a small proportion of production, the majority being for Coastal Command, duties in North Africa and as long-range fighters in the Middle and Far East. These aeroplanes proved to be very versatile and in due course were to carry a large range of weapons and equipment; notably torpedoes, rockets or bombs and specialised radar.

Mid 1941, these Beaufighter IF front fuselages, the closest for X7646, were being fitted-out in the south-west corner of the No. 2 Erecting Hall by some of the many girl workers that had recently been drafted into the Oldmixon Factory (Bristol via C. R. Butt)

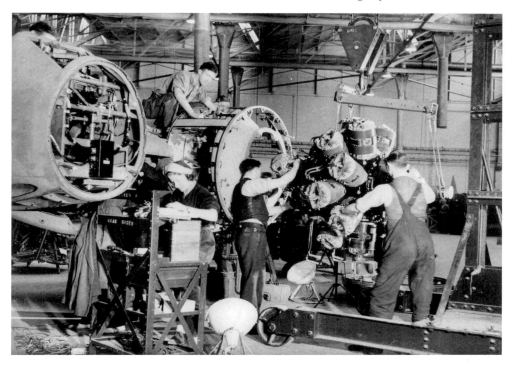

Above: This Beaufighter IF in the No. 2 Erecting Hall, whilst still in its Aircraft Assembly Jig is having a Hercules engine offered-up to the port engine mounting (Bristol via C. R. Butt)

Below: About to join one of the four production lines, this Beaufighter IF sometime in August 1941 was being lifted out of No. 2 Erecting Hall's Aircraft Assembly Jig No. 6 by a Special Double-Lifting Crane, and then having its undercarriage locked in the down position (*Aeroplane* via C. R. Butt)

One of the two lines of Beaufighters on the south side of No. 2 Erecting Hall's very substantial blast wall that divided the building lengthwise into two equal areas (Bristol via C. R. Butt)

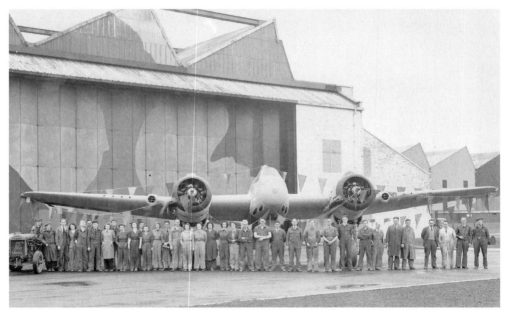

Oldmixon's one-thousandth Beaufighter JL762, a Mk VIC with the new dihedral tailplane outside No. 2 Erecting Hall in the winter of 1942. Airscrews would be fitted in the Flight Shed. The production achievement is celebrated by the workers with bunting in the usual Bristol fashion (Bristol via The Bristol Aero Collection)

Some of the senior managers that made the eventual, very impressive, production rate of Beaufighters possible. In front of the 1,000th machine, left to right: F. Jefferies — Chief Production Engineer, H. Carnall — No.2 Erecting Hall Superintendant, H. Smith — No. 1 Flight Shed Supervisor, H. S. Butt — Factory Manager, R. Ellison — Chief Test Pilot (Oldmixon), H. V. Perman — Sub-Contracts Manager and W. Yeadon — Works Office Manager (Bristol via C. R. Butt)

As early as April 1941, Weston's factories had been associated with the first torpedo-carrying Beaufighter when Mk VIC X8065, a Banwell-built Coastal Command machine had been rapidly modified to cover an urgent requirement for the Command to carry a British 18 inch (46 cm), or an American 22.4 inch (57 cm), torpedo under its belly. Flown to Filton for initial acceptance, in early May it was passed to the TDU at Gosport, but trials were prematurely curtailed on 16 June when, following an engine failure, it rolled and crashed into Fort Road, Alverstoke. In spite of the machine's loss, the installation was already proving a great success and a further sixteen Mk VICs, to be modified in a similar way, were ordered to form the complement of a trials squadron. The changes soon began to be retrofitted to some of the existing and new Mk VICs. The Mk VIC with the torpedo installation was known as the Interim Torpedo Fighter (ITF) and unofficially as the 'Torbeau', and a total of sixty were built. With the success of this machine, it was decided to develop it still further into what would become the Beaufighter X, the prototype being completed at Oldmixon by basically installing the more powerful low-altitude variant of the Hercules VI power plant — the Mk XVII. By May 1943 Bristol's Accrington Factory and its new No.2 Engine Shadow Factory at Patchway would between them be producing 430 Hercules XVIIs a month, thus permitting all of Oldmixon's future Beaufighters to be Torpedo Fighter Xs or the 'TF X' as it became known, or the Mk XI which was a TF X without the torpedo equipment.

This was only the beginning of the Beaufighter TF X/XI, as there were many further modifications earmarked for eventual installation. The main ones were Fairey-Youngman bellows-type dive brakes and modified flaps, an elevator with an increased chord, an enlarged dorsal fin-fairing, a BLG tail wheel and provision for the carriage of additional fuel comprising of an under-fuselage 200 gallon (909 litre) drop-tank whilst structural stiffening would give strengthened engine nacelles and main undercarriage fittings. Provision would also be made for: increased amounts of ammunition for the machine's 20mm canons, a rear-firing Browning .303 machine-gun mounted in the observer's blister, the carriage of a 2,000 lb (907 kg) bomb load and the carriage of up to four 3 inch (7.5cm) rocket projectiles beneath each wing. Avionic-wise, the Air-Interception (AI) Mk VIII radar adapted for Air-to-Surface Vessel (ASV), that in development was proving to be excellent for tracking submarines, would be installed in what was now becoming the standard thimble nose-radome, and additional radio and navigation equipment that included radio altimeters would be introduced. All-up weight for the TF X would eventually come out at 25,400 lb (11,521 kg) as against 21,000 lb (9,525 kg) for the other machines.

With these and the other changes envisaged and with the necessary security aspect of some of the modifications, funding for the erection of a dedicated DTD hangar, where prototypes belonging to the DTD could be worked on in secrecy, was requested. As a consequence, by early February 1943 work on a Robin-type hangar, now more commonly known as the Experimental and Modification Shop, had commenced. Progress on the structure, which was located directly opposite the doors of Oldmixon's Erecting Hall, proceeded extremely slowly due to a shortage of steel, but by early August it had been completed. Most Beaufighter trial-installation development work was done at Filton, and the DTD hangar would generally be used to introduce already proven major modifications to certain production aircraft prior to them being introduced to aircraft on the production line. The first DTD Beaufighter earmarked for the hangar was Mk IF X7579 and in August 1943, returned from Filton, work commenced to replace its AI Mk IV radar with the new Mk VIII installation, under supervision of the new shop's superintendent Walter Watkins and foreman Horace Jeffrey.

The Minister of Aircraft Production, Sir Stafford Cripps, who had replaced Lord Beaverbrook in 1942, visited Filton, Oldmixon and a new facility at Bridgwater on Saturday 7 August 1943 during his round of visits to the various aircraft factories, and was most pleased with what he saw. At Oldmixon he gave an address after a spirited flying display given by Ronnie Ellison flying Beaufighter TF X LZ114 carrying a Mk XV torpedo. In this address, amongst his other words of wisdom he remarked about Oldmixon that "With the factory being just beneath the lush Mendip Hills in a very picturesque position — it was a Factory in a Garden". Beaufighter TF Xs proved to be an immense success and Oldmixon went on to produce 2,095 of them. Even toward the war's end, such was the urgency to still get Beaufighter Xs delivered that when, during the night of Friday 15 December 1944, one being worked on in No.3 Flight Shed caught fire resulting in approximately 50 per cent of the aircraft being damaged, within thirty-six hours MAP had authorised its repair and the replacement of components. It was ironic that the 15th was coincidentally the day in which Sir Stafford Cripps had paid a further visit to the Weston and Bridgwater factories, and, early the following week, Oldmixon's Works Manager Herbert Butt received a note from Sir Stafford to say "that he was pleased to observe again the smooth and competent running of both factories" — he probably hadn't yet heard of the incident!

It was intended to develop the Beaufighter TF X still further at Oldmixon into the Beaufighter TF XII by fitting Hercules Mk 27s that had the American Bendix pressure carburettor, which didn't cut or go rich in violent manoeuvres. However, in trials it wasn't a success and in due course was replaced with the new Hobson RAE injector unit that worked well. Although Mk VI EL393 had been returned in November 1943 from Filton to act as the prototype, the TF XII contract was cancelled in early February 1944. In an obscure way Weston had already been associated with the Bendix carburettor. To prove the system, at Filton, Beaufighter VI X7881 had been suitably modified and on 9 June 1943, two hours into a fuel consumption test flight, near Weston its starboard engine failed and severe vibration from the unfeathered airscrew caused an engine fire. Heat and fumes soon entered the cockpit, soot formed on its interior, and during an approach to Weston Airport with forward vision almost completely obscured, a heavy landing resulted, and the starboard undercarriage leg collapsed. Although the crew managed to extract themselves from the machine, emergency services were unable to put the fire out and the aircraft was completely burnt out.

On 8 July 1943, a meeting between Bristol and the Ministry discussed a more radical approach to replacing the Beaufighter TF X. The aircraft under discussion was the new twin-finned, twin Bristol Centaurus-powered Type 164 Brigand Torpedo Fighter that was intended for the Pacific Theatre of Operations. Designed at Filton with many components common with the Buckingham, it would rectify various Beaufighter TF X shortcomings including the separation of crew members and the lack of navigation facilities, and as soon as technical clearance had been affected an initial 200 machines under contract Acft 3379, in the serial range RH742 to RH998, would start to be assembled at Oldmixon, where in due course output was expected to reach

Taking-off towards the east 7 August 1943 from the initial 1000 yard concrete runway, Beaufighter X LZ114 carrying a Mk XV torpedo was at the start of a demonstration flight for the Minister of Aircraft Production (*Aeroplane* via Airbus)

A few minutes later LZ114 was heading east along the runway (with the new dive-brakes open) towards the TDU's dispersal that was unfortunately directly in-line with the new runway, and shortly to be demolished. Two Lancaster IIs and an Albacore belonging to the TDU can be seen next to the building (*Aeroplane*/www.aeroplanemonthly.com)

Shortly after Ronnie Ellison was putting LZ114 through a very low, high 'g' turn demonstrating manoeuvrability of the Beaufighter and his skill in handling this big aeroplane at low level (*Aeroplane*/www.aeroplanemonthly.com)

sixty a month. Introduction into RAF service was pencilled in for the end of 1944, although, with the aircraft still being in its early stages of design, early 1945 was thought to be a more likely date. Like the proposed Beaufighter TF XII, the Brigand TF I was expected to be manufactured mainly by Oldmixon's existing subcontractors, but as early as November 1943 Austin and Standard had rejected any Brigand commitments, as they intended to resume motor car manufacture at the cessation of hostilities. In spite of this setback, by early March 1944, subcontractors for all main components of the Brigand had been arranged. The drawing position was also fairly satisfactory with fifty to sixty being received each week from Filton, but as yet there were insufficient at Oldmixon to form complete assemblies. By May, it was realised that aircraft design and component manufacture was running so late that Oldmixon's production plans would be thrown out. Tooling could not be started as certain components were not yet finally determined, also with delays there would be a problem in reserving subcontractors and their manufacturing capability for an extended period. The final setback occurred 1 October 1944 when the Brigand contract was transferred from Oldmixon to Filton. By now there were substantial raw materials at Oldmixon for subcontractors, and with it being decided that Filton would now make nearly everything for the aircraft, materials and proprietary items were transferred there and contracts with Midland subcontractors cancelled. Although the machine was ultimately not to be built at Weston, in the 1950s several Brigands did operate for a time from the Hutton Moor Flight Shed in the hands of the Aircraft Torpedo Development Unit.

A Requirement for Spares Manufacturing

Around May 1941, Filton acquired Brinton's carpet factory on the A38 (Bristol Road) at Bridgwater as a detail fitting shop, but with Oldmixon taking an ever-increasing role in Beaufighter production and with its lack of manufacturing facilities, on 1 March 1942 Brinton's was handed over to Oldmixon for use as a combined machine and detail fitting shop and it became known as the No.3 Factory. This was to put further stress on Oldmixon's limited storage facilities and the Parrett Bath Brick Company at Bridgwater and premises at Axbridge, Orchardlea Farm, Claverham and Clist & Rattles were commandeered. Although originally not intended to manufacture Beaufighter components, the multitude of spare parts required to support Weston's in-service aircraft, up to now provisioned by Filton and its subcontractors, from early 1943 at MAP's request was to be provisioned by Oldmixon with No.3 Factory providing much of the output. It was also proving difficult to obtain suitable workers for this factory. In May there were only 129, and a request to the Ministry for a broadcasting facility so that *Music While You Work* could be enjoyed was put on hold until numbers had doubled. In addition to now having No.3 Factory, a Spares Hangar identical to the Experimental and Modification Shop was also erected at Oldmixon. It was located to the north, between the Quarantine Store and the railway siding, but due to the shortage of steel, building work proceeded extremely slowly, and it wasn't until around the end of August 1943 that it was ready for equipment and benches to be moved in. Like No.3 Factory, this facility would also require off-site premises for the storage of raw materials and components, and these, in due course, were provided at the Dorothy Coach Depot at Clevedon, Oak House Café at Axbridge, Millier's Stores at Burrington, Palmer Row Store at Weston and Old Junction Farm on Hutton Moor.

Weston's Wartime Exports

Of Weston's Beaufighters, two early F I night-fighters, X7610 fitted with Mk IV radar and X7818 equipped with the Mk VIII version were sent to Wright Field USA for test and evaluation in October 1941 and January 1942 respectively. More were provided direct to American night-fighter units in Europe at a later date, the majority being Filton-built, although a number were from the Rootes Blythe Bridge Factory and a few from Weston.

Oldmixon, starting in June 1943, had 117 of its Beaufighters (thirty-five Mk VICs, sixty-two Mk Xs and twenty Mk XICs) allocated to the Royal Australian Air Force (RAAF). These were to complement the initial seventy-two Mk ICs delivered by Fairey in 1942 that had created a profound impression on arrival in Australia. This had brought about a follow-on order from the same source for twenty-eight Mk VICs, a proposal for the setting up of Australian factories to produce home-produced Beaufighters, and the Oldmixon order which was to largely keep the RAAF going until the home-produced machines became available. Except for its Hercules power plants and a few other components, like the Beaufort that was already being built in Australia, it would be completely manufactured in-country.

The new Australian production line, which would go on to build 365 Beaufighter Mk 21 with the Australian designation A8, was for an aircraft based on the RAF Beaufighter XIC with the Rocket Projectile installation, but it would be equipped with Hercules XVIIIs, the torpedo installation replaced by one designed to carry a 2,000-lb (907-kg) bomb, four 0.5 inch (12.7 cm) Browning machine-guns replacing the six .303s and provision for a Sperry autopilot in a bulge on the upper nose. However, neither radar nor the dorsal fin fairing would be fitted. Even with the similarities to its predecessor, manufacturing would be a major task with hundreds of Australian companies and organisations eventually involved. To smooth the way, Oldmixon in 1943 provided certain Beaufighter TF X tools, together with a sample rear fuselage, stern frame, front fuselage and various pipes and fittings. Some 62,000 microfilm negatives containing around half a million images of blueprints needed for local manufacture of tools, equipment and aircraft components were also sent from Britain to assist with the task. The majority of engines supplied to Australia for its interim British-built Beaufighter and the later Australian home-produced Mk 21, although mainly from Bristol's Accrington Shadow Factory were delivered to the customer via Oldmixon's No.3 Bridgwater Factory where they were equipped with bulkhead and engine-mountings, ancillary equipment and cowlings to become power eggs, and Banwell where a power egg packing section loaded them into shipping crates. On completion of the various contracts, the first commencing March/April 1942, over 900 power eggs had been assembled, crated and sent by sea to Australia.

End of the War

Oldmixon continued to assemble only Beaufighters and would do so until 21 September 1945 when SR919, a TF X, and the last of 5,562 built, 3,336 of them at the Weston factories, came off the production lines. Of the Weston machines, no less than 1,800 had been flight tested by Ronnie Ellison who had also test-flown the 1,000th, 2,000th, 3,000th and the last. Now with the war over, there was a chance to review the factory's short history. From the beginning Bristol's directors had doubted that the newly-formed organisation and factory could achieve the standards and output demanded, but they were wrong. The standards and output had been made possible with guidance of some first-class engineers and managers who, having acquired their skills at Filton, had trained an enthusiastic and dedicated workforce at Weston. Amongst Oldmixon's production achievements was the output of 100 aeroplanes a month during October 1943 and May 1944, the latter being all the more notable due to the great disruption caused following the air raid on Weston 27/28 March and the resultant knock-on effect that it caused with all goods by rail destined for Oldmixon being stopped at Bristol and their content having to be collected by road. One hundred Beaufighters were again produced in July, and in August, in spite of the factory holiday period intervening, output was a remarkable eighty-five aircraft in only nineteen-and-a-half days!

Considering the many machines that had been assembled and repaired at Weston's factories during the 5-year wartime period there were very few accidents, which was remarkable considering that most of the workforce was initially untrained. The first of the only known accidents to involve Oldmixon-built Beaufighters operating from Weston occurred on 5 July 1942 when EL235, a Mk VIC collected by lady pilot First Officer S. E. Mitchell from No.2 ATA Ferry Pilots Pool at Whitchurch, on take-off from Weston Airport had an engine cut. In the attempted return, the machine undershot, hit wires and belly-landed on the north side just outside the airport near the flak tower. The crew managed to escape unhurt, but although it didn't appear to be too badly damaged the aircraft had to be written off. The reason for this crash is thought

Bristol Hercules Power-Egg Assembly in No. 3 Bridgwater Factory (Bristol via The Bristol Aero Collection)

JM123, a Beaufighter XI in early 1943 at the commencement of its assembly in Aircraft Assembly Jig No. 13. Note, to save valuable time, rather than using the previous laborious method of fitting an engine and then adding around it the various associated components, Hercules Power Eggs from No. 3 Factory at Bridgwater are laid out to be fitted (Bristol via C. R. Butt)

to have been a problem with fuel, for during the month of July there had been ten unexplained engine failures during run-up at the Oldmixon Factory. The second accident occurred 15 January 1944 when a TF X flown by Reston in rather foggy conditions was, for reasons unknown, force-landed at Bleadon. The event appears to have been hushed-up, and the aircraft not badly damaged was dismantled on-site, its recovery back to the factory for repair being a long and difficult process. As far as is known, the only accident occurring to a Banwell-built aircraft was on 30 May 1945. Ronnie Ellison was on a test flight in Hawker Tempest F II MW404, and whilst flying straight and level at high speed the port undercarriage leg extended and its door broke off. On landing back at Weston Airport, the leg which couldn't be locked down collapsed. Not badly damaged, after repairs the aircraft went on to serve with the Royal Indian Air Force as RIAF HA557.

Post-War

Aircraft production finished at Banwell in August 1945 and, with Hutton Moor Flight Shed empty, to assist Filton and to retain as many employees as possible, a number of Buckinghams were flown down to be modified to meet the latest RAF requirements. With this work completed, the next aircraft task was to come from an unlikely source — British Overseas Airways Corporation (BOAC) at Whitchurch Airport. Prior to moving to Hurn, BOAC was looking locally for a temporary maintenance base with a runway long enough to operate a small number of Handley Page Halifax heavy bombers on loan from the RAF. The corporation intended to open up a passenger route to Accra in West Africa, and as a stopgap until purpose-built airliners became available, a number of civilianised Halifaxes (Haltons) were to be obtained. With the agreement of Bristol/Ministry of Supply (MoS), in September 1945 three 10-seat Halifax C 8s, PP325, PP326 and PP327, were flown into Weston from Whitchurch and in the flight shed fitted-out by personnel belonging to Banwell's repair section

SR919, a TF X with all the latest modifications embodied, and the last of 3,336 Weston-built Beaufighters on a dispersal at Oldmixon in September 1945 (Bristol via Airbus)

Oldmixon-built Beaufighter TF X RD805 'J' of 45 Squadron in early 1947 at its RAF Negombo, Ceylon (Sri Lanka) base (E. Johnson)

with special experimental equipment to suit the type for operation in tropical conditions. Frequently seen around the town in early October being air tested, on Friday 19 the first completed machine ballasted-up to simulate a full load of passengers, and with a crew of five left the airport for Hurn at the start of a fast desert route to Accra. Flown at a cruising speed of 200 mph (322 kph), this 4,474-mile (7,200-km) journey proved the equipment and until November, when the machines transferred to Hurn, there was an ad hoc three flights a week air service that started at Weston.

MAP control of the Oldmixon and Banwell Factories continued until 1 January 1946 when Filton took over. Meanwhile, Weston-built aircraft were still in the news with Beaufighters exported to France, who took nine, Dominican Republic (ten), Portugal (seventeen), Turkey (twenty-four and twelve Beauforts), while the Indian Air Force took thirty-two of the fifty Tempests. There was also an illegal export of refurbished Beaufighters to Israel, six supplied to a buyer who said they were to be used in the making of a movie. One, however, crashed leaving five that were next seen in the colours of the Israeli Air Force. The Beaufighter remained in RAF Squadron service until February 1950 at Tengah, Malaya, where 45 Squadron 'The Flying Camels' had been engaged in 'Operation Firedog' using cannon and rockets against insurgents. Just after the war another use was found for the Beaufighter TF X when thirty-five were converted at Filton for target towing, and as TT 10s, continued in RAF service until 16 May 1960 when the final sortie was flown by RD761, an Oldmixon-built aircraft, from its Seletar, Singapore, base.

Prefabricated Aluminium Buildings

With the Allies consolidating their landings in Normandy and the steady advance towards Germany from the west, and knowing that the Russian armies were making similar progress in the east, the end of the war in Europe had been anticipated. For some time, behind the scenes at the Bristol Aeroplane Company, thought had been given as to how skills of its Shadow Factory workforce could be applied to volume production of a peace-time requirement. The desperate need for new houses highlighted by the widespread destruction of property across the country, especially during the Blitz, persuaded the company's directors to investigate the possibility of producing prefabricated buildings. As a result, mid-war, plans of a prefabricated single-storey building were obtained from the Tennessee Valley Building Estate Corporation of the USA. Using these as a basis, Jimmy Rush, a senior design office manager at Oldmixon was tasked to develop the design, and by the war's end had ready for production a bungalow, predominately made from aluminium and soon to be widely known as a 'Prefab'. This building would be assembled at Oldmixon against a government contract under the auspices of the newly-formed Aircraft Industries Research Organisation for Housing (AIROH) Trading Co. Ltd. In early 1945, as the last batch of Beaufighters was being completed, the prototype prefab was coming along well with flooring being manufactured and assembled in the No.1 Flight Shed (about to be renumbered Shop 4), its tubular roof structure being assembled in the No.2 Erecting Hall (about to be renumbered Shop 8), and its aluminium sheet wall-panels being formed by a large brake press in the Quarantine Store (about to be renumbered Shop 7). The Banwell Factory was also getting geared up to support Oldmixon with the programme.

Following considerable preparatory work and testing, including proving the building's structural integrity by subjecting it to the 70 mph (113 kph) storm-force slipstream from airscrews of an Oldmixon Beaufighter, the first bungalow was completed during the week ending Friday 13 February 1945 and sent to the Tate Gallery in London for display. Re-erected at Filton, it was subsequently dispatched to Chester for the benefit of the Vickers Group. Meanwhile, with the Ministry agreeing that Filton would take over Oldmixon on 1 January 1946, the Aircraft Division Board at Filton was approving production of the first government contract for 2,500 bungalows, by what was now the Bristol Aeroplane Company (Housing) Ltd. With Banwell and four other concerns supplying major components to Oldmixon, when in full production, bungalows were completed at an average rate of 126 per week with peak output reaching 200. This equated to one coming off the line every thirteen minutes. With its sub-assemblies having been moved by road from Oldmixon, one of the first of these 'Green and Cream' buildings to be erected for occupation was opened for inspection by the Lord Mayor of Bristol, at Shirehampton, Wednesday 18 July 1946. Fordson tractor units were initially the prime movers for road delivery that stretched over the length and breadth of Britain, and for distribution further afield, and for the bringing in of raw materials, the railway line to Oldmixon's coal dump was extended to the easterly end of Shop 8. Less than two years later on 8 May 1948 production came to an end and the last of the 11,250 bungalows was transported to a housing estate in Sevenoaks, Kent.

Oldmixon continued to develop the aluminium bungalow's prefab concept and diversified the range into buildings for other uses, and the single-storey unit was soon superseded by 2-storey semi-detached 'Alcrete' (aluminium/concrete) houses. A further development was in 1948 when a prototype aluminium school building was completed and its design was in due course modified for use as hospitals, telephone exchanges, post offices, hotels, churches, coal mine pit-head bath houses and laboratories, etc. Although the line in Shop 8 had been closed down, building work continued in Shop 5 (formerly the Experimental and Modification Shop) on schools and hospitals. Since the days of Beaufighter experimental work, the shop's surface area had been extended to the east and south 3-fold and a railway line laid that went from its easterly end to the factory's railway siding. Although Weston's factories were capable of high output, more often than not production was limited by availability of raw materials, with as late as December 1951 supplies of aluminium being restricted to 280 tons (258.5 tonnes) per month.

In late March 1949, the Bristol Type 170 Freighter, another of the company's post-war triumphs, was involved in the school programme when a 2-classroom unit was transported by air from Oldmixon to Paris for exhibition. Afterwards, the building was used in France as a pattern for licence production by Société Nationale des Constructions Aéronautiques du Sud-Ouest (SNCASO), later a part of Sud Aviation and responsible for design of the SA330 Puma and 341 Gazelle helicopters that would be built in later years at Oldmixon. Four Freighters belonging to Cie Air Transport were involved in the ferry operation, with the first leaving Weston Airport Friday 25 March and the last the following Thursday. One foreign visitor to show keen interest in school and hospital production was 18-year-old King Hussein of Jordan, who whilst at Sandhurst for military training was shown around Oldmixon on 6 March 1952. A year later, on 2 March 1953, the King returned for a further visit to see progress on the latest buildings, this time accompanied by his uncle, Prince Nasir Jamil. Of the many school buildings produced, the largest consignment was for twenty-six which on 7 February 1950 left Oldmixon by rail for Avonmouth for shipment to Australia onboard SS *Trelyon*, thus fulfilling part of an order from the Government of Victoria for 100 buildings, thus perpetuating Oldmixon's involvement with that country.

Further Diversifications

By the early 1950s, Bristol had decided to sever building work from Oldmixon's other engineering projects and at the beginning of 1952 Bristol Aeroplane Company (Housing) Ltd became Bristol Aeroplane Company (Weston) Ltd, and by November 1953 plans were afoot to move all building work to Banwell. Bristol, anticipating a decline in demand for prefabricated buildings, had been looking for opportunities to obtain other work including general military and aviation-related contracts. It was intended that the 230-foot (70-metre) span

Production line of AIROH bungalows in Shop 8 (formerly No. 2 Erecting Hall). Only a few months before, this building was full of Beaufighters (Bristol via S. Terrell)

One of the many DUKWs that passed through Henlys Shop 8 in the 1940s/50s for refurbishment, in this case 73 YP 34 that left the company 21 December 1956. It was displayed on the Beach Lawns in 2008, having again been completely rebuilt, this time by Scootopia of the Oldmixon Trading Estate (E. Johnson)

Bristol Brabazon airliner would be assembled at Oldmixon, but extensive tests only confirmed those of 1940, that the subsoil was unsuitable for factory and runway enlargement. Had conditions been satisfactory, a massive assembly hall would have been built and the runway increased in width to 100 yards (92 metres) and extended towards RAF Locking to give a length of 2,750 yards (2,515 metres). As it was, in September 1948 the Oldmixon Factory and an adjacent part of the airport, some 52 acres (21 hectares), was compulsorily purchased by the MoS, due, it was said, to the recent war-work carried out which had been funded by the Crown, and this coincided with Bristol relinquishing Shop 8 and it being leased by Henlys of Bristol for refurbishment of military vehicles under a War Department contract. Eventually eleven lines would be set up including ones for Willis Jeeps, Humber Estate Cars, Merryweather and American fire engines, Austin Champs, Antars, Diamond Ts, Trailers and DUKWs. The latter were initially checked for leaks in a specially widened part of Cross Rhyne, formerly the Main Storage Rhyne, brakes were tested on a stretch of Winterstoke Road outside the factory and finally vehicles were tested in the sea from Uphill. Other parts of the factory had also been given over to non-Bristol work, with by May 1950 Andrews Brothers Ltd, who specialised in fabricating and finishing stainless-steel milk road-tankers, brewing and milk-processing equipment and stainless steel domestic cooking pots and pans in the 'Elizabeth Anne' range, occupying Shops 4 and 6. The company left Oldmixon for Liverpool in March 1952.

Bristol's directors continued to look for aircraft and armament work for Oldmixon and considered taking on the manufacture or assembly of complete aircraft, but this was soon discounted as it would have meant Bristol taking over Shop 8 and its labour from Henlys. However, the departure of Andrews Brothers was timely, for in 1951 arrangements were made with the Ministry to take over all remaining buildings at the factory and absorb the Andrews Brothers workforce. This would allow for armament subcontract work to be taken on from Filton, and from September capital equipment to be obtained for a newly-arranged aircraft contract, production of components for the DH Venom FB I jet fighter, for which early in 1951 Bristol together with de Havilland had been awarded substantial production orders.

By February 1952, large sums of money had been invested in re-equipping Shop 3 (formerly No. 3 Flight Shed) and Shop 4 for the Venom contract. Skilled labour for this work, however, was still difficult to obtain, and towards the end of 1951, with concern that more defence work would over burden Oldmixon, the company started to take on apprentices as a safeguard for its future. Unfortunately, by mid-year Venom work was at an end as the aircraft had failed to achieve status as NATO's standard fighter bomber, and Oldmixon was again looking to other parts of the company for business. Filton's armament work was by then already established in Shop 6 (formerly the Dope Shop), with fitters repairing and refurbishing Bristol B17 dorsal 0.79 inch (20 mm) cannon gun turrets from Avro Lincoln heavy bombers and refurbishing and modifying Bofors Mk VIII and Mk IX Anti-Aircraft Guns. By mid-November, sixty-eight B17 turrets supplied by A. V. Roe had been stripped and examined, but due to a shortage of spares from Filton and poor supply of turrets from A. V. Roe, their re-assembly was impossible and in May 1952 the contract was cancelled and replaced by one for repair of Frazer Nash FN4 B turrets, again from Lincolns. Bofors Gun output was also not meeting targets, again due to lack of spares and conversion parts, but in June materials from the Aircraft Division were promised to meet the programmed output of 120 guns per month. Other armament work also found its way from Filton to Oldmixon's Shop 6 when in 1953 it was subcontracted to fabricate the structure of a small number of rockets. Known as Project 12-20, this mysterious code covered design and development of highly secret Experimental Test Vehicles (XTVs) for the MoS that could be powered by different types of booster motors, and would eventually evolve into the Bristol-Ferranti Bloodhound ramjet-powered surface-to-air guided missile. The person responsible for arranging the aviation work for Oldmixon was Walter Strachan, who from 28 March 1954 as general manager had taken direct control of Weston's section of the Aircraft Division.

When Shop 6 in 1954 was required to become an aircraft component store, its turret and Bofors work was transferred to the westerly end of Shop 7 where it joined a few Bristol Freighter outer wing panels resting on leading edges that had been deposited there as spares. The other end of the shop was now given over to various aircraft-related departments including detail fitting, machining, welding, routering, inspection and electrical component assembly, whilst the northern part of the building had again taken on its original function of being a quarantine store for raw materials. Unlike several years before, few people visited the factory by air, probably the only ones in 1954 being on board Airwork's DH Dragon Rapide G-AKUB from Haverfordwest that flew in on 14 May. It would be another year before the next visit, this by Sycamore HR 14 XG503 brought in from Filton by test pilot Peter Moore on 23 May 1955, it probably being the first helicopter to fly into Oldmixon.

Production of Motor Cases for Missiles and Research Rockets

Shortly after the war Bristol had become involved with the design and development of motor cases for both military missile and research rocket projects. Carried out by the Bristol Engine Division at the Rodney Works, by the early 1950s this activity was beginning to outgrow the facility which luckily coincided with Walter Strachan's search in early 1952 for work to replace Oldmixon's cancelled contracts. British Messier Ltd, a wholly-owned subsidiary of Rotol Ltd (Rolls-Royce/Bristol) that had also become involved in rocket-motor design and the production and development of motor cases and pressure bottles using advanced welding techniques, also became involved and it was agreed that work from both companies could be subcontracted to Oldmixon. As a result, in April 1952 a contract was awarded for Oldmixon to assist Rodney Works and British Messier in the manufacture of a number of 16 inch (41 cm) motor tubes for the MoS and there was a promise from the Ministry's Guided Weapons Division that if results were satisfactory additional work would be forthcoming. In September, certain key members of British Messier were taken over by Oldmixon and the necessary machine tools and equipment provided, so that by the year's end ten tubes had been completed in the recently refurbished Shop 3. In the meantime, British Messier agreed to complete any work that Oldmixon couldn't handle, such as heat treatment, as in December work was still underway with the excavation of a massive pit in Shop 3 for installation of the essential furnaces and quench tanks. This business at Oldmixon continued to expand steadily with the transfer in April 1953 of all rocket-motor tube work from the Rodney Works, a part of it being the repair of around fifty units, whilst Rotol agreed that in December Oldmixon would take over the design and manufacture of its pressure-bottles.

New Aircraft Work

Filton in the early 1950s also provided Oldmixon with other aircraft subcontract business. It had been hoped that towards the end of 1952 there would be repair work on Canadair-built RCAF Sabre jet fighters, but with its lower overheads, Western Airways, which was already producing Bristol Freighter sub-assemblies for Filton, picked up the contract. The work eventually provided was for the Britannia airliner, and it involved the manufacturing of components and their assembly to speed up the new production line at Filton, and a second, soon to be set-up line at Belfast by Short Brothers and Harland. Shorts, coincidentally, had an alliance with Bristol and was its agent for the manufacture and erection of its aluminium houses in Northern Ireland.

Subsequently, starting at the end of 1952 and lasting until the late 1950s, many Britannia detail fittings were manufactured in Shop 7, and in Shop 5 the aircraft's 56-foot span (17-metre) tailplane, cabin floor structures, wing trailing-edge sections, dinghy boxes, cabin doors, control pedestals, luggage racks and baggage and pantry fittings were assembled. With the shortages of supplies and the inadequacy of some tools and drawings, work was slow to get going, and to lessen the risk of losing skilled men due to lower-than-expected pay and to put the factory on a sounder economical basis, attempts, albeit unsuccessful, were made to obtain component work from Gloster on its new Javelin delta-winged jet fighter. Early in 1954 the manufacturing of Bristol plastic drop-tanks was offered to Oldmixon, but by then, due to the other work provided, space and labour was now at a premium.

Bristol's Helicopters

Towards the war's end, Bristol had not been slow to recognise the need to move on from its traditional product range and this was demonstrated with Oldmixon's involvement in aluminium houses. At Filton work was also going ahead, designing the giant Brabazon and Wayfarer/Freighter and developing the Beaufighter, Buckingham, Brigand and Buckmaster. Turbo-prop and jet-powered aircraft, not to mention various engine and armament projects were also being worked on. Another product that Bristol at that time had become interested in was the helicopter, which during the earlier war years had made tremendous progress especially in Germany and the United States of America.

Having no previous experience with rotary-winged aircraft, towards the end of 1944 the company started to look for a designer who would head up a helicopter design and development team. The person eventually selected was Raoul Hafner, who, before the war, had been involved in Austria and later in Britain designing and developing helicopters and gyroplanes. More recently, he had been engaged with a team at the Airborne Forces Experimental Establishment at Sherburn-in-Elmet developing rotary-wing gliders for troop and vehicle delivery into Europe. Hafner accepted the position as Chief Helicopter Designer, joining the company in November 1944, and by early 1945 had gathered together the nucleus of a design team at the Banwell Factory. Some of the team, such as Sam B. Weller, George Mickie Walker and Charles Bradbury came with Hafner from Sherburn-in-Elmet. The task before them was to design and build under an MoS contract a 4-seat passenger helicopter in the 4,000 to 5,000 lb (1,814 to 2,268 kg) AUW category suitable for both civil and military use. To help with the task, the team brought with it preliminary drawings of wooden rotor-blades designed to carry an Army Valentine Tank into wartime Europe, a scaled-down version of these being considered suitable for the new helicopter. In addition, arrangements had been made for two RAF Sikorsky R4B Hoverfly Is to be allocated to the project, KK988 arriving at Banwell on 6 March and KK991 on the 27th. These machines would be used to discover the helicopter's strengths and weaknesses, and it was decreed by Hafner that the team should be given air-experience flights in them so that the intrinsic limitations of a helicopter could be appreciated. However, in June the team left Banwell and moved to Filton from where all basic development and early production work would be carried out.

The team's first helicopter, the Type 171 Mk 1 with a 450 hp American P & W Wasp Junior engine flew on 24 July 1947 and another similar prototype followed. The rotor control system employed was based on the very successful one perfected by Hafner pre-war that, using a spider, imparted simultaneously on the rotor-blades both cyclic and collective pitch, through what these days is the normally accepted cyclic stick and collective lever. As soon as the British Alvis Leonides 550 hp engine became available, the design was modified, and with seating increased to five, named 'Sycamore'. Under the guise of various mark numbers, ninety-three of this type were built at Filton over the following eight years. Most went to the British Army, the Royal Air Force, Royal Australian Navy, the Belgian Ministry of National Defence, British European Airways and Ansett-ANA but Bristol also retained two or three for its own use.

After the Type 171 came the Type 173, a medium/short-range 10-seat passenger tandem-rotor design for proposed civil and military operators to trial. With this machine Bristol was breaking new ground, it being the first tandem-rotor to have two engines and was not much more than two Type 171s joined together by a passenger cabin. Initially, two prototypes were built for the MoS, the first known as the Mk 1 G-ALBN (XF785), which flew on 3 January 1952, and the second known as the Mk 2 G-AMJI (XH379), which flew 8 May 1953. Early trials resulted in substantial modifications to both aircraft as it was clear that the first, especially, suffered from ground resonance, they were underpowered and suffered from Dutch Roll instability and the second machine near unsteerable on the ground. These shortcomings resulted in three further prototypes being ordered by the MoS. Known as the Mk 3, XE286, XE287 and XE288 had amongst other changes the more powerful 850 hp Alvis Leonides Major and up-rated gearboxes, and were the third, fourth and fifth prototypes respectively. Before completion, the fifth machine XE288, was extensively modified at Filton following Royal Navy trials with the Mk 1 to reflect navy sea-going requirements.

Amongst the changes was the fuselage being shortened and provided with a 4-poster undercarriage that gave it a sit-up and beg appearance with the pilot's eye-level now almost 10 feet (3.05 m) above ground level. The main reason for the high forward fuselage was that any future navy machine would have to carry its weapons in an under-cabin weapon bay that would be loaded from between the front legs of the undercarriage. At the time the torpedoes being developed for the aircraft also had to be kept warm in an internal bay.

As a result of encouraging flight trials using the first two Type 173s, and the promise of improved performance with the three Type 173 Mk 3s, the MoS place a production order with Bristol for a variety of new military tandem rotor helicopter totalling ninety-four machines. The order announced by Duncan Sandys in the House of Commons on 17 May 1954 was for three Type 191 Series 1 helicopters powered by two 850 hp Alvis Leonidies Major piston engines and sixty-five Type 191 Series 2s powered by two 1,500 hp Napier E165 (Gazelle) gas turbines (XG354 to XG398 & XG419 to XG441), all for service with the Royal Navy. Four other navy machines were also ordered (XG473 to XG476), these being Type 193s which were almost identical to the Type 191 Series 2 but designed around a Royal Canadian Navy Requirement for eventual manufacture in Canada. The remaining part of the order was for a mixture of twenty-two Type 192 Series 1 and Series 2 helicopters for service with the Royal Air Force, and these would have similar engines to the Type 191 Series 1 and Series 2 machines respectively; later the Series 1 was cancelled and the order for Series 2s increased to twenty-six.

The navy machines that closely resembled the fifth prototype Type 173 were for anti-submarine warfare work and to be capable of carrying dunking ASDIC (sonar) in the forward cabin and two 'Dealer B' (Mk 30) 18 inch (46 cm) homing torpedoes and a variety of other ASW stores in a massive 19 feet (5.8 m) long under-floor weapons bay. They were to have a crew of two in the cabin and as a result were given few windows, and cost implications resulted in the RAF's Type 192, which would have to carry up to eighteen fully-equipped troops in the cabin having to accept the same sit-up and beg geometry of the navy machine, although a concession was the cabin floor level being lowered slightly, not an ideal arrangement for loading and deplaning troops from the cabin door with its ledge around 5 feet (1.5 m) above ground level! An unusual aspect of the tandem-rotor order was that there were no true prototypes, the machines being built straight off the drawing board using production tools and jigs.

The Move to Oldmixon

In the early 1950s the design and manufacturing capability of the company's Filton Works was stretched somewhat, it being spread between supporting the helicopters and all of the other Bristol projects which now also included missiles, plastic drop-tanks and motor cars. A solution to this overload was Walter Strachan being asked at the end of 1953 to survey available capacity at Oldmixon, and keen to fill it with aircraft-related work confirmed the practicability of accommodating the manufacturing of complete helicopters together with the existing Britannia and armament work.

Once agreed, a start was made in mid-1954 to transfer the Helicopter Design Office (HDO), and initially this was from Filton to temporary accommodation in Kenn Road, St George, Bristol. Meanwhile, with the completion of the buildings contracts, Banwell was somewhat under-utilised and the rocket motor work was transferred there thus freeing-up Oldmixon's Shop 3 for what would become the Sycamore Flight Shed. In addition to Sycamore production being established and further Type 173 development, there would also be the task of putting into production the new Type 191/192 and Type 193 that had already been largely designed at Filton/Kenn Road for the British and Canadian Ministries respectively. There was of course a considerable amount of building work required to make Oldmixon suitable for helicopters; it would also be necessary, as in 1940, to make arrangements with the Weston Town Council to house key Filton personnel. By the autumn of 1955, sufficient reorganisation had been completed for the transfer to commence, and with the move almost completed, it was announced on 1 January 1956 that the various divisions of the Bristol Aeroplane Company were now officially companies in their own right, and the facility at Oldmixon was now the Helicopter Division of Bristol Aircraft Ltd.

Early in the year, a new HDO for the people relocating from Kenn Road had been completed and a new paint bay, large enough for tandem-rotor

AID Inspector Francis Boreham at work in Shop 4 contemplating the front rotorhead of the first prototype Type 173 (Westland)

helicopters had been added to the south-west end of Shop 4, and in Shop 5 Sycamore and Type 191 and 192 production jigs had been set up alongside the Britannia tailplane jigs. On open ground, preparations were also being made for construction of a rotor test-tower and gantries for ground-rig running. The large heat-treatment furnaces, quench tanks and welding machines for rocket-motor tube work in Shop 3 were transferred to Banwell, and following floor repairs the company's and resident Ministry-owned Sycamores were moved in from Filton. The first two Type 173 Mk 3s were brought down from Filton by road during July/August, the Mk 1 was flown down and all were located in Shop 4, which now became the Tandem-Rotor Development Flight Shed. The Flight Test Department also arrived with engineers located in wooden buildings on the hard-standing to the east of Shop 4 and test pilots moved into their original wartime office. To complete the loop so that Ministry flying could recommence, the small band of helicopter AID inspectors at Filton also relocated to Oldmixon, and came under the control of Mr Goodfellow, who had been there since the Beaufighter days. One of the inspectors was Francis G. Boreham, who for many years had been employed by the Ministry and had at one time or another looked after its interests at Cierva, Saunders-Roe, Westland and Bristol. As a result of this association he was partially deaf, the consequence of spending much time in and around piston-engined helicopters, especially the mighty Rolls-Royce Merlin-powered Cierva Air Horse.

Now an old and rather eccentric gentleman, Francis, known by all as 'The Old Professor', was the much respected AID inspector in Shop 4 and operated from a small office in a corner of the hangar. Behind its red door there was always a smell of fuel for engines of model aeroplanes, and the filing cabinets that should have contained Ministry documents were topped-up with a strange assortment of flying machines. At Oldmixon he was often to be seen, glasses perched on top of his head, trotting after one of his gyrating machines. Most models, although rather rough and looking not particularly realistic flew extremely well. One of his designs, the 'Jeticopter', manufactured commercially by the Jetex Company of Southampton and powered by two of its solid fuel rocket motors was extremely popular and in the late 1940s and the 1950s was sold worldwide to much acclaim.

Sycamore Production Re-established

With Sycamore production re-established, by February 1956, five HR 14s were being fitted-out adjacent to the sliding doors of Shop 5, with XG545 on its wheels and ready to be towed to Shop 3 for ground-running and initial flight-trials. With trials successfully completed, although still unpainted, on Wednesday 14 March it was given a public airing. In a strong, chilly easterly wind, the factory's workforce and press were gathered on the apron outside Shop 3, and at noon precisely, with Bristol Aircraft's new managing director, Peter Masefield, in the port seat and Weston's mayor, Councillor Richard Ivens, in the back, 'Sox' Hosegood lifted the machine off for a short demonstration flight. Other test pilots at Oldmixon at that time were Peter Wilson, Bob Smith, Don Farquharson, Peter Moore and Ian 'Willie' Wilkinson. XG545 and approximately thirty other Mk 14s would eventually swell the fleet of Sycamores already delivered to the RAF and British Army. A few would be painted yellow and used for Air Sea Rescue duties whilst others given a silver finish would be used by the Central Flying School. Most, however, were to be camouflaged and serve in the jungles of Malaya and in Cyprus supporting the Army in its fight against Communist terrorists and EOKA respectively. Several early camouflaged machines were also delivered to the Joint Experimental Helicopter Unit at Middle Wallop, one XG548 the 100th and the fifth Sycamore built at Oldmixon being delivered to the unit 19 June 1956, only a few days after its first flight on the 13th.

Several other Sycamores built at Filton were brought to Oldmixon and used as test beds and for display and demonstration purposes. One was Mk 3 G-ALSX that had been previously displayed at various Farnborough and Paris air shows, taken part in the Festival of Britain, carried out sea-trials aboard *HMAC Triumph*, and helped in rescue operations in the disastrous Dutch floods of 1953. In 1958, sold to Dr Williamson of Williamson Diamonds of Nairobi and reregistered VR-TBS it was flown out from Oldmixon to Uganda in the hold of Bristol Freighter F-BFOU. But with the unexpected death of its

Oldmixon's longstanding helicopter test pilots. *Upper left:* Chief Helicopter Test Pilot, Charles 'Sox' Hosegood. *Upper right:* Peter Wilson being briefed by Bristol's Chief Helicopter Designer Raoul Hafner. Hafner during pre-flight briefings on occasions pronounced that he had 'made the calculations and taken a calculated risk' with regard to the flight test about to be undertaken. On one particular occasion, this was too much for Hosegood who exclaimed, 'It's all very well *You* making the calculations, but it is *Me* who is about to take the risk!' Hafner's reply is not known. *Lower left:* Bob Smith facing forward in the cockpit. *Lower right:* Don Farquharson (Westland)

In Shop 5 on 13 February 1956, the beginnings of Oldmixon's Bristol Sycamore production line with XG545 the 96th and first Weston-built machine in the foreground (Westland)

With Peter Masefield on board, Sox Hosegood lifts off Sycamore XG545 14 March 1956 for a short demonstration flight (Westland)

Shop 3, the Sycamore Flight Shed on 28 June 1957 with George Dawes and others, inspecting a Sycamore's wheel. At this time the shop contained a collection of development, and some new machines for West Germany. One of two Sycamore transmission test-rigs is at the far end in front of the door which led to the Gearbox Shop (Westland)

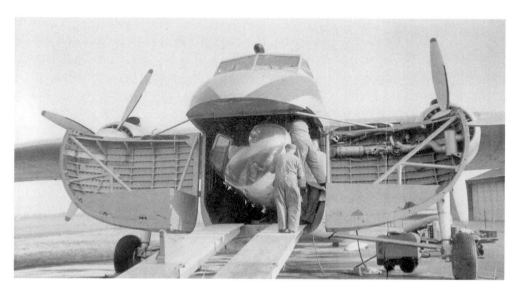

'Bristol' Sycamore Mk 3 G-ALSX being loaded into the Freighter for its trip to Africa (Westland)

new owner, it was returned to England on 1 December 1959 and put back to work in the Type 192 development programme, its main task being to prove a new nose-mounted pitot/static system for the Type 192, that in the factory was known as the OMD (Old Maid's Delight), for reasons that become obvious when seen. With the eventual takeover by Westland, in-service Sycamores still had to be supported, and G-ALSX as G-48/1 was used under B Conditions at Oldmixon and Yeovil for wooden rotor-blade production clearance. In May 1969, after eighteen years of faithful service and having treated many VIPs and Bristol employees to the delights of flying in a helicopter, it was again declared redundant and acquired by Elfan ap Rees who would eventually display it in The Helicopter Museum (*see chapter 4*). Another Sycamore to reside at Oldmixon was G-AMWG, one of the two Mk 3As built, and one of the trio of Sycamores operated by British European Airways (BEA), and the first British-designed helicopter to fly regular services. With the delivery of the larger Westland-built Sikorsky helicopters to BEA in 1956 WG was returned to Oldmixon, repainted in the new red and white Bristol livery and following miscellaneous work, in 1958 was chartered by John Laing and Sons, and flown by test pilot Bob Smith assisted in construction of the first long-distance British motorway, the M1. When of no further use, in July 1958 it was sold to the Australian operator Ansett-ANA as VH-INQ.

By 1956 the Sycamore Mk 4 and the Mk 14 military variant had become well established as the ultimate in the line of Sycamores. The prototype Mk 4 G-AMWI which first flew in May 1953 was the second company demonstrator; it too arrived at Oldmixon in 1956 and between June 1957 and January 1958 was used to give type-conversion to a number of West German helicopter pilots. When this task was completed, it was modified and sold in May 1961 to the Royal Australian Navy as an HR 51. A further Sycamore to arrive was WT933; it was the fourth Mk 3 and one of several MoS trials aircraft. A much-travelled machine, not long before, it had been transported to Nairobi in a Bristol Freighter for tropical trials and then shipped to Canada in 1956 and used in the development of electric de-icing equipment for the Type 192's wooden rotor-blades. At Oldmixon, it was used for flight trials of a fin intended for the Bristol Type 203 and in the development of metal rotor-blades for the Type 192. WT933 now resides at the Newark Air Museum. An early HR 14 XE308, was also to stay at Oldmixon for long periods. In 1964 it too was equipped with metal main rotor-blades intended for what was now the Belvedere and sent to Canada for icing trials. Its blades were similar to those fitted to WT933, but in this application, each had seventy-six jets spaced along the leading edge fed with de-icing fluid from a tank in the luggage bay.

These metal rotor-blades were built around a light-alloy spar machined from a hollow D-section extrusion. This work executed on a Wadkins spar-milling machine previously used at Filton and moved to Oldmixon for Britannia tailplane spar and the blade work, had its long bed set up with great precision on Shop 7's concrete floor. However, the completed blade spars were found to suffer from unexplained and unacceptable variations in wall thickness, and after much deliberation it was concluded that the only cause for the irregularity was Weston's tide affecting the water table beneath the factory and thereby changing alignment of the mill's bed. This finding took one back to the two drilling tests, the first in 1940 that showed subsoil in the locality to comprise deep deposits of peat and areas of moist shifting sand.

Receiving much praise for its mechanical and flying qualities, the Sycamore's main drawback to larger worldwide sales was its high initial price and the fact that problems had been experienced with its wooden main rotor-blades when operated in conditions of high humidity, and Bristol being unable or unwilling to offer a guarantee to prospective customers that metal blades would be an option. The blade problem first highlighted in Malaya during 1953, reached a peak in early 1959 when two Sycamores crashed in Malaya killing all onboard. With it being thought that the main rotor-blades had disintegrated in flight, the seriousness of the problem was forcibly brought home to everyone. Burnt remains of the last aircraft to crash were sent back, laid out behind a roped-off area in Shop 10 (formerly the the Spares Hangar but now the Tool Room), and the jigsaw of blade parts following reassembly confirmed suspicions.

The problem was eventually solved when blade-spar and external joints were completely sealed to prevent ingress of moisture, and a heavy mass-balance weight added to the blade tip to reposition the centre of gravity, much of this work being carried out in the Railway Siding's Romney huts. After successful flight trials at Kuala Lumpur and Seletar, modified blades were fitted to the fleet and from February 1960 Sycamores resumed operational flying in

Sycamore Mk 4 G-AMWI on 21 January 1958; here being used by Don Farquharson to train pilots of the West German Armed Forces (Westland)

Sycamore Mk 52s CA+328 and CA+327 for VIP use in the West German armed services in formation over Uphill on 13 March 1958 (Westland)

Malaya. Other failures had to be contended with during the machine's service life; slipping main-drive torque-limiting clutches caused by oil contamination was a particular problem and in 1962 a disintegrating tail rotor grounded the fleet for a short time. During their service in Malaya both Bristol-built and Westland-built helicopters had their fair share of problems with failings exposed by the harsh operational environment.

Timber rotor-blades were not a problem in Europe and on 8 March 1957, after much competition between the world's helicopter manufacturers, the Federal German Government placed an order for fifty Mk 52 Sycamores for use by its armed forces. This was one of the largest orders ever placed for helicopters and some workers found it strange to see uniformed members of the Luftwaffe, only a few years after the war's end, walking around the factory where not so long before Beaufighters had been built to fight possibly the same Luftwaffe pilots. On completion, the Sycamores were flown to Germany, the first two leaving Oldmixon on 31 May 1957 on a 600-mile (965-km) delivery flight piloted by Bristol test pilot/instructors Peter Wilson and Peter Moore. Later, aircraft were delivered by German crews. With between three and four Sycamores completed each month it would be March 1959 before the final aircraft was delivered. The last complete Sycamore produced was XN450, an HR 51, which left Shop 5 in December 1958. In total 178 Sycamores were completed, although airframe components for a further two were produced, one set being used on the first prototype Bristol Type 203, an 11-seat turbine-powered Westland Whirlwind replacement that was partially built at Filton in 1958. Although the last RAF Sycamore in service, Filton-built XG544 was retired on 11 August 1972, several of the fleet of Mk 52s that had been retired from military service in 1969 were civilianised, and as late as 2008, CA+328, now registered HB-RXB and in the colours of Mk 14 XG544 was said to be still airworthy in Switzerland.

Type 192 (Belvedere) Development

Regrettably, in 1956 the Type 191 order for sea-going RN anti-submarine tandem-rotor helicopters was cancelled by the British Government, the Westland Wessex HAS I being ordered instead, and shortly afterwards the Canadian Government likewise cancelled its order for the similar Type 193. By this time airframes of three piston-engine Type 191 (Series 1s) that were very similar to the fifth Type 173 were almost complete and modified into rigs, two being fitted with the new Napier Gazelle gas-turbine to become ground-test rigs for the RAF's Type 192 (Series 2) of which twenty-six were to be built, the only part of the large order to survive. With the embodiment of the Gazelle, the two Type 191s effectively became Series 2s.

Once support equipment had arrived and key staff transferred from Filton, development carried on apace with the Type 173. Continuing with trials aimed at reducing vibration and Dutch Roll instability, it had been decided to equip the second prototype with new 4-bladed rotors and replace its 'V' tail with a new 'H' configured unit. The first flight with these rotors at Filton 11 February 1955 was followed by a debriefing where there was much satisfaction when it was reported that vibration inherent in the type had been greatly reduced. After returning from the 1956 Paris Air Show in June, the machine was prepared for its long-awaited full evaluation by BEA. Following three weeks of simulated passenger-carrying with the airline, the aircraft was flown to Oldmixon for the new tail to be fitted. Early trials showed great promise but unfortunately, just before the helicopter was due to be returned to BEA, it flew into the ground on Sunday 16 September during a flying demonstration at the 'Families at Home'

2-day show at Filton, fortunately with no injury to the pilot and just a sprained ankle sustained by the flight test engineer. Prior to take-off at Oldmixon, the forward cabin had been loaded with ballast weights, and so long as the two crew in the cabin's rear remained seated, the machine's centre of gravity would remain within design parameters. However, at Filton the cabin crew got out for a cup of tea and the aircraft took off without them for the demonstration, with dire results! The following week in Shop 4, the crashed machine's slightly-damaged 'H' tailplane was removed and after repairs fitted to the first prototype which by then had also been equipped with 4-bladed rotors. The machine flew quite well in this configuration and continued to be operated from time to time for another two years in the Ministry's tandem-rotor development programme. This machine is now displayed at the Bristol Aero Collection Museum at Kemble. The only other Type 173 to fly was the third prototype (the first Mk 3) XE286, but due to various problems, carried out only limited hovering in November 1956. Following cancellation of the MoS development contract in 1956, the fifth prototype was offered to BEA for trials. Anticipating a positive response, Bristol registered it G-AORB and painted it in their colours, but when the trials didn't materialise, it was put into storage. Together with the damaged second prototype, and the fourth prototype, it was cut up in 1959. Meanwhile, the six now-redundant Alvis Leonides Major engines which belonged to the MoS and designed specifically for the Mk 3s, were returned to Alvis to be modified to rotate in the opposite direction and re-allocated to Westland at Yeovil for their Whirlwind Mk 5/7 programme.

The Type 192 although looking very similar to the Type 173 was a completely new helicopter. It was twice as heavy as the Type 173 Mk 3 and with its two 1650 hp Napier Gazelles effectively had more than twice its power and was the first gas-turbine powered helicopter for the RAF. With delays caused by transfer of production facilities from Filton to Oldmixon and the training of a new workforce it was May 1958 before XG447, the first Type 192, and the first of a number of development machines was moved from Shop 5 to Shop 4 for fitting out with test equipment. Some 250 hours of engine and transmission testing had to be completed before being allowed into the air, but most of this had already been carried out using the two Gazelle-engined Type 191 ground test rigs.

By July the various trials had been successfully completed and on Saturday 5 July, Sox Hosegood lifted off the all-white insectlike machine for thirty minutes of hovering and low-speed manoeuvres. To everyone's relief there were no serious problems and there was no sign at all of the dreaded ground resonance that had plagued the first Type 173 during early trials at Filton. With this hurdle overcome, an early start could be made in the exploration of the full flight envelope, and a few days later, after the addition of large tabs to the endplate fins to trim the machine to starboard, and a weight in each fin tip to damp vibration, and the addition of fuselage RAF roundels, XG447 was taken clear of the airport for a circuit of Weston in the start of its flight test programme.

Upper: The second prototype Type 173 XH379 at Oldmixon on 28 August 1956 with its newly fitted 'H' tailplane (Westland). *Bottom left:* The unfortunate incident at Filton (D. Pitchford). *Bottom right:* The end result (Westland). The crash caused Bristol a certain amount of trouble, for the machine, which was owned by the Ministry, had been signed off by AID Inspector Francis Boreham for a local test flight with no landings away from Oldmixon. As it had put down at Filton prior to the crash, Bristol was faced with funding the repairs

The third prototype Type 173 XE286 during the forty minutes of hovering-flight on 9 November 1956. After this airing, it never flew again and with nose and rear fuselage cut off was relegated to become a cabin mock-up of the proposed civil Type 192C. In the background, a Lincoln of the ATDU climbs away for the range (Westland)

The fifth Type 173 XE288 beneath the gantry at Oldmixon in BEA colours during 1956. At Filton it had been shortened, and the longer forward undercarriage legs embodied to give the sit-up-and-beg appearance (Westland)

However, it was quickly established that there were major problems to be solved before the Type 192 would be allowed into RAF service. The Type 192 as with the earlier 171 and 173, using the spider had fully manual flight control systems and although Hafner had insisted that no power assistance should be provided, it soon became apparent that a single pilot didn't possess the strength to fly the new, much heavier aircraft in anything but sedate flight, the approach to landings being particularly difficult, and because of this it was mandated that two pilots would be required to fly each aircraft. As with the Type 173 there was also still a tendency to Dutch Roll in cruise flight and for vibration to be fed back from the rotors to the pilot's controls, and of course it was still equipped with the same type of wooden rotor-blades fitted to the Sycamore.

With Sycamore production re-established, Type 173 development flying again underway, and Type 192 build progressing, other aircraft now came in greater numbers to the Oldmixon end of the airport. There were yellow North American Harvard IIBs FT375, KF183 and KF314 from A&AEE, Boscombe Down bringing in test pilots, KF183, in an earlier life having been with the ATDU at Gosport, and a frequent visitor to Weston Airport in 1947. There were also camouflaged Edgar Percival EP9s XM797 and XM819 and various Westland Whirlwinds bringing in Army and RAF pilots from Middle Wallop, and German Percival Pembroke C 54s with crews to ferry new Sycamore Mk 52s to Germany. DH Doves also brought in VIPs, such as on 25 April 1958 when Aubrey Jones, the Minister of Supply, arrived in G-AJOT, and from Filton on the same day the attractive red and white Bristol-converted DH Chipmunk G-AOTM with blown canopy and wheel-spats, albeit odd ones, was flown in by Peter Masefield.

At the end of June 1959, employees at Oldmixon were surprised to see an unusual tandem-rotor machine arrive. This was the first prototype Vertol 107 N74060 which had flown in after its recent debut at the Paris Air Show. The reason for its visit was an interest by the RAF and Bristol in a Belvedere replacement. All and sundry walked through the machine that lunchtime, and at 2 p.m. it took off with Raoul Hafner onboard for a demonstration flight.

The Takeover by Westland

The visit of the 107, however, probably needs to be put in perspective. At that time, the Vertol machine was a competitor as Bristol had been actively involved for some time in designing a more suitable civil/military replacement of the original military Type 192 with the Types 192C and D, and the Type 194 48-seat civil machine powered by four DH Gnomes with off-loading wings on the stocks, and it was important to evaluate the Vertol without showing ones hand. These Bristol machines, with government assistance, could have resulted in the production of quite impressive helicopters that would have been true

The three Type 191s built as a part of the RN anti-submarine helicopter contract being converted in Shop 4 mid-1957 to ground-rigs. In the foreground, Rig No.2 had already been modified to accept Napier Gazelle gas-turbines, and at the far end Rig No.1 is similarly modified. Between the two is Rig No.3, which was to remain structurally unmodified and be fitted with exciters to vibrate the flying controls and thereby discover at an early stage any mechanical weaknesses. At the steps near the vacuum cleaner, charge-hand Pete Smith gives advice to one of the fitters and in the cockpit Les Curtis adjusts a part of the helicopter's structure (Westland)

By 20 July 1958, RAF roundels and a 'cut here' black dashed rectangle had been painted on the fuselage of the first Type 192 XG447. The long nose-mast was to monitor yaw and to check accuracy of the aircraft's own short pilot tube located just in front of the windscreen. A quick fix were blanks over the front engine air-intakes, added in an attempt to improve cooling of the front rotor gearbox. The Oldmixon Factory is in the distance and what was the Sands Aerodrome is beneath the helicopter's nose (Westland)

Shop 5 on 31 July 1959 looking to the south. Eight of the production run of twenty-six Type 192s can be seen in different shades of green primer. In the back row, on the left XG449 and next to it XG461 (Westland)

The busy scene in Shop 4 on 31 July 1959 as Type 192s recently delivered from Shop 5 are prepared for development flight trials. First prototype Type 173 XF785 at the far end is almost at the end of its useful life and will soon be delivered to RAF Henlow for preservation (Westland)

competitors to the American company's products, however, things were about to change. In 1959, under Government pressure, the Yeovil-based Westland Aircraft Ltd commenced the acquisition of Britain's helicopter manufacturers. Initially Saunders-Roe with its sites at Eastleigh and Cowes, Isle of Wight, was taken-over, and in March of the following year the Helicopter Division of Bristol Aircraft at Oldmixon and a little later Fairey Aviation with its sites at Hayes and White Waltham followed. Under the new management, work continued at Oldmixon on the Type 192 replacement with delivery of much technical literature, drawings and manuals, from what was now Boeing-Vertol to support various proposals to build for the RAF and RN, an anglicised version of the large CH-47 Chinook tandem-rotor machine that would be powered by three or four DH Gnome turboshaft engines. Design of the Type 192C (also known as the Belvedere Mk 2), the Type 194, and a new Type 193 'Westonian' for the RAF and RN with three DH Gnomes engines that now resembled the Type 194 and utilised parts of the Wessex main gearbox and its rotor blades, but with Type 192 rotor hubs and wings replaced by sponsons, also continued. Another project, the WG1, also known as the 'Westonian' that resembled the Chinook but was slightly smaller and possessed many Type 192 design features and powered by three or four DH Gnomes was also proceeded with. However, due to government indecisions over several years, all schemes eventually came to nought, but it is ironic and sad to note that the CH-47 Chinook had to be eventually bought for the RAF in some numbers directly from the USA.

As is the case with the majority of takeovers by one company of another, there was the usual resentment and animosity to the new management, particularly so at Oldmixon by those who considered that Westland did not design helicopters, all their helicopters having been based on American Sikorsky designs. With the takeover, Oldmixon became the Bristol Division of Westland Aircraft and it wasn't long before its new headquarters at Yeovil instructed Oldmixon's paint shop to adjust the paint scheme of G-ALSX, and overnight the fuselage marked 'Bristol Sycamore' became 'Westland Sycamore'! Introduction of these and other changes resulted in the departure of some managers, designers and senior pilots. Sox Hosegood joined SWEB to fly its new Augusta-Bell 47J-2 G-ASLR from Lulsgate, Bob Smith eventually joined Ferranti Ltd as chief helicopter pilot, and in due course several high-ranking designers moved to Boeing's plant in Philadelphia to work on its tandem-rotor designs, however, most opted to stay at Oldmixon or be transferred to Yeovil or Cowes. At Oldmixon, work still steamed ahead on trying to cure some of the Type 192's problems, and by the summer of 1960 sufficient modifications had been approved; amongst them the fin trailing edge being offset to starboard, the 'H' tail replaced by a large anhedral 'Barn Door' unit and a bungee trimming-system introduced to improve handling of the flying controls, thus allowing for an initial three pre-production Type 192s — XG453, XG454, and XG456, by now named the 'Belvedere HC I', to be handed over at Oldmixon on 13 October 1960 to the RAF Belvedere Trials Unit (BTU) based at RAF Odiham.

Under the wing of Westland, the Type 192 had been named Belvedere, and on Thursday 13 October 1960, XG453, XG454 and XG456 were handed over at Oldmixon to the RAF Belvedere Trials Unit (Westland)

Following the handover, XG454 flown by Flying Officer J. H. Martin was taken around Weston on a demonstration flight (*Flight* via R. Dudley)

As soon as time allowed, experiments were initiated with a rearranged tail in an attempt to eliminate Dutch Roll. Initially flights were made using XG447 with fins removed and then with fins inverted and swapped port for starboard (R. Dudley). The next change was to lower the tail and cant the fins inboard (Westland). However, these were quick fixes for test purposes. The end result was the 'Gull' tail. Note the machine is now equipped with the OMD developed on Sycamore G-ALSX and metal rotor-blades (Westland)

Meanwhile, work was continuing in parallel with that on the pre-production machines to provide an answer to the aircraft's major problems. The fifth development, Belvedere XG452, now displayed in The Helicopter Museum, was mainly used for this work, and with most of the required modifications embodies, in June 1960 it carried out a record-breaking proving flight to Idris, North Africa, where hot weather trials were to be conducted. The modifications that had been embodied in the machine included: metal rotor-blades, a double-anhedral 'Gull' tail that utilized all components of the original 'H' unit, a single hydraulic power-operated flight-control system with manual reversion instead of the fully manual system, a modified engine-control system which automatically doubled power of the good engine following an engine failure, a stand-alone IPN engine-starting system, larger wheels, sliding doors rather than the original upward-hinging type and the new OMD pitot/static system. The OMD, because of its very accurate reading capability, was in due course also fitted to Westland's new Wessex HAS 3. On return, XG452 was further modified, the initial single power-operated flight-control system being replaced with a new dual power-operated flight-control system with no manual reversion located in an under-nose bulge, and with this modification approved, other machines were progressively converted, allowing delivery in August 1961 of the first fully-productionised Belvedere HC I XG457, with a further five machines, to the BTU. The new machines then made up the initial complement of 66 Squadron, the ceremony taking place on 15 September, and the pre-production aircraft were returned to Oldmixon for conversion.

Under the new management, aircraft continued to visit the factory. There was the Auster AOP 9 flown in on 24 August by Bob Smith just before the 1962 Farnborough Air Show. Bob, in addition to being a Bristol test pilot was also a major in the Territorial Army and at weekends flew its machines. Arriving from over the Bournville Estate in a shallow dive, the Auster in a beat-up sped through the factory below hangar height. No sooner had it been landed and the engine stopped, it was whisked away to Shop 6 so that modifications could be carried out to the cabin roof for it to accept a large 'Shepherd's Crook' hook that would hopefully allow for the aircraft to be aerial-launched and recovered from a latching device attached to the underside of Belvedere XG453. At that time all Belvederes were grounded due to the unexplained crash on 30 July of XG465 in West Germany and, unfortunately, for Westland, results of the crash enquiry which was eventually found to have been due to the front engine failing and the rear engine not automatically doubling its power, came too late to allow the type to be ungrounded for the early September Farnborough display.

The Product Support Manufacturing Centre

With the takeover, Westland became responsible for support of the Bristol, Saunders Roe and Fairey range of in-service aircraft, and after a few months Oldmixon was given the responsibility of establishing the factory as the company's Product Support Manufacturing Centre, specialising in the refurbishment of helicopters and the design and manufacture of modification kits, spare parts and ground equipment. The initial mainstay of the 1,600 workforce at Oldmixon, Weston's largest single employer, was the conversion of piston-engined Westland Whirlwinds/WS-55s/S-55s owned by the RAF, Royal Navy and Bristow, into Mk 10, Mk 9 and Series 3 turbine-engined machines. Starting with XJ729, eighty-one machines were to be involved, two being HCC 8s XN126 and XN127 that arrived for conversion in May 1964, having recently been in the Queen's Flight. The Bristow machines were only part converted to the Series 3 turbine configuration with the work being completed at the company's Redhill, Surrey facility. Around the end of this programme, which was carried out in

Ministry trials Sycamore HR 14 XE308, under the supervision of Danny Reardon, is crated for its trip to Canada to test metal rotor-blade de-icing for the Belvedere (Westland)

XG457, the first fully productionised Belvedere HC I. All Belvederes left Oldmixon in the white/blue/silver Transport Command colour scheme but soon those of 66 Squadron out in the Far East were being camouflaged green/brown with water-based Walpamur Emulsion (Westland)

Shop 5 and often required extensive reskinning of the airframe, the workforce considered its long-term future was probably assured when in 1973 Westland bought the freehold of the Oldmixon Factory from the Ministry of Defence.

Keeping the Belvedere supported until withdrawn from service in 1969 was another important role for the factory. Production machines that had been equipped with the very volatile IPN engine-starting system, in-service seemed to explode at the drop of a hat. Incidents of this were so common that pilots tried various ways of engine starting by remote means, some in the RAF resorting to using a long stick to depress the start button in the cockpit roof. Such was the unreliability of the system that armour plate was eventually fitted between the front engine bay and cockpit to protect pilots from injury. This of course didn't stop explosions and fires, and a succession of damaged machines came back to Oldmixon for repair. At Seletar, Singapore, one such explosion in XG475 caused the pilot to break a leg when leaping from the cockpit, and the nose of the helicopter eventually separated and fell to the ground. Due to this event, the station ran out of foam and all flying had to be temporarily suspended for the day. Despite this, the aircraft was rebuilt with a nose grafted on from another Belvedere which had had its rear engine bay destroyed by a similar event.

Refurbishment of Belvedere rotor-blades had been carried out in Shop 7, but in the mid-1960s a Metal Rotor-Blade Facility had been set up in the west end of Shop 5 to handle refurbishment of Whirlwind main rotor-blades, and in due course those for the Scout/Wasp and later, Wessex, Sea King and Puma. The original rotor test-tower was converted to accommodate some of these and used until mid-1981 when the contract covering Whirlwind blades came to an end, by which time some 6,000 blades had been manufactured/refurbished and tested at Oldmixon. Meanwhile, because the original tower was unable to test Wessex blades, in early 1981 an all-purpose tower was built to the south of Shop 4 and for many years was to share the testing of refurbished blades with the tower at Yeovil.

Following completion of the Whirlwind/WS-55/S-55 rebuild programme, other similar work, both British military and that from the company's export customers came the way of Oldmixon. There was also a large amount of BN-2 Islander subcontract work from Britten Norman on the Isle of Wight which lasted from 1968 until 1972, and in Shop 7 many wings and fuselages were built for assembly on the island. Alongside the Islander jigs, Sea King cockpit canopies, cargo doors and cabin structures were produced for Yeovil, and this carried on well into the late 1990s. There was also a line for Sea King crew seats of which over 1,000 had been built by the end of 1981.

By 1963, Belvederes were rapidly building up flying hours and there was an urgent requirement to extend the machine's useful life until the RAF could procure a replacement helicopter. The Type 192 designed for a fatigue life of only 1,000 flying hours had been tested in rigs and a limited amount of strain-gauge work had been carried out at Filton in 1958-59 on the ninth airframe.

In 1963, the proposal had been made to extend airframe life to 5,000 flying hours, but this was soon reduced to a more achievable 3,000 flying hours, and in 1964 further structural-fatigue testing was carried out when XG450 was flown extensively from Oldmixon with instrumentation that would give an overall pattern of imposed loads. Vibration meters were also fitted to all in-service Belvederes, and rotating exciters fitted to sections of damaged aircraft showed airframe lives in excess of the 3,000 hours were possible, provided that the fuselage was strengthened. But to complicate matters, there was also concern about fatigue in the flying controls caused by the higher than expected vibration, and this resulted in the life being extended to only 1,700 flying hours. The first machine to attain this figure (actually 1,698.55 hours) was XG466, it being struck off-charge and reduced to spares in May 1968. The ever-diminishing fleet of Belvederes remained in service with 66 Squadron at RAF Seletar, Singapore, until 1969, with the disbandment ceremony, that included a fly-past of the remaining six aircraft, each carrying an under-slung Howitzer, taking place on 20 March.

Anglo French Collaboration

With the need for both the British and French to replace their aging fleet of military helicopters, in May 1965 an Anglo-French Memorandum of Understanding was signed which in due course led to the new Westland Group (WG) and the British Government proposing WG13 (Lynx) and the French Government and helicopter manufacturer Sud Aviation (later Aerospatiale) proposing the SA330 (Puma) and SA 341 (Gazelle), each to be jointly built in Britain and France with design leadership of WG13 Westland and the other machines Sud Aviation. In Britain, Lynx and Gazelle were to be built at Yeovil and Puma at the former Fairey factory at Hayes.

Puma Production

Following closure of the Hayes site in 1972, the few Puma HC Is remaining to be produced, and the repair and modification work together with many staff were transferred to Oldmixon. The first in-service Puma to come in for repair and overhaul XW218 arrived early 1976 and was delivered back to the RAF at the end of August. The production line, however, was shut down once the forty machines ordered had been completed, but several years later the RAF requested eight new aircraft and the line in December 1978 was reopened in Shop 4. The first ZA934 flew on 7 May 1979 and was handed over to the RAF on the 23rd. The next machine was completed in the following January and the others were produced at a rate of approximately one a month, the last ZA941 for RAF Farnborough being finished in the Establishment's red, white and blue

Locking Moor Road's north-easterly airport entrance gate was still being used to deliver aircraft to Oldmixon as late as the early 1960s. In this case it was Whirlwind HR 4 XJ727 late of 228 Squadron on a Queen Mary being brought in for conversion to HAR 10 configuration (A. Smith)

In the early 1960s, Shop 4 was the flight shed and housed Sycamore G-48/1 (G-ALSX), the odd Belvedere, various turbine-engined Whirlwinds and a Sycamore transmission test-rig (Westland)

The Shop 5 Metal Rotor-Blade Facility on 4 January 1977 (Westland)

colour scheme. ZA934 subsequently returned to Oldmixon in 1982 for major modification in preparation for winter icing trials in Denmark.

Puma kits were also produced for the main assembly line at Aerospatiale's Marignane Factory in Southern France. These consisted of roof and cabin structures, which included cabin doors and rear hatches. In addition to Sea King work, Shop 7 completed a nominal six of these each month and by 1988, when production ceased, 950 sets had been delivered including some for the AS332 Super Puma. In addition to the new build, repair and modification work, one Puma captured from Argentina in the South Atlantic (Falklands) Conflict came in for rework. But unlike the Westland-built SA330E, it had long-range fuel tanks, and as ZE449 after refurbishment left Oldmixon in 1985 to swell the RAF's diminishing fleet of Pumas.

Miscellaneous Work

Following the takeover by Westland, the content of Shop 10, the Tool Room, was transferred to Banwell and in 1974 it became Westland's new Transmission Repair Centre. Concentrating on the reclaim/rework of transmission system components, with fifty-four pieces of machinery, it worked in conjunction with Shop 8, vacated by Henlys in 1965, that had since handled the repair and overhaul of various in-service helicopter transmission systems. Then, to be more centrally located, in 1983 the machinery was moved to Shop 8 to free up space for the arrival from Yeovil of two Wadkins spar-milling machines for Sea King rotor-blade spar work. One had originally been at Oldmixon on Belvedere blade-spar work and for the last twenty years had been machining spars for Wessex and Sea Kings. To ensure there was no recurrence of the previous problems with Weston's tide, this time each mill was mounted on a specially reinforced and stress-tensioned concrete bed. The first Oldmixon Sea King spar was completed at the end of April 1984 but following an announcement in May 1985 that the Ministry of Defence (MoD) was to buy composite blades for its Sea King fleet, it was realised that the metal spar contract would probably be short-lived. Following machining, the spars went to Yeovil for trailing-edge pockets to be bonded on and then it was back to Oldmixon for finishing. The complete transfer of metal blade manufacture from Yeovil to Oldmixon occurred in mid-1985 when Lynx work was transferred to Shop 8, but like the

On 4 April 1986, some of the 950 sets of Puma roof and cabin structures that were in due course built in Shop 7 could be seen. At the far end is the Detail Fitting Area. In the mid-1950s, this central area was the Machine Shop and the foreground area was used for the refurbishment of turrets and AA guns; up to the mid-1940s it was full of Beaufighter sub-assemblies (Westland)

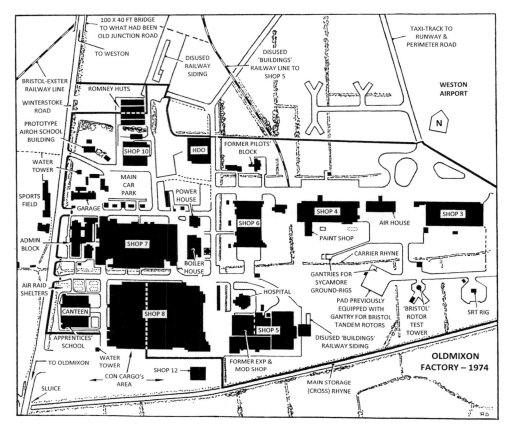

The Oldmixon Factory as it appeared in August 1974. The last five of the wartime air raid shelters (each held eighty workers) in front of the Canteen, after a struggle were demolished in the summer of 1983 (R. Dudley)

Sea King, this helicopter too was already earmarked for composite blades.

In 1982 Con Cargo, a company that for ten years had been occupying a large area of floor space in Shop 8 manufacturing containers and glass-fibre boat-hulls moved into a smaller building, and in early 1983 the Metal Rotor-Blade Facility in Shop 5, that by now was also manufacturing and refurbishing tail rotor-blades, moved in. Taking the now vacant 10,000 sq. feet (929 sq. metres) in Shop 5 was the company's new Central Hydraulic Facility, a super-clean area making, amongst, other items hydraulic manifolds and nose undercarriages for the Lynx that, as a result of a company reorganisation, had been moved down from the Westland (Sandall) Helicopters, Milton Keynes, Bletchley site.

Because the Oldmixon Factory was fairly remote, quite a few trials that could be considered noisy were carried out on its open land. In addition to the various Bristol-built rotor rigs whose noise had produced many complaints from the local populace, in the late 1960s Westland, very interested in the tilt-wing convertiplane Short Range Transport (SRT) concept, had a tall Rolls-Royce

Gnome-powered rotor-rig built behind Shop 3 to help perfect the technology. Installed inverted with thrust directed upwards to avoid the ground-cushion effect, noise from its rotor was monitored from a helium-filled balloon flown above, that carried test equipment such as microphones. There was also a trial with a supersonic rotor that, although small in diameter, produced a horrendous noise that could be heard all around the factory. A further test facility was a purpose-built 6-cell test house erected alongside the old Bristol rotor-blade whirl tower. Completed in mid-November 1982 it was for production clearance of the Weslake Aeromarine Engines Ltd (WAM) 342 30 hp piston-engine used in the Westland Wideye remotely piloted vehicle (RPV) rotorcraft. The project was managed by a newly set up propulsion division in Normalair-Garrett Ltd which was 52 per cent owned by Westland and shared its Yeovil Factory site.

Gazelle and Wasp/Scout Work

With the need for extra space at Yeovil to set up a Gazelle production line, in 1971 the Westland/Augusta-Bell Sioux AH I and the civil Augusta-Bell 47G-4 work that by then was beginning to tail off had been transferred to Oldmixon. After several years the Gazelle work was also nearing completion, and in mid-1977 this line was moved to Oldmixon's Shop 7, thus enabling Yeovil to expand Sea King/Commando production and set up a Lynx line. The first Oldmixon-built Gazelle XZ338, an AH I for the British Army had its first flight in the hands of Jerry Tracey on 28 October 1977, and by April of the following year ten new Gazelles had been delivered, and from then on an average of three were built a month. In addition, in-service Gazelles were also being repaired and fitted with a range of new equipment that included radios, TANS, SIGMAT, etc. for the British armed forces. Meanwhile, the production line had been moved to the north-east side of Shop 6, and, almost five years to the day after Gazelles had gone into production at Weston, work started on a second batch of thirty-eight machines of which twenty-five were for the British Army, nine for the RAF and four for the Royal Navy. The first HT 3 ZB625 flew in April 1982 and the ninety-first and last Gazelle from Oldmixon, ZB649 an HT 2, was handed over to the Royal Navy on 3 February 1984. Gazelles continued to pass through Shop 6 for Category 4 repairs and trial installations and, as of early 1984 there were still a dozen machines undergoing modification work. As with Puma, many sub-assembly kits were also produced at Oldmixon for Aerospatiale's Marignane Factory.

In the early 1970s with pending closure of the Hayes Factory, Oldmixon started to become involved with the completion of some of the last few new Hayes-built Wasps. The last new Wasp to be flown from Oldmixon was AH-12A 247 for the Royal Netherlands Navy, it having its initial flight in mid-1974. Coinciding with testing the newly-built machines, some Royal Navy Wasps came up for retirement and a long programme commenced in Oldmixon's Shop 4 covering the rebuild/refurbishment of these aircraft for other customers, and

Oldmixon's original Gazelle production line as set up in Shop 7 during 1977 (Westland)

Mid-1973, one of the Wasps of the politically-sensitive follow-on order for South Africa about to be taken by road to the Yeovil Factory for flight testing (Westland)

Shop 6 on 6 February 1976 with British Army Scouts being refurbished. A Puma is under assembly in the far jig (Westland)

over a number of years the machines were delivered to the Brazilian Navy and the Royal New Zealand Navy who were already Wasp operators. In September 1976 the Royal Netherlands Navy became the first foreign customer to receive the Navy Lynx, and its AH-12A Wasps, some having been in operation for fifteen years, became surplus to requirements. In this case the Indonesian Navy took over the entire fleet and spares, and of these, six needed to pass through Oldmixon's shops, whilst four others that were in good order were delivered to the new customer direct from Holland. The last refurbished Wasp, which was one of those that had gone direct to Indonesia but was later sent to Oldmixon for refurbishment, was handed over in September 1985. Alongside the Wasps, some two dozen British Army Scouts were also refurbished, some of which were also equipped with trial installations such as the Hawkswing missile system. The first Scout to undergo Category 4 repairs was AH I XV131, which was handed back to the Army Air Corps on Tuesday 2 September 1975. Another requiring repair and overhaul was XT627, it arrived the following year having been recovered from 6 feet (1.8 metres) of water in Hong Kong Harbour. In early 1982 five Scouts were also brought in for major structural changes to allow for the embodiment of emergency flotation gear for the South Atlantic (Falklands) Conflict.

Last of the Fixed-Wings

Since the Beaufighter, no complete fixed-wing aircraft had been brought into the Oldmixon factory for refurbishment, and it was of some interest to the employees when they discovered that the Fairey Gannet AEW 3 overhaul and modernisation work that since closure of the Fairey White Waltham Factory had been carried out at Westland's Ilchester Works (Yeovilton), was to be transferred there. The work on a number of these bulky twin-engined carrier-based machines was to be executed in Shop 6 and from 16 August 1974 when XL450 was test-flown until 12 February 1976 when XL494 was handed back to the Royal Navy, XL471, XP226, XL482, XL472, XL497 and XL456 had also been through the shop and test-flown by Keith Chadbourn, the only Westland test pilot cleared to fly the type. XL494 made its first post-refurbishment flight on 3 February and, following further flights at RNAS Yeovilton, it returned to Weston for final checks and handover on Thursday 12 February. This marked the end of an era, being the last fixed-wing aeroplane to leave a Westland factory by air. One other Gannet was down for refurbishment, but due to defence cuts, work was cancelled part-way through the programme and the aircraft left by road in October for Yeovilton to become a 'Christmas Tree' providing spares for others. It is understood that the few Gannet under-nose radomes still in store as spares became garden pond-liners, but it's unclear how they left the factory! The untimely withdrawal of the Gannet AEW 3 'Eyes of the Fleet' from service, due to there no longer being an aircraft carrier for it to operate from, brought about 'Project Last' in 1982 during the South Atlantic (Falklands) Conflict. This was the urgent embodiment of Modification 700, the fitting at Yeovil of a retractable radome and associated equipment that converted two Sea King HAS 2s into AEW 2s. This conversion work for the new 'Eyes of the Fleet', would in future years create much work for the Oldmixon Factory.

Wessex Work

Bristow Helicopters, a company formed in the late 1940s by an ex-Westland test pilot, for a time became the world's largest operator of civil helicopters, with many of the machines being Westland S-55s and Wessex 60s. In August 1981 one of its Wessex's crashed in the North Sea under mysterious circumstances with the loss of the thirteen men onboard, and following a much-publicised crash enquiry, the company reluctantly offered to take the machines off Bristow's hands, probably hoping that an order for the new W30 would follow. As a result, seven of these helicopters came to Oldmixon for storage with the hope of a future sale, but there was a distinct lack of interest from any prospective customers. Two others had been sold and, having starred in US Marine Corps markings in the 1987 film *Full Metal Jacket*, were obtained by what was then the British Rotorcraft Museum and these were joined in due course by the machines from Oldmixon.

XL494, the last Gannet to be refurbished, is towed from Shop 6 for the demonstration flight on 12 February 1976 (Westland)

Shop 6 on 15 April 1982. Gazelle production is now in the north-easterly corner with much floor space taken up with ex-Bristow Wessex 60s returned after the 1981 North Sea crash (Westland)

Around 1984, Oldmixon also took over Wessex product support that since 1970 had been carried out by Westland's Cowes, Isle of Wight Factory, and early in 1984 the first Wessex for some time arrived for the trial installation of a new inflatable life raft module and a radio intended for all RAF Wessex HC 2s. In fact, it was a Wessex that had heralded Oldmixon again becoming a flight test centre. For several years prior to June 1975, helicopters following repair/overhaul at Oldmixon had been delivered by road to Yeovil for test-flying and customer acceptance, but in June there was a breakthrough when a Wessex HU 5 that had arrived eighteen months previously to undergoing Category 4 repair was test-flown from the factory, and then delivered directly back to the customer for further service, in this case the Fleet Air Arm.

Helicopter Services Ltd

In 1978 Westland Helicopters entered into a contract with the Arab Organisation for Industry (AOI), the partners in which were Egypt, Qatar, Saudi Arabia, the United Arab Emirates and the Arab British Helicopter Company (ABH) of which Westland owned 30 per cent. The object was to build an initial 250 skidded Lynx with the majority assembled by ABH in Egypt, but in May 1979, following the Camp David agreements, AOI announced that the organisation would be terminated with effect from 1 July 1979. This led to the cancellation of all contracts, with Westland promised compensation, but due to a difference of opinion in the Egyptian Government the claim was not settled. This resulted in Westland initiating in 1980 proceedings with the AOI to recover the cost of setting up the Lynx production facility. Concerned that its contracts in other parts of the region would be affected by the arbitration proceedings, a new subsidiary of the Customer Support Division was formed that didn't include 'Westland' in its title. Thus Helicopter Services Ltd (HSL) was born with headquarters in Winterstoke Road, Oldmixon. Its task to undertake advisory, consultancy and project management services for current and prospective users of helicopters.

Meanwhile, to facilitate its future plans, Westland decided to buy Weston Airport. Weston Town Council had spent £60,291 on the airport by February 1939, and after six years of threats of compulsory purchase, was forced to sell its freehold to the MoS on 20 September 1956 for a mere £42,000, and in the following years it was to spend much time and effort in trying to get it back again. For a long time the airport had been a thorn in the side of Weston Borough Council (later the Woodspring District Council), as it was considered that the large area of land it occupied prevented the town's natural development evenly outwards. The council was therefore looking forward to the end of 1978 when it was expected that Straight's Airways Union would relinquish its operating licence. Considered a foregone conclusion that it would obtain the 375 acre (152 hectares) site, the council meeting on 10 October had been set aside to decide on how to proceed with its purchase. But unknown to the council,

Westland, which originally wanted to retain only the 140 acres (57 hectares) immediately adjoining the Oldmixon Factory, changed its mind and expressed interest in buying a much larger area of 335 acres (136 hectares) that wouldn't include the rectangular area on the northern side that stretched from Locking Moor Road past the Hutton Moor Flight Shed occupied by EMI. Much to the annoyance of the council, with MoD backing Westland started what was to be over four years of negotiations with the Government's Property Service Agency to obtain the land. By early 1984 agreement had been reached and on 23 March 1984, with a purchase price of some £750,000, the land became the property of Westland plc. This, together with its 90-acre (36-hectare) Oldmixon site with 523,000 sq. feet (48,588 sq. metres) of factory space, made the company one of the largest private property owners in the Weston area. Coinciding with this acquisition, Westland was also granted a new licence by the CAA for commercial flying to recommence from the airport.

In addition to taking over support of the Egyptian Air Force's thiry-three Sea King/Commandos, HSL gained a repair and overhaul contract for Egyptian Air Force Russian-built Mil Mi 6 and 8 helicopter transmission systems, the latter work carried out in Shop 8 under the cover of 'Project 47'. In 1982 it also set about forming a rotary-wing flight-training school at Weston Airport to take pilots and ground crew through the same syllabus as that of the British Forces, Westland setting its sights on training pilots of many of the world's air forces that had bought the Gazelle. Amongst early contracts was a relatively small amount

One of the Nigerian Navy Lynx Mk 89s together with Helicopter Services Ltd instructors and Nigerian Navy trainees (Westland)

of modification work for HSL on several civil Gazelles, but probably the most interesting was that for the refurbishment of the two Arab Republic of Egypt Air Force VIP Westland Commando Mk 2Bs that in 1975-76 had been handed over at Yeovil to carry President Sadat of Egypt and his entourage. Each helicopter would remain at the factory for several months. The first, 725, for the ferry flight from Egypt registered SU-ARR, arrived at Weston on 13 September 1982 in an all-over rather abrasive sand scheme. After a detailed survey followed by overhaul and refurbishment in Shop 6, it was redelivered in November of the following year. The second machine, 726, also registered SU-ARR for its ferry flight arrived on 31 May 1983, and after a similar programme of rework was redelivered in April 1984. As had been noticed with interest some years before by Western Airways personnel when seeing-off refurbished Bristol Freighters belonging to Middle-Eastern customers, the foreign crews for these Commandos must have also arrived with long shopping lists, as they obtained every conceivable item from Weston's shops for the journey home.

April 1983 saw the arrival of staff to run the flight-training school, and the completion of G-BKLU, the first of five ex-US corporate French-built SA 341G Gazelles that had been under refurbishment since December of the previous year at Oldmixon. The other machines operated by HSL were Gazelles G-BKGL, G-BKLT, G-BKLV, G-BKLW, and Bell Jet Ranger G-HRAY which was used for instructor courses and air-charter work.

The first active contract for the school was one from Westland Helicopters to train the air and ground crew of the Nigerian Navy Air Arm on the Lynx Mk 89, three of which had been ordered in 1982. Selected from crews of Nigerian Navy ships, in most cases the prospective pilots had never flown an aeroplane before, let alone a helicopter. From the beginning fixed-wing training was at Air Service Training, Perth, in Scotland, and helicopter conversion at Hamble. Flight conversion onto the Lynx was carried out for the most part at Weston Airport, which by now had been purchased and relicensed by Westland, who had had its original control tower and associated buildings refurbished. The three Lynx arrived from Yeovil in March/April 1984 and were, like the other training machines, hangared and maintained in Shop 3 where the first squadron of the Nigerian Navy Air Arm, No. 101, was officially formed following a period of night-flying training, which was especially unpopular with local residents. The helicopters departed Weston early in 1985 for Stansted from where they were flown out to Nigeria in a Short Belfast belonging to Heavy Lift. With the conclusion in 1986 of an 18-month contract to train helicopter pilots for the Bahrain Defence Force and completion of work on an AS Dauphin belonging to Bond Helicopters, little business came the way of HSL, and in August 1987, coinciding with return of HSL personnel from Nigeria, the company was wound up and the staff made redundant. By this time too, the control tower building, which in one position or another had been in almost constant use since 1937, was abandoned and essential equipment relocated to new landing pads within the Oldmixon Factory enclave.

Lynx Work

At the end of the 1970s, occasional Lynx work started to appear at Oldmixon, mainly for the survey and rebuild of damaged machines and the manufacture of mechanical, electrical and avionic training aids. The first Lynx to arrive for rebuild was AH I XZ172. It had flown on 4 May 1977 at Yeovil and was the first for the Army Air Corps (AAC). But soon after delivery, whilst being ground run at Middle Wallop, an engine explosion and the resulting fire destroyed much of the fuselage. Arriving in Shop 6 towards the end of July for rebuild, due to the extent of the damage, when handed back to the AAC in mid-December 1981, about the only original parts left on the machine were the cockpit and lower fuselage.

One of the mechanical training aids was for the German Navy which had taken delivery of the first of twelve Lynx Mk 88s at Yeovil on 15 June 1981. This involved Oldmixon building its one-and-only new Lynx. Assembled in the repair jig in Shop 4, it was identical to the real thing except that there were no flying controls nor rotor-blades and only one engine, which was a slave unit, and at the end of September 1982 it was flown to Germany from RNAS Yeovilton in a German Air Force Transall. Oldmixon was also responsible for initiating the Super Lynx programme when it converted two HAS 2s, ZD249 and ZD267, into aerodynamic prototypes of what would eventually become the Lynx HMA 8, the first being delivered back to Yeovil in good time to be readied for the 1986 September Farnborough Air Show.

W30 Work

In 1979 Oldmixon started to contribute its skills in the construction of the WG30. This was basically a larger version of the Rolls-Royce Gem-powered Lynx, it having around 85 per cent of its components and designed to carry a crew of two and up to twenty-two passengers in a box-type cabin. The rear fuselage for the first prototype G-BGHF, now on display in The Helicopter Museum (*see chapter* 4), was constructed freehand in Shop 7, and with the helicopter successfully flown at Yeovil on 10 April 1979, Oldmixon was tasked to build two dozen production rear fuselages, the first delivered to Yeovil for what was now known as the W30 Series 100 on 22 July 1981. Oldmixon would also supply the machine's cabin and cockpit floor structures. Late in 1983 in-service W30s also started to appear at the factory for modification work. The first to arrive were the three British Airways Series 100 machines G-OGAS and G-BIWY in November and G-BKGD in December for mandatory modifications to the tail rotor control mechanism and AFCS, the former modification resulting from the crash of an Airspur-operated machine in the USA.

Other W30 work came to Weston over the following years, including at the end of 1984 a Type-Test Transmission Maturity Rig that had a new high-speed reduction gearbox for the W30 General Electric CT7-2B-powered Series 200. Planning permission for this rig had only been granted after a W30 flown up from Yeovil had been hovered over the proposed site to check out noise levels. There was also the fitting, developing and flight testing over a 3-month period of new side-facing engine air intakes to Series 160 G-BLLF for cold-weather trials in Denmark. The W30 was not a commercial success with only forty built, included in this number being twenty for India. Others found their way to the USA, but after being withdrawn from service, came to Oldmixon for storage and eventual use at The Helicopter Museum, with them joining HF, GD, the Series 200 and 300 prototypes and the Series 200 maturity rig.

Westland Industrial Business Division

In 1980, the Westland Industrial Business Division formed two years previously obtained an 18-month contract from British Aerospace at Filton to help with conversion of five commercially-operated Standard (ex-Gulf Air), and four Super (ex-East African Airways) VC10 passenger airliners into in-flight refuelling tankers (designated Mk 2Ks and Mk 3Ks respectively) for the RAF. Involved was the manufacturer of component sets, comprising ballast floor-panels and blocks for the forward cabin tank area, cabin frames and floor beams with the necessary tooling, all to be supplied to Filton's Brabazon Assembly Hall where the conversion was to be completed. Around this time a contract was also obtained for loom-work for the BAe 146.

The South Atlantic (Falklands) Conflict

The South Atlantic (Falklands) Conflict in 1982 created a British Task Force which in Westland-built helicopters alone comprised nearly 200 machines. These Sea Kings, Lynx, Wessex, Wasp, Scout and Gazelles between them flew some 23,000 hours, performing 11,000 sorties and nearly 20,000 deck-landings, mostly in atrocious weather. The Sea Kings in particular were operated at ten-times their normal peace-time usage rate and were often launched at an AUW 20 per cent beyond their normally permitted limitations. During the conflict, Oldmixon received some 400 priority requests from the MoD to keep the Task Force operational, this requiring at Oldmixon extra shifts giving twenty-four-hour, seven-days-a-week cover, particularly so in the Shop 8 transmission build area. The Conflict, however, did have a temporary benefit for the workforce, and that was a delay in announcing a redundancy of 350 workers at the Yeovil and Oldmixon Factories, resulting from a general fall-off in orders.

The W30 Series 200 Maturity Rig at Oldmixon, July 1984 (Westland)

Loss of the AAC-Westland A-20 Wamira

Issue of Air Staff Target (AST) 412 in June 1981 by the MoD came near to bringing a fixed-wing aircraft production line back to Oldmixon, and in so doing securing the jobs of some 350 of its workers. The requirement was for an order of at least 130 almost off-the-shelf, turbo-prop tandem-seat, high-performance aircraft to replace the ageing and expensive-to-operate RAF Jet Provost. Four designs were eventually short-listed, three of them from overseas, and for those to be considered they had to be presented to the MoD by a British aircraft manufacturer. One proposal from the Australian Aircraft Consortium (AAC) that had the side-by-side seat A-10 Wamira due to fly mid-1985, was in partnership with Westland (AAC-Westland). The task for Oldmixon would be to convert the A-10 into a tandem-seat machine with its cockpit based on that of the RAF's British Aerospace Hawk advanced jet-trainer; to manufacture 50 per cent of its airframe; to carry out final assembly and flight testing and to look after product support of the machine. A full-size mock-up of what would be the A-20G shown at the Farnborough Air Show in September 1984 was taken back to Oldmixon where it was to remain for some weeks, but at the end of 1985 due to a change in requirements, the AAC-Westland proposal was excluded from the competition. The winning design was the Brazilian Embraer Tucano, which in due course was built by Shorts.

Loss of this contract was to have a very damaging effect on Westland which had strong hopes of securing in return the sale of military W30 Series 300 Tactical Transports to the Royal Australian Air Force. Although Wamira had been lost, a variety of work continued to be found in the mid-1980s to occupy Oldmixon's workforce. Shop 4 was working on a number of rigs and training aids for customers including a large avionic rig for India associated with purchase of the Sea King Mk 42B, and three EH 101 test-rigs for the Anglo/Italian Sea King replacement programme. Amongst MoD contracts obtained in 1986, there was one that brought in a number of British military helicopters for paint strip and respray, and in early 1987 one of the machines that came in was a tandem-rotor, but this time an RAF Chinook.

The Capital Restructuring Plan

Following what was called the Westland Affair in the summer of 1985, during which the company almost went to the wall, a capital restructuring plan was conceived that would involve major changes to the Westland Group. With only limited options available, it was decided in March 1986 to bring in United Technologies Corporation (UTC-Sikorsky) of America and Fiat of Italy as minority shareholders. A part of the plan was also for the company to diversify into civil markets, and on 1 October 1987 what had been a part of the Customer Support Division at Oldmixon was split into two. The manufacturing element became Westland Industrial Products Ltd (WIPL) and the design element was renamed Westland Design Services Ltd (WDS). In addition to providing support for Westland, the new companies would also offer their services to other sections of the aircraft industry.

With this reorganisation, most of Weston Airport was sold for a reported £7 million to Coastal & Countryside Properties. It then passed through the hands of Peter de Savary, Leisure Investments, Alfred Walker Ltd and then the Receiver, who by 2004 had sold it to the Persimmon Group for £20 million! With the reorganisation, all WIPL work was now consolidated into Shops 5 and 8 and the seventy employees from the Helicopter Drawing Office moved into the old canteen which became WDS. The remaining part of the factory was then also sold. The total number of employees on the site, now referred to as the Winterstoke Road Facility, which had been 1,241 as recently as early 1987, stabilised at around 290. Under this arrangement WIPL obtained both military and civil contracts, some of the largest being the manufacture of all doors for the Bae 146, Jetstream 31 and later the Jetstream 41 and Dornier 328 airliners. A further contract was for manufacture of Jetstream 31 rear fuselages which included the tailplane and fin, and design of certain Airbus structures. There were also the established contracts involving repair and overhaul of helicopter structures, transmission systems, rotor-blades and electrical systems. WDS on the other hand was also involved in design work for most of these and other subcontract work for the Westland Group and other manufacturers.

Another part of the recovery plan occurred in early 1987, when WIPL started on a major contract from Sikorsky Aircraft to repair and overhaul transmission components of S61N helicopters used by North Sea operators. To run for five years, it involved rotor-heads and gearboxes and was part of a 2 million man-hour agreement made with UTC, and in the case of Oldmixon was for the turn round of approximately three sets a month of rotor-heads and main, intermediate and tail gearboxes and the machining of gearbox casings for the Sikorsky Black Hawk. However, towards the end of 1988, unfortunately for the factory, this work was returned to Yeovil. In October of the following year, it was announced that the GKN company had acquired Fiat's shareholding and together with other shares obtained, now owned 22.02 per cent of Westland and the company's name was duly changed to GKN Westland.

The end of the Gulf War of 1991 brought more work, when WIPL won a contract for a major rebuild of forty-nine rather tired RAF Pumas. Over several years they were flown into Yeovil, stripped and then taken by trailer to Shop 5 where main lift-frames were replaced and engine and transmission top-decking repaired. It was then back to Yeovil where assembly and flight testing took place. The first refurbished Puma was handed back to the RAF on 21 February 1992, although many would return to WIPL at a later date for a new RACAL navigation system to be embodied.

During 1997 a lucrative Puma transmission refurbishment contract was lost and this was to have a lasting effect on WIPL's financial position and in the numbers of employees required. The loss was to some extent offset by a contract to manufacture detail components for the Lynx AH 7 and EH 101 that were then made into major sub-assemblies for the production lines at Yeovil and Italy respectively. During the year WIPL also delivered the first two of three Sea King AEW 2s that had been converted from HAS 5s. Other Sea King work came to the factory with the arrival in 1998 of seventeen HAR 3s for the fitment of the Night Vision Goggle Installation, four machines also being equipped with a Global Positioning System. Belgian Sea King Mk 48Bs also came in for their original AFCS to be replaced with the new Smiths Newmark SN500 system.

Another Chinook made an appearance at Oldmixon in 1998 on Wednesday 10 June when ZH892, a new HC 2, was flown into the factory by Westland test pilot Ted Mustard accompanied by Sandy Sproule, for WIPL to design and fit a trial installation of the new complex Smiths Industries Health and Usage Monitoring System (HUMS). This work was part of a major £4 million contract that would include eventual fitment of the modification into the RAF's fleet of over forty aircraft. Following extensive flight trials with ZH892, the modification was installed in the other Chinooks at Odiham by Westland working parties.

WIPL again became the responsibility of Customer Support Division within Westland Helicopters in 1999 and moved away from the civil market back to

WIPL carrying out ISR work on early in-service RN Merlins, and the refurbishment of what were now fairly ancient RAF Pumas (Westland)

its traditional area of helicopter support for mainly in-service Sea Kings, Pumas and Lynx and a variety of these in-service machines went through Shop 5 for modification work. Even with the latest contracts, there was a need to offload some of the 400-strong workforce, and in January 2000 it was announced that eighty-five employees would be made redundant. With the new streamlined organisation, in Shop 5, now renamed the 'Aircraft Centre', RAF Pumas were equipped with Ferry Fuel Tanks, Sea King HC 4s were fitted with a new Enhanced Communication System and four Sea King AEW 2s were converted by embodiment of a Mission System Upgrade into AEW 7s. Tail rotor-blades for a variety of types also continued to be manufactured together with a wide range of spares and electrical looms.

In 2000, WIPL was also to handle the major In-Service Retro (ISR) modification of the Merlin HM I, this being set in motion shortly after the first prototype Merlin I ZF649 (PP5) was flown in during the last week of July for decommissioning. ISR, involving fitting the fleet of around forty RN machines with main rotor-blade and tail-pylon automatic folding facilities, emergency avionics and emergency egress lighting and enabling the troublesome rotor brake, was to give Merlin a ship-operating capability and the programme commenced with the arrival of RN 11 on 2 August. Also passing through the Aircraft Centre at that time were Sea King HC 4s being equipped with Radar Warning Receivers. WDS meanwhile continued to obtain contracts, typical being the design of various Sea King mid-life updates, designing sections of the Nimrod MRA 4 wing and providing contract staff to other organisations such as DERA at Boscombe Down.

Coinciding with the setting up of the Agusta/Westland joint venture in 2000, some major contracts were coming to an end and there was a need to combine the WIPL facilities with those on the main site at Yeovil. This resulted in an announcement on 10 January 2002 that the manufacturing element of the Winterstoke Road facility would shut in April, but as it happened it would be the end of September before the last employee left. During the rundown, the last Sea King to leave, HU 5 XV670, was flown out on 30 August, but the last helicopter of all to depart was a Merlin which left on 6 September on completion of its ISR update. At this point, there remained on site just ten WIPL employees and the flight team employed by Westland that totalled twelve. It is interesting to note that in 2010, except for the Pilots' Block and a few other small buildings, all of the original factory buildings remain intact and in diverse uses.

The Banwell Factory Post-War

With the Banwell Factory joining with Oldmixon in the peace-time activity of producing houses, aluminium-alloy wall frames and roof trusses soon started to take up the floor space recently occupied by the Hawker Tempest IIs. The early 1950s decision to take all building work from Oldmixon resulted in June 1954 of all that work being transferred to Banwell, and by Christmas the drawing office and all equipment that included the large brake press and raw materials had been moved to what was now the Building Division's new home with Mr P. W. Lawson its General Manager. As with the Oldmixon Factory, the opportunity was now taken to give the major buildings shop numbers, and No.1 Erecting Hall became Shop 2, the Quarantine Store became Shop 1, the Garage became Shop 9 and the building attached to the Administrative Block became Shop 11.

Until 1955 all schools had been of a single-storey design known as the Mk 1A System, but now the first of a number of Bristol Mk II System multi-storey (up to three) designs that had been conceived and constructed at Banwell was erected at Coventry. In essence, the Mk II buildings consisted of standardised steel frames carrying precast concrete floors and aluminium-framed wall panels and many were sold. But with the high cost of aluminium and with the eventual greater availability of conventional building materials and labour, the company ran down the building work, and on 1 July 1955 the Building Division was disbanded and the factory absorbed into the company's Aircraft Division. One of the most notable buildings produced was one of the last, a 420-room, 75-bed military hospital that left mid-1956 for erection in the desert some 4 miles (6.4 km) from Benghazi, Libya. Remarkably, some AIROH buildings that had been intended for only a short lifespan were still being used at the commencement of the twenty-first century. The legacy of this venture was the establishment of an independent company in Weston called 'Alumin',

One of the three Sea King AEW 2s converted from an HAS 5 by WIPL in the late 1990s (Westland)

Chinook ZH892 lands on 10 June 1998 for embodiment by WIPL of HUMS (Westland)

which specialised in aluminium doors and windows and led in turn to the local development of the uPVC double-glazing industry.

With the development and production of rocket motor cases now allocated to the factory, a large pit was excavated in Shop 2 (formerly No.1 Erecting Hall) for the heat-treatment furnaces and quench tanks, and during one weekend in the summer of 1956, the complete rocket motor-case machine shop, together with other equipment, was transferred to the new site. Around that time, a team from British Messier, which had developed the Magpie motor and gas-storage pressure vessels for the DH Firestreak air-to-air guided missile, was also relocated to Banwell to join with the Bristol team. Up to this point the company had produced rocket motor cases mainly for meteorological research rockets such as Skua, Skylark and Raven, the latter being used to propel Britain's high-altitude research vehicle onto the edge of space. Development was also being carried out on motor cases for British surface-to-air and air-to-air missiles designed by the MoS. Its factories were the Rocket Propellant Research Establishment (RPE), later known as the Propellant and Explosives Research and Manufacturing Establishment (PERME) at Westcott near Aylesbury, Buckinghamshire, where motors were named after birds, and the Summerfield Research Station (SRS) where motors were named after dogs. There was a change to this practice in 1965 when SRS motors received land battle names.

Along with the rocket and bottle work, Bristol Aero Engines Ltd also maintained a very large parts store at Banwell. Known as the Engine Spare Parts Stores, in a part of Shop 1, it held some 40,000 items for the company's piston and jet engines that, on receipt from the engine factories, were pre-packed, packed and dispatched to all parts of the world. The store continued in being for some years, later under the auspices of Rolls-Royce, and would eventually move to Oldmixon where it occupied Shop 3.

During 1957, Aerojet General Corporation of California, wanting to exploit its polyurethane solid propellant technology and attempting to enter the European market, made overtures to the Bristol Aeroplane Company about the possibility of the two companies joining forces. Bristol had for some time appreciated the need for it to have a propellant facility and be able to offer filled motors, and after high-level discussions with both the British and US governments, on 18 December it joined with Aerojet, who would supply rocket motor and propellant technology to the new company — Bristol Aerojet (BAJ). Bristol had now gained a powerful associate which reinforced its already strong position in the increasingly important field of solid rocket motor development. The new firm would have exclusive rights to exploit Aerojet's rocket motor and solid-propellant products which included those for the Minuteman and Polaris ICBMs. Aerojet was also doing extensive liquid-propellant rocket motor work for a variety of missiles. Bristol too was a significant contributor to the partnership, it providing the vast experience accumulated in the manufacture of the majority of British guided weapon motor cases, and the helical welding

The enormous pit being dug in Banwell's Shop 2 during January 1956. Completely excavated by hand, it was now close to receiving the furnaces and quenching tanks from Oldmixon's Shop 3 (S. Parsons)

of high-tensile steel which was unique in Europe and probably the world. The company also had a wealth of experience in design and manufacture of gas-storage pressure-vessels used in civil and military aircraft.

Although the company name had changed, Banwell carried on as normal with Managing Director Walter Strachan looking after production of Gosling booster motor cases for the Bristol/Ferranti Bloodhound and English Electric Thunderbird ground-to-air missiles, Bullpup motors for NATO missiles, Magpie and propulsive motor cases for Firestreak. Cases were also being made for Wagtail, Sea Wolf, Deerhound and Blue Water and other military and space projects. After 1965, Blackcap solid-propellant motors and Troy cases were also built for Rapier, a larger version of Skua named 'Petrel' was developed and booster motors were built for Seaslug (Retriever) and for Seacat for which the company supplied some 3,000 Sealyham boost motors. The end of the 1960s also saw Banwell build the solid-propellant apogee-stage Waxwing motor for the 3-stage all-British Black Arrow satellite launcher. This rocket motor, based on the RPE Kestrel, was to launch payloads of up to 200 lb (91 kg) into a 350-mile (563-km) circular polar orbit. However, the expected transfer of technology to Britain from Aerojet never fully materialised as there were no firm orders from the British Government for the type of missile motor that the American company was able to offer.

The Bristol Aeroplane Company's original connection with the company was to become a bit more tenuous on 31 March 1959 when Bristol Aero Engines Ltd officially joined forces with Hawker Siddeley Group Ltd and the organisation became Bristol Siddeley Engines. This was not entirely unexpected as it had already been announced that from 28 April 1958 the company would be coordinating activities with Armstrong Siddeley Motors. In 1966 there were further changes in the UK element of Bristol Aerojet's management team, with amalgamation of the British aero-engine industry under the mantle of Rolls-Royce. In this new grouping with Aerojet, meteorological and research rockets continued to be produced, Troy was further developed and solid and liquid motor research work was carried out for what would become Chevaline, a large solid and liquid rocket motor development.

During the 1960s, the Banwell Factory was associated with work for the atomic energy industry and the French company Eugene on a number of projects including the handling of radioactive materials and with the fast reactor programme. It also endeavoured to exploit Aerojet's automated package-handling technology and two companies, Welding Construction Ltd and J. Baker Conveyors Ltd, of Avonmouth, were acquired and traded as SORTRAC in what proved to be a highly competitive materials-handling business, but in 1969 heavy losses were sustained that brought about the rapid demise of the company resulting in a major downturn in BAJ's overall finances.

Again there were substantial changes for the organisation in 1971 when BAJ's first managing director retired and Rolls-Royce went bankrupt, and yet again in April 1979 when the receiver was able to sell off this branch of the company to the Vickers Engineering Group. By now the company had also produced motors for Flagstaff, Tigercat, Sea Wolf, Sea Skua, USD-501, Fulmar and the INTA Flamenco. An anglicised version of the Sparrow motor named 'Hoopoe' was also being built for the Skyflash missile and some Stinger motor cases were produced for the USA.

Rationalisation and restructuring of the Vickers Group in the mid-1980s caused BAJ to be identified as non-core and placed on the 'For Sale' list, and 24 April 1985 saw company control go to a management buy-out team for £4 million. The buy-out proved to be very successful for what was now BAJ Holdings Ltd, and, under the name Maltalton, five separate businesses were set up: Rocket Motors, Pressure Vessels, Coatings, Electronics and Composites. After two years, the company had made such an impact that there was a queue of suitors wishing to acquire it. Eventually, on 5 June 1987, Meggitt Holdings plc, which was an expanding British engineering group, won the acquisition race and bought out the fledgling company for £14 million. All institutional investors were very pleased with the result in financial terms and BAJ Ltd became a wholly-owned subsidiary of Meggitt. A new chapter had begun! Without the

Booster rocket motor-case production
underway in 1957 by what was now BAJ.
Clockwise from left: A glowing motor-case
is taken from the furnace for quenching in
oil. A spectacular burst of flames and smoke
as the case is quenched. Cases are checked
for soundness of welding. Completed motors
ready for delivery (Bristol via R. Dudley)

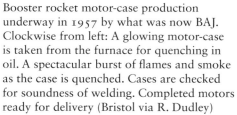

financial backing of a large organisation the new company, although making valiant efforts to find new contracts, found the going difficult and the only volume rocket motor production was that of Chevaline, Blackcap and Hoopoe, although during the Gulf War of 1991 additional work unexpectedly came from an order for almost 1,000 alarm booster motors and sustainer cases for the Bayard motor used in Operation Desert Storm.

With the Cold War's end, there was a general rundown in rocket engine work and although a further joint venture was attempted with the American Atlantic Research Corporation, it was stillborn. Meanwhile, the Meggitt Surface Coatings Division had become most successful, having at Banwell a facility much used in the aircraft industry that applied a unique range of composite abrasion-resistant coatings to components, such as tips of jet engine compressor blades to dramatically extend their lifespan. However, the business that had been BAJ's mainstream activity was no longer operating profitably and in 1990 a decision was taken to cease trading. With legal matters settled agreement was finally reached at the end of June 1991 and the rocket motor business, including all manufacturing plant and tooling, passed into the hands of Royal Ordnance. The highly successful Meggitt Coatings Division was in due course taken over by the American company Praxair Surface Technologies and relocated to the Oldmixon Industrial Estate from where it continues to provide the aviation industry and others with a unique service.

The Bristol Aero Collection

After a break of nearly sixty years, in 1991 the Banwell Factory started to house aeroplanes again when Meggitt's Managing Director Stephen Parsons provided a temporary home to exhibits of the expanding Bristol Aero Collection, however, there was a proviso that it could be asked to move at six-months notice. The collection displayed aeroplanes, components and documents associated with the Bristol Aeroplane Company and its subsidiaries. Included were Britannia 308F G-ANCF, the forward fuselage of Britannia 101 G-ALRX that Bill Pegg had put down on the frozen mudflats of the River Severn near Aust, Sycamore HR 14 XJ917 and a Bloodhound surface-to-air missile with its Banwell associations also on show. Because it was impossible for the low-loader carrying the Britannia forward fuselages to negotiate the narrow humpback bridges along Locking Moor Road, they were delivered to the Banwell Factory via the Oldmixon Factory and east along the airport's runway, and then finally out onto the A371.

When in 1995 the inevitable happened and Meggitt requested that the collection vacate the factory as it was to be sold, a new home was found on Kemble Airfield, Cirencester, Gloucestershire. The exhibits were moved out, and for the Britannia forward fuselages the route was now down the realigned Locking Moor Road and out on to Somerset Avenue. The large glass case that in earlier days had been in the factory gatehouse also found its way to Kemble, and is now used to house members' name badges. After several years in the planning stage, in mid-October 1998 developers George Wimpy started to demolish the Banwell Factory to make room for Elborough Village, a development that would provide some 173 homes. Sadly, efforts by North Somerset Council to have the original Rocket Test House preserved as a part of planning permission fell through and a JCB destroyed the building before preservation action could be taken. In doing so another piece of Weston's and Britain's aviation heritage was lost. Lasting reminders of the factory and one of its products can be found in two of the village's road names — Shadow Walk and Beaufort Close, whilst the wide approach from the A371 is still a reminder of the days when aircraft were towed from the factory to the airport.

January 1999 – all that remained of the Banwell Factory (E. Johnson)

3

WESTON'S ASSOCIATION
WITH THE MILITARY

Wartime Military Activity Around Weston

Most types of Allied aircraft were seen over and around Weston during the war years, and all except for the oft-seen BOAC airliners from Whitchurch were military. Some aircraft were from units based at Weston and there were those from service stations relatively close at hand such as Filton, Colerne, Charmy Down, Yatesbury, Hullavington, Zeals, Middle Wallop, Boscombe Down, Gosport, Warmwell, Culmhead (Church Stanton), Exeter, Chivenor, Merryfield, Yeovilton and Weston Zoyland. There were also aircraft from stations on the South Wales coast that included Pengam Moors, St Athan, Llandow, Stormy Down, Fairwood Common, Pembrey and Pembroke Dock. Stations on both sides of the Bristol Channel supported fighters, and they at times could be seen going about their task of protecting the towns and cities and industrial areas such as Weston's shadow factories. There were also many machines on flight trials from manufacturer's airfields in South-West England that included: Filton and Weston (Bristol), Brockworth, Staverton and Moreton Valence (Gloster), Christchurch and Portsmouth (Airspeed), Eastleigh and Keevil (Supermarine), Yeovil (Westland), Cowes (Saunders-Roe/Vickers-Supermarine), and there were those from the Royal Aircraft Establishment at Farnborough and the Aeroplane and Experimental Establishment at Boscombe Down. From early 1942 aircraft also started to be brought into Britain from the USA for the war effort, and soon it was possible to see from around Weston, with the aid of binoculars, transport vessels and modified tankers on their way to the docks at Newport, Cardiff and Avonmouth loaded with cocooned North American P-51 Mustangs, Republic P-47 Thunderbolts, Lockheed P-38 Lightnings, Noorduyn UC-64 Norseman, Douglas A-20 Havocs and North American AT-6 Texans. Other aircraft came crated including troop-carrying gliders. When shipments ceased in 1945, 2,167 aircraft had been delivered to Avonmouth, 210 to Cardiff and 275 to Newport, and many of these had been assembled and test-flown by USAAF Station 803 Aircraft Assembly Depot at Filton.

Bombers and transports from further afield also came through the local airspace after departing for, or returning from war missions, and the adjacent

Bristol Channel coast also brought in many aircraft to take advantage of the locations offered for developing and testing ordnance and to practise its delivery. These were mainly in mid-channel at air-to-air gunnery areas located near Flat Holm and Steep Holm and around an old ship used for bombing practice, and closer to Weston at an air-to-surface and a bombing range at Sand Bay. There were also bombing ranges at Pawlett Hamms to the north of Bridgwater, and at Stert Flats near Burnham-on-Sea. Anti-aircraft ranges were also located near Weston at Brean, and a more distant one at Doniford near Watchet, and these were supported by aircraft from Weston Zoyland that were frequently seen operating from Weston Airport.

Some aircraft were attached to Weston that stayed short term, whilst others, like those from the Torpedo Development Unit that stayed at the airport from 1941 until 1956, were medium-term residents. The Technical Training Camp (RAF Locking) built during 1938, in the different guises of No.5 School of Technical Training and later No.1 Radio School stayed in being until 2002 and was the longest of Weston's military residents. These specialist schools, in turn, generated the need for various support units. Initially there was Locking's Station Flight and in the 1950s and '60s the Colerne Communications Squadron and Locking's Varsity Flight. As a by-product, the general need for pre-service military training units such as the Air Defence Cadet Corps, which quickly evolved into the Air Training Corps and the female equivalent, the Girls Venture Corps, would all provide the various services over the years with recruits from Weston. These cadet organisations, some of which are still in being, would in turn also generate the need for their own support units such as No.87/621 Gliding School which was at Weston from 1943 until 1993.

Early short-term visitors would be No.5 Air Observer and Navigation School (5 AONS) that opened at Weston in November 1939, No.16 Operational Training Unit that made a brief visit mid-1940, No.10 Elementary Flying Training School that moved in during September of that year, No.286 Anti-Aircraft Co-operation Squadron that visited in 1942 and a detachment of No.116 Anti-Aircraft Calibration Squadron that arrived in 1943. That year the airport was also used by No.10 Operational Training Unit with its Armstrong Whitworth Whitleys for emergency landing training, and between June 1944 and July 1945 No.3 Flying Instructors' School, based at Lulsgate Bottom, used Weston Airport as a relief landing ground for its Airspeed Oxfords and Miles Masters. There was also much aerial activity by the Luftwaffe, especially in the early years of the war when formations of bombers on their way to various targets in England and Wales, using Weston with its piers and the headlands of Brean Down and Sand Point as distinctive navigational aids, overflew for Cardiff, or a right-turn made, to fly up-channel for Bristol and the northern towns and cities. With all this air activity, it was inevitable that many friendly and enemy aircraft would be forced to come down in the locality, luckily more often than not on open ground, and those machines, if not mentioned in the relevant chapters, can be found listed in Chapter 5.

No. 5 Air Observer and Navigation School

By the time No.5 Civil Air Navigation School was formed at Weston on 2 September 1939, it had become apparent that due to the deteriorating situation with Germany there would be little civil work for it to do in the foreseeable future. Reflecting this, on 1 November, 'Civil' was dropped from the establishment's title and, still under the auspices of Western Airways, it became the No.5 Air Observer and Navigation School (5 AONS) with Neville Cumming as its commander. Equipped with twelve RAF Avro Anson Is that included N5312, L7956, N5252, N5132, N5313 L7955 and L7947, all of which had been converted into navigational trainers by Western Airways, a part of the modification being the cutting of a hole in the cabin roof to accept an astrodome, they were used to train navigators, mainly over the Bristol Channel and the Irish Sea. Trainees for the last course, which was to last five weeks, arrived in July 1940, and when completed, half went to Turnberry and the others went to the Bristol Flying School at Yatesbury. Amongst the instructors were Pilot Officers Cameron and Lewis, Flying Officer O'Grady and Sergeant Ironmonger. Another instructor was Edward Crundall who some years previously had flown Avros from Hutton Moor with the Cornwall Aviation Co. Ltd. The unit, absorbing No.3 AONS in June 1940, stayed at Weston until 22 August, when it commenced a move to South Africa with some twenty Ansons to become a part of the Empire Air Training Scheme. Shortly before departure on 19 August, whilst on a cross-country flight, N5132 piloted by Cameron flew into a tree at Littleton Lane, Wellow, 4 miles (6.4 km) south of Bath, and sadly the pilot and three crew members were killed.

No. 16 Operational Training Unit

In May 1940, three Handley Page Hampdens of No. 16 Operational Training Unit RAF Upper Heyford were transferred from their temporary base at Stormy Down near Porthcawl, South Wales, for a 6-week period to train air-gunners. Operating in pairs over the Bristol Channel, one towed a drogue and the other carried the trainee gunners. Dispersed in the north-east corner of the airport near the GWR railway line, the aircraft were flown most days, weather permitting, between 7 a.m. and 7 p.m. On one sortie on 26 May, two of the aircraft were lost in a collision, with L4156 crashing into the sea and L4158 ditching. Landings were usually over Locking Moor Road and this caused certain problems with passing traffic when sometimes there were near misses, and occasionally the towed drogue, released a fraction too early, landed in the road.

No. 10 Elementary Flying Training School

Following the departure of 5 AONS, No.10 Elementary Flying Training School (10 EFTS) moved on 7 September 1940 from Yatesbury with a reported sixty-four RAF DH Tiger Moths. Operated for the RAF by the Bristol Aeroplane Company, the school was commanded by Squadron Leader T. W. Campbell AFC, one of his instructors being Flight Lieutenant David Cubitt, recently a senior pilot with Western Airways. As well as aircraft, instructors and mechanics, the school also brought with it a wireless set and a couple of machine-guns, one of which was set up for airport defence on a hillock just outside the airport boundary behind Western Airways. Because of the limited hangar space available, many of the Moths were picketed out in the open, this always being a bit risky especially in the winter with strong westerly winds blowing in from the Bristol Channel. On the night of 12 November 1940 the inevitable happened during a hurricane-force storm when eleven of the school's machines were badly damaged, some being blown across Locking Moor Road, and two ending up against the Passenger Terminal building. When the move from Yatesbury was being considered, it had been recognised that Weston Airport would have difficulty in handling the extra ground and air activity and a search was made for a Relief Landing Ground (RLG). In due course a suitable site was found at Cornerpool Farm, which was on high ground some 12 miles (19 km) away to the east near the village of Lulsgate Bottom, and here a number of fields were requisitioned. With the removal of hedges and a certain amount of levelling the RLG was ready for dual training to commence on 28 September 1940.

So that Lulsgate Bottom (for a time known as RAF Broadfield Down but changed to avoid any confusion with Boscombe Down) could be rebuilt as a fighter station for 10 Group with taxi-ways, runways and hangars, it was closed on 10 June 1941, resulting in aerial and airport movements at Weston being dramatically increased. The Tiger Moths were considered to be a nuisance by other users of the airport and a source of irritation to the local barrage balloon unit that arriving in May, had to recover some of their envelopes each morning before flying training could commence. By mid-July, construction of the 1,000 yard (914 metres) concrete runway for Weston's shadow factories was well underway and Squadron Leader Campbell was forced to express his concern to the factory manager regarding disruption to the school's flying-training programme caused by the building work. Air exercises and practice forced landings were carried out over the moorland on the southern side of the Mendips and, as to be expected with the large number of training aircraft, there were quite a few incidents and accidents in that area. There were also a number at Weston Airport, mainly when the machines were at their most vulnerable, during landing and taxiing. 10 EFTS remained at the airport until the end of September, when areas of waterlogged grass, together with the previously mentioned problems and the need for more hangar space to be made available to Western Airways enforced its departure. The unit's remaining fifty-four aircraft, plus the staff and equipment, which included what had been until February the airport's only defensive armament, then departed for Stoke Orchard in Gloucestershire.

No. 286 Anti-Aircraft Co-operation Squadron

In the first part of the war the RAF, with the exception of the TDU, had used Weston Airport only as a base for training units, but on 10 October 1942 No. 286 Anti-Aircraft Co-operation Squadron moved in from Colerne. Formed from 10 Group AAC Flight at Filton in November 1941, the squadron until May 1945 provided targets for AA gunners around the West Country. It brought with it three Boulton Paul Defiants, a Miles Martinet, an Airspeed Oxford, and a Hawker Hurricane that belonged to its commanding officer 'Digger' Coburn, it having his personal codes 'DC' on the fuselage sides. Dispersed to the north-east corner of the airport, the local ATC cadets soon found they were able to persuade some of the pilots to take them on sorties in the Defiants, mainly up and down the Bristol Channel area. 286 stayed at Weston until April 1943 when it departed for Zeals near Wincanton. Returning to Weston in July, it stayed until 29 November when it moved again, this time to Weston Zoyland.

No. 116 Anti-Aircraft Calibration Squadron

Shortly after the departure of 286 Squadron, a detachment of twelve Airspeed Oxfords of No. 116 Anti-Aircraft Calibration Squadron arrived from Croydon and was dispersed behind Western Airways at the two Blister hangars. Its primary task was the calibration of predictors and anti-aircraft guns throughout the country, and during its stay would be supporting gun and radar sites in Wales and South-West England. With some fifty personnel, it was given a crew room in the old farm cottage just behind the Blister hangars and aircrew were billeted at RAF Locking. Ground crew, however, together with the unit's mascot, a black Labrador named 'Chips' were billeted in huts off Laney's Drove behind Western Airways. The type of flying performed by the unit was very boring, with accurate and steady speeds and heights having to be maintained, and to reduce the drudgery, every opportunity was taken to give the unit's ground crew and cadets from local ATC squadrons air-experience flying; this also applied to Chips who was also always keen to get airborne. Because the detachment was a non-operational unit, the loss of any squadron colleague was always deeply felt, and this was especially applicable during mid-July 1944. There had been a period of prolonged rain, and the all-timber aircraft had been parked in the open and were extremely damp. The remedy in these circumstances was to fly them for extended periods to dry out, but on 22 July Oxford EB724, sent up for such an airing, whilst over the town was seen in a near vertical dive. Its wing separated from the fuselage and the aircraft came down in a field close to the gasworks killing the pilot, Warrant Officer Macklin, a Canadian, and LAC Day the unit's tractor driver. The squadron is believed to have left Weston in November 1944.

Some Interesting Arrivals

With the Second World War over for some sixty-five years, and with no surviving log of wartime airport movements, nor reports in newspapers to survey, the task of providing a comprehensive narrative of military events at Weston Airport was a near impossible task. However, over the years snippets of information and the few diary notes made by aircraft spotters were noted, and information gleaned by studying the small number of surviving surreptitiously-taken photographs of visiting aircraft. The end product follows, which it is hoped will give a flavour of the activity around Weston Airport during that time.

On 8 April 1941, Westland's chief test pilot, Harald Penrose, on a test flight from Yeovil in a Whirlwind fighter experienced a loss of oil pressure in one of its underdeveloped Rolls-Royce Peregrine engines and a precautionary landing

In front of one of the Blister hangars, 116 Squadron's personnel and 'Chips' with one of its Oxfords (Via K. G. Turner)

was carried out at Weston Airport. The Whirlwind's existence had been a closely guarded secret in the early stages of the war and it was still on the 'restricted' list. Whirlwinds had been seen over Weston quite often on their way to the Sand Bay range, but this was one that could be inspected at close quarters. With its renowned high speed and unusual high-set tailplane, nose cannons and Fowler flaps and the possibility of a few words with the famous test pilot, its arrival was quite an event!

One of the most interesting arrivals did not in fact land at the airport but just to its north in a field behind the electricity company's premises. On 28 December 1941, Armstrong Whitworth Whitley Z9297 of the Overseas Aircraft Delivery Unit operating from RAF Honeybourne, piloted by Flight Lieutenant Ramsey, was on its way to Gibraltar with gold bullion, and to prevent the consignment falling into enemy hands had been instructed to ditch the Whitley if trouble was experienced outside territorial waters. Making its way down the Bristol Channel to the South-West Approaches, one engine unfortunately cut and it was decided to make a precautionary landing at Weston Airport. Approaching from over Worlebury Hill, the circuit was joined from an easterly direction and eyewitnesses reported that suddenly the aeroplane pitched down sharply as though it had hit a barrage-balloon cable and it rapidly descended, luckily in a semi-controlled fashion. The bomber caught fire almost immediately and eventually burnt out with just its tail unit remaining. However, the crew managed to escape without injury, the pilot later reporting that on selecting flaps-down the aircraft became uncontrollable, probably due, he thought, to the heavy cargo being incorrectly positioned or not secured sufficiently well. The gold was quickly recovered by personnel from RAF Locking and impounded at the camp for safekeeping.

Towards the end of July 1942 a Douglas C-47 named *Flying Sack* of the 18th Troop Carrier Squadron of the 64th Group, 51st Troop Carrier Wing USAAF became one of the first aircraft of the USAAF to land at Weston Airport. With 21-year-old Radio Operator Bill Cleland on board, the C-47's pilot, along with others, had been tasked to fly to Britain using the new northern ferry route and on the way drop off GI aircraft mechanics at various staging posts that were to shortly receive P-38 Lockheed Lightnings. The journey was uneventful until approaching Prestwick when severe weather was encountered and a precautionary landing made at an RAF Coastal Command station on the Isle of Lewis. Next day the weather had cleared and the C-47 flew on to Prestwick. Within a couple of hours of landing it was airborne again and heading for Weston Airport where the remaining mechanics disembarked. Then after beating-up the airport, it headed for Ramsbury near Hungerford where on 18 August it, with others, was assigned to the Eighth Army Air Force.

Further American visitors were to arrive, including a Bell P-39 Airacobra which had left its base at Atcham near Shrewsbury, the pilot looking for Newquay. His name, Lieutenant Jones, was in bold script on the side of the cockpit and he wasn't sure if Newquay was in Wales or Cornwall. Landing

Left: Air Gunner Staff Sergeant
Frank T. Lusic of B-17 Fortress
422954 'Meat Hound' that landed
at Weston in 1943 (USAAF)

Below: The C-46A Commando
with a group of Western Airways
inspectors during the winter of
1943 (Bob Cooke)

east to west, he had taxied to the Oldmixon Factory where after refuelling and having some discussion with the flight shed's superintendant and others, and expressing concern about taxiing and a take-off with 'a belly full of gas' (his drop tank), he was pointed in the direction of Portreath and was soon away. This aircraft, along with many other British and American aircraft including P-39s, from December 1942 through to the early months of 1943 were flown to North Africa with a sometimes hazardous crossing of the Bay of Biscay.

During 1943 and 1944, large formations of Boeing B-17 Fortresses and Consolidated B-24 Liberators of the USAAF were often seen returning from operations over western France, and during this period, due to fuel running low, a number of precautionary landings were made across the south-west counties. One such, B-17 229524 VK-K, adorned with nose art identifying it as *Meat Hound*, with tail markings of the 303rd Bomb Group, 358 Squadron, around September 1943, following a mission to Nantes, landed at Weston Airport. Although there were no obvious signs of battle damage, it is believed that the aircraft landed so that one or more casualties could be taken to Weston Hospital for emergency treatment, and until departing for its Molesworth, Huntingdon, base early the following morning, it was parked parallel to Locking Moor Road.

With the build-up to D-Day, units of the United States Army started to arrive in Weston. Initially B Battery of the 116th Anti-Aircraft Gun Battalion (Mobile) of the First US Army Coast Artillery Corps, it trained on the Promenade sighting its guns on various passing aircraft. It was probably this unit's activities that brought to the pre-war Sands Aerodrome on a day in December 1943 two US Air Force Cessna UC-78 Brass Hat twin-engine communications aircraft, that parked near the open-air swimming pool. Next day they were at Weston Airport beside Locking Moor Road and then they were gone.

In the winter of 1943 the airport was to be visited by a Curtiss-Wright C-46A Commando of the USAAF. This type was the largest and heaviest twin-engine aircraft to see operational use with the USAAF and for a short time was parked on the grass in front of the small hangar of Western Airways. With its two mighty 2000 hp Pratt & Whitney R-2800-51 piston radials, each driving massive 4-bladed 13 foot 6 inch (4 metre) propellers it grossed at 56,000 lb (25,455 kg) and had accommodation for a crew of four and fifty troops.

On 3 January 1944, two of a flight of eight B-24 Liberators of the USAAF 44th Bomber Group, 'The Eight Balls', returning from a raid on St Nazaire, and short of fuel landed at Weston Airport. Visibility had been poor during their mission and for support and guidance on the home journey the aircraft joined a group of B-17s heading for South-West England, but unfortunately they proved to be off course and headed up the Irish Sea. The B-24s, desperately short of fuel, turned to the east and, finding the Bristol Channel, began to look for airfields on the Pembrokeshire coast but with little success, two making wheels-up landings in fields whilst another, putting down at Talbenny, was wrecked when an engine was lost on the approach. The Liberator crews, who were fortunate to find Weston, were apparently unaware that they had been shadowed by at least two Focke-Wulf Fw 190s. Just as the B-24s completed their nose-to-tail landing run from the east, these fighter-bombers sweeping in low from the direction of the Mendips, and, judging by engine noise flying at very high speed, released what were believed to be AB 250 bomb containers. Landing close to the B-24s, because of low release height the hundreds of bomblets that were scattered weren't armed and were later safely recovered. The next day the aircraft departed for their base at Shipdham and the bomblet containers found their way to the local pig farmer who for many years put them to good use as feeding troughs.

Enemy Action

With RAF Locking, Weston Airport and Western Airways already in being and a shadow factory under construction, all within a mile or two (1.6 to 3.2 km) of Weston, the local populace considered they were vulnerable and faced the war with a certain amount of trepidation. It was therefore of no surprise when, following the German occupation of France in June 1940, the Luftwaffe started to show an interest in Weston. Until then, at night, aircraft were occasionally seen held by searchlight beams, but in daylight it was more often than not just lone aircraft passing over at altitude, probably on photo-reconnaissance missions capturing on film the latest developments at the local and distant military and industrial establishments. The German occupation of France also coincided with commencement of the delivery of parachute mines and attacks on shipping in the Bristol Channel.

1940

Probably the first time Westonians would have heard the distinctive sound of enemy aircraft was on the night of 19/20 June when two Heinkel He 111 bombers flew up the Bristol Channel towards targets at Filton and Portishead, but their bombs fell in the sea and mud off Battery Point, Portishead. However, the first alert was not to sound in Weston until shortly after midnight on the 26th, and the first brush with the enemy around the town came at 12.43 a.m. on the 30th when a bomb fell a few miles away at Weare and three fell at Wrington.

It was not until 4 July that the enemy was actually engaged over the town when in the mid-afternoon Supermarine Spitfires of 92 Squadron from Pembrey intercepted a Heinkel He 111P of 4/KG54 which subsequently crashed at Gillingham in Dorset. Between the 10th and 12th, bombs also fell on Congresbury, Redhill, Burtle, Huntspill, Mark, Edithmead, Bleadon and Edingworth. On the 18th, bombs fell at Bleadon, Mark and Cossington.

Bombs also fell on Burnham where two people were killed and a number of houses damaged, and at 2.17 a.m. a bomber held briefly in the searchlights over Wrington dived low, firing its machine-guns in an attempt to extinguish the light. Another Heinkel, this time an He 111 H4 minelayer of 1KG4 was attacked on the 26th by Pilot Officer J. R. Cock in a Hawker Hurricane of 87 Squadron, Exeter, over East Portishead Point and it crashed just inside the Devon county boundary at Longfield Farm, Smeatharpe, near Upottery. Bombs also fell near the Anchor Inn at Bleadon; landing on Air Ministry property (the top-secret Starfish Site). Initially there was to be a certain amount of confusion as to the organisation to deal with the event, which concerned unexploded bombs — the RAF, the Police or the Civil Defence! From this time on, enemy bombers flew over Weston most nights to targets in Bristol, Cardiff, Swansea, the Midlands, Manchester and Liverpool. But for the time being, bombs tended to be dropped in rural areas and this in itself was to cause a logistic problem associated with the speedy filling in of craters and their camouflage to prevent the enemy from being able to note navigational errors when studying aerial reconnaissance photographs.

On 2 August, leaflets reporting Hitler's 19 July speech in the Reichstag entitled 'Hitler's Last Appeal to Reason' were dropped on Berrow. Parachute mines continued to be delivered but not always to the right address. Some were blown inland where they detonated with huge explosions that made enormous craters, one on the 9th causing a 50-foot-deep (15 metres) crater at Middle

Wadham Street after the 4 January 1941 raid (P. Warrilow via A Kingsmill)

Lane Farm, Kingston Seymour. A further sortie on the 14th to attack Cardiff
Docks with Heinkel He 111Ps of 9/KG27 was intercepted in the late afternoon
over Glastonbury by Supermarine Spitfires of 92 Squadron, Pembrey, and
three of the raiders were shot down. One force-landed at Charterhouse near
Cheddar, another dived vertically into Toogood's Farm, near Puriton, and
the third came down in Bridgwater Bay. Two had fallen to the guns of Flight
Lieutenant Robert Stanford-Tuck who went on to become one of the most
successful fighter pilots, and by the year's end had destroyed eighteen enemy
aircraft. In the late afternoon a Junkers Ju 88 from 1/LG1 also dropped five
bombs, four exploding on the beach at Weston where the southern of the two
model-boating lakes was partly demolished. These were the first bombs to fall
in the borough. During this raid, Banwell, Burnham, Berrow, Congresbury and
Yatton also received bombs. On the 16th, just before midnight, bombs fell on
Brean, Locking and Hutton Woods, and one 500 lb (227 kg) bomb landed on
Wrington Road at Congresbury but didn't explode. One of the first George
Medals to be awarded went to Lieutenant Reynolds for his bravery in defusing
this bomb which was equipped with a new time-delayed fuse. Between the 20th
and 28th, bombs fell at Worle, Lympsham, Axbridge, Congresbury, Bleadon,
Weare and Wick St Lawrence.

The first substantial damage to residential property in Weston came at the
end of the month when, during the late evening of the 30th, just three bombs
from a force of 109 aircraft dispatched to raid various targets were dropped
onto Albert Quadrant and Landemann Circus, but fortunately there were no
serious casualties. The one landing on Albert Quadrant didn't explode, and was
the first to hit a house in Weston and for a time was exhibited in the nearby
Tivoli Cinema. During September, bombs dropped in previous raids that hadn't
exploded were discovered almost daily. On the night of 3 September a force of
twenty-one Heinkel He 111s belonging to KG55, with Avonmouth Docks its
main target, scattered some of its load onto Worle High Street. Three people
were killed and they became the first of Weston's many eventual fatalities. On the
night of the 4th, one of a force of some forty-seven bombers making for Bristol
and Avonmouth jettisoned its bombs onto Banwell where approximately 100
buildings were damaged, including the post office and telephone exchange and
seven people were killed and fifty injured. In addition, bombs were dropped by
other aircraft around Clevedon, Portishead, Loxton and Locking, and in the
sea off Weston. On the night of the 10th, bombs were dropped on Banwell,
Oldmixon, Hutton, Southwick and Mark. A raid on Cardiff just after midnight
on the 12th led to bombs again being misdirected and these fell in the mud
off Knightstone Causeway and at Greenwood Road, Worle, where there were
casualties and considerable damage.

The Bristol Aeroplane Company's Filton Works which had already been
attacked on a number of occasions by single aircraft and by small groups,
on the 25th was subjected to an intensive attack during daylight by a force
of fifty-eight Heinkel He 111s of 1, 2, 3 and 5/KG 55 with an escort of some

fifty Messerschmitt Bf 110s of ZG26. Seen by most of the Weston's population as it overflew the town at 11.38 a.m., the formation approached the target by turning north-east and flying along the coast, losing Heinkel He 111P G1+DN Nr 2126 of 5/KG 55 to the guns of 236 Battery, 76 Heavy Anti-Aircraft Regiment, Gordano, which crashed between Weston and Bristol on Racecourse Farm, Failand. Two days later on the 27th, Sergeant Mike Bush of 504 (County of Nottingham) Squadron on detachment to Filton to help defend Bristol's aircraft factories against a possible follow-up attack, due to low fuel, made a precautionary landing at Weston Airport in Hurricane N2669. He had been positioned near Exeter in anticipation of a raid on Westland at Yeovil, but the raid didn't materialise, although ten Messerschmitt Bf 110C fighter-bombers of Erpr Gr 210 supported by an escort of forty-two Messerschmitt Bf 110Ds of ZG26 headed for Parnalls of Yate which was producing Frazer-Nash gun turrets. Hangared overnight, the Hurricane departed from Weston the next day to rejoin the squadron at Filton that had successfully dispersed the Messerschmitts the previous day.

On the evening of 14 October a stick of twelve bombs from a Dornier Do 17 from 2/606, thought by its pilot to have been dropped on Avonmouth Docks, was actually despatched in a north-westerly direction across Weston's Ashcombe Park. One narrowly missed the Bristol Waterworks pumping station on Milton Road, but although not exploding it wrecked the water tank beneath the adjacent children's sailing pond that had been opened as recently as 30 September 1937. Incendiaries also fell close to the airport, and a property just under the woods at Leewood Road was hit. Early the following morning, an unsuccessful attempt was made by a Heinkel He 111 of 3/KG55, returning to France after an abortive raid on Filton, to bomb a goods train moving slowly through the cutting at Uphill; its other bombs fell on the Old Hutton Golf Course whilst Bleadon Hill and the Totterdown Lane area received oil bombs. Bombs had already been aimed at Yatton back in August but on 24 October, a lone Junkers Ju 88 dropped eight bombs which blew up the main Bristol — Exeter (Weston) line about half a mile (0.75 km) west of the railway station causing all trains to be diverted, and the bomber was seen from Weston as it flew southwards near Congresbury at low-level.

On 6 November bombs fell on Rooksbridge, Churchill and Brean Down. Congresbury received a number of bombs during the nights of 3 and 4 December but fortunately there were no serious casualties. However, an electricity sub-station was put out of action but was quickly repaired. Incendiaries also fell harmlessly to the east of Weston in fields at Puxton. Many bombs had similarly fallen harmlessly in the woods and fields around the town, with others falling in the sea off Berrow and Brean Down. On the 21st there was another incident in Weston when a Heinkel He 111 of 3/KG27, one of a strong force raiding Liverpool and Birkenhead, suffering engine problems dropped its four bombs near the Langford Road level-crossing causing damage to four properties and the utility services, but luckily no serious casualties resulted. During 1940, the town's air-raid sirens had sounded 387 times which gives some indication of the frequency of the perceived threat of attacks that fortunately for Westonians were mostly intended for other towns.

1941

At the beginning of January, flares were dropped over Worle, and during the night of the 2nd, incendiaries fell on Mark Moor and in fields around Bleadon; bombs also fell between Blagdon and Wrington.

Weston was to suffer its first sustained attack on the 4th. Starting at 9.55 p.m. and lasting for over three hours, a bomber force comprising of forty-two Heinkel He 111s from 1/KG 26 and 2KG 27, and twenty-five Junker Ju 88s from 3/KG 77, in two waves dropped an estimated twenty bombs and some 3,000 incendiaries onto various properties in and around the town. The attack began in Sand Bay when the Birmingham Convalescent Home was damaged and had to be evacuated. Then moving over Weston Woods to the town, in the Grove Park area, Grove Road, Glebe House, Grove Park House, Grove Park Concert Pavilion, Lovers Walk, St John's Church (east window), the Civil Defence Ambulance Depot No.1 in Wadham Street, Wadham Street Baptist Church and its Church House were damaged. Near the gasworks, Rectors Way was badly hit with many casualties; also hit was the corner of Mendip Road and Locking Road where Pang's fish and chip shop was destroyed. In the Whitecross Road area, bombs and incendiaries caused damage, with St Paul's Church being destroyed by fire and its Whitecross Hall damaged. Bournville Estate was particularly heavily hit with many houses in Argyle Avenue, Stonebridge Road, Downside Road, Bournville Road and Lonsdale Avenue being badly damaged or destroyed. Moseley Grove at Uphill was also hit and many bombs fell onto the sands and into the sea with one impacting in the dunes between the Sands Aerodrome and Weston Golf Course making a 30-foot-wide (9.1 metres) crater that was claimed by club members to be the 'Biggest Bunker in the World'. The raid, in which thirty-four were killed, eighty-five injured and 430 buildings damaged had been intended for Avonmouth Docks, but after the first wave had unloaded its bombs onto the docks, due to deteriorating weather the target moved south with Clevedon and Blagdon receiving incendiaries and bombs, and then it was Weston's turn, it receiving bombs from the further two waves of aircraft. Had it not been for the very effective Starfish Site on Bleadon Level which took hits from some fifty bombs and many incendiaries there would have been even more death and destruction. On the 17th, incendiaries were dropped on Locking, Wedmore, Mark and around Rooksbridge, and bombs fell on Congresbury but little damage resulted.

Around midday on 22 February, Heinkel He 111 H-5 1G+GM Nr 3247 of 4/KG27 was observed as it emerged from low cloud over the Mendips and then again seen very low over Weston Woods as it turned up-channel towards

In the Stonebridge area of the Bournville Estate after the 4 January 1941 raid (P. Warrilow via
A Kingsmill)

'The Worlds's Largest Bunker', 5 January 1941; behind can be seen Weston Golf Club's club
house and The Sanatorium (P. Warrilow via A. Kingsmill)

Clevedon. Its intended target was apparently the Parnall Aircraft Factory at Yate, and shortly after passing Clevedon the raider was spotted at the Portbury gun site, but its gunners only had time to open fire with a Lewis gun as it disappeared into the mist and cloud. The gun crew of B troop, 236 Battery, 76 Heavy Anti-Aircraft Regiment at Gordano heard the approaching aircraft and fortunately their 3.7 inch (9.4 cm) guns were loaded and set and they opened fire blind. At least one shell hit the bomber which then fouled a barrage-balloon cable and exploded on Portbury Mudflats, its pilot the only survivor. Between the 26 February and 1 March, bombs fell on Loxton and Banwell.

During the night of 3 March, it looked as though another raid was starting when a number of parachute flares illuminated Weston, but these were for navigation purposes as the bombers then headed for Cardiff and Avonmouth. Although the main raid was on Cardiff, bombs were also dropped on Banwell, Locking Moor, Winscombe, Sidcot and around Shute Shelf. During the night of the 16th, in an 8-hour raid on Bristol, ten bombs fell near Wrington and there were extensive fires on Blackdown where there was another Starfish Site.

On the night of 3/4 April, during raids on Bristol there were green flares over Knightstone and Heinkel He 111 H-5, 1H+ED Nr 3595 of 3/KG26 was intercepted over the outskirts of Weston by Flying Officer Edward D. Crew and Observer Sergeant Guthrie. Flying Filton-built Beaufighter IF R2252 of 604 Squadron based at Middle Wallop, after a short engagement the raider was hit, crashing on farmland at West Hewish. Two of the crew were killed and three parachuted to safety. During the raids, bombs also fell at Wrington and Southwick, and between the 9th and 11th, bombs fell on Sand Bay, Wick St Lawrence, Wrington and Langford. On the 12th, during another raid on Bristol, bombs were dropped in Woodspring Bay. Beaufighters were continuing to find targets over Somerset and on the night of 7 May a 604 Squadron machine from Middle Wallop, piloted by Squadron Leader John 'Cats Eyes' Cunningham with Observer Sergeant Jimmy Rawnsley, destroyed Heinkel He 111P-2, 1G+DR Nr 1639 of 7/KG27 bound for Liverpool. Crashing at Weston Zoyland near Bridgwater, it became a well-reported event since its interception had been witnessed from afar by King George VI during a visit to the Ground Control Interception Station at Sopley near Bournemouth. Closer to Weston, Heinkel He 111P-2, 1G+NA Nr 1647 of KG27 also heading for Merseyside was shot down by a Beaufighter of 600 Squadron, Colerne, piloted by Flying Officer John Howden with Observer Sergeant Fielding, it crashing a mile (1.6 km) south-west of Wrington at Stock Lane near Langford House (now the School of Veterinary Science). The crew of five parachuted to safety and the aircraft was completely burnt out. On the 19th, there were flares over Uphill, Berrow and Brean, and bombs fell around Bleadon. To round off the month, on the 31st a bomb landed on Weston's Promenade breaking windows and setting fire to a gas main. There was an unexpected arrival on 24 July when following a sortie to Birkenhead, Junkers Ju 88A-5 4D+DL Nr 3457 of 3/KG30 piloted by Uffz Wolfgang Hosie, heading back to its French base at

Lanvéoc in misty conditions was the victim of poor navigation, compounded by a British radio beacon at Lympsham working on the same frequency as the German beacon at Audierne. Believing they had crossed the English Channel, after flying past Weston, Broadfield Down (Lulsgate Bottom) which was still being reconstructed for Fighter Command was spotted and a landing made on the partially-completed runway. Immediately confronted by men of the King's Own Royal Regiment, the crew was detained and a guard placed on the aircraft, and quite a few 10 EFTS pilots flew their Tiger Moths from Weston to their former RLG to view the prize. Shortly afterwards, the Junkers was flown to Farnborough where as EE205 it was flown by the RAE.

Between the 7th and 10th of October, parachute mines were dropped around Wedmore, luckily without exploding. Mine laying continued through the year, and on the 28th, mine-laying Junkers Ju 88A-4 4D+MR Nr 1436 of 7/KG30 crashed at Wembdon near Bridgwater, following an attack by Flight Lieutenant Selway in a Beaufighter of 604 Squadron. In November there were reports of up to twenty-four incidents in the Channel area with a number of them being parachute mines falling on land rather than into the sea. Between the 27th and the 30th, unexploded parachute mines were found on Berrow Sands and near Lympsham Church. Others exploded high up in the Mendips and some came down in Woodspring Bay. On the night of the 24 November, two mines had been dropped in Weston Bay, one exploded between the Grand Pier and Knightstone Harbour making doors and windows rattle and minor damage was caused to some thirty-seven properties. The other mine was recovered in the bay some 500 yards (457 metres) from the Trans-Atlantic Cable pole. As recently as April 2008, a 2,200 lb (1,000 kg) LMB magnetic parachute mine was washed up on Stert Island where it was blown up by a Royal Navy Bomb Disposal Unit. Also witnessed from Weston around that time were some of the devastating attacks on towns and cities on the Welsh coast only some 12 miles (19 km) distant. The sounds of exploding bombs and gunfire could be clearly heard and the flashes and bursts in the sky from both heavy AA gunfire and rockets from the Z Sites seen above the smoke and fire. During 1941, the town's air-raid sirens had sounded ninety-eight times, the last being on the 28 November.

1942

The first air-raid warning of the year was on 24 March and no incidents were reported. Weston's turn came again on two consecutive clear moonlit nights in June when in the early hours of Sunday 28th and the early hours of Monday 29th it suffered what would be its worst attacks of the war. During each, which was carried out by a mixture of some fifty Dornier Do 217s and Junkers Ju 88s from units KG2, KG6, KG100, 7/Kfg100 and Kfg106, the second at low level, an estimated 11,000 incendiaries and ninety-seven

The scene on Weston Sands 14 April 1942 as munition-workers witness demonstrations by the Army of their products. An Army Co-operation Tomahawk participated in the display as did the Spitfire Vbs of a Polish squadron seen flying overhead that fired at an off-shore target. The newly rebuilt wall of the model boating lake damaged by bombs on 14 August 1940 is very noticeable (Mac Hawkins Collection)

The devastated Lances Corner after the 28 June 1942 raid. In the far distance, Christ Church
Spire that in May 1938 was insured against possible damage caused by low-flying aircraft
(P. Warrilow via A. Kingsmill)

The Tivoli Cinema destroyed 28 June 1942. The façade that was all that remained of the cinema,
for safety reasons within a day or two was also reduced to rubble (Mac Hawkins Collection)

The extensive damage caused to Prospect Place on 29 June 1942 (P. Warrilow via A. Kingsmill)

All that remained of the Town's Railway Goods Station, 29 June 1942 (P. Warrilow via A. Kingsmill)

bombs were dropped onto the town centre and surrounding areas. This was to result in 102 civilians being killed, 400 injured and 3,500 houses destroyed or damaged. Either by accident or design, the Luftwaffe had chosen a part of the Midland's Wakes Week for these raids, and although they had been warned not to travel, many of the casualties had been holidaymakers who shouldn't have been in Weston.

On the first raid, amongst the properties damaged and destroyed were ones in Grove Road, Grove Park Road, Queens Road, All Saints Road, South Parade, The Boulevard, the High Street, Meadow Street, The Drive, Hazeldene Road, the Milton area, the corner of Moorland Road and Devonshire Road, Sunnyside Road and Stradling Avenue. Some of the notable buildings destroyed or damaged in the raid were the Tivoli Cinema, Douglas Maurice Stores, the London Hotel, the Boulevard Congregational church, the Assembly Rooms, Lances Corner with Lance & Lance the local Department Store, Marks & Spencer (M & S) and other High Street stores, Wrights Printing Works on the corner of West Street, Thos. Adams, the Number Ninety Pub, the Rugby Ground's Grandstand, Moorland Sanitary Steam Laundry, Etonhurst School, Uphill's St Nicholas Church, the New Inn at Worle and the Birmingham Convalescent Home at Kewstoke. One seafront building to narrowly escape being damaged was the Guards Armoured Division School where an unexploded bomb was found.

During the second raid, the Beach Road, the Royal Parade, the Marine Parade, Oxford Street, Regent Street, the High Street, Waterloo Street, Orchard Street, Prospect Place, Winscombe Road, Longton Grove Road, Southside, Victoria Quadrant, Worthy Place, St Paul's Road, Malvern Road, Selworthy Road in the Bournville Estate, and parts of Hutton were hit. Amongst the more notable buildings destroyed or damaged in this raid were the first-aid post at the Swimming Pool, Pruens Garage in Oxford Street, Bournville School and five of the six road-over rail bridges in the town were left with craters around them. Weston's Brunel railway terminus then being used as a goods station together with many other railway properties that included the East Signal Box were also badly hit.

The numbers of military personnel killed and injured during the raids was also very high, amongst them were some ten RAF airmen belonging to the No. 14 Recruiting Centre located at the Beach Hotel in Regent Street, who were killed as they ran for slit trenches located along the sea wall near the Swimming Pool. Some bombs didn't explode and were to cause many problems for some time afterwards. Following the raids, to give resolve to the rescue services and those that had been personally involved, on 15 July, the Duke of Kent visited the town and toured the worst affected areas. To some people the two raids appeared to be a response by the German High Command to the publicity given to a display held on the sands on 14 April that gave munitions factory workers in the West an idea of the capability of the aircraft and weapons that they were producing. The event, considered to have been an impressive success, was reported in one national newspaper as a 'Holiday Invasion in Town Where Nobody Seems to Care' and showed thousands watching Curtis Tomahawks swooping in low over the beach and the Army firing its Bofors, anti-tank and other weapons. However, on reflection the response to that event would have been more appropriate if the bombers had attempted to wreck the Oldmixon Factory. On balance it was probable that the attacks were a part of the so-called Baedeker reprisal raids for the Allied raids on German cities in which Hitler had ordered that towns and cities featuring in the pre-war Baedeker tourist guide be heavily hit, although it is believed that Weston did not in fact feature in the guide.

Such was the importance of these attacks on Weston to the German High Command, that Radio Berlin featured them in its Monday-morning broadcast, announcing that heavy damage had been caused to military installations and munitions factories, which of course was blatantly untrue. What was in fact true was the report that all aircraft had returned safely to base and that daylight air reconnaissance had shown Weston to be under a pall of thick black smoke with fires still raging. This statement was also not strictly true as by midday on the 29th, all fires had been put out or damped down and it was thought that sea mist drifting across the town when the enemy reconnaissance aircraft arrived overhead was mistaken for smoke. Another radio report, this time from Calais in English on the following Thursday, reported that, resulting from the raids, all rail traffic from the town was still disabled.

On 28 August at 9.30 a.m. Bristol suffered a devastating daylight attack caused by a single high-altitude Junkers Ju 86R from Beauvais piloted by Feldwebel Horst Gotz, who had participated in many operations over Britain during the Blitz. He had crossed St Albans Head at 39,000 feet (12,000 metres) on course for Bristol, too high for accurate anti-aircraft fire to be effective, and dropped a 250 kg (550 lb) bomb onto the busy thoroughfare of Broad Weir, a street near the city centre that was being used as a temporary bus terminus, wrecking three buses, and killing forty-eight and injuring more than fifty people. Following the attack, Gotz headed back towards North-West France along the North Somerset coast where his presence was reported by Oldmixon Factory's Raid Spotters perched on the water tower. Two Westland Whirlwinds were reported to have given chase but could manage no more than 31,000 feet (9,000 metres) in their attempt to intercept the high-flying raider. Due principally to the machine's high-aspect ratio wings and relying on the limited capability of the optics then available to the Raid Spotters, and being unfamiliar with the latest high-altitude pressurised cabin versions of the obsolete Junkers, the spotters (one of them a co-author of this book) together with others in the locality incorrectly registered it as a Heinkel He 177. On 30 November the last siren of the year, No. 513, was sounded.

1943

On 12 March, the Starfish Site on Bleadon Level was bombed and in the early hours of 18 May 1943, two Dornier Do 217E-4, one from 2/KG2 and the other from 3/KG2, a part of a force attacking Cardiff, collided over the Bristol Channel, with both coming down on the mud of Woodspring Bay. Only one crew member survived and he managed to swim ashore at Clevedon. Other than these incidents, there was little enemy activity during the year with only seventeen siren warnings being given.

1944

Weston's last raid of the war was on the night of 27 March. Some 112 German aircraft had been plotted over Southern England and at Weston conditions were clear, but thick low-lying mist was being driven in from the sea. When bombers did arrive over the town, they dropped a number of large incendiaries, one canister coming down on Weston Airport where an Airspeed Oxford was damaged by splinters, but most landed in the vicinity of the Bournville Estate. Bungalows along the Oldmixon Road that led to Hutton were also hit by a bomb and four killed; many bombs also landed around Weston in gardens and on railway embankments and adjoining rail/road bridges, where, due to the soft earth, they luckily failed to explode. Hedges over a wide area were liberally sprinkled with German 'Window' anti-radar foil and there were a number of unexploded bombs and craters next to the A370 beside the Bleadon Hill Road junction. Only two houses were set alight in the town itself, one being in Albert Road adjacent to Ellenborough Park which was crammed full with US Army vehicles and equipment amassed for the forthcoming D-Day.

Except for these incidents, little damage was caused. The misty conditions had the unfortunate effect of blanketing and muffling the sound of the aircraft, and Weston's AA gunners had to fire blind. However, some hits were claimed on a Junkers Ju 88. Within seven minutes of the raid starting, RAF night-fighters had arrived on the scene and chased off the bombers, and their remaining bombs were jettisoned between Weston and Highbridge with the Starfish Site on Bleadon Level attracting a number of them. The bomber hit by AA fire was Ju 88A-4 B3+UA Nr 141211 of KG54; three of the crew bailed out and the aircraft crashed just before midnight on a turf pit on Tadham Moor, Wedmore. That night the Luftwaffe lost a total of thirteen aircraft, the three crashing in Somerset being a Junkers Ju 188E-1 of 5/KG2, a Junkers Ju 88A-4 of 2/KG5 and a Junkers Ju 88A-14 of 3/KG54; with two others coming down in Devon and Dorset.

In the early months of the year, German raids across the West-Country were tailing off in frequency and intensity with sporadic attacks continuing until May. In April, the Luftwaffe claimed to have attacked Bristol with 117 aircraft, but whilst thirty-five aircraft were reported over the West-Country, no bombs fell in the city. There was further enemy activity over Somerset on 15 May and it proved to be the county's last raid of the war. It was also the last time that German aircraft were shot down over Somerset with a Dornier Do 217K of 7/KG2 falling near Yeovilton and a Junkers Ju 188A-2 of 2/KG6 crashing in the grounds of Inwood House, Henstridge.

Weston had its last air-raid siren of the war, its 536th, on 13 June at 5.10 a.m. There was no enemy activity in the area but the date was notable, it being the day when the first four VI Doodle Bugs fell in South-East England. When there was time to tot-up the totals of ordnance dropped on the Weston area, it was believed that some 343 high-explosive bombs (149 of which didn't explode), 31,500 incendiaries, a number of oil bombs and twelve magnetic parachute mines had been dropped and 8,447 buildings in the Borough of Weston damaged or destroyed. On the plus side, at least nine enemy aircraft had been downed within 12 miles (19 km) of the town.

Royal Air Force Locking

The RAF Technical Training Camp (Locking) built to the east of Weston during 1938 soon took on the mantle of No.5 School of Technical Training (5 SoTT), a part of No.24 (Training) Group Halton. Unlike most RAF camps there would be no facilities for flying aeroplanes, this having to be done from Weston Airport about a mile (1.6 km) down the A371. However, the school would need ground instructional aircraft to provide the necessary hands-on training, and these were to be brought in, usually on Queen Marys, although still-airworthy machines would be flown into the airport and then towed through the north-east gateway onto the road and thence to the camp. Large by any standards, the camp cost at least £570,000 to build and comprised many timber huts, four spacious workshops, four Bellman hangars and a number of ancillary buildings, sufficient in fact to accommodate and train 4,500 RAF and Fleet Air Arm personnel in trades as diverse as Flight Mechanic Airframes or Engines, Rigger, Fabric Worker and Parachute Packer. Soon other trades would be catered for, such as Carpenter, Boat Builder, Fitter Marine, Flight Engineer, Navigator, Light Anti-Aircraft Gunner, Field Engineer and Cook. Courses would usually be of 8-months duration and it would not be long before there were more than 6,000 trainees on daily parade rather than the planned 4,500, with many of the overflow billeted in bell tents pitched on the large areas of grass.

On 2 January 1939, the camp's first Commanding Officer, Group Captain J. McCrea and a skeleton staff of seven officers formally opened the establishment in readiness for arrival of the first intake of 1,000 trainees. These young men, most having come on two special trains from RAF Hendon, arrived at Milton Halt during the first weekend of March and were marched along Locking

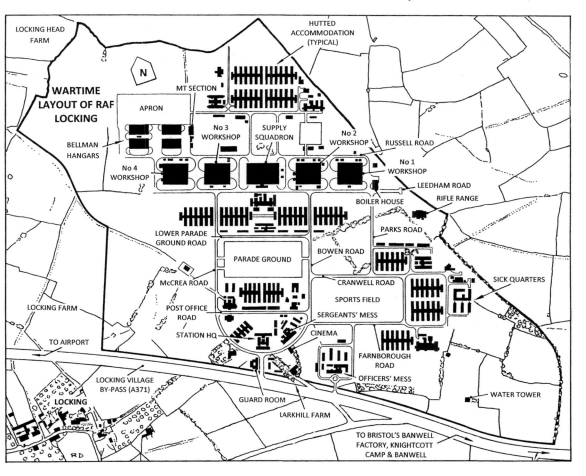

The wartime layout of RAF Locking (R. Dudley)

Moor Road and past the airport to their new home. On arrival they were probably surprised, and no doubt somewhat relieved, to find that work was still in progress on the workshops and parade ground. The first aircraft to be delivered was a Westland Wapiti, closely followed by three DH60M Moths and the Vickers Vespa VII K3588 that on 16 September 1932 had gained the world altitude record of 43,976 feet (13,403 metres). Another machine delivered was a Saro Cloud that had been towed to the camp from the airport. The machines allocated were either prototypes or early production models that had been retired after completing their allotted development tasks or damaged in service and beyond economical repair. During the war years numbers and variety of aircraft grew so that soon there existed a good cross section of machines then in RAF and FAA service. Early on there were at least four DH 93 Dons, three Fairey Battles, twelve Hawker Demons, five Fairey IIIFs, three Gloster Gauntlets, fourteen Fairey Gordons, seven Hawker Harts, one Hawker Hector, three Hawker Hinds, fourteen DH 60 Moths, one Fairey Seafox, one Blackburn Shark II, two Supermarine Spitfire Is, four Avro Tutors, a Supermarine Walrus and a Westland Wallace. There were also two DH Puss Moths, G-ABNZ and G-ABPB, the latter having previously been owned by Norman Edgar of Western Airways. As time went on some machines were replaced by later or more relevant types including Bristol Blenheims, a Blackburn Botha, a Westland Lysander and DH Tiger Moths, Airspeed Oxfords and Avro Ansons, three of the latter being Mk 1s, K6304, K8822 and K6155. Many aircraft were destined to be left in various stages of disassembly in the workshops, whilst the others remained fully rigged so that instruction could be given to Flight Mechanics and Flight Engineers in setting up procedures, ground running and taxiing techniques. In addition to obtaining the necessary trade skills, the flight engineers also received parachute training using towers, and air-to-air gunnery practice in a dome trainer. These buildings were located at a small satellite that was almost opposite the camp on the other side of the A371 just to the east of Bristol's Banwell Shadow Factory. Known as Knightcott Camp, towards the war's end it was given over to housing girls of the Polish WAAF and, after the war, some 200 German POWs. These days the group of buildings is known as the Knightcott Industrial Estate, and is cut off from its original access by the M5 motorway.

Censorship that had been in force since the outbreak of war ceased at the beginning of September 1945 and, only a few days later on the 15th, Battle of Britain Day, which was the fifth anniversary of the greatest victory scored by Fighter Command over the Luftwaffe in September 1940, the public having been advised to leave cameras at home, was allowed to look inside the perimeter fence of RAF Locking for the first time. Along with another eighty-nine RAF stations, Locking was 'at home' for inspection and visitors were able to see displays covering the training courses then in being. In the open they saw many aircraft, amongst them a Chance Vought Corsair II being run-up and having its wings alternately spread and folded. It had a jury-seat rigged up outside the cockpit in the slipstream where initially the pupil sat taking in the various checks and procedures from the instructor, and then, once sufficient experience had been gained, they swapped seats. Bristol Beaufighters and Blenheims, Airspeed Oxfords, Grumman Avengers and Hellcats, Fairey Fireflys and two Handley Page Halifax heavy bombers were also on display. In the workshops there were many RAF and FAA machines, including Corsairs and Fairey Barracudas. Also, in one hangar was an early simulator; known as a Synthetic Control Trainer it had been produced from a damaged bomber and introduced into Locking's flight engineer training programme in August/ September 1945.

Commemorating the sixth anniversary of the Battle of Britain, observed during the period 9 to 15 September 1946, the officer commanding RAF Locking, Group Captain R. J. M. de St Leger, made available for public display on the M & S bomb site in Weston, a fine selection of the school's smaller aircraft.

Chosen were a Gloster Meteor jet fighter, Hawker Hurricane, Miles Martinet and an AOP Auster. These, together with a collection of ASR and aircrew safety equipment, gave the town its own version of the large RAF exhibition then being staged in London on Horse Guards Parade. The exhibition was very popular with mothers who left their offspring in the enclosure whilst they shopped (one child was noted to have been there for three hours!). Allowed to climb over the aircraft, the youngsters were given access to the cockpits and had great delight in being pretend pilots. One boy even managed to select the correct combination of switches and levers in the Meteor that jettisoned some 30 gallons (136 litres) of fuel over the ground.

On Saturday the 14th, the camp itself was opened for inspection again and most of the aeroplanes from the previous year could still be seen, but now there were also DH Mosquitos, Hawker Typhoons and Hurricane IICs, a Consolidated Catalina being broken up and Avro Lancaster PD418 recently of 467 Squadron. In the hangars and workshops were Hawker Typhoons and Tempests and a number of Gloster Meteors. At that time, Locking had on its strength Meteor F1s EE225 delivered in March 1945, DG202/G, the first prototype that had spent four busy years of testing and F1 EE228, both delivered in February 1946. That year the Victory fly-past over London was intended to be extended to encompass the southern counties of England, the route taking in Selsey, Beachy Head, Portsmouth, Southampton, the Isle of Wight, Bournemouth, Weymouth, Exeter, Weston-super-Mare, Bristol and Salisbury. Weston, however, would only see the multi-engine types as single-engine machines with their limited range would be forced to break off at Bournemouth, but due to deteriorating weather, the flying was unfortunately cancelled. Other Meteors were soon to arrive, DG208, the seventh prototype, was delivered in November 1946, F3 EE391 in July 1948, the first F2 prototype DG207 in November 1948 and F3s EE493 in Ocober 1948 and EE420 in May 1952.

RAF Locking survived the early post-war cutbacks, and by May 1947, when boy entrant training started again, the total number of trainees that had passed through the gates was a staggering 83,110. Of these, 74,700 had been airmen, 2,800 airwomen and 5,610 naval ratings. As a prelude to that year's Battle of Britain commemorations, an RAF mobile exhibition was set up on the sands and many prospective boy recruits were drawn inside by the attraction of seeing a sectioned Rolls-Royce Derwent jet engine and a GEE navigation aid. In September, as in previous years, Locking opened, and again some new aircraft were to be seen. Included were Avro Lancaster NG340 that at one time had been on the strength of 617 (Dam Busters) Squadron and the last of some sixteen Spitfires held by the school Mk XIVC RM694 from the Central Fighter Establishment. A Spitfire of 501 Squadron, based at Filton, flown by a Battle of Britain pilot, gave a thrilling aerobatic display and it was said that this particular aircraft had featured in the film *The First of the Few* about the Spitfire's designer, R. J. Mitchell. There was also a radio station where visitors could communicate with the crew of an ATDU Avro Lincoln flying low overhead.

In 1948, it was back to the High Street M & S bomb site, when from 13 to 19 September, a Gloster Meteor F3 and various German and British jet engines could be inspected. The previous week, the site had been visited by some 30,000 people to view Field Marshal Hermann Goering's bullet-proof car. On Saturday the 18th, Locking also opened, but aircraft were now few and far between, a DH Mosquito and a partly dismantled Lancaster being the only ones in the open. In 1949, the Beach Lawns were used again, this time for a June RAF recruiting drive called 'The Man Takes Wings'. At Locking in September, the public could see a Gloster Meteor, a Hawker Tempest and a Lancaster being ground run, whilst in the air a Supermarine Spitfire was again demonstrated, as was a Meteor and a target-towing Bristol Beaufighter TT 10 that dropped its drogue in front of spectators on the parade ground. Aircraft overflying Weston that year were RAF Avro Lincolns and Boeing B-50 Super Fortresses of the USAF. The following year Short Sunderlands were to feature.

In the early post-war years RAF requirements were rapidly changing to meet the need to strengthen training in radio and radar. One consequence of this policy was Locking Camp being given over to the training of airmen to use and maintain the large range of radar and ground- and air-communications equipment then coming into service. As a result, the aircraft and equipment associated with 5 SoTT was withdrawn and the school closed on 15 May 1950. Then on 25 May the station was transferred to 27 Group Training Command, and in October a detachment from No.1 Radio School Cranwell (1 RS) which brought its name, equipment and new commanding officer, Group Captain H. A. Evans-Evans with it, moved in. This was followed on 1 December 1952 by the apprentice element of the school, some 600 boys that had stayed at Cranwell also relocating to Locking, now commanded by Group Captain A. T. Monks. The school had been at Cranwell since 1929 and until 1943 was known as the Electrical and Wireless School. Before 1929 it had been at RAF Flowerdown, near Winchester. Ground-instructional aircraft were still needed for the new duties but this time the emphasis would be on antenna and oscilloscopes rather than engines and mechanical systems. Airframes initially allocated for training were a Meteor, two Lincolns equipped with H2S and a night-fighter Mosquito and night-fighter DH Venom NF 2 prototype WP227, both equipped with Airborne Interception Radar.

Battle of Britain commemorations in 1951 were once again on the Beach Lawns, and featured three Gloster Meteors ranged around a marquee containing radar equipment and a radio station. Here members of the public could communicate with RAF Locking, or, more interestingly, with the crew of an Avro Anson that frequently flew low overhead. Unfortunately, during the week, Weston suffered from the usual strong winds and, to prevent damage occurring, the Meteors had to be hurriedly faced into the wind. Other displays were to follow. In 1952, two Hawker Tempest Vs positioned side by side with their noses pointing out to sea greeted passers-by who could also see an impressive selection of RAF equipment and model aeroplanes. Battle of Britain Week continued to be celebrated, but in 1953, at Locking it was a rather low-key affair, with the weather having grounded all but those aircraft based at Weston which managed to complete a limited flying display.

The 1955 celebrations were on Saturday 17 September when between 2 p.m. and 6 p.m. Locking was one of forty-seven stations opened to the public. This time the weather was fine and the RAF had laid on quite a reasonable flying display. On the previous day Percival Provost T I WV568 from RAF Ternhill and Gloster Meteor F 8 WK942 from RAF Waterbeach had flown into Weston Airport ready for Saturday's activities and Locking's own DH Chipmunk WB721 had tested radio-communications with a small transmitter set up at the camp. Early on the Saturday, the Army Air Corps at Middle Wallop sent over to Weston Airport Auster T 7 WE592, and at 10.20 a.m. Lieutenant Duddridge took it on the short hop to Locking, it landing on a specially mown strip on the sports field. This could well have been the first powered fixed-wing aircraft to land at the camp. The flying display proper began after lunch with Flying Officer Hubbard going through a thrilling aerobatic routine in the Provost, then Flight Lieutenant Boult in the Meteor carried out mock attacks on a Bofors gun emplacement manned by the RAF Regiment, and then he finally went through a high-speed aerobatic routine. Followed by Squadron Leader Francis flying the Chipmunk overhead in a speed- and height-judging competition, it was joined by a Bristol University Air Squadron North American Harvard in an aerobatic display. Finally a Bristol Sycamore dispatched from the Oldmixon Factory showed what a helicopter could do. Interspaced with the above, Lieutenant Duddridge gave demonstrations of short-field take-offs and landings that culminated in a demonstration of supply-dropping by parachute. The annual fly-past was by small formations of Short Sunderlands, DH Vampires, English Electric Canberras, Meteors and Vickers Valettas of the RAF and by Republic F-84F Thunderflashes of the USAAF.

Battle of Britain Days at Locking continued until 1971 when they were replaced by the Flowerdown Fair. Named after the original wireless school, they revolved around the parade ground with no access to the workshops. However, there was still a flying display, mainly by RAF aircraft and the attendance of an RAF recruiting stand and the ATC. At the final fair in 1996, there was the usual low-level air display by RAF jet and turboprop aircraft, and on the ground one could climb into the forward fuselage of a Nimrod, actually DH Comet IV G-ALYN suitably modified and used by the RAF as a recruiting aid.

The instructional aircraft at Locking continued to be replaced by more modern types and, in 1957, DH Venom NF 3 WX801 from 141 Squadron, Gloster Javelin FAW I XA564 from Filton, Hawker Hunter F I WT616, an engine-trials aircraft from the A&AEE, and the first production Hunter F I WT555,

Locking's last Lancaster during the 'At Home' 18 September 1948 (*Weston Mercury* via J. Bailey)

a handling-trials aircraft also from the A&AEE were delivered. However, in 1958, due to space constraints at Locking, these aircraft were towed along the A371 to occupy part of the Hutton Moor Flight Shed. EMI of Wells, behind a dividing canvas screen, would be the other occupant. Since the departure of the ATDU in 1956, the hangar had been used by Western Airways for the storage of Bristol Freighters, by Bristol for the storage of redundant Bristol Type 173 tandem-rotor helicopters, and, for a short time, it was the temporary home for gliders of 621 Gliding School. Over the years, other RAF aircraft would be delivered and parked outside on the hangar apron. These were English Electric Canberra B 2 WD936 from the Station Flight at RAF Khormaksar delivered 31 October 1958, Vickers Valetta C I WD171 that had served with the Royal Radar Establishment and was delivered 13 June 1960, and Avro Shackleton MR I VP289 from the MOTU Kinloss, it flying in on 6 September 1961. Also arriving in 1961 was Handley Page Victor B I XA919, the fifth production machine. Many onlookers gathered on 16 May to watch the landing, which turned out to be uneventful, with Squadron Leader Jack Cook making three practice approaches before touching down and using braking parachute and wheel-brakes. Much to the surprise, and perhaps a little to the disappointment of some onlookers, only two-thirds of the runway was used. It was discovered later that the squadron leader had indeed made full-use of the available runway, for the rear pair of wheels of each bogie had been placed on the grass several feet short of its threshold, the indentations being evident for some weeks.

The last instructional airframe to arrive was Javelin FAW 5 XA699 delivered 14 February 1964 from 151 Squadron, and it and the others were to remain at Hutton Moor until EMI needed more space and greater security for its activities. The Shackleton, Javelin and Victor were then moved to the Oldmixon end of the airport and here a team from the MU at Bicester removed the Victor's tailplane and fin, for it was to occupy Shop 3 which, although devoid of helicopters, was not able to take the fully rigged bomber. With insufficient room, the Shackleton had to remain on the apron outside. When the ground-instructional aircraft were no longer needed by No.1 Radio School, Hunter WT616 and the Valetta were relegated to fire practice duties. Javelin XA564 and the other Hunter were moved to the Aerospace Museum at RAF Cosford where they joined Meteor DG202/ G which had found its way there some years before via Yatesbury, whilst the Canberra was struck off charge on 28 October 1963 and the Shackleton in April 1966. The Victor was dismantled in September 1966 and sections returned to its Radlett birthplace for use in structural test rigs. In addition to turning out skilled men and women to maintain the wide range of communication equipment and radars, RAF Locking, from 1976, was also involved in the training of personnel to service and maintain flight simulators.

With instructional machines gone, the only ones left on the school's strength were the gate-guardians. Spitfire LF IXe MK356 had arrived in 1961 and then appeared in a non-flying role in the 1968 epic film *Battle of Britain*, and in

Some of No.1 Radio School's aircraft parked on the apron outside the Hutton Moor Flight Shed in the late 1950s. They comprise: Canberra B 2 WD936, Valetta C I VL276, Javelin FAW I XA564 and Hunter F I WT616 (R. Dudley)

A later arrival, Shackleton MR I VP289, outside Hutton Moor Flight Shed on 8 March 1964 (R. Dudley)

All-white Victor B I XA919 about to touch-down on 16 May 1961 (Robbie via R. Dudley)

September 1966 target-towing Meteor T 7 WL360 from 229 OCU Chivenor was brought in. In early May 1970, it was joined by Spitfire F21 LA198 which had also featured in the *Battle of Britain* and, in an earlier life, been on the strength of the Whitney Straight-run No.3/4 CAACU at Exeter. It was replaced in April 1974 by Canberra T4 WH840, and it in turn by Locking's last aeroplane Folland Gnat T I XM708, which arrived in October 1986 and was withdrawn in 1996.

Locking's Station Flight

DH Puss Moth X9400 (ex-G-ABLB), taken on charge by the RAF on 5 April 1940, was to form the foundation of Locking's Station Flight that was to later use a Miles Magister, two Percival Proctors and an Oxford. RAF Halton's Station Flight also provided aircraft from time to time; in the mid-to late 1940s these were a Percival Proctor coded THA and DH Dominie NR739 coded THA H. Many aircraft from other air stations brought in visitors to RAF Locking whilst others were brought in as required to provide air-experience flying for the station's trainees and ATC cadets at annual camp, a long-standing resident being DH Chipmunk WB721. Hangared in the Hutton Moor Flight Shed alongside the ATDU Lincolns, it was frequently airborne in the summer months, being flown exclusively by officers, who over several years included: Messrs Pressley, Morgan, Bobart, Thomas, Robinson, Linnard, Muggridge, Hobbs, Hooper and Francis.

RAF Colerne's Communication Squadron

With the change over to a radio school in 1950, requirements changed and aircraft such as Airspeed Oxfords, Handley Page (Miles) Marathons, Avro Ansons and Vickers Valettas and Varsities equipped as radio/navigation trainers were brought into Weston Airport on an as-required basis to assist with Locking's training programme. No.62 Group Communications Flight, which, at the end of July 1952, became RAF Colerne's Communication Squadron was to provided the majority of these machines. Most of its aircraft were Ansons, including: Mk XIIs, PH663, PH704, PH775 and PH769; Mk XIXs VL348, VM358, VM365 and VS602; T 21 VV365 and T 22s VV358 and VV362, and they were flown by an equally varied group of officer and NCOs/Master Pilots. When required, and this was on most days of the year, one, two or three of these machines would be flown into Weston with the first arriving at about 8 a.m. There would then be a steady supply of apprentices/boy entrants requiring air-experience/navigation or radio-training flights of between thirty to ninety minutes duration and this often resulted in some thirty Anson flights during a day. In the mid-1950s, in the busier parts of the year, Varsity WJ892 would also be dispatched to Weston to provide air-experience flying for Locking's trainees and ATC Cadets on annual camp, and these would often be of two hours duration around Somerset, Devon and Cornwall.

With the number of movements by Colerne's Ansons from Weston Airport, there were one or two incidents. On 29 April 1955, T 22 VV358 piloted by Squadron Leader C. W. Scott had taken off from Lyneham at 2.24 p.m. for Weston. With a flight sergeant co-pilot and two passengers the machine landed at 2.52 p.m. and dropped off the passengers. Taking off for Colerne seven minutes later for the 15-minute flight home, just after becoming airborne, the port engine failed, due, it was later discovered, to a malfunctioning fuel cock. Not having the power to climb away, the Anson made a wheels-up landing in fields just to the south of the Oldmixon Factory. When it was realised that the Anson had force-landed, the airport fire engine set off in a spirited way heading towards the airport gate on what had been Hutton Moor Lane adjacent to 621 Gliding School, where it was thought access could be gained to the crash site. However, a rather substantial gatepost got in the way of the brass hose fittings on the fire engine's side which were wiped off. Luckily the Anson didn't catch fire! The following day (Saturday), the squadron leader was airborne at 9.05 a.m., this time in Anson VS602 with the squadron engineer to survey the damaged machine. Although having skidded across two fields and rhynes, damage was slight, but the Anson was considered to be beyond economic repair and a few days later broken up. This incident was followed on 13 June when Anson T 21 VV365, flown by Sergeant Emmett, after returning from a local flight with four apprentices on board, had his starboard tyre burst

One of the two Ansons and the two Provosts that arrived 22 July 1955 from RAF Ternhill, mentioned in Chapter 4's 'A Typically Busy Day at Weston Airport' (R. Dudley)

The relative position of RAF Locking to Weston Airport can be clearly seen in this photograph taken 21 August 1996. To the right of the far workshop are foundations of the four Bellman hangars, the last demolished in 1993. The 'T'-shaped buildings alongside the workshops are the living quarters for apprentices that in the late 1960s replaced the old timber huts (R. Dudley)

on landing. The aircraft showed no sign of damage and, after a wheel change, was flown back to Colerne for a more detailed inspection.

The Varsity Flight

From around 1959, the demand for airborne training in radio and radar was such that two, and sometimes three, radar-equipped Vickers Varsity T I 'Flying Classrooms' were based at Weston Airport. Usually WJ914 B, WL641 and WF408 Z, these silver and day-glo machines, maintained by a crew from Western Airways, formed the nucleus of the 'Varsity Flight'. Normally parked on the dispersals near the control tower, their activities were controlled by the officer commanding, Flight Lieutenant D. Curtis, from what had been the post-war passenger terminal. In 1965, when requirements changed and Air-Radio apprentice training was transferred to No.2 SoTT Cosford, the Varsity Flight also moved there. Varsity WF408 was withdrawn from flying in 1973, and, until scrapped, was exhibited at the Aerospace Museum at RAF Cosford. Whilst operating from Weston, the Varsity Flight was also to experience several incidents/accidents.

On 7 June 1960, WJ914, having taken off from Weston Airport with a crew of five from RAF Locking, collided over Cambridge with DH Vampire T 11 XD549 from RAF Oakington and the occupants of both aircraft were killed. The Varsity, which broke up in the air and crashed at Comberton, 3 miles (4.8 km) west of Cambridge, had been crewed by pilot Flight Lieutenant Z. W. Kaye, co-pilot Flight Lieutenant W. H. Jackson and two further officers and an NCO. The Vampire had been piloted by Flying Officer A. J. Lakeman from Exeter, accompanied by a South African student. A particularly firm landing by one of the Varsities on Thursday 7 July 1960, resulted in the tyres on both legs of the main undercarriage bursting, and on Tuesday 12 November 1963, there was a more serious incident when a landing had to be made with the nose gear stuck in the retracted position. Following repeated attempts to shake it down and a slow fly-by for a visual inspection, Master Pilot J. Beaton executed a textbook landing with only the tips of the airscews and undernose skinning being slightly damaged.

The End of RAF Locking

With the ending in the late 1980s of the Cold War, and with it the need for defence cuts, although much money had been spent in updating the station with new accomodation blocks and facilities, after some years of discussion the Ministry of Defence announced that Locking Camp would be closed on 31 March 1999 to save a reported £6 million a year. The last 'Freedom of the Borough' parade for the RAF took place on Wednesday 23 September 1998, forty-two years after being granted this honour, the march along Weston seafront being over-flown by Supermarine Spitfire IXe MK356, that had at one time been gate guardian at Locking, and now with the RAF Battle of Britain Memorial Flight. No.1 Radio School then moved to RAF Cosford and its non-technical and civilian staff were

WL641 of the Varsity Flight at Weston, 3 March 1963 (R. Dudley)

either made redundant or dispersed to other stations. After lying dormant for a time, the camp was sold in April 2002 to the South West Regional Development Agency and English Partnership for £10 million.

Fund Raising for Spitfires

Amongst the many Supermarine Spitfires defending Britain during the early war years was Mk II P7925. Built at Castle Bromwich in February 1941, it had been funded to the tune of £5,000 (although £12,000 was thought to be a more realistic cost) by the citizens of Weston and carried the town's name on each side of the fuselage. Confirmation that this presentation aeroplane actually existed was given by a photograph of it surrounded by snow outside the factory in the *Weston Mercury* for 19 April 1941. After delivery to 12 MU, the aircraft served in several squadrons and survived the war, it being declared non-effective at 39 MU on 4 January 1945. P7925 was one of more than 1,500 Presentation Spitfires funded during the war by individuals, organisations and the general public.

Funds for this presentation aircraft and others were obtained by various means. Probably the most common was the holding of exhibitions on various sites in the town, the most popular being on the M & S bomb site in Weston High Street. The first involving an aeroplane was during the 1943 Wings For Victory Week, when during the period 3 to 10 April, excluding Sunday 4th, the

The remains of a shot-down Messerschmitt Bf 109 on general display near the Winter Gardens was used as a means of fund-raising for Weston's war effort (*Weston Mercury* via J. Bailey)

RAF allowed the public to inspect a Spitfire and a Hawker Hurricane, both announced as being Battle of Britain veterans. In this case, the object was to raise funds for the RAF to purchase nine American-built Consolidated B-24 'Liberator' heavy bombers. The target was the saving of £360,000, and this was to be achieved by the public buying savings bonds, national war bonds, defence bonds, savings certificates and saving stamps through local banks, the Town Hall, Howe's Tea Rooms at Uphill, and the aero-modelling supplies shop at 42 Moorland Road. The Liberator had been chosen due to its name meaning so much to those living in the Nazi-enslaved countries of Europe. During the week, there were also barrage balloon handling demonstrations at the site on Station Road, and the frequent display by a friendly aircraft flying low over the Beach Lawns being driven off by an anti-aircraft gun crew. There were also other displays, one in Locking Road's King's Hall of equipment from RAF aircraft that included a dinghy, a bomb-release mechanism and a bombsight, instrument panels and Lewis, Vickers and Browning machine-guns, and another in the town hall where model aircraft, a Rolls-Royce Merlin, aircraft equipment and a selection of *Daily Mail* aviation photographs, featuring such pioneers as Alcock and Brown and Amy Johnson, could also be seen. Weston's Wings for Victory Week proved to be a great success with £375,060 saved, enough, it was said, to purchase the nine Liberators, and, in addition, three Spitfires!

With RAF airmen assisting and eager ATC cadets looking-on, a Spitfire on the M & S Bomb Site, a part of the 1943 'Wings for Victory Week' celebrations, is inspected by Colonel C. H. Welch of the USAAF (*Weston Mercury* via J. Bailey)

Weston's Cadet Corps

In the last few years before the start of the Second World War, a group of private citizens came together in an effort to further promote Britain's future youth capability in aviation by recruiting and providing opportunities for young men to be trained in aviation skills. Named 'The Air League of the British Empire' and headed by Air Commodore (retired) J. A. Chamier CB, CMG. DSO, OBE, as a result of its efforts, in 1938, the group formed the Air Defence Cadet Corps (ADCC) with Chamier executive secretary and Marshal of the Royal Air Force, Sir John Salmond chairman.

In Weston this resulted in the formation, on 25 July 1939, of No.159 Squadron ADCC at the County School for Boys (later the Boys Grammar School and now Broadoak Comprehensive), with the school's headmaster, Mr T. E. Lindfield, being made its commanding officer and some of his teachers becoming officers. By September, with fifty-six boys enrolled, eight officers, ably assisted by other members of the teaching staff, were instructing such subjects as aircraft rigging, the internal combustion engine, theory of flight, navigation and map-reading, signals, meteorology and first aid. The shared scout hut was soon found to be too small, and replaced by rooms within the school, the hall being used for parades, drill instruction and lectures, in particular those on aircraft recognition when an epidiascope and aircraft models were used. The popularity of this study, and the necessity of having Raid Spotters at the school, soon brought about the formation of a branch of the National Aeroplane Spotters' Club. Instruction in drill, initially given in the hall, but in the better weather on the playing field, was by Warrant Officer Harry Bradley, recruited from the local Boys' Brigade where he had served as a very dignified drum major. His brother Roy, after a short spell working for the Bristol Aeroplane Company, would complete flying training in the FAA, and post-war become a test pilot and flying instructor with Westland.

Some of the theoretical training was put into practice at Weston Airport, with work-experience sessions at Western Airways on engine-overhaul, general hangar work, parachute packing and aerial photography, and at the gasworks' indoor rifle-range where most cadets had their first opportunity to fire live rounds. With the imminent arrival of a working Napier Lion V aero-engine and Vickers Vildebeest III K6398 delivered by the RAF on 6 December 1940, a purpose-built Air Shed was rapidly erected alongside Broadoak Road, the task supervised by the school's woodwork master, Arthur 'Robbie' Robinson, who had also become a pilot officer in the squadron. The Air Shed continued to fill when, in due course, Weston Airways supplied the wings and tailplane from a Hillson Praga, with the promise of its fuselage. Later still, Hawker Demon I K8190 was also provided by the RAF.

With numbers increasing, the squadron was split into three flights, B and C comprising school pupils, and A for old boys who could only meet in the evenings or at weekends. In 1940, the government took over the ADCC, and in February 1941, the Air Training Corps (ATC) was established with

Air Commodore Chamier its first commandant. At 159, this resulted in Mr Lindfield becoming a flight lieutenant in the Volunteer Reserve Training branch of the RAF and given the responsibilities of co-ordinating officer in the newly-created Somerset Wing of the ATC. Flying Officer J. R. 'Curly' Hay, the school's chemistry master, who, since the squadron's formation, had been adjutant, and, to relieve the headmaster of some of his other responsibilities, the active officer commanding was then made the commanding officer. An advantage of having good connections within the organisation was that the school/squadron, to expedite cadet entry into the RAF, had arranged with the Service and a Dr Hill, who normally practised from his surgery on Beach Road, a fast-track scheme whereby boys that were close to wanting to join the RAF were given a preliminary fitness examination at the school.

Flying was to play an important part in the ATC's activities. Most cadets couldn't get enough of aeroplanes, and with the arrival at Weston Airport of visiting RAF units such as 116 and 286 Squadrons, unofficial flying was privately arranged by cadets, and it wasn't long before one or two smartly turned-out lads were making a nuisance of themselves. One Cadet, D. Chapman, was very lucky going on a cross-country in the gun turret of a Boulton Paul Defiant of 286 Squadron piloted by Sergeant Pilot Ralph K. Hofer of the RCAF. An American who had joined the RCAF in 1941, after training Hofer had been posted to England and 286 Squadron but when the United States came into the war, as Lieutenant Hofer, he became a member of 334 Squadron, 4th Fighter Group USAAF, flying Republic P-47 Thunderbolts and later North American P-51 Mustangs. Before being shot down and killed on 2 July 1944 over Mostar, Yugoslavia, he had become the 4th Group's highest scoring ace. Cadets also managed to get flights in the Avro

Cadets from 159 Squadron together with others from London at the 1942 ATC Summer Camp, RAF Halton, 18 August (Via E. Johnson)

159 Squadron's 1943 ATC Annual Camp at Staverton with a Hurricane being used to best advantage (Via E. Johnson)

ATC cadets from Weston's 290 Squadron and those from the Burnham/Highbridge Squadron during 1954's Summer Camp at RAF Chivenor. Amongst the cadets, who are in front of one of the station's Canadair-built Sabres, are Flying Officer R. Ivey of 290 and Flying Officers Ruskin and Hoey of the Burnham/Highbridge Squadron, who were at that time also teachers at Worle Secondary Modern School (Via R. Dudley)

Manchester and Lancaster heavy bombers of the resident TDU where some of the keener ones even had their own parachutes reserved in lockers. Although a certain amount of unofficial flying had been carried out, it wasn't until 1943 that cadets had their first official air-experience flight, and that was at Lulsgate Bottom in a DH Dominie, brought in from RAF Yatesbury by Group Captain C. D. Barnard of Air Tours Circus fame, who, in 1931, had visited Weston. From mid-1943, there was also flying at Weston Airport with 87 Gliding School.

Flying was also available when at camp, most being under canvas at RAF stations. One, in 1942, at No.1 SoTT Halton, allowed the first USAAF Boeing B-17 Fortresses to be seen flying over on their return from Rouen, their first operation; and another camp at Staverton provided cadets with confirmation of secret jet developments with the prototype Gloster Whittle E28/39 seen flying over most days. In early 1944, a camp at RAF Honiton, Whitney Straight's pre-war Clyst Honiton (Exeter) Airport, gave sight of 610 Squadron's new Spitfire XIVs, and the chance for one of the cadets to have an exciting ride in Canadian 406 Squadron Beaufighter VIF ND221. Night flights were also laid on in Airspeed Oxfords of 595 Squadron that were engaged in searchlight/radar-calibration and there was also a visit to the RAF ASR unit at Exmouth. A later camp at RNAS Yeovilton provided a visit to the Westland Factory at Yeovil where Supermarine Seafires were in production. 1947's camp was again at RAF Honiton, the highlight for the cadets this time their herding into a roped-off arena in the middle of the airfield where they were repeatedly beaten-up by a Supermarine Spitfire and a Gloster Meteor coming in at nought feet! There was further excitement later in the week when low-level trips were given along Torquay Beach in an Avro Anson.

Although the war had ended, the squadron remained very active until the Boys' Grammar School became Broadoak Comprehensive and 159 became a detached flight of the Town Squadron. When the resident flight's commanding officer, Flight Lieutenant Ewart Alford, and incidentally the head of Broadoak School's science department, retired in October 1975, the last of 1,644 cadets that had been with 159 since 1941 transferred to the Town Squadron. As a matter of interest, Ewart Alford had been twenty-five years in the ATC, eighteen of them as the commanding officer of 159 Squadron and had also, for a number of years, been an instructor with 621 Gliding School.

The Town Squadron that had absorbed the remnants of 159 was No.290. It, like many others, had been formed early in 1941, and by May was firmly established in a temporary headquarters at Kings Hall on Locking Road, and detached flights were being formed at some of the smaller towns and villages in North-West Somerset, such as Winscombe, Axbridge and Langford. Meeting three times a week, its impressive nucleus of some thirteen instructors, amongst them Flying Officers G. G. Clutterbuck, Walter, and H. C. Evett who was the adjutant and would in due course become No.87 Gliding School's first commanding officer, taught airframes, engines, theory of flight, map reading and navigation, maths, wireless/signals, airmanship, aircraft recognition and

During a visit to Weston Airport for air-experience flying, Miss Freydis Leaf discusses with girls of the town's WJAC an important feature of *Grey Dove* (Via B. Passmore)

aeromodelling. As with 159, 290's cadets also visited RAF stations, aircraft factories and enjoyed air-experience flying. Drill was also to feature strongly, it usually being taken by Warrant Officer E. J. Burton.

On 12 August 1941, a move was made to a more permanent headquarters at the senior boys school on Walliscote Road, but with growing numbers, a further move was made to the Territorial Army (TA) drill hall at Langford Road. But with around 120 cadets on its books and the need for it to supervise additional detached flights, there was a high priority for permanent accommodation, and, in the summer of 1948, this was provided adjacent to the drill hall. Opened on 11 June by Admiral of the Fleet Sir James Somerville GCB, GBE, DSO, the new headquarters comprised two timber huts located parallel and close to the loop-line leading to Weston Railway Station. One hut was partitioned into three, the west end having a signals room with numerous Morse key positions and a VHF radio transmitting and receiving station. The other end of the building was fitted out as an engineering workshop with a great variety of aircraft components for instruction, pride of place going to a beautifully sectioned DH Gypsy Major; between these rooms was the CO's office and a storeroom. The other hut was used for drill, PT, film-shows and had a tearoom.

Even with the war over, there were still many reasons for adventurous boys to join the ATC; it was also said that being in the corps guaranteed one's entry into the RAF for National Service. Amongst the early post-war activities, on

Sunday 26 May 1946, at Sand Bay some 250 Sea, Army and Air Cadets, all armed to the teeth, were involved in an exercise that revolved around the bay being attacked from the sea, and the invaders and defenders being bombed with bags of flour by a cadet in a North American Harvard with hood slid back and six cadets sitting on the floor of an Avro Anson heaving flour bags out through the cabin doorway. There were also semi-regular flights from Weston Airport in the ATDU's Avro Lincoln heavy bombers, the first group of forty cadets having 30-minute trips on Sunday 27 October 1946.

There were also visits to local aircraft factories; in 1947, cadets saw the Bristol Brabazon being assembled at Filton in the massive new Assembly Hall, and whilst in the Main Erecting Hall, Freighters and Brigands were seen in assembly. In 1954, the annual camp was at RAF Chivenor and there was flying in a Boulton Paul Balliol, an Auster 6A and an Anson, and cadets were able to climb over the station's Canadair-built North American Sabres and its two Hawker Tempest V target-tugs. There was also a trip from Ilfracombe in an RAF ASR launch. Semi-regular air-experience flying was also available two or three times a year from local air stations such as Yeovilton, Filton, Colerne, and at Merryfield and Weston Zoyland where cadet NCOs were often lucky enough to be flown in Gloster Meteor and DH Vampire jet trainers. There were also occasional air-experience flights from Weston Airport in Ansons, probably the last being on 27 September 1958 when Mk XII PH587 of 61 Group Communications Flight, Biggin Hill, gave 30-minute trips around the town and the Mendip area.

Around 1963, 290's Langford Road timber-hutted headquarters was demolished and replaced by a modern building located nearby, which unfortunately had none of the aeronautical trappings of the original huts. This building too, in its turn, was replaced by another more permanent one on the other side of the parade ground and this is used by the squadron to this day.

Also based at Langford Road TA drill hall was Weston's Woman's Junior Air Corps (WJAC). Formed in 1947 with the assistance of personnel from RAF Locking, like its male ATC counterpart it was for youngsters aged between fourteen and twenty years. Under the leadership of former cadet Barbara White, tuition was given in theory of flight, unarmed combat, drill, Morse code, navigation, meteorology, engine theory and air traffic control. Instruction was also given in less aviation-oriented subjects such as service to others, child care, health, hygiene and crafts. To most, the highlight was the summer air-experience flight in the corp's own 4-seat Fairchild Argus 2 G-AIYO. Obtained in 1947 and named *Grey Dove* by HRH the Duchess of Kent in July 1948, the machine was flown to various airfields across the country by Miss Freydis M. Leaf, an ex-ATA pilot who had a licence endorsement for instruction, was a licensed ground engineer and the unit's aviation advisor. Weston Airport was one of the approved venues and, by the end of the second year of operation, some 2,500 flights had been given nationwide. With a nominal sixteen cadets on the books, Weston's unit remained in being until around 1959.

No. 87/621 Gliding School

When the Air Training Corps was formed in 1941, the training and opportunities provided lacked one very important feature, there was no basic official hands-on flying training available to a cadet. However, it was recognised that there was a reasonably cost-effective solution available, and that was the one used for many years in Germany with great success, 'The Glider'. Soon, orders had been placed by the Air Ministry with Slingsby Sailplanes of Kirbymoorside for the Kirby Cadet Mk I and Fred Slingsby also kindly offered the plans to schools and other organisations for glider construction. The first ATC gliding school was opened in 1942 at Kirbymoorside for instructor training and development flying, and, starting in 1943, Elementary Gliding Schools started to be set up so that, by 1945, there were eighty-four spread across the country, training cadets over the age of sixteen years to fly gliders. To go gliding, a boy would already have had to pass the cadet 'Proficiency' test at his local squadron.

In July 1943, No.87 was established at Weston and located in an area on the south side of the airport that straddled what, before airport enlargement in 1940, had been Hutton Moor Lane. Subsequently, the school was provided with two Nissen huts and a single-bay Great World War-type Bessoneaux hangar whose canvas-covered timber structure was believed to date back to 1923. Neither gas nor electricity was connected to the school and when it became dark, hand-held oil lanterns provided light. There was, however, a water supply and a telephone. The easterly Nissen hut housed the CO's office and a small lock-up store, but most of the area was given over to general storage and workshop facilities, whereas the westerly hut was split, giving crew-room facilities for the instructors and cadets.

Initially equipped with a Slingsby-built Dagling open-framework single-seat primary trainer, in due course it was joined by two yellow/dark earth camouflaged Kirby Cadet Mk I single-seat gliders PD637 and PD690. These had been built for the school by tradesmen at 5 SoTT RAF Locking and given a superb internal and external finish. Of wood and fabric construction, they had a parallel wing chord and had neither flight instruments nor wheel and had to be dragged around on the timber nose-skid. The gliders were launched using a worn-out winch that had come from a barrage balloon unit, and were retrieved together with the winch cable by an old cut-down RAF staff car and a Beaverette light-armoured vehicle that had been discarded by the Ministry of Aircraft Production; any other equipment was scrounged or made by instructors, such as the lightweight trailer that sported two Spitfire wheels. Although the school's vehicles consumed quite large quantities of petrol, there was no bulk storage facility and fuel had to be brought in jerry cans from RAF Locking, and, along with dope and thinners for glider repairs, stored in an adjacent concrete pillbox.

With this rudimentary ground equipment and the Dagling, in early 1943, a small band of volunteer aviators was given training in instructional techniques

No. 87 Gliding School's Bessoneaux hangar around September 1951. The surrounding equipment comprises, left to right: the Beaverette, Cadet Mk 3 WT875, Cadet Mk 2 VM667 and a late Cadet Mk 1. The Mk 1 and Mk 3 are in the post-war silver/yellow trainer scheme whereas the Mk 2 is still in the late wartime overall yellow scheme. Behind the gliders is the school's newly received Bedford 15-cwt truck and a barrage balloon winch. In the distance is Oldmixon's Shop 3 (P. Stride)

in readiness for arrival of the first cadets. The training was initially given by the internationally known pre-war racing driver HRH Crown Prince Birabongse of Siam, now a pilot officer in the RAF, who, on 16 July, performed the school's opening ceremony. The Crown Prince, in 1945, became chief test pilot of Slingsby Sailplanes in Yorkshire, and for a time would be a frequent airport visitor, when in his Miles Messenger G-AIDH a stop would be made for fuel *en route* to his home in Cornwall. Soon after their initial training, and now under the command of Flight Lieutenant H. C. Evett, the newly qualified instructors were able to start cadet instruction. The commanding officer's tenure, however, only lasted until September 1944 when Flight Lieutenant Jarman took over. Gliding was initially on Sundays when generally there was reduced airport activity and, with the early machines especially, it was all in a straight line. When slightly improved gliders became available, a circuit of the airport was possible, but normally only by an instructor, who on a soaring flight was limited to a maximum altitude of 1,000 feet (305 metres) and not straying further than 2 miles (3.2 km) from the airport. However, because of the 'sea breeze effect', there were few thermals and most flights were down-hill all the way. Because of this and due to the location of several nearby barrage balloons, it was essential that the circuit was kept close to the airport's boundary.

Having only single-seat gliders, there was of course no dual instruction, the cadet's first flight was solo and the glider attrition rate was obviously fairly high. Initially, with the glider positioned into wind and with the instructor standing-by, the cadet first learned how to keep the wings level. Then hooked up to a winch cable, he attempted to keep the glider straight and wings level whilst being pulled at low speed along the grass towards the winch, this was known as doing a 'ground-slide'. After a number of ground-slides had been successfully carried out, the instructor showed the cadet where to keep the stick and rudder pedals; the winch would then be opened up a little more than for the ground-slide, and the glider would have sufficient airspeed to just lift off the ground. After covering a few hundred feet, still with the cable attached, the winch driver throttled back and the glider automatically landed itself. Over the next few flights, the cadet was allowed to experiment with the controls, but would be limited by the winch driver to a height of about 5 feet (1.5 metres). These were called 'airborne-slides'. Airborne-slides continued, with the winch driver pulling in the cable progressively faster, allowing the cadet to fly higher still to an altitude of about twenty to thirty feet (8 to 9 metres), after which he would attempt a controlled landing with the cable still attached. This was called the 'low-hop'. With a few of these performed safely, the winch driver wound in the cable faster still, allowing the cadet to actually make the glider climb, using the stick, to an altitude of about 100 feet (30 metres). The cable was then released by the cadet pulling a yellow knob, and the glider landed straight ahead, the result hopefully being a flight of at least thirty seconds duration. This, known as a 'high-hop', was the 'passing-out' stage, and in due course the cadet received the coveted 'A' Gliding Certificate of the Federation Aeronautical Internationale, issued in Great Britain by the Royal Aero Club.

By the end of the war, the complement of staff at the school comprised four officers holding Air Ministry instructor categories and three civilian instructors under training, and was equipped with two barrage balloon winches and therefore known as a '2-line' school. In August 1945, there was a further change at the top when the school's adjutant Flying Officer, Arthur 'Robbie' Robinson, one of its original civilian instructors, was promoted to the rank of Flight Lieutenant and became the school's commanding officer. His boss was the chief gliding officer of South West Command who was Squadron Leader A. H. Phillips MC, OBE, a post that expired with his retirement in the mid-1950s. Robbie was already well known to some of the cadets, being woodwork master at the County School, and, until the end of 1944, on the staff of its cadet squadron. He was instantly recognisable, having a large shock of hair and a prominent chisel chin jutting out from the leather helmet and goggles that he always wore when flying. The ensemble was completed by a brown Sidcot suit and fur-lined flying boots.

The ending of hostilities in 1945 also saw changes to the operation of Weston Airport, and, in September 1946, responsibility for its running was transferred to the Ministry of Civil Aviation (MCA). Its main interest was the running of the newly reintroduced Weston — Pengam Moors ferry service, and it was this activity that was to be partly responsible for gliding at Weston being banned for a year. During this period, gliding continued in a reduced way at Lulsgate Bottom and at Halesland, a group of undulating fields on top of the Mendip

Probably taken in September 1951 shortly after delivery of the school's first two Cadet Mk 3s (P. Stride)

Hills just behind Cheddar Gorge, that in 1946 had been opened by the ATC for instructor training.

The ATC's standing was improved in 1946 when it was brought into the RAF proper as a part of Reserve Command, and the thirty-four gliding schools that had been operating mainly from non-Air Ministry property, such as large farm fields, were shut down or merged and their equipment redistributed. This also resulted in the gradual replacement of the old Cadet Mk 1 with a newer Mk 1 equipped with an instrument panel and a wheel behind the skid, and at Weston, the delivery in 1947 of the first Cadet Mk 2 VM667; this was similar to the later Mk 1 but the wing had a larger span with tapered outer panels. The big improvement, however, came in 1949/50 when WB991, delivered 27 March 1950, and WB929, delivered 9 August 1949, arrived at Weston. These were 54-foot-span (16.5-metre) Slingsby T21B Sedbergh TX 1 side-by-side, 2-seat, intermediate soaring machines. It had a high-lift wing section with spoilers on the upper surface that could be raised when landing to disturb airflow over the wing and thus reduce lift. A variometer was also fitted that gave indication of lift by a green ball rising in a tube, and sink by a red ball in another tube rising. The glider was soon to be nicknamed *The Barge* for obvious reasons. Another big day was on 13 September 1951 when WT874 and WT875, the first of the school's Slingsby T31 Cadet Mk 3 2-seat tandem trainers were delivered. The Mk 3 was similar to the Mk 2 but it had a slightly longer fuselage with a cockpit for the instructor beneath the wing.

The older machines, which included Cadet Mk 1s RA916 and VW503 and Cadet Mk 2 VM635, were now progressively withdrawn from service and the school, when up to full strength, was to hold three Cadet Mk 3s and two Sedberghs. Together with the new gliders, Mk 4 'Wild' barrage balloon winches, suitably modified, were also provided but, like the earlier ones, still proved difficult to keep serviceable with battery and ignition problems during the winter months resulting in unorthodox procedures being used for engine starting. At this point, an RAF Bedford 15-cwt truck was also provided to tow the new winches, and Land Rovers replaced the old car and Beaverette.

There was now also the need for a revised training syllabus aimed at achieving higher standards of flying proficiency and, when introduced, it included exercises such as the 'effect of controls', 'recovery from unusual attitudes', 'spin recovery' and 'cable break' procedures, most of them featured reduced 'g' and were guaranteed to initially take the cadet's breath away. Stressed for a more adventurous style of flying, the Sedbergh could attain launch heights of around 1,300 feet (396 metres) and allowed *ab initio* cadets to be given air-experience flying, whilst staff cadets and instructors too could benefit, being shown soaring and basic aerobatics. Circuit work and solo flying was reserved for the Mk 3s and, until withdrawn, the Mk 2s which could only make about 800 feet (244 metres) on launch. With these dual-control gliders, cadets could now be trained up to the 'B' Gliding Certificate standard where, after completing some forty dual launches and having been checked out by an independent instructor, three separate solo circuits of the airport were flown. One was left-hand, one right-hand and the other in a direction of the cadet's own choosing.

Ideal for *ab initio* training, the Mk 3, like the Mk 1 and Mk 2 before it, was built of spruce and ply, fabric covered, extremely strong and put up with much misuse. With most flights being of no more than three minutes duration, each aircraft during its life would have made thousands of less-than-smooth touch-downs. Their strength was well illustrated by inspection after the occasional landing incident in which the pilot and aircraft more often than not escaped with only a few scratches. An early casualty to this type of training at Weston was a Cadet Mk 1 flown by a lad who was a local GPO messenger boy. Due to inexperience on his first high-hop, after cable release the glider was unintentionally allowed to stall and it dived to the ground. The nose splintered, folded back, and its upper spine went through the cadet's neck pinning him to the cockpit bulkhead. The fast-thinking winch driver pulled out the jagged piece of wood, stemmed the bleeding, and after hospitalisation, the lad luckily made a full recovery. Another incident was on Sunday 5 October 1952. On that day, a 17-year-old from Bristol who already had his 'C' Certificate (a soaring flight of five minutes duration above the launch height, which in the ATC gliding movement approximated to a flight of fifteen minutes), whilst completing a turn at 400 feet (122 metres) in VM667 to start the landing approach, allowed airspeed to drop and the machine entered an incipient spin. Although control was regained, he was too low and forward progress was arrested by the airport's boundary fence and the glider disintegrated around its pilot. Extracted from the wreck, the lad was rushed to Weston Hospital by St John's Ambulance, and luckily was allowed to return home that evening.

On Sunday 12 January 1964, there was another accident when the school lost
WT874, one of its first two Mk 3s. Training was being carried out in marginal
conditions with low cloud and snow flurries sweeping across the airport from
the north-east. Senses were probably a bit dulled in the bitter weather and the
unfortunate instructor allowed his cadet to start the final turn at too low an
altitude. The machine was still turning when it touched down and the port
wing and fuselage contacted the frozen ground simultaneously. In a cloud of
dust, the fuselage broke off just aft of the wing and, still held together by the
elevator and rudder-cables, swung round to lie alongside the nose.

With a stalling speed of just 28 mph (45 kph), the Sedbergh when in lift,
with its large wing, could out-perform most other machines. In a thermal with
ASI showing just above stalling speed, the glider could easily be made to go
round and round with bank held off, the stick back and the rudder used to
keep the nose just below the horizon. With its cut-away cockpit sides, in a
thermal, both of the crew had a marvellous view of what was happening on the
ground, which came in useful on Sunday 4 September 1960. By mid-1960, a
lot of development flying had been done by the Bristol Aeroplane Company at
Oldmixon on its Type 192 tandem-rotor helicopter, and under the new wing of
Westland it had just been named 'Belvedere' and granted an initial CA Release
for limited service use. Three pre-production machines, XG453, XG454 and
XG456, were close to being delivered to the Belvedere Trials Unit at RAF
Odiham and they were due to be handed over 17 October 1960. However,
the machines very nearly didn't make it, for on that Sunday a fire in Shop
6, which was now used as the Belvedere production flight shed, destroyed
much equipment and was close to spreading to and consuming the almost
completed helicopters. The one to be thanked for discovering the fire was the
pilot of Sedbergh WB991 who had the glider in a thermal over the factory, little
knowing the source of lift. When the smell of burning attracted his attention to
the thin wisp of smoke curling up from the vents along the length of the hangar
roof, an emergency let-down and a 999 call in due course brought the Banwell
Fire Brigade tearing across the airport. Meanwhile, the fire, which involved
about half of the hangar floor area, was being tackled with fire extinguishers
by two 621 instructors who had gained access through an office window and,
by the time the fire brigade arrived, were close to exhaustion.

As well as operating the Weston site, from August 1946, the school also took
on the responsibility of helping to set up and maintain for the ATC a small
ridge-soaring site on the Mendip Hills high above Cheddar. The land, discovered
by Squadron Leader Phillips following much exploration in his Auster, after
protracted negotiations with the Ministry of Agriculture and Fisheries was
rented from one Farmer Hales. It was therefore of no great surprise when, after
a time, the site became known in the ATC gliding movement as Hales Land, later
by usage, Halesland. The squadron leader was a staunch believer in the need to
raise the standard of gliding in the ATC and for the last two years had run an
instructors school at RAF Charmy Down, just to the north of Bath. At Halesland

he would be able to gather together some pre-war sailplanes and teach thermal and ridge-soaring techniques to ATC instructors in a similar way to that carried out pre-war at civil soaring clubs. As a matter of interest, gliding in the Mendips had been carried out as early as May 1932, when on the 1st and 2nd of the month, an exhibition was held in the hollow between Crook Peak and Wavering Down. Two machines were involved, a home-made primary trainer flown by Major Sykes of Pilning and a Skud sailplane piloted by Mr L. C. Williams of London. Unfortunately, the large crowd were to witness flights of only short duration, there being little wind over the slope to support the machines.

Much effort was spent in clearing a 30-foot-wide (9-metre) strip some 100 feet (30 metres) long that allowed an experimental instructors course to be run in August 1946 using a Grunau Baby. There was no hangar for the aircraft and it had to be picketed behind an old stone barn. The main problem with this site was that it was too far from the slope and the pilot often ran out of altitude before reaching lift. In 1948, a better site was found adjoining the original one, and serious thought could now be given to the establishment of a permanent base for the squadron leader's instructors' school, and in October, a Robin Hangar and timber hut were erected at the easterly end of the site next to a very steep and narrow lane that went down the hillside coming out near The Red Lion Inn at Draycott. Equally tricky to fly from, the 'new' Halesland was usually only operated when a stiff breeze blew from the south-west over the strawberry beds of the Cheddar Valley to provide lift from the 800-foot-high (244-metre) slope. With the addition of Halesland, the school now became a '3-line' unit, and its commanding officer, Flight Lieutenant Robinson, was promoted to the rank of Squadron Leader.

Halesland was so undulating, with the winch being out of sight of the launch point, that because of the short land-line, a signaller with a bat had to be positioned at a strategic position to relay telephone messages to the winch driver. Unpopular with the signaller, the system was soon replaced by a full-length line partially hidden in the base of a drystone wall that bordered the collection of fields. However, there was a downside to this as the sheep that inhabited the area, and always had to be corralled before gliding commenced, had a liking for the line's insulating material, which necessitated a thorough visual inspection of the system before each day's flying. Typical of the early courses run from the new site was 62 Group's third, held at the end of August 1948. For this, two Grunau Babies, two Cadet Mk 2s and a Cadet Mk 1 were used, with the machines picketed at night in the lee of trees with trailers and winch drawn up around for protection from the wind. The course lasted a week, and during it there were 162 flights totalling 30 hours 27 minutes. Between courses (there were three in 1948), gliders were de-rigged and stowed in a marquee erected near the trees that was guarded by two airmen.

From the early 1950s, the hangar at Halesland always held at least one Sedbergh, and a T30A Prefect TX I, which was also a Slingsby design. This 45-foot-span (14-metre) glider was an advanced trainer, based on, but reckoned

A Prefect landing at Halesland in the mid-1950s. Behind the school's buildings the road starts to drop away down the steep hillside to emerge near the Red Lion at Draycott. The site is now used by the Mendip Gliding Club (P. Stride)

Robbie was the first to try out, on 16 June 1963, the new 'solo' nose ballast-weight installation fitted to Sedbergh WB929 that replaced a sand-filled sack going under the name of 'Gertie'. On the wing-tip is instructor Chris Parkman, and in the group of instructors Graham Light, John Stride and Alan Harden (R. Dudley)

Sedbergh WB991 seen 28 July 1984 in the new red and white RAF Training colour scheme had now been at Weston for thirty-four years. Just behind the glider is one of 621's yellow Cadet Mk 3 retrieving trailers delivered in the early 1960s hitched-up to a Land Rover. In the distance, the Woodspring Gliding Club is operating on the far side of the runway (R. Dudley)

On Saturday 3 May 2003, to commemorate its sixtieth anniversary, the gliding school/squadron returned to Weston Airport complete with its three Vikings and borrowed Sedbergh XN151 (R. Dudley)

to be not as good as, the Grunau Baby. It was, however, much better than the Cadet Mk 2, it having a wing with similar refinements to the Sedbergh's and an almost enclosed cockpit. It also had speed-limiting air-brakes that made it ideal for operating out of small sites such as Halesland. Initially, the one allocated was WE983 but Squadron Leader Phillips heard that there were ten others in storage at RAF St Athan that nobody seemed to know about, and in double-quick time he managed to get hold of two of them.

With the Sedbergh and Prefect, staff cadets and selected senior cadets were now also able to enjoy the delights of ridge-soaring the Mendips, and during dual instruction were shown landmarks such as the 'T of trees', 'The Rocks' and 'The Tradesman's Entrance', etc., that would help in safely navigating their way around the area. Trips to Halesland in the late 1950s were normally by Land Rover as the Bedford 15-cwt's transmission system was getting rather worn, the vehicle often having to be reversed up the steep hill from Draycott to the gliding ground as its gearbox tended to lose oil pressure when in a steep nose-up attitude. In July 1952, the first of many advanced gliding courses for cadets was run by the school, and over the following eight years around 280 cadets were converted to the Prefect at Halesland. Once in ridge-lift, Cheddar Gorge could be easily reached and there was a rather juvenile challenge from the early days that had over the years been passed down from pilot to pilot. That was, on reaching the great gully in the Mendips for the first time solo, the pilot had to spit over the side onto the winding road some 1,500 feet (457 metres) below. The advanced gliding courses continued until 1960, when 621 was requested instead to organise and monitor weekly visits of the country's other gliding schools to the site. These visits were to continue until new high-performance glass machines replaced the original fleet of Slingsby gliders. Other gliders to have seen service at Halesland were a Falcon III, Grunau Babies VD178 and 204; Dart Tottenhoe VD199; Gull 1 VW912; Cadet Mk 1 RA960; Sedberghs WB956, 964, 943, 987, 966, 983, 980, XN151 and WB974; Prefects WE990, 981, 980, 987, 993, 982, 990, 984 and 989 and Slingsby Swallow XS650.

In addition to Robbie, who retired in September 1970 taking with him an MBE awarded in 1959 for services to the cadet gliding movement, other RAFVR (T) instructors of long standing were John Stride and Hobby Hopkirk. John had been at the school since being an ATC cadet during the war and took over as commanding officer with the rank of Squadron Leader when Robbie retired in 1970. Hobby was with 92 Gliding School at Colerne prior to moving to Weston where he became CFI; he also retired in 1970 and was replaced by Flight Lieutenant Brian House who, as a member of 159 ATC Squadron, had soloed at the age of sixteen and by 2008 had been forty-seven years with 621 GS and amassed some 1,900 hours in 19,500 launches. In February 1979, Squadron Leader Dave Simmons in turn replaced John Stride and he was in due course replaced by Squadron Leader Sean Stent in August 1987.

At the end of September 1985, 621's Sedberghs and Mk 3s, now between thirty and thirty-five years old, and having completed sterling service, were replaced by five Viking T Is (German Grob 103s), ZE610 to ZE614. Top-of-the-market 2-seat sailplanes, they were built of glass-reinforced plastic and had a maximum permitted airspeed of 156 mph (251 kph). Shortly after their delivery, the Eagle winches that had replaced the barrage balloon winches in 1960 were in turn replaced by the more powerful Munsters Van Gelder 6-drum units, and likewise a Bedford 4-ton truck provided for towing purposes to replace the earlier Austin 1-ton truck that had in-turn replaced the Bedford 15-cwt. Other Cadet Mk 3s to have seen service at Weston were: XA310, XA308, XN248, WT898, XN251, XN240, WT877, XE793, XE791 and WT908.

Over the years, there had been a number of changes in the gliding school's title. 1955 saw the school numbering system come under review, and, on 1 September, No.87 GS became No.621 GS, thus reflecting the fact that it had long belonged to 62 Group Southern Reserve of RAF Home Command. In 1984 all schools were renamed again and No.621 Gliding School became No.621 Volunteer Gliding School, and, in November 2005, the school, along with the others, was renamed yet again, it becoming No.621 Volunteer Gliding Squadron. With general aviation flying ceasing at Weston Airport in 1978 and the school and Westland Helicopters becoming the only operators, by the end of 1988, 621 was an unwelcome lodger at the airport with uncut grass, collapsing drainage courses and unannounced events being held, adversely affecting the school's training programme. The result was frequent inactivity and a hunt was on for another Ministry-owned airfield with Merryfield, Yeovilton and Keevil being considered. Finally 621, which was now one of only thirty schools, was forced into moving to RAF Hullavington in Wiltshire, its last flight from Weston being on 27 June 1993, almost fifty years to the day from when the school commenced operations from Weston Airport.

Weston's Ranges

Air-to-sea gunnery practice had been carried out over the Bristol Channel from before the war with much of it being onto floating targets located in mid-channel. This hazardous activity caused several accidents, one witnessed from near Weston's Birnbeck Pier on 12 December 1940 when, in hazy conditions, P6980, one of a flight of Westland Whirlwind I fighters of 263 Squadron operating from Exeter Airport with guns firing, failed to pull out of a dive. The other aircraft then broke off the exercise and headed back towards base.

Air-to-air gunnery practice over Weston Bay, commencing in the late 1930s, continued until well after the war's end and was probably discontinued due to public safety, or lack of it, as vividly demonstrated on Wednesday 21 August 1946 to several hundred passengers on board the Campbell saloon paddle steamer, *Ravenswood*. Less than three months after Birnbeck Pier had been reopened on Thursday 6 June, the steamer had set out in the morning for a pleasure cruise to Clevedon. On its return, in the vicinity of the McKenzie buoy near the Holms, two RAF aircraft, one towing a drogue, were seen circling low over the sea. All the children went to the ship's rail to wave at the pilots, whereupon bullets started to hit the surrounding water and one actually struck a companionway narrowly missing the ship's mate. The attacking aircraft then passed so low over the steamer that many thought that it had hit the topmast. It must have been a memorable trip!

The Sand Bay air-to-ground firing range was on the south side of Sand Point promontory at Swallow Cliff, where four rectangular whitewashed canvas targets, two small and two large, were supported on scaffolding. Used mainly by fighters and ground-attack aircraft stationed in South-West England, the first to use the range were Gloster Gladiators of 263 Squadron prior to their departure to Norway, with one of their number, N5623, whilst formation flying, coming to grief in the sea near Portishead on 7 April 1940. From then on, a variety of aircraft used the range including Supermarine Spitfires, Hawker Hurricanes, Westland Whirlwinds of 263 Squadron, Bristol Beaufighters, DH Mosquitos, Lockheed P-38 Lightnings of the USAAF and Hawker Typhoons, one being Mk IB JR301 from 3 TEU Aston Down, which suffered engine failure on 29 August 1944 on the run-in and exploded on Middle Hope (Woodspring Priory) when anti-invasion blocks were hit. The last type to use the range, just prior to it being closed just after the war, was the Gloster Meteor. The range, approached by diving-in over Weston Woods and then remaining low over Sand Bay, resulted in many thousands of .303, 20 mm, 40 and 35 mm

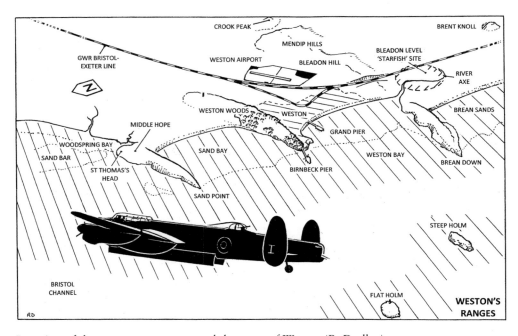

Location of the weapon ranges around the coast of Weston (R. Dudley)

cartridge cases falling into the sea. But on low tide, with the red warning flag down, the locals were quickly on the scene making their way out through the mud and deep gullies to recover the ejected brass cases, a lucrative practice that continued through into the 1960s.

As far as Sand Bay was concerned, the toll collectors on Kewstoke Road that led to the bay, early in the war were replaced by armed Royal Navy sentries and barbed-wire barriers were erected, and from 1941 the bay itself was operated by the Admiralty as a bombing range, and mainly inert weapons were dropped by aircraft of the TDU/ATDU based at Weston Airport. The main reason for this site being chosen was that it was fairly remote, and the rise and fall of the estuary tide, the second highest in the world, made recovery of the stores at low-water by landing craft relatively straightforward. This operation, however, was complicated somewhat by some 3,000 anti-invasion stakes that, until the end of 1947, lined the foreshore of Kewstoke and Sand Bay. With the opening up of Sand Bay after the war for civilian use, the bombing range was relocated to Woodspring Bay on the far side of Sand Point. Here the ATDU continued to use the facility and the RAF also started to show an interest in using the range, and, from 1948, its machines, operating at altitudes as high as 35,000 feet (10,668 metres), bombed a raft moored in the bay. Although practice bombs were normally dropped, on one day in mid-1948 an Avro Lincoln carried out ten runs, and on each released a live bomb into the sea near St Thomas's Head; 1,000-pounders (454 kg), each went off with an enormous thump that raised a great column of water into the air. This episode, together with the noise and vibration from previous bombing and explosive experiments brought a storm of protests to the Admiralty from those living in the locality. When RAF Hullavington also wanted to use the range for practice bombing, the local authorities became worried about its increasing use and the resulting enquiry was a drawn-out affair. In 1951, however, permission was given for continued use of the range by piston-engined aircraft operating at altitudes from between 50 feet (15 metres) and 25,000 feet (7,620 metres). When the ATDU departed Weston Airport in 1956, the range at St Thomas's Head continued to be used by a contingent of the Naval Torpedo and Mining Establishment that had relocated to RAF Locking. Later, a building was erected at St Thomas's Head for the RAF and Ministry of Defence explosive experts, who, early in the twenty-first century, were still using the area.

Some of the wartime aerial activity around Weston had been associated with the requirements of the Admiralty-run Department of Miscellaneous Weapons Development (DMWD) located at Birnbeck Pier, which for the war's duration was HMS *Birnbeck*. One of the challenging trials undertaken by the department was the development of a means of rapidly deploying a large army store from an aircraft that was conventionally dropped using an array of slowly-descending parachutes. For the trials, which were to take place over land and over water, a large concrete block, equipped with a bank of reaction rockets, represented the store, and dropped from an Avro Lancaster, the store's rapid, stabilised free-fall would be arrested by the rockets firing just prior to touchdown. Overland trials had already been successfully completed and over-water trials were now due to be done off the pier. These required the bomb aimer to make the drop so that the store arrived close to the pier, for its landing to be studied and filmed. The initial drop was from 2,000 feet (610 metres) and the store came down too far away. A second drop was then requested with the Lancaster crew being asked to position the store this time as close as possible to the pier. A couple of dummy runs obviously allowed the bomb aimer to get his eye in, for when finally dropped, the block scored a direct hit on the department's workshop at the end of the pier! Decommissioned on 1 March 1946, the pier would need much repair work before pleasure steamers could again use its facilities.

Not all the stores launched into the bay were recovered at the time and, in the summer of 1967, there commenced a prolonged hunt by bomb disposal teams. Sometimes the teams were assisted by a Westland Whirlwind HAR 10 from RAF Chivenor and an FAA photo-reconnaissance aircraft from Yeovilton, as many of the rusting wartime relics were lying buried in the mud and inaccessible by boat or foot. The weapons eventually recovered included parachute mines, bombs, aerial depth-charges, torpedoes, hedgehog anti-submarine missiles and a number of unidentified objects.

The anti-aircraft range at Brean was an altogether much smaller undertaking than that at Doniford. Opened in August 1942 as No.4 (Gunners) Wing, it was run by RAF Regiment personnel from RAF Locking. In October 1942, its name was changed to RAF Regiment Wing No.1 Anti-Aircraft Practice Camp, and until closed down in August 1944, some three and a half million rounds of .303 and three quarters of a million rounds of 20 mm had been fired at drogues towed principally by Miles Martinets from 1 AACU Weston Zoyland that flew up and down the beach. These yellow and black aircraft were often seen dropping drogues at Weston Airport, completing the circuit and then landing to pick up another target. Brean Down was also used early in the war by the RAF for the initial training of navigators and bomb aimers, the latter aiming bags of chalk at a target marker on the Down. At the war's end, the Air Ministry proposed to open up a further range using the Down's south side specifically for air-to-ground rocket-firing practice. However, the public outcry caused the project to be abandoned and Brean Down was finally relinquished by the Air Ministry on 27 May 1947.

Aircraft Torpedo Development Unit

An important arrival at Weston Airport in the early war years was the Torpedo Development Unit (TDU). Formed at RAF Gosport, Hampshire, on the pre-First World War airfield Grange in November 1938, it carried out tasks for both the Fleet Air Arm and Royal Air Force using both service's aircraft and crews operating over the nearby Stokes Bay Range in the Solent. Administered

Squadron Leader Thomas Murray in Manchester L7378 EM-A about to depart snowy Boscombe Down on 1 February 1942 for the TDU at Weston (Via N. Franklin/Bob Kirby)

Bombs being recovered at low tide from the mud of the Sand Bay Range (Mac Hawkins Collection)

from Thorney Island by the RAF, it was split into two flights, one dealing with the aerial delivery of torpedoes and the other mainly with parachute mines, special bombs and pyrotechnics. It was the flight specialising in the latter type of weapons that on occasions also dealt with torpedoes, known as the 'Special Flight', that, in August 1941, was detached to Weston. On arrival, the unit took over the large shed alongside Locking Moor Road that had been built several years before for airport ground equipment, and on either side temporary hard-standings were laid for the aircraft.

There was a lot of work to be done by the Flight to clear the airdrop characteristics, and constantly vary the fuse settings of these top-secret weapons, especially the mines, as the Admiralty, who was responsible for this type of store, hadn't ordered any until July 1939. At Weston, the proving of these weapons was to be carried out from the Sand Bay bombing range where the high tidal range allowed stores to be dropped into deep water on high tide and recovered at low tide just six hours later. To make full use of the high-tide 'window', aircraft carrying bombs and mines often took off from Weston as early as 6 a.m. and could be heard over and around the town for between one and two hours whilst clawing their way to weapon release altitude, and then completing a number of runs. The weapons were dropped at varying heights and speeds as close as possible to a yellow floating target and, after recovery, with circuits and fuses re-adjusted, were again dropped until they performed perfectly. The flight worked in close collaboration with 'boffins' from Farnborough, who supplied the torpedoes, and a Royal Navy team from Station MX at the Naval Torpedo and Mining Establishment, HMS *Vernon*, Portsmouth, who supplied the mines.

The unit's crews, like their aircraft, were a mixed bunch and were given little or no information regarding the flights except on a need-to-know basis, and the flights were normally listed as 'Trials'. Based at Gosport, pilots were flown to Weston as required, but the flight engineers were effectively posted to RAF Locking where they were always on hand for aircraft ground-handling and engine-running. Selected for their experience, flying in the multi-engined machines, they remained ever watchful of the less experienced pilots, most in this category being FAA that were used to operating single-engined machines from the decks of aircraft carriers. They had particular difficulty in converting to the bombers, and ignored advice sometimes resulted in aircraft undershooting and tyre marks and damaged kerbstones appeared in Locking Moor Road, but, fortunately, nothing more serious. Once familiar with the new machine, 3-engine approaches and practice overshoots tended to be conducted from the grass runway that extended north-west from West End Farm. A further advantage of using this runway was no road traffic to contend with and noise annoyance to those living in Bournville was reduced.

Two Avro Manchesters, R5773 and R5774, initially formed the mainstay of the unit at Weston, but if both became unserviceable at the same time other Manchesters were borrowed, with 207 Squadron at Bottesford in 1942 supplying L7378 EM-A, L7432 EM-J *Kipper's Kite*, L7515 EM-S, and R5835. These heavy bombers and their pilots, which included Flight Lieutenant Huntley-Wood, Squadron Leader T. C. Murray and Flying Officer D. Green, already with many operations over Germany, were also to experience various problems during their time with the unit, but these were mainly with the aircraft's two unreliable Rolls-Royce Vultures. Other types were also brought in as necessary, and with combinations of Vickers Wellingtons, Handley Page Herefords and Hampdens, Bristol Beauforts and Beaufighters, Fairey Swordfish and Albacores being loaded with stores, the area around this part of the airport frequently resembled that of an active RAF station. In January 1943, two Bristol Hercules-powered Avro Lancaster B IIs, DS632 and DS687, were semi-permanently attached to the Flight and the Manchesters were withdrawn. Together with the second prototype Lancaster I (P) DG595, still with its yellow under-surfaces, they operated alongside other, newer types of aircraft that came via Gosport and included a DH Mosquito XVI, a Douglas Boston, a Fairey Barracuda and Hawker Typhoon and Tempest Vs.

The 1,000-yard (914-metre) concrete runway laid down for Oldmixon's Beaufighters in 1942, was unfortunately directly in line with the TDU's dispersal building and, with a 400-yard (365-metre) extension to be added, there was an urgent need for it to be moved. This occurred in 1943/44 when the building was demolished and two concrete dispersal pans, a Bomb Shop and other buildings specifically for the unit were built nearer to Western Airways, and the new complex, together with Western Airways, was connected by a new taxi-track to the end of what was now the lengthened runway. There was also another change around this time when, on 11 November 1943, 'Aircraft' was added to the unit's title, it becoming the ATDU.

When, after the war, Bristol gave up its Hutton Moor Flight Shed, the ATDU moved in, and at last it was provided with good accommodation for its ground crew and aeroplanes. In 1946, the Lancaster IIs were progressively replaced by Avro Lincoln B Is. Although the first was almost immediately lost in a crash, it was soon replaced by RE231, and this, somewhat later, was joined by RE281. The Lincolns, which were to remain at Weston until 1956, for the first few years enjoyed the company of the constantly changing fleet of aircraft. Included were Swordfish NR933, NF399 and NF389 (now in the FAA/RN Historic Flight); DH Tiger Moths BD188 and T6702; Beaufighters LX856, NV290, NV316, NV361, and NV451; Sea Mosquitos TV458, TW228, TW230, TW284 and TW242; Barracudas RJ948, MX795, ME230, RJ925; North American Harvard KF183; Blackburn Firebrands EK744 and EK745; DH Sea Hornet TT188 and Hornet PX219 and Bristol Brigands RH773 and RH746. Communication flying was usually in Airspeed Oxfords V4321 and PH325 and Avro Ansons NK384, NK940, LT764 and NK790.

The first Lincoln RE285 had been lost on the night of 8 November 1946 whilst returning from a cross-country flight to Northern Ireland. It had a crew of three that included Flight Lieutenant R. H. Clark and Flying Officer Richard Williams and, in addition, three ground crew had gone along for the ride, and, unusually, all had taken parachutes with them. The expected time of arrival at Weston was 6 p.m., but whilst in transit the aircraft's radio was said to have failed, and in poor weather and darkness the pilot had become hopelessly lost. Weston Airport, which had no Ground Control Approach (GCA) was over-flown and with fuel running low the aircraft was abandoned, crashing at Chirton near Devizes in Wiltshire. All occupants landed safely near Boscombe Down and, returning to Weston the following day, had some tales to tell. In later years, GCA equipment operated by trainees from RAF Locking would be positioned adjacent to Weston's runway, and gave a certain amount of assistance to RAF aircraft landing at the airport.

Left: Some of the ATDU's
mechanics in 1949 in front
of one of the Lincolns
(R. Vallan)

Below: An ATDU Lincoln
in early 1955 outside the
Hutton Moor Flight Shed
waiting to be bombed-up
(R. Dudley)

November 1946 proved to be very bad month for the unit with two serious events following the loss of the Lincoln. Just four days later, on Tuesday 12th, DH Hornet F I PX229, *en route* to Weston from Farnborough in low cloud, flew into trees on high ground at Charterhouse-on-Mendip just 11 miles (18 km) short of the airport. The pilot, Lieutenant Commander Thomas Bentley, was killed and the wreck guarded until removed by a crash-site crew from RAF Locking. Worse was to come when, on Friday 22nd, the accident waiting to happen occurred.

Heavily laden and high-performance aircraft, during landing approaches from the east, usually came in rather low over Locking Moor Road to make an early touch-down on the runway. There was no supervision of traffic on the road but there were 'Danger' and 'No Parking' notices displayed. On that Friday, the runway was being resurfaced and take-offs and landings were being made on the adjacent grass, from where, during the morning, Boston III AL467 had taken off after a period of heavy rain from what was a very soggy field. Flown by Flying Officer Richard Williams, who had been co-pilot on the ill-fated Lincoln, Flight Engineer Bill Watson, and the unit's sergeant fitter IIE who had gone along for the ride, the mission was to deliver four 500-lb (227-kg) bombs to RAF Llandow, 15 miles (24 km) to the south of Cardiff.

On their return to Weston, they made a low pass over the runway to assess the condition of the grass landing area before joining the circuit and making a long, low approach from the east. The pilot and flight engineer were both partially blinded by the setting sun and didn't see the second of three green Bristol Tramways double-decker buses that was carrying fifty-seven airmen from Locking Camp to Weston Railway Station for weekend leave. The driver of the bus appeared not to see the approaching aircraft and witnesses said there was no evidence of an attempt to stop or reduce speed and seconds later there was an almighty crash as the two collided. The undercarriage and starboard airscrew struck the roof of the bus which was ripped off and, tragically, eight airmen on the top deck were killed and fifteen injured. With a severed nose leg which fell just inside the airport boundary and a collapsed starboard main leg, the Boston came to a rapid halt some 400 yards (366 metres) from the road as it dug into the soft ground alongside the runway. The main structure of the aeroplane had remained intact and, remarkably, the bus had stayed upright with not a window on its lower deck broken, and after receiving a new roof in Bristol, returned to Weston to see further service. Having to field answers to the difficult questions as to why three aircraft attached to the unit had crashed within such a short period of time was Squadron Leader Allison. His comments on the accident were widely reported, and there was even a full-page artist's impression in colour of the collision in the Italian newspaper *La Tribuna Illustrata*.

To eliminate any recurrence of this type of accident, the airport manager was instructed to have constructed on the airport a sterile area 470 feet (143 metres) wide and 180 feet (55 metres) deep adjacent to Locking Moor Road to

The end result of the ATDU's Boston hitting a double-decker bus on 22 November 1946 (*Weston Mercury* via R. Dudley)

One of the ATDU's Mosquitos being serviced in the Hutton Moor Flight Shed (R. Vallan)

be defined by white concrete strips and chevrons let into the grass, and a wide yellow threshold line painted on the runway, this was intended to ensure that pilots would bring aircraft over the road at an altitude of at least 50 feet (15 metres). The new arrangement was successfully tried by one of the Lincolns, and used in anger a short time afterwards when an Air Lingus DC3 full of passengers on the scheduled Dublin — Northolt route, due to bad weather at its destination, was forced into making a diversionary landing at Weston. In addition to the markings, road traffic control was also introduced using Air Ministry policemen when larger types of aircraft were involved. Another, but smaller, aircraft on the unit's strength at that time was Hawker Tempest F II PR857. On 1 July 1947, Flight Lieutenant T. G. Neach whilst carrying out a high-speed mine-clearance sortie, diagnosed failure of the wheel-brake system and, not wanting to wreck the aircraft in an uncontrolled landing, made a successful wheels-up landing at Llandow.

Following this unfortunate spate of accidents, there was a lull in events until Wednesday 7 July 1948 when another aircraft of the unit came to grief, again with fatal results. This time it was to be DH Sea Mosquito TR 33 TW284. At 3 p.m., having already been airborne three times that day, Squadron Leader David Alistaire 'Scottie' Robertson DFC, accompanied by Flight Lieutenant Anthony G. Nichols, the ATDU's armament officer, took off for a local flight, in which it was understood the pilot intended to give his passenger some excitement. This seems to have been the case, for twenty-four minutes later the Mosquito was back, being brought in from the north-east inverted at an altitude of around 250 feet (76 metres), and then, as the pilot rolled the aircraft the right way up, those watching on the ground, including armourers bombing-up a Lincoln, heard a very loud 'Crack' and the port wing immediately began to fold and break away. Some parts of the aircraft fell onto Locking Moor Road and one wing and its engine narrowly missed hitting the control tower, but the rest of the aircraft impacted on the grass just to the north of the runway in a mass of smoke and flames, instantly killing the crew. A Weston Aero Club Auster also came close to being hit by the falling wreckage as it taxied out for take-off, and passengers for the Weston — Pengam Moors ferry service alighting from the airport bus were delayed for a time until permission was given for their DH Dragon Rapide circling overhead to land.

After the war, with the bombing range being relocated a bit further to the north at Woodspring Bay, the floating target was also moved and this time positioned over a sand bar that made recovery of bombs, mines and torpedoes easier, as they were always clearly visible on the sand at low-water. The Swordfish and Barracudas continued to be used for torpedo work and surprisingly one of the Lincolns was also adapted for the purpose, this aircraft also being equipped with a flight recorder in its spacious bomb bay. Torpedoes then under test were of British and American origin comprising 18-inch (46-cm) and 21-inch (53-cm) devices which had some unusual nose and tail configurations, and test-drops were now made on the St Thomas's Head range, and released close to the shore from low altitude. On one occasion, a Swordfish about to release a torpedo nearly came to a sticky end. Approaching the dropping area at about 50 feet (15 metres), the usual release procedures were completed, followed by the simultaneous rapid forward-stick movement to prevent the aircraft rearing-up, only for the pilot to discover that the store had hung up and the aircraft had instead dived and was running its wheels through the choppy water. An equally rapid heave back on the stick brought the machine back to a safe altitude, and the weapon was successfully released on the next run. There was also an incident with a Barracuda that at the end of a torpedo-dropping sortie had one leg of the machine's peculiarly ungainly undercarriage stick up, and after trying to free it by bouncing the aircraft on Weston's runway, it headed off to RAF St Athan where better facilities were available to cope with this type of incident.

Weapon recovery was the responsibility of a team from the Naval Torpedo and Mining Establishment at HMS *Vernon*, Portsmouth. Based at Weston Airport, the establishment operated an Admiralty 60-ton landing craft from Wick Wharf, Kingston Seymour, and, on Thursday 2 February 1950, in severe weather whilst several miles offshore, one of its two engines failed. At the height of the gale, distress flares alerted Weston's lifeboat and a Lincoln was scrambled to carry out a search. The landing craft was duly located and, following a difficult transfer to the lifeboat, the crew of sixteen was landed at Uphill; a tug sent from Bristol relocated the landing craft and managed to tow it to Cardiff for repairs. At times, helicopters were also brought in to assist in store recovery and other trials. The first had probably been towards the war's end, as the ATDU at Gosport had on loan Sikorsky R4B Hoverflys KK989, KL111 and KL112. However, there was a visit by R4B KL104, coded P9-T, from the Air-Sea Warfare Development Unit at Thorney Island when, in the first week of February 1948, during coastal survey work, it landed for fuel. Probably the next to visit was Westland Dragonfly HR 3 WP503, an A&AEE machine. It was flown in from Gosport by Lieutenant Chaplin on 18 July 1955 and stayed for seven days. Westland S-51 Mk 1 WB801, belonging to the MoS and operated by the A&AEE, was next to arrive on 31 August. Unusual, in that it had been converted from a civil machine and had only one fuel tank instead of the normal two, it also had small bomb racks beneath the fuselage to carry gas canisters. Like WP503, it was also flown in from Gosport by Lieutenant Chaplin.

In the early to mid-1950s, the two Lincolns were still at Weston and from time to time were joined by aircraft from the earlier period, but there was also a variety of new machines from Gosport, including Barracuda VX381, DH Dominies X7396 and NR739, Boulton Paul Balliol VR590, Brigands RH742, RH743, RH746 (the fuselage of which is now at Kemble in the Bristol Aero Collection), RH747, RH749, RH750 and RH772 and Lincoln RE381. In 1955, Westland Wyvern S 4 VZ760, on 20 July, also took up temporary residence at Weston. Flown by Lieutenant J. G. Marshall, the unusual sound produced by its gas turbine-powered contra-rotating airscrews, until returning to Gosport on 18 August, was frequently heard around the town as it dived to drop parachute mines onto the range. Pilots involved with flying the resident machines and the visiting aircraft from Gosport now included Squadron Leader Grubb, Lieutenant Marshall, Lieutenant Commander Wynes, Flight Lieutenants D. Stoten, McGlashan, J. F. Pinnington, Leggett, Nuttall, A. Twigg, Flight Sergeant Bill Pitt, Flying Officer W. J. Burnett-Smith and Pilot Officers A. B. Frazer and Turley.

Other aircraft associated with weapon trials but not necessarily based at Gosport arrived from time to time for short stays. Gloster Meteor T 7 WH231, an RAE machine from Farnborough, flew in on 7 April 1954 and later in the day took off for Filton. Avro Shackleton MR 2 WG553, from the Anti-Submarine Warfare Development Unit at St Mawgan, flew in 2 June 1954, and Shackleton MR I WG527 of 42 Squadron at St Eval flew in on the 30th. Lincoln B 2 WD125, an A&AEE machine, came in from the Bombing Trials Unit (BTU) at West Freugh on 15 July and, again, this time from its Farnborough base, on the 19th. Lincoln B 2 RF341 flew in from St Athan *en route* to its home base at Debden on 20 September, whilst, on 12 October, another of Farnborough's Lincolns, WD129, touched down and stayed the night, did a local flight the next day and then returned to base. On 25 October, DH Venom FB I WE267 arrived from the Armament Flight at RAE Farnborough to carry out a series of dive-bombing trials over the range with 1,000 pounders (454 kg). Piloted by Flight Lieutenant Tanner, it returned to base two days later. On 6 November, Grumman Avenger AS 4 XB447 from Anthorn flew in accompanied by a DH Dominie, both returning to base the following day. In the following year, Lincoln B 2 RE422, on 18 April, flew in from the BTU at West Freugh and, later in the day, returned to its base.

During the mid-1950s, there was an unscheduled stay at the Hutton Moor Flight Shed for a Vickers Valetta from RAF Chivenor that followed an emergency landing at Weston by one of the station's Hawker Hunters. Low on fuel, the relatively inexperienced Hunter pilot was making haste down the Bristol Channel hoping to make base before the tanks ran dry. Approaching Weston with only a few minutes of fuel left, he decided on an emergency landing at Weston Airport. Made at high speed, the tyres burst on touchdown and a lot of rubber was deposited on the runway, and, reporting the incident to his commanding officer over the telephone, it was said that the colour of the young pilot's face matched that of his bright ginger hair. There was a quick response from Chivenor, replacement wheels were loaded onto the Valetta and flown to Weston, and meanwhile, with the Hunter's undercarriage resting on makeshift sledges, the machine was recovered to Western Airways. When the Valetta arrived, the new wheels were unloaded and the Valetta directed to the flight shed where it would stay overnight. Unfortunately, one of the aircraft's wing-tips collided with a rather substantial obstruction and was extensively damaged. Not a good day for Chivenor, but perhaps this incident took some of the heat off the unfortunate

What would have been Oldmixon's first production Brigand TF I RH742 at Filton, probably January 1946. After serving with the Empire Central Flying School and then the A&AED it was on the strength of the ATDU at Gosport and until June 1956, when it was struck off charge, was a frequent visitor to Weston Airport (Bristol via Airbus)

The Hutton Moor Flight Shed on 22 July 1955 with doors open exposing, left to right: Locking's Chipmunk WB721, and being refuelled the ATDU's Lincolns RE281 and RE231. Wyvern S 4 VZ760 has just been shut down by Lieutenant Marshall (R. Dudley)

Dragonfly HR 3 WP503 outside the Hutton Moor Flight Shed in July 1955 (R. Dudley)

Hunter pilot. The following day, with new wheels fitted, the Hunter departed for its base, leaving the disabled Valetta awaiting a repair party.

Soon there was a new requirement to drop mines accurately from much higher altitudes than had previously been attempted, up to 20,000 feet (6,096 metres). The Mk 14 bomb-sight had so far been used when appropriate, but for these trials other arrangements were made, including what was described as a Heath Robinson device consisting of wires on poles positioned some 40 yards (37 metres) apart with distance markers positioned along them. The ground control officer, in this case the ATDU's armaments officer, in communication with the aircraft, would attempt to 'fly' the aircraft giving the accepted 'Left, Left, Right, Steady' instructions to the pilot and a countdown of five and 'Off' to the bomb aimer. In one instance the count of 'Five' was followed by 'Round Again', but it was too late and the store had gone. It was a mine released from 15,000 feet (4,570 metres), suspended on three parachutes that landed some distance from the aiming point, and it was thought by the crews that at times it was the parachutes that were being tested rather than the weapons.

On 25 April 1955, at Weston there were nineteen Brigand movements, the first at 7.25 a.m. when RH749 piloted by Flight Lieutenant McGlashen took off for Gosport. This sort of activity was not unusual, and occasionally caused the odd scare. On 1 June 1954, whilst airborne in RH747, Flight Lieutenant Twigg called an emergency following failure of his starboard engine. A successful landing was carried out, but it was three days later before the machine was airborne again on a test flight. The following year, on 23 April, Flight Lieutenant McGlashen also had a similar experience whilst airborne in Brigand RH749, having to land with the starboard airscrew feathered. On the ground, there had also been the odd incident, one being the accidental release of two long, cylindrical mines from the bomb bay of a Lincoln onto the concrete apron, due, it was said, to the inexperience of the unit's armaments officer who was standing-in for the regular bomb aimer. On another occasion, a malfunction of the release mechanism in one of the Lincolns resulted in the aircraft returning to the airport with a new type of flare canister lying on the closed bomb-bay doors, giving the armourers some anxious moments as they supported the canister as the doors were inched open. However, the incident that had occurred on the 11 October 1945 was certainly the most alarming and potentially the most dangerous when a mother preparing breakfast for her family of five was given a severe fright when a parachute mine fell from an aircraft, making a large hole through the roof and ceiling of 7 Albert Road in the town, coming to earth alongside the lady in her kitchen! With this type of incident in mind, approaches to the airport over Weston were to be avoided, but as in this case, due to wind direction, it was not always possible.

There was one more incident when an aircraft came to grief, fortunately no one was hurt but perhaps the pilot suffered a loss of face and there was damage to one of the communication Dominies in two instalments. On 16 January 1956, NR739, piloted by Flying Officer Burnett-Smith, was taxiing towards the runway for departure to Gosport when heavy braking lifted the tail and brought the nose and airscrews into contact with the Perimeter Road. The unfortunate pilot was later ferried back to Gosport and would have the daunting task of explaining to the officer commanding flying, Squadron Leader Grubb, just how he had managed to stand the aircraft on its nose. In due course, the engines were removed and the Dominie was parked in the open in the lee of the flight shed. There it remained until a particularly windy Sunday in the summer when air traffic control saw it travelling tail first at a fair rate of knots across the airport directly towards the tower. In spite of desperate efforts to steer the machine clear by pulling on a wing-tip, it unfortunately buried itself in the side of the adjacent crew room. NR739's damaged remains survived and were sold on 21 June 1957 and delivered from Weston on the 26th to Hants & Sussex Aviation.

In May 1956, the station at Gosport closed and, on 18 May 1956, the ATDU moved to RNAS Culdrose where runways were longer and there were better facilities for the operation of jet-powered aircraft. Later in the year, the flight left Weston, and its aircraft were withdrawn from ATDU use.

EMI of Wells

In the 1950s, for a short period, the ATDU shared the Hutton Moor Flight Shed with EMI of Wells. At that time, the company had been contracted by the Ministry of Supply (MoS) to develop the guidance system for a new ram-jet powered missile believed to have been the C.F. 299 Sea Dart. The work at Weston commenced with Vickers Valetta VX560, on loan from the MoS and operated by Airwork of Blackbushe, being ferried to the airport where over a period of months at the westerly end of the shed, it was converted by six Airwork and EMI employees for preliminary trials. A large diesel-powered generator installed in the fuselage between the two wing spars, that violently shook the aircraft when started, provided the necessary 240 volt supply to the large number of black boxes that were put in every conceivable space. Operating with a crew of four or five, the machine, normally piloted by Alfred 'Dusty' Rhodes who lived in Banwell, was usually accompanied by Flight Engineer Don Clow and Engineer Ray Teague (all Airwork employees), the project leader from EMI at Wells, Professor Gilmore, and other boffins from EMI and the Ministry.

A wheeled Bofors gun-carriage, obtained from the Army and fitted out with tracking equipment, was a part of the ground test equipment, and this was initially positioned on top of Sandford Quarry. With two EMI personnel operating the hand-wheel traversing system, it was used to manually track the Valetta as it approached and passed over. Disturbing the local cattle population, the device was eventually moved to Birnbeck Pier where the Valetta was then flown at low level over the Bristol Channel, and tracked as it circumvented the

Valetta VX560 with various wing-bulges rests on the Hutton Moor Flight Shed compass-swinging pad part-way through its Airwork/EMI trials (R. Teague)

various local headlands. Trials were also, for a time, undertaken from Weston Airport with the aircraft homing onto equipment carried beneath a weather balloon towed by a Land Rover. As the system matured, the missile guidance system was reduced in size, and, with it installed in a large under-fuselage radome, carried out further trials over the snowfields of Cumberland, and the Aberporth, Cardigan Bay range in Wales. Trials from Weston started in the second half of 1955, when, between 4 August and 20 September, the Valetta completed eighteen flights. Most were local of one to two hours duration, but several were to and from Airwork's bases at Blackbushe and Gatwick where the machine was serviced. Eventually, to give more hangarage space to the ATDU, the Valetta and the development team moved away from Weston to a sectioned-off part of the Bristol and Wessex Flying Club hangar at Lulsgate Airport.

EMI returned to the Hutton Moor Flight Shed in 1958 to share it with ground instructional aircraft belonging to Locking's No.1 Radio School. Here, unadvertised and behind a dividing curtain, the embryo National Radar Target Modelling Centre (NRTMC) was set up. This organisation, run by EMI in co-operation with the Royal Signals and Radar Establishment (RSRE) at Malvern on behalf of the Defence Ministry, carried out much secret work, most of it involving checking the radar signatures of very accurate scale models of new Ministry aircraft, missiles, ships and vehicle projects. The models, some made by Western Airways, were hung or supported on a stem, and then rotated whilst being scanned by various radar devices. The object of this exercise was to minimise the model's radar signature (make it more stealthy) by, if necessary, subtly remodelling parts of it. With the radar return optimised, the information was passed back to the designer for the full-size machine's shape to be similarly modified. It is believed that the Victor, which for a time shared the hangar with NRTMC, was also used for experiments, as at that time the bomber was a part of the country's prime nuclear deterrent, and it was essential that the force should be well on the way to its target before being observed by enemy radars.

Eventually, to give more space to EMI for their expanding research projects and to improve building security, No.1 Radio School's aircraft were dispersed to other locations. In the early years of the twenty-first century what was now Thorn EMI was taken over by the French company Thales Defence Information Systems and an early task was to borrow Westland W30 Series 160 G-BKGD from The Helicopter Museum on the other side of the airport so that an evaluation could be carried out on radar signatures given by Lynx-type tail rotors. In early 2004, it was announced that the facility at Weston would be shut down and, in early June, nine of the twenty staff were made redundant, and those that survived were transferred to the Wookey Hole Road, Wells Factory, and the Weston site was decommissioned before being handed back to its owner, the Ministry of Defence.

4

END OF A DREAM

Western Airways — Early Post-War Contracts

With the return of peace the size of the armed forces started to rapidly contract. Personnel were demobbed and many RAF and RN aircraft were flown to Maintenance Units (MUs) for storage or scrapping and spares recovery. At Western Airways, most Ministry contracts were terminated and the remaining Ansons in for rebuild were either completed and ferried to MUs or written off, some burnt on site. One of the last wartime Anson Is in for rebuild, N4877, was ready for collection on 25 March 1946, and, following demob, on 14 July 1950 eventually found its way, via the Skyfame Museum at Staverton, to Duxford's Imperial War Museum, where today it is displayed in a pristine RAF wartime colour scheme.

Immediately post-war, Straight Corporation's management was still very depleted, having as managing director Whitney Straight and secretary Stanley Cox with head office 'The Airport', Weston, and the London office at Bush House, Aldwych, WC2. Western Airways on the other hand, was slightly better off with Managing Director Whitney Straight, General Manager Frederick Jeans and Test Pilot Lew Lisle. For these management teams there was now the urgent matter of deciding on the immediate way forward. Initially, as a part of the greater Ministry spares-recovery programme, a small contract was obtained for three fitters to remove generators and certain other electrical components such as Sperry Panels from 200 Airspeed Oxfords lying at MUs at Silloth, Lichfield, Kirkbride, and one in Northern Ireland, but, although bringing in the necessary funds, the job was to last for only a few weeks.

In this period, new Ministry contracts for aircraft work were to prove difficult, if not impossible to find and, to fill the gap until they again became available, Western Airways reluctantly took on a contract to refurbish a range of wartime Army vehicles, mainly 3- and 5-ton Austin trucks, ambulances and low-loaders, until the late 1940s, the area around the factory complex was full of these vehicles awaiting their turn for rebuild. The work carried out in the large hangar, with the remaining Anson refurbishment behind curtains at the building's easterly end, included engine removal for overhaul and reconditioning in Bristol and the stripping down to component parts of chassis, gearboxes, axles and brake units. When rebuilt and tested, many were exported to friendly countries such as India. However, Western Airways was lucky to obtain one new Ministry aircraft contract and that was for the repair and refurbishment of 140 Slingsby Kirby Cadet Mk 1 gliders for the ATC. Brought in from all over Britain three at a time in a purpose-built pantechnicon, the work, under the supervision of manager and woodworker Jack Newbury, continued from mid-1946 until the end of 1948 and was carried out in the timber building that, during the war, had been used to produce aircraft recognition models and was now known as the Glider Hut. Also within a year or two, Western Airways would become area agents for Slingsby Sailplanes and, as late as the early 1950s, de-rigged gliders could still be seen around the site awaiting collection.

With the likelihood of there not being much new Ministry aircraft work, the decision was made to start on a programme of converting war-surplus military aircraft for civil use. Carried out in the small hangar, the first to be tackled was ex-RAF Percival Proctor I P6197 that had been purchased in January 1946, and, as G-AGWV, it carried out a number of runs to Pengam Moors until sold in June. Three Piper Cub-Coupés were also obtained in March 1946; these machines, BV990, ES923 and DG667, had belonged to the Straight Corporation pre-war and were in due course overhauled, returned to their original registration and then sold on. In the early summer, DH Hornet Moths W5779, W5750, W9388 and AV952 were also purchased and, after being overhauled, had their respective pre-war registrations of G-AFDT, G-ADKL, G-ADLY and G-ADSK restored. All were then sold, except for G-AFDT, which had been with the company before the war and was to become the first aircraft in the about-to-be-reinstated Weston Aero Club.

War-surplus aircraft for conversion continued to be purchased, three being ex-RAF Percival Petrels P5637, P5640 and P5634, the latter having been allocated to the King's Flight and later used by the C-in-C Bomber Command. These machines were military versions of the Percival Q6, the type used by Western Airways pre-war, and after conversion were sold on as G-AHOM, G-AHTA and G-AHTB respectively. G-AHOM, however, because of a crash in bad visibility near Dungeness when on its way back from Paris on Christmas Eve 1946, was returned to Western Airways for rebuild, arriving Saturday 11 January 1947 on a low-loader after a 250-mile (402-km) road journey. In the autumn of 1946 Western Airways also secured two Supermarine Walrus II amphibians from Wroughton. Although allocated civil registrations, G-AIKL (ex-HD915) and G-AIEJ (ex-HD903), only the latter received a C of A and it had a relatively short but chequered life in civvy street. Amongst other duties, in 1948 it was flown up the River Thames by Western Airways pilot Group Captain R. Louis with a cameraman in the nose, the footage was obtained for the film *London Belongs to Me*, and then in August it took a photographer from *Life* magazine to obtain stills of Olympic yacht racing in Torbay. Shortly

Sometime in 1948, Walrus G-AIEJ on the apron outside Western Airways. A Lincoln of the ATDU and the airport bus are just behind (From the collection of North Somerset Studies Library)

after performing a number of practice take-offs and landings in Weston Bay, it was flown to Glasgow for another job, but was written off in a storm. Another Walrus, this time a privately-owned Mk 1, G-AIIB (ex-X9467), arrived in September 1946 and was due to be flown to Australia, but it was wrecked at Weston Airport during a gale.

Another military aircraft to come the way of Western Airways in 1946 was Avro 621 Tutor K3215. Civilianised and registered G-AHSA, it had its C of A flights on 19/20 July 1947 and after a few years appeared in the film about the life of Douglas Bader, *Reach for the Sky*. It would eventually revert to original pre-war military markings in the ownership of the Shuttleworth Trust. Other aircraft seen in the workshops in 1946/47 included Auster G-AJJB (ex-Auster V TJ520), Miles Hawk Trainer IIIs G-AJHE and G-AJHB (ex-Magisters N3777 and N2259) respectively, DH Moth Minor G-AFPH (ex-X5133), Taylorcraft 'C' G-AFTN (ex-Taylorcraft 'Plus C/2' HL535) and BA Swallow II G-AEZM, named *Puddlejumper II*. There was also DH Queen Bee LF863, recovered after a lengthy stay in a hangar at RAF St Athan. This aeroplane was to be flown to Weston by Lew Lisle, but experiencing two forced landings due to engine failure before leaving Cardiff airspace, it was finally delivered dismantled and used for spares by Western Airways. A Miles MIIA Whitney Straight also appeared, but spares were unobtainable and it was scrapped in 1948.

Reintroduction of Commercial Flying Training

Just after the end of hostilities, there were changes that affected the way Weston Airport was run. During the war, its control had passed through the hands of various RAF commands and the Bristol Aeroplane Company, and on 3 September 1946, responsibility for its operation was transferred to the Ministry of Civil Aviation (MCA) with Mr R. A. Hobday being made airport manager. This tied in well with Straight's post-war vision, for he had in mind the company again becoming active, predominately in civil flying activities. He had already put in place the refurbishment of light machines that would be suitable for aero clubs and was now about to resurrect flight training on a commercial scale. With this in mind, William Cumming, by now Group Captain OBE, DFC, following war service with RAF Coastal Command, was re-engaged as Director of Training and tasked with re-forming Straight Aviation Training Ltd. Established in the basement of Bush House, the Central Navigation School and Link Trainer Centre was to provide comprehensive training to the many pilots and navigators leaving the services that were looking for a career in civil aviation.

Also in 1946, Francis Chichester, the pre-war record-breaking pilot and navigator who in 1931 had made the first solo long-distance seaplane flight from Brooklands to Sydney and then on to New Zealand, was made a director of the company. During the war, Chichester had been senior navigation officer at the RAF Central Flying School and produced for the Air Ministry, amongst other notable items, *Navigation Notes for Instructors and Students*. With this background, in 1947, he spent ten days at Weston Aero Club assisted by its CFI, Bobby Wardle, simplifying the standard RAF navigation manual to make

G-AIOA, one of Straight Aviation Training Anson Is resting between navigation sorties at Willingale on 4 July 1948 (E. J. Riding Collection)

G-AITJ, one of the two Anson Is modified to the passenger-carrying configuration in front the Western Airways large hangar. Note the Austin lorries awaiting their turn for refurbishment (E. J. Riding Collection)

Six FAA radar-equipped Anson Is await rebuild by Western Airways early post-war (Via E. ap Rees)

it more appropriate for the training of private pilots. Other directors, some also from Straight's pre-war operations were brought into the new company and these were Roland King Farlow, Owen Roberts and Louis Strange. Whitney Straight was managing director and again Stanley Cox was secretary.

Avro Ansons were selected as navigation trainers for Straight Aviation Training Ltd, and, in 1946, Western Airways procured eight ex-RAF Mk 1s: NK728, EF928, EG593, EG391, DJ492, MG281, NK601 and NK843. These machines, registered G-AIEZ, G-AIFA, G-AIFB, G-AIFC, G-AIFD, G-AINZ, G-AIOA and G-AIOB respectively, over a period of several months were overhauled and finished in Straight's new post-war silver and crimson colour scheme that retained the pre-war horizontal stripes on the rudder. From 1946 until 1948, these machines, mainly flying from Willingale, an ex-American bomber base at Chipping Ongar, Essex, provided training to crews from the air forces of Holland, Pakistan, Iraq and India. One of the Indian Air Force officer cadets to be trained was 18-year-old Nevek Nehru whose uncle was Prime Minister Pandit Nehru. He arrived late for the course, and Chief Instructor R. C. Cheshire moved to Weston for a time to give this rather important cadet private tuition. Most of the Ansons would, in 1948, return to Weston and be parked in the open until sold, some gaining a certain notoriety, having been illegally disposed of by a third party to the Israeli Air Force. Straight Aviation Training Ltd ceased operation in 1949.

Two further Anson Is, MG874 and W2628, were also purchased, and they were extensively modified, having seven passenger seats installed and the 'glasshouse' replaced by five small windows on each side. Registered G-AITJ and G-AITK and finished with extra crimson trim to their nose and engine nacelles, the aircraft were retained by Western Airways for a number of civil transport duties, usually in Britain but sometimes much further afield. Early in 1948 one was chartered by a French Count for a safari to French Equatorial Africa. The pilot for this 4,000-mile (6,438-km) trip, which left on Thursday 5 February, was Wing Commander 'Daddy' Crundall DFC, AFC, recently returned to Western Airways following wartime service with an anti-aircraft co-operation squadron. Not long before, he had taken Compton Mackenzie around the Second World War battlefields of Italy in a Western Airways machine chartered by the War Office. The Anson, in turn, was accompanied on some of the 3-month tour by an Auster flown by Mr C. Rushworth. Shoehorned into the machine's tiny cabin was a long-range fuel tank, emergency survival equipment and a ground-service engineer who would look after both aircraft on their long trip around Central Africa. The Auster, which had no wireless, after reaching Khartoum returned to Weston and the Anson carried on alone. With the increase in civil flying and passengers no longer being able to use the pre-war Terminal Building as the airport entrance, a new access was required. This was cut through from an enlarged roadside car park to join with the south ATDU dispersal and, it connected with two new timber buildings, one of which was used as the passenger terminal.

In addition to looking after its own Ansons, others passed through the workshops of Western Airways, with NK842 being converted to G-AJHK for Aerial Transit in May 1947 and MG676 converted and delivered to the Royal Hellenic Air Force in June 1947. These were followed by six Royal Navy Anson Is, including NK173 and NK951 that had previously been used to train Fairey Swordfish, Firefly and Barracuda ASV/ASH radar operators. Arriving with a variety of hitherto-unseen scanners, blisters and aerials, they eventually left after complete rebuild for further service in the Navy as standard Anson Is.

Resurrection of the Aero Clubs

As soon as possible after the wartime ban on private flying was lifted on 1 January 1946, the Straight Corporation, anxious to get its pre-war aero club activities back on stream, began to consider where they should be set up. The first, obviously, would be at Weston and this was reinstated on Friday 7 June. It had been hoped to open the club earlier but occupation of the airport by the military prevented this happening. Plymouth's Roborough Airport and Exeter Airport would also again be given clubs, but the other pre-war clubs would be replaced by a new one named the 'Home Counties Flying Club' and, as its name implied, serve those living in the Home Counties and would operate from the Handley Page aerodrome at Radlett and the one at Willingale. Exeter, decommissioned towards the end of 1946, was transferred to the MCA on 1 January 1947, and Bill Parkhouse who, at the beginning of hostilities had joined the RAF and left as a Wing Commander, with Bill Dann was dispatched there from Weston to re-establish it as a civil concern with an aero club run under the auspices of Exeter Airport Ltd, who leased it from the Ministry.

The club at Weston, around which all of the company's aero club aircraft were based, now became registered as Weston Aero Club Ltd with Wing Commander Richard John Bennett 'Jack' Pearse OBE, AFC its chief flying instructor. Pearse, also registered as CFI of the other clubs was a very experienced pilot, in February 1938 having become Plymouth Airport's pre-war manager and CFI of its aero club. During the war he had served in Bomber Command OTUs and at its end was personal assistant to Dr Roxbee Cox of Power Jets (R & D Ltd). His stay at Weston proved to be of short duration, for, at the end of March 1947, he went back to Plymouth to again become airport manager and CFI of the new club. In 1956, on the retirement of Bill Parkhouse, he would become managing director of Exeter Airport Ltd and remain in that position until 1969.

At the end of June, Weston Aero Club's first aircraft, DH Hornet Moth G-AFDT was joined by Taylorcraft 'Plus D' G-AHUM. Like the Ansons, they were also finished in the overall silver and crimson scheme and could be flown dual or solo for £3 an hour. Also in June, three ex-RAF Miles Magisters T9672, L8210 and R1914 were obtained for the clubs. These trainers had come from a batch of 100 military light aircraft made available by the government at a

Celebrating the re-start of Weston Aero Club. In front of the club's first machine Hornet Moth G-AFDT are left to right: Jack Pearse, Freddy Jeans, Stanley Cox, Mr. Herring (the first pupil) and Lew Lisle (*Aeroplane*/www.aeroplanemonthly.com)

G-AJOY was one of the ten Argus obtained in 1947 and converted by Western Airways for distribution to the various Straight-run aero clubs (E. J. Riding Collection)

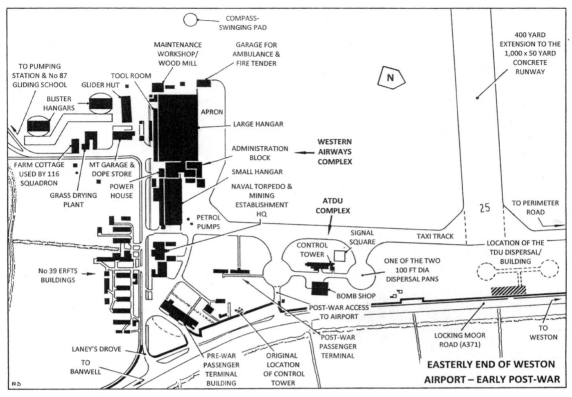

Layout of the easterly end of the airport early post-war (R. Dudley)

Looking north from the Western Airways complex in the summer of 1947. The Proctor (NP324) and the Dominie (NR739) are from RAF Halton's Station Flight; the latter when transferred to the ATDU, in mid 1956 nearly wrecked the timber buildings alongside the tower (Bob Cooke)

Looking east from the Western Airways complex. In this and the previous photo, many of the aircraft converted by the company to civil configuration immediately after the war can be seen (Bob Cooke)

nominal £10 apiece to enable post-war aero clubs to get going again. Many of these machines, however, proved to be something of a liability, most being in poor condition. Of the three Magisters, L8210 (although registered G-AHUL) was scrapped with its components being used for spares, and R1914 (registered G-AHUJ) was exchanged for DH Tiger Moth G-AHWE, belonging to the Lochleven Aero Club of Kinross. However, T9672 converted to Hawk Trainer Mk III standard, and registered G-AHUK, stayed at Weston to become the club's third machine. At this time, a further Tiger Moth EM929 was also obtained, converted to G-AHVV, and in due course operated by the Home Counties Aero Club.

To see how the country's aero clubs were coping with the early post-war constraints, in mid-August 1946, officials of the Royal Aero Club headed by Whitney Straight, the recently elected chairman of the Association of British Aero Clubs, flew in prototype DH Dove G-AGPJ to a number of them. At Weston, as chairman of Western Airways, he was no doubt delighted to learn that the first of his post-war clubs had made such a promising start with 122 members already having completed a respectable 570 flying hours. Straight, however, was about to resign as chairman of Straight Corporation as some of his interests in aviation were about to conflict with his other business activities.

Following departure of Jack Pearse to Plymouth, Bobby Wardle took over as CFI and manager of the Weston club with Philip R. Sparrow his deputy. First job for the new team was to collect another Magister from 51 MU at Lichfield for Western Airways to rework. Another type of aircraft to join the aero club fleet at that time was the single-engined American Fairchild Argus 4-seat high-wing monoplane, ten being obtained from RAF stocks, with the first FK315 in the workshops for conversion in April 1947, and ready to fly in May. In due course, two of the machines were operated by Weston Aero Club, one by the Plymouth club and the others by the Home Counties club. Two further training aircraft to join the Weston club in mid-1947 were new Auster Autocrats G-AJUM and G-AJUO. One was owned by club member Mr F. H. Wheaton and, on Friday 20 June, accompanied by Mr R. Penny, they became the first club members after the war to fly one of the club's aircraft to the Continent. 1947 had also proved to be quite a successful year, for during the last six months alone, using the two Austers, the Hawk Trainer and an Argus, club members flew a total of 1,016 hours and gained fifteeen 'A' Licences.

Weston's club, like most others in the country, was mainly equipped with old wartime aircraft, and manufacturers were desperately trying to persuade clubs and individuals to purchase more up-to-date equipment. Western Airways had become area agent for Percival Aircraft, and, on Saturday 21 June 1947, a Proctor V was flown in by a Percival demonstration pilot and some club members were given a chance of flying it. On Sunday 29 February 1948, the new Elliots of Newbury, Eon G-AKBC, in a striking pale-blue colour scheme, was flown in by test pilot Mr R. Antill, accompanied by Chief Designer Mr N. Carroll, to give club members probably their first experience of flying a light aircraft with a tricycle undercarriage. During the winter months when the days were short, there were also occasional talks and film shows put on in a clubroom in the pre-war Terminal Building. Guest speaker, in February 1948, was Raoul Hafner, Chief Helicopter Designer of the Bristol Aeroplane Company, and he gave some 130 members the background to helicopter development and his rather ambitious thoughts on the future of air travel by helicopter. He predicted that, by the late 1950s, there would be a helipad on top of Weston's Beach Bus Station that, with others at Cardiff, Bristol, Bath, Reading and London, would be used for a scheduled airline service by a fleet of his soon-to-fly Type 173 tandem-rotor machine.

Although 1947 had been a very good year for the Weston club, 1948 saw a downturn which slowly continued into 1949. One factor affecting operations was the new MCA regulation introduced on 1 April 1949, requiring many extra hours to be flown before a trainee pilot could obtain a full licence, and the government discontinuing the fuel subsidy. Another factor was operating costs of the Argus, for, although having a low initial cost, its thirsty 165 hp Jacobs radial proved to be an extravagant luxury when fuel was relatively expensive and difficult to obtain. Resulting from these problems, in October

1949, Western Airways announced that it would no longer be supplying the club with aircraft, and neither would it continue to sponsor its activities, which in the previous year had resulted in only 480 hours being flown. The club was now officially disbanded with CFI Captain R. E. Roberts and deputy CFI Captain Denys Axel-Berg receiving their notice. Western Airways did suggest that flying training could restart the following spring but this didn't happen and it was to be some years before the airport had another aero club. Although the club was no more, visiting light aircraft continued to use the airport and its facilities, one rather obscure machine of note being GAL Cygnet G-AGAX, a light low-wing aeroplane with a tricycle undercarriage. It arrived on 5 September 1949 for overhaul shortly after taking its young pilot on his first, and epic, trip around France.

With the general reduction of aircraft activity, the Blister hangars were given over to other uses, with Somerset Crop Driers Ltd, a subsidiary of Airways Union, leasing them from the MCA. The problem of spontaneous combustion associated with the storage of grass on the night of Wednesday 18 May 1949 caused a fire that consumed the northerly building. Detected at about 11 p.m., the conflagration which, until the fire brigade arrived, was fought by men from the RAF and the Naval Torpedo and Mining Establishment led by Lieutenant F. W. Furzman, destroyed many bags of grass, two fuselages, one (probably the second) Western Airways Walrus, and a number of aero engines, their burning mag-alloy castings adding to the fire's intensity. Surprisingly, an aircraft in a packing case only feet away from the building escaped unscathed. The remaining hangar, which was beginning to shed its corrugated-iron cladding, after the fire was only used to store the pre-war Chance floodlighting and airport grass-cutting equipment.

The Ferry Service Restarts

Meanwhile, there had been a very welcome event in July 1946 when the Weston — Pengam Moors ferry service was reintroduced, not by Western Airways, as would have been expected, but by the silver and black DH Dragon Rapides of Great Western & Southern Airlines, the first setting off for Pengam Moors on 31 July being G-AERN, piloted by Captain H. J. King DFC, DFM. This and other routes in Britain were now licensed and run by the newly formed nationalised airline, British European Airways Corporation (BEAC), its deputy chairman from August 1946 being Whitney Straight. The government had announced, in November 1945, that BEAC was to absorb all private British airlines and then decide the routes to be served and by which aeroplanes. Thus it was in early June 1946 that the MCA stated that the ferry service would recommence in July, with six return trips each day, a single fare being 9s (45p) and a return 16s 6d (82.5p); this including travel to and from the Beach Bus Station. Of the many ferry flights from the airport in 1947, four were arranged by sea cadets belonging to TS *Weston*. Chartered to fly a contingent of boys to Cardiff for the Special Empire Youth Parade held over the Whit weekend, one of the Rapides G-AIHN was to give the eight boys in it more excitement than expected, for it overshot the landing strip at Pengam Moors and ended up standing on its nose.

However, the service didn't last, as BEAC, in a countrywide cutback, announced that the Weston — Pengam Moors and some other services would have to stop by 5 October 1947; in fact, the last flight from Weston was on the following day. There had been a problem with what was considered to be an exorbitant charge made by the MCA by way of landing fees, £1 5s per landing (£15 per day), but, in fact, the number of passengers carried during the worst period of the year, October 1946 to March 1947, had exceeded the numbers carried in the same period by Western Airways in 1938/39, and in the thirteen months to September 1947 some 35,000 passengers had been carried. Western Airways, however, always quick to seize an opportunity, through the aero club then offered the public flights to Pengam Moors in an Argus at £2 18s (£2.90) return (three seats), and in an Auster at £1 19s (£1.95) return (two seats). Failure of BEAC to run these services at a profit was somewhat unfortunate, for Weston Airport, under direction of the MCA, had regained some of the national prestige enjoyed pre-war, as at the end of 1947 it was announced that a total of 511 flights had been logged in October. Of these, the number of movements by private aeroplanes, which amounted to 310, was higher during that month than at any of the country's other fifty MCA-controlled airports. Even though the ferry service had been withdrawn, the success of the MCA was again reflected the following year when over 8,500 arrivals and departures were logged.

In 1948, succumbing to external pressure, BEAC again allowed the independent airlines to operate their own aircraft on scheduled services, but only in association with the corporation. Long-term rivals Western Airways and Cambrian Air Services now decided to bury the hatchet and jointly apply to operate six flights a day between Weston and Pengam Moors, this being the first time since 1935 that the two companies had worked together. In the arrangement, Western Airways would operate its two passenger-carrying Ansons and Cambrian its two cream and maroon Rapides, G-AKUB (Glamorgan) and G-AKUC (Monmouth), recently bought from the RAF specifically for the service.

With the approval of the MCA, the service commenced for an experimental 12-month period on Tuesday 25 May 1948, with Captain Jack Peacock piloting a Rapide carrying the Lord Mayor of Cardiff on the first trip from Pengam Moors, and an Anson carrying Weston's mayor in the other direction. Landing fees had been reduced allowing for a single fare of 14s 6d (72.5p) and £1 2s 6d (£1.13) return, and the service was now provided in some style with passengers escorted to and from the aircraft by a stewardess. This escort service wasn't all it seemed as it had been introduced partly to prevent fuel being wasted whilst passengers ambled aboard and to avoid the unattractive alternative of shutting down engines as they had to be restarted by winding a crank-handle. In slack periods, a fitter was carried to Pengam Moors in the co-pilot's seat to assist in restarting after shutdown. As a legacy from the machine's earlier days, due to the manually-operated undercarriage retraction/lowering system still being fitted, the gear was usually left down for the channel crossing.

The service certainly attracted passengers, to the extent that right from the beginning the number of day-return flights during the summer was increased from six to thirteen, and by the year's end over 9,000 passengers had been carried. But the number of ferry service aircraft movements was only a small proportion of the total of 8,847 aircraft arrivals and 8,837 departures during the year at Weston. Even with the numbers carried, profit margins were small and, although further Rapides were introduced mid-1949, the service, as it was, continued only until the end of the summer when, with the reduction in holiday traffic, it became uneconomical for Western Airways to continue. Cambrian, however, still soldiered on with its service handled by Western Airways at a cost of 10d per passenger, but this was only until Saturday 29 October when its last flight left Weston.

Meanwhile, by the autumn of 1948, the active fleet at Weston had been reduced to just the two Ansons, two Argus and the two Austers; many of the other machines were still on site but awaiting disposal. Even with the reduced fleet, 1949 commenced well with Weston Airport again being highlighted as one of the busiest in Britain, but, by the year's end, there had only been 6,287 aircraft arrivals and 6,307 departures. Of these, 1,225 had been on the ferry service, 1,284 on charter flights, 2,914 on private flights, and the remainder by military flights. However, in June and July, there was still much activity; the weather was good and there was a great deal of charter work. On 2 July, Captain Roberts flew the Minister of Agriculture from Exeter to Shrewsbury for the Royal Show; the event was also well attended by local farmers who were flown there from Weston, as they were to many of that month's national race meetings. There was also a charter to Northern Ireland, and, on the 13th, Harry Gold and his orchestra, performing at Weston's Winter Gardens, were flown to Croydon and back by 'Daddy' Crundall for a BBC broadcast. A less typical charter flight was the arrival on Saturday 16th of a DC3 belonging to the Scandinavian Airline System, which brought in from Malmo, via Northolt, a party of fifteen Swedish students destined for Wills Hall, Stoke Bishop, Bristol. The aircraft left forty-five minutes later with another party of twenty students for the return journey to Sweden.

Although the passenger-carrying Ansons were then sold, Weston would continue to see Cambrian's Rapides, for the company was awarded a contract to carry out Army co-operation flying over South Wales. This operation continued until 1950 with flying during the day from Pengam Moors and at night from Weston where Gooseneck flares were available. The last Argus G-AJOX was sold in 1951 to an operator in Finland for £550, and, registered

OH-FCE, on Wednesday 16 May, it set out on its way across Europe to a new home. However, Western Airways had decided to stay in the charter business and, in 1949, obtained two Percival Proctor Vs, G-AHBH and G-AHTF, and they were to remain in service until sold in 1953/54.

A Change of Direction

By April 1949, Straight's operations had become basically a West Country affair with the Head Office of Airways Union Ltd registered at Weston Airport with its holdings: Straight Aviation Training Ltd, Straight Corporation Ltd and Whitney Straight Ltd, and, with a desire to have more anonymity, on 20 April, Straight had these titles changed to Weston Airport Ltd, Southern Aviation Training Ltd, Airways Union Ltd (the new parent company of Western Airways Ltd, Exeter Airport Ltd and Plymouth Airport Ltd), and Aviation Associates Ltd respectively. Thus, on a single day, Whitney Straight's name was effectively removed from his company's titles. At this time the new Airways Union's senior executives were Chairman Roland King-Farlow, Owen Roberts, General Manager Stanley Cox, Managing Director Fredrick Jeans, Chief Pilot Jack Pearse, Director Bill Parkhouse and Chief Engineer and test pilot Lew Lisle. Senior executives of Western Airways Ltd at that time were Chairman Roland King-Farlow, Joint Managing Directors Fredrick Jeans and Stanley Cox, who was also company secretary, Bobby Wardle Operations/Commercial Manager and Chief Pilot, the Lady Apsley, Basil Watling (now MBE), and Frank Allen, Accounts Director. The test pilot was still Lew Lisle.

In addition to the 'active' companies associated with Airways Union Ltd, others of mainly pre-war origin, were still active but in name only, probably for tax purposes. Around 1950, these, together with a few current ones, were Exeter Aero Club Ltd, Glamorgan Aero Club Ltd, Haldon Airport Ltd, Home Counties Flying Club Ltd, Inverness Airport Ltd, Inverness Aero Club Ltd, Ipswich Airport Ltd, Ipswich Aero Club Ltd, Plymouth & District Aero Club Ltd, Ramsgate Airport Ltd, Somerset Crop Driers Ltd, Straightaway Ltd, Southern Airways Ltd, Weston Aero Club Ltd and Woodason Aircraft Models Ltd. Whitney Straight, however, would continue to reign over the company and had annual flying visits to Weston and Exeter, often using BOAC's DH Dove G-AMZY in which he would share the piloting.

The Western Airways element of the ferry service closing down at the end of summer 1949, followed in October by the folding of Weston Aero Club and the change of direction of the company, also had an effect on the responsibilities of Chief Engineer/test pilot Lew Lisle, who now replaced Mr Jordan as Weston's airport manager. Although Western Airways had changed its focal point, it still ran the airport and continued to have frequent movements of both military and civil aircraft. Most civilian movements were by light aircraft belonging to clubs in the southern counties, many from Air Service Training of Hamble with its large fleet of Tiger Moths, Austers, and later, Chipmunks. There were also visits by training aeroplanes from other Straight aero clubs who used Weston for practice cross-country exercises. Weston was also a convenient refuelling point for those on company business, one using the facility being Bill Parkhouse who regularly arrived from Exeter Airport for meetings at Western Airways in a club machine, or in his own DH Hornet Moth G-AESE. Even now, passengers were occasionally brought in and out on charter aircraft, such as on 20 July 1955 when, early in the morning, Cambrian Air Services' Douglas Dakota 4 G-AMSW, piloted by Captain Bill 'Wingco' Elwin, AFC, in two flights brought in seventy passengers from Cardiff's Rhoose Airport for a day in Weston and ferried them back in the evening. As a matter of interest, all civil flying had been transferred from Pengam Moors to the new Cardiff (Rhoose) Airport on 1 April 1954.

From the RAF side of Filton Airfield also came Bristol University's Air Squadron North American Harvards on short expeditions to the seaside. When replaced by DH Chipmunks, they could also occasionally be seen during an away day at Weston Airport, lined up in front of the tower, and when the runway at Filton was being repaired, the Air Experience Flight Chipmunks also transferred to Weston for a while.

Aircraft Manufacturing and Refurbishment

Commercial operations had all but disappeared by the early 1950s and Western Airways' management made a decision to concentrate its resources on the repair, overhaul and maintenance of aircraft and the manufacture of aircraft components, with early contracts coming from Westland and de Havilland on the Wyvern and Vampire respectively. The Bristol Aeroplane Company at Filton, very busy at this time, was coming under increasing pressure to meet orders for the Bristol Type 170 Wayfarer and Freighter, and as a result, the manufacturing of components was subcontracted to various companies, Western Airways being one, and initially it manufactured the aircraft's control surfaces and doors. However, once sufficient experience had been gained, the company was also awarded contracts associated with assembly of the machine's large nose-doors and tailplane. Having impressed Bristol as to its manufacturing capabilities, in early 1953, a Freighter production line was laid down in the larger of the two Western Airways hangars. This coincided with the return of Bill Dann from Exeter who would be helping to set up the line, and soon large Freighter sub-assemblies were on their way from factories in various parts of the country.

In July, only fourteen passengers had travelled from the airport in six aircraft movements, while military, aero club and private air movements totalled 250. Recognition of this downturn in passenger flying and the recent gearing-up for aircraft manufacturing at Western Airways occurred officially on 1 October. On that date, the MCA gave up control of Weston Airport and the Ministry of

Hornet Moth G-AESE, up from Exeter on 5 December 1954 awaits its owner Bill Parkhouse. The machine in pristine condition, still resides in the West of England flown by owner, Geoffrey Green, and Ben Cox of RVL Group (R. Dudley)

The first Western Airways-built Freighter in the process of being joined-up (Via Bob Cooke)

Supply (MoS) took over and Western Airways was allocated its own discrete R/T call-sign of 'Shovel'.

There were two models of Freighter to be manufactured, initially the Mk 31, joined, slightly later, by the Mk 32. Like the wartime Beaufighter built at the other end of the airport, these Freighters also had Bristol Hercules engines, in their case the 1980 hp Mk 734. The Freighter Mk 31 was able to carry twenty passengers or the equivalent of two motor cars, and the Mk 32, on the other hand, which was often referred to as the Super Freighter, was 5 feet (1.5 metres) longer than the Mk 31 with a fin and tailplane of increased area, allowing for the carriage of up to sixty passengers or three cars and fifteen passengers. Unfortunately, it was impossible to get a Freighters fin inside the building and this was circumvented by the construction of two sheds under Bill Dann's instructions that could be moved around on wheels, each completely covering the empennage of a Freighter sticking out through a gap in the hangar doors. Although this solved one problem, care was still needed as there was very little distance between the top of the aircraft's cockpit canopy and the hangar roof girders, which were on occasions used by the more daring fitters to move between aircraft.

Major subcontractors included Harris and Sheldon of Birmingham who supplied wing outer-panels and lower fuselage sections and Freddie Laker's Aviation Traders of Southend who supplied wing centre-sections. Hitherto, the fuselage had been manufactured by Bristol at Filton, but, as experience and confidence grew, jigs for the fuselage were transferred to Weston, and, shortly after, a jig for the main spar was moved down, it being used long after aircraft construction had been completed in the refurbishment of wings from in-service Freighters. Meanwhile, for a time, there were two production lines with Western Airways personnel being trained on the Filton line to fit out cockpits, fuselages and wings with the various systems, and, in due course, with experience gained and with all relevant equipment transferred to Weston, the last Filton-built Freighter left the Erecting Hall in March 1955 for service as 9700 in the Royal Canadian Air Force (RCAF), and the Weston line carried on alone.

The first Western Airways Freighter was a Mk 31 for Cie Air Vietnam, and on Monday 28 September 1953 after six months in assembly, G-18-142 left on its maiden and delivery flight to Filton, crewed by Ronnie Ellison who had been Bristol's wartime chief test pilot at Oldmixon, accompanied by Freddy Jeans strapped in alongside in the co-pilot's seat. Departure was made to the accompaniment of cheers from the workforce that now numbered some 300, and after two low passes, it headed towards Filton for further test flying and painting in readiness for the first stage of its delivery flight as F-VNAR to French Indo China the following week. During the first year and a half of production, machines left the factory, on average, one every three weeks for fitting out at Filton. A number of Bristol test pilots were available for the short delivery flight and were brought into Weston, usually on a Friday, either by

On Monday 28 September 1953 after six months in assembly, the first Freighter with the temporary registration G-18-142 heads for Filton and further test-flying (Via Bob Cooke)

Bristol's own rather tatty Airspeed Oxford G-AHGU or by Freighters on test flights from Filton. The last new Freighter to be completed was Mk 31 G-APLH, it being painted in Dan Air colours on 23 March 1958 and delivered a few days later.

At the beginning of March 1955 with the workforce further increased, Western Airways had met the initial backlog of new machines and for a time took on the repair and overhaul of in-service Freighters. These were usually flown in-and-out by the operator's own pilots coming from their bases, many on the other side of the world. The very nature of the Freighter meant that most aircraft were completing many short, heavily-laden flights. A good example of this was the 125,000 take-offs/landings with 215,000 cars, 70,000 motorcycles and 759,000 passengers flown by Silver City's fleet of Freighters during their first ten years of cross-channel operation. It was quickly established that the stresses imposed on the airframe under these conditions could lead to premature component failure and it was mandated by the certification authorities that wing main-spar lower-booms would have to be replaced after 25,000 landings. This operation could be done up to three times and was to ensure much work for Western Airways over a number of years. Another problem associated with the spar was the shearing of rivets attaching the boom to the web on the outer wing panels. This was well illustrated to employees by one Freighter being flown back for repairs, for on touchdown the wing was seen to actually flex down as rivets failed. The remedy was to support the wing, peel back its leading-edge skin, drill out the hundreds of rivets in the spar and replace them with special high-tensile steel 2BA bolts inserted in reamed holes. Western Airways became the only organisation allowed to perform this operation.

Two notable examples in for repair were shipped back from New Zealand and delivered by road to Western Airways. One ZK-AYG operated by SAFE had suffered heavy damage following an engine failure on take-off on 3 February 1954. It was repaired and made ready for its ferry flight to Filton in March 1955. The other was NZ5901 of the Royal New Zealand Air Force which had crashed at Karachi; it too was repaired and flown to Filton on 20 September 1955 by Walter Gibb. Later, other aircraft which had gone for export would return for repair, including those supplied to the RCAF. One Freighter, in 1956, was to even become a film star, playing alongside the well-known British actor Jack Hawkins in Ealing Studio's *Man in the Sky*. In the film, Hawkins took on the role of a test pilot working for a firm developing a rocket-boosted challenger to the Freighter. The machine used was a Freighter belonging to Silver City suitably modified with under-wing pods, and Hawkins, to familiarise himself with the aircraft, spent a couple of days at Western Airways with test pilots Ronnie Ellison and Hugh Statham.

Towards the end of the Freighter activity, after runway, taxiway and apron strength had been checked, a further contract was obtained from the Bristol Aeroplane Company for the fitting out of Britannia airliners. The first G-ANBB in BOAC colours was brought in from Filton by Walter Gibb, now Bristol's chief test pilot, at 11.55 a.m. Monday 14 January 1957. With 277 flying hours, it had been delivered to Shorts for refurbishment but the work was transferred to Western Airways. It was the largest aircraft to land at Weston Airport, but by approaching from over the sea it got in easily, and using reverse-thrust used only half the runway's length. Next day, it was fitted in the hangar, not an easy task bearing in mind the overall size of this aeroplane. G-ANBB, G-ANBA and G-ANBH, all of which had been test aircraft, were in the first batch for refurbishment, and by 30 July had been delivered back to Filton.

The contract, which was mainly concerned with major modifications to the electrical and fuel systems, and the installation of new cabin furnishings, lasted for several years, and during that time Bristol-built machines in BOAC colours, and unpainted Belfast-built machines, amongst them G-18-1, arriving 21 June and G-18-2, arriving 24 July 1957, for a time could be seen parked on the apron or with their large rear-fuselage sticking out of the hangar. Most machines from Belfast arrived at Weston on their maiden flight with undercarriage locked-down and stayed for around four or five months. As with the Freighter, it was a tight fit to get a Britannia into the hangar, and because of its large wingspan only two could be undercover at a time. Each was swung in with its nose-wheels closely following a painted line, the outer main wheels

G-ANBB, the first Britannia to come into Western Airways for refurbishment and modification has just been shut-down, 14 January 1957 (E. ap Rees)

traversing a specially laid bulbous concrete extension to the apron. With the machines inside, there was only about 18 inches (46 cm) to spare between the tip of each 142-foot 3-inch span (44-metre) wing and the hangar structure. Vertical clearance was also at a premium, the undercarriage oleos having to be deflated to enable the upper fuselage to clear the low hangar entrance. When it came to undercarriage retraction tests, these were carried out over three wells dug in the hangar floor. Once in RAF service, Britannia tailplanes, wing leading-edges and seats were returned from time to time for refurbishment by Western Airways.

In parallel with the initial Freighter contracts, miscellaneous aircraft repair and overhaul work was also in progress. During the early 1950s, the RCAF had around 300 Canadair licence-built North American Sabres (USAF designation F-86) operating in its No.1 Air Division, Canada's NATO contingent in Europe. Rather than returning them to Canada for repair and overhaul, agreement was reached with the Bristol Aeroplane Company for the work to be carried out at Filton, and Western Airways was subcontracted by Bristol to repair and refurbish the empennage, wings, fuel tanks and parts of the nose. Additional work also came to Weston from Filton, including the manufacture of rocket nose-cones which were spun from sheet metal, assembled to rockets at Filton and test-fired over the ranges at Woomera in Australia. Other RCAF aircraft passed through the Western Airways workshops in the late 1950s and early 1960s, these being Beech Expeditors, DHC Otters, Bristol Freighters and Douglas Dakotas that came in for repair and refurbishment and for modifications to be embodied. In 1962/63 many were fitted with new avionic equipment such as Freighter Mk 31M 9850 equipped with nose-mounted weather radar, whilst Dakota KP221 was fitted out with a VIP cabin and galley. Several aircraft were also repainted, Freighters being generally resprayed in a camouflage scheme whereas Dakotas were stripped and either left in a mainly natural metal finish or, like KG563, re-sprayed white for work with the United Nations. Western Airways didn't have any test equipment for checking out the aircraft radios, so a novel method was used. At Weston, one of the Dakotas was loaded with the numerous receiver/transmitters and flown towards Bournemouth, it stooged around Hurn Airport for several hours whilst a licensed radio engineer plugged into the Dakota's radios one by one, to check out their glide slope, localiser and other facilities using Hurn's approach aids.

Four of the Freighters that had been refurbished at Weston in the early 1960s were to return in 1967/68 to be civilianised and sold on to Wardair, already a Freighter operator. These were 9698, 9699, 9850 and the last Filton-built machine, 9700. In addition to having military equipment removed, they had the latest modifications embodied, and following overhaul and repainting emerged as CF-WAC, CF-WAE, CF-WAD and CF-WAG respectively. All four aircraft returned to Canada via Prestwick, Iceland, Greenland and the Arctic Circle route to Edmonton. One was still airworthy as late as 2008.

At this time, DH Mosquitos were also frequent visitors to Weston Airport. They belonged to No.3/4 Civilian Anti-Aircraft Co-operation Unit (CAACU) based at Exeter that had been formed on 18 March 1951 as the No. 3 CAACU with the assistance of Bill Dann. Initially commanded by Bill Parkhouse, it was operated for the Ministry by Exeter Airport Ltd which, like Western Airways, was a part of the Straight Corporation. A civilian/military concern with a staff of around seventy its duties included radar-calibration and target-towing for the Royal Air Force, the Royal Navy and the Army. The reason for the visits to Weston was the bringing in of John Stokes, a licensed radio engineer, to sign off radios on aircraft about to be delivered by Western Airways. Equipped with a variety of aircraft, which, in 1962, included fifteen Mosquitos, mostly TT 35s, in 1963, the majority were to take starring roles in the film *633 Squadron*. The pilot who normally flew into Weston was Harry Ellis, chief pilot of the unit, and it was he who checked out Flight Lieutenant D. Curtis, Officer Commanding RAF Locking's Varsity Flight, to fly Mosquitos in the film. Ellis' arrivals and departures were normally without incident but, on Tuesday 17 July 1962, VP191, a TT 35, came to grief on take-off, finishing up on its belly in a very sorry state in a field at the westerly end of Weston's runway. Although a write-off, both Ellis and Stokes emerged from the wreck bewildered but unhurt. Harry Ellis would later become Exeter Airport's Managing Director. Other aircraft that became familiar for a time in the early 1960s were Exeter-based Westpoint Aviation Ltd ex-BEA Dakota 3/Pionairs G-ALYF and G-AMDB, which were overhauled by Western Airways. Meanwhile, visiting aircraft

RCAF Otter 3677 outside Weston Airways in the summer of 1960 (R. Dudley)

Two all-white RCAF C-47s outside Western Airways in May 1961; KG563 rests on the concrete apron extension laid-down for the Britannia work (R. Dudley)

Mosquito TT 35 VP191 from Exeter's No. 3/4 Civilian Anti-Aircraft Co-operation Unit, having failed to get airborne on 17 July 1962; the Oldmixon Factory is in the background (R. Dudley)

RCAF Hercules 10301 outside Western Airways on 25 July 1962 has onboard (*left*) a refurbished RCAF Otter being secured. This Hercules, unlike RAF transports of the era, was a very plush affair with a red carpet in the cockpit (R. Dudley)

Freighter RCAF 9850 of 157 Transport Flight, having recently been refurbished and equipped with nose radar, awaits engine-runs on 17 February 1963. Eventually, it returned, and demodified, it became CF-WAD for Wardair (R. Dudley)

continued to make use of the airport's refuelling facilities, some were flown by students, dual or solo, on practice cross-country flights; others, like Dragon Rapides G-ALBA and G-AFFB of Trans-European Aviation, came in for fuel on their way from the Channel Isles to the Midlands with fuselages packed out with consignments of strawberries, vegetables and flowers.

Western Airways continued to get subcontract work from Filton, some of it involving the manufacture of components for the BAC/Aerospatiale Concorde, and during assembly of the first British machine 002, British Aerospace, under pressure to meet production targets, contracted Western Airways to provide a working party of twenty, complete with inspector and foreman, to travel daily to Filton. Around that time work also came in from Rolls-Royce Derby for the manufacture of acoustic side-panels for its RB211 engine.

Diversification of Interests

By 1958, Western Airways had decided to diversify its interests and the small hangar was given over to non-aircraft-related work. The company to occupy the building was Barber Electrical Services Ltd, a Birmingham light-engineering concern run by Arthur A. Barber who now became a director of Airways Union and Western Airways, and in due course his company was renamed 'Barber Weston Ltd'. With upwards of 130 employed, it acted as a buffer for the ever-diminishing aircraft maintenance and repair work carried out in the adjacent hangar. The company specialised in the design and manufacture of a very large range of industrial products including conveyor systems, hospital equipment, wheelchairs and tubular furniture, cigarette and ticket vending machines, the

The Imperial Tobacco Group's Beagle 206 G-AVCJ at Weston in 1972 (P. Turner)

The fleet of Bristol Air Taxi aircraft at Weston sometime in 1979 (P. Turner)

The Campbell Cougar built by Western Airways in 1972/3 now resides at The Helicopter Museum (R. Dudley)

latter being for London Underground. Much of the design work was carried out in a Barber-designed and manufactured prefabricated building erected within the small hangar, and many of these steel-framed buildings were sold, a large number being bought by the Little Chef chain of eating-houses.

Whitney Straight continued to take an interest in the activities at the site, attending regular board meetings in the old Terminal Building. By the late 1960s, with the retirement of aging members, faces had changed somewhat. On the board of Airways Union there was Stanley Cox, Arthur Barber and Frank Allen and there was a new Chairman and Managing Director Lieutenant Commander Peter H. Lucy, whose wife happened to be 'Dorothy Perkins', sister of Whitney Straight's wife, Lady Daphne. In addition, Bill Dann represented Western Airways, but by now subsidiary companies of Airways Union were only Western Airways Ltd, Somerset Crop Driers Ltd, Straightaways Ltd and Barber Weston Ltd.

Resulting from Western Airways itself diversifying to non-aircraft work in the 1950s, Straightaways Ltd had been formed under the umbrella of Airways Union to design and manufacture at the airport, prams and pushchairs for Mothercare, chicken hutches, and electrically heated clothes-horses. There was also the refurbishment of food-mixers that came from the London beauty salons that also dealt with health foods that traded under the name 'Dorothy Perkins'.

Interspaced with the larger aircraft contracts, general maintenance and conversions was carried out in 1958 on a number of military light aircraft.

Typical was the conversion of ex-RAF Chipmunks WB757 and WB725 to a civilian standard to become G-AORE and G-AORV for the Exeter and Plymouth Aero Clubs. Western Airways continued to provide a charter service, albeit in a small way, with Cessna 310F G-ARMK obtained in 1962. Often flown by Peter Lucy, who also flew his own F8L Falco 1 G-APXD from Weston, it was used mainly for taking company representatives to subcontractors involved with Straightaways; typically Silco at Denham who owned Mothercare and to Exeter for meetings with Kingfisher Luggage who produced upholstery for the pushchairs and prams.

With completion of the larger contracts, space also became available in the large hangar and aircraft operators in the area were encouraged to use Weston as a base for their operations. Those taking up the offer of cheaper hangarage and maintenance initially were the Imperial Tobacco Group, Bowyers of Trowbridge and Koda Computers. The first of Imperial Tobacco's machines to arrive was DH Heron G-AOGU, replaced on 5 April 1968 by Beagle 206 G-AVCJ. Imperial Tobacco's aircraft needed to operate at night and, towards the end of 1968, the airport was equipped with electrically powered runway and approach lighting and a Non-Directional Beacon (NDB) was also installed in the roof of a barn 1.5 miles (2.4 km) to the east of, and in line with runway 25. Moving into the jet age, on 2 October 1969, Weston was to receive its first resident jet when Imperial Tobacco's HS 125 G-AXPS arrived to be looked after by Western Airways. Previously owned by film star Liz Taylor, at Western Airways its sumptuous interior was replaced by a standard executive fit. Being used extensively for semi-regular daytime trips to Scotland required that maintenance, including engine changes be carried out overnight. Regular early-morning take offs brought many protests from people living under the flight-path, although these were to end following a fatal accident on 20 July 1970 during crew training at Turnhouse.

Other contracts obtained at that time were for the servicing of aircraft belonging to Bristol Air Taxis, and the Canadian Kenting Aviation Inc. which was carrying out geo-physical aerial surveys in Africa. Owned by Trevor Lansbury, Bristol Air Taxis was a charter company with Chief Pilot Paul Weeks, late of Imperial Tobacco, Training Captain Peter Turner and Captain Paul Deegan, both late Achilles School of Flying. From 1972, it operated Piper Turbo Navajo G-AWOW and Piper Aztecs G-AWVW, AVTS, BBRA, BBOM and BBYK and stayed at Weston until airport closure when it relocated to Lulsgate. In mid-1972, also taking advantage of the facilities that Western Airways had to offer, was Twyford Moors (Helicopters) Ltd of Chandlers Ford, Southampton. Its two very noisy Hughes 269Bs, G-AVZC with skids and G-ASTZ with floats, more often heard than seen, were employed on what would have been a long-term contract for the Gas Board, had not the helicopter side of Twyford Moors folded shortly afterwards.

At the beginning of the 1970s, Western Airways, which already had a contract with Campbell Aircraft Ltd of Membury Airfield for the welding-up of tubular-steel fuselages for its small gyroplanes, was awarded a contract to construct the single-seat prototype of what would in production be the 2-seat Campbell Cougar gyroplane. Registered G-BAPS, it was completed by the end of March 1973 and carried out a number of short hops on 20 April. With no troubles experienced, the next day it flew the length of Weston's runway and again with no problems, on 12 May, a circuit of the airport was completed. Flown to Le Bourget for the Paris Air Show in June, although gaining a lot of interest, money had run out and with no firm orders forthcoming, production plans for four machines a month were abandoned and it was stored at Western Airways until its C of A expired in 1974. Presented to the embryo Helicopter Museum but loaned for a time to the local Woodspring Museum, it is now preserved in The Helicopter Museum next door to where it was built.

Pleasure Flying

Pleasure flying, or joy-riding as it had been known pre-war, had always been popular with Weston's holidaymakers during the summer months, when for a few shillings a 10-minute flight from the airport out along the beach was exciting and, to many, a new experience. This activity had restarted after the war using Weston Aero Club's aircraft, then following the club's closure, aircraft and pilots were brought in for the season. Some years the machines were leased, whilst other years they were loaned by the Straight-operated Plymouth & District Aero Club. The hired pilots obviously did most of the flying but Airport Manager Lew Lisle would also do the occasional flight to keep his hand in and to give the regular pilot a break. In 1954, Auster 5 G-ANDU and DH Dragon Rapide G-AHKV were leased from Sky Neon Aviation Ltd of Croydon Airport with flights available from 15s (75p). The busiest day for the service was on Tuesday 3 August when the Auster did twenty-four flights and carried fifty-nine passengers and the Rapide did seven flights and carried fifty-three passengers. The following year flights were still available from 15s, but this time in Plymouth club aircraft. The aircraft flown up from Roborough were Miles Gemini G-AKHW, Miles Messenger G-AKBM and Auster J/1 Autocrats G-AJUM and G-AJUO. The 3rd August, a Wednesday, was again the busiest day of the season, when G-AJUM did thirty flights and carried sixty passengers whilst the Messenger did seventeen flights and carried forty-eight passengers, many of the customers being bussed in from the nearby Sand Bay Pontins Holiday Camp.

During the many years of pleasure flying, there had been very few incidents at the airport. A relatively minor one occurred on 19 July 1960 when the Messenger was taxied into DH Chipmunk WP836 of 3 AEF Filton which was parked near the tower, but fortunately there were no injuries. As a result neither aircraft flew again. However, regrettably, the airport's excellent accident-free civil operation would soon suffer a severe setback.

For the following year's pleasure-flying season, the Messenger was replaced by Auster 5 G-AKPI leased from Anglian Air Charter Ltd and flown by Peter

Longest serving of Weston's pleasure-flying machines the silver and red Messenger G-AKBM; in the mid 1955s it did a roaring trade with holiday-makers from Pontins (J. Strickland via A. Smith)

The pleasure-flying team in front of Auster G-AMZV. Left to right: Deputy Airport Manager Monty 'Steve' Stevenson, the resident pilot, Airport Manager Lew Lisle and Gerry Mallett (Via E. ap Rees)

Lucas, and occasionally by Lew Lisle who lived within minutes of the airport making it easy for him to take the first flight of the day. The aircraft replacing the Messenger long term, however, was Auster J-5G Cirrus Autocar G-AMZV, leased from Mell-Air Ltd and, as in the past, various pilots were engaged for the summer seasons with Lew Lisle filling in. Lew, airport manager and company test pilot for many years, was always keen to take an opportunity to get airborne, and, on Sunday 28 August 1966, he took the first early-morning flight with three passengers. Soon after take-off, the Auster was seen by eyewitnesses to be inverted at about 800 feet (245 metres). Remaining inverted with engine spluttering, just above the ground the aircraft appeared to lose flying speed and it dived into Ten Acres, a field adjacent to the Electricity Board's Depot in Locking Road, instantly killing the four on board.

After this sad event, Monty 'Steve' Stevenson, who had been Deputy Airport Manager for many years, was made Airport Manager, and for the 1967 passenger-flying season Malcolm Burke, was engaged as pilot. However, in August, as a result of personal problems he was unable to continue. Western Airways, in urgent need of a replacement, was very fortunate to obtain the temporary services of one of the country's best-known and respected lady pilots, Jackie Moggridge from Taunton. A South African, she gained an 'A' Licence when seventeen and arrived in England just before the outbreak of war. Joining the ATA, she went on to ferry more aircraft than anyone else and for this was awarded a King's Commendation for valuable services in the air. Post-war, she flew jets in the RAFVR, aircraft of the Exeter Aero Club, captained airliners of Channel Airways, and by the time she started pleasure flying at Weston, had amassed some 10,000 flying hours. In her smart captain's uniform, Jackie, complete with black leather flying boots and gauntlets, was for a time a familiar sight at the airport.

A Typically Busy Day at Weston Airport

Friday 22 July 1955 would have been classed as 'a typically busy day at Weston Airport'. Both Lew Lisle and Steve Stevenson had arrived at the control tower earlier than the normal 8.00 a.m. and the airport fire wagon had been warmed-up and ready for the first arrival. There was also early morning activity around the tower as on the following Wednesday HRH the Princess Margaret was due to arrive from RAF Marham in Vickers Viking VL247 of the Queen's Flight, and the grass was being tidied and a white line painted on the taxiway indicating where the aircraft should stop.

RAF Colerne's Communication's Squadron was down to provide navigation/ radio training for some of RAF Locking's apprentices, and three of its Ansons had been readied for an early start. The first machine, T22 VV365, piloted by Flying Officer Bowtle, left Colerne at 7.33 a.m. and fourteen minutes later was slipping in low over Locking Moor Road. This was closely followed by T22

VS602 flown by Sergeant Pearce and a further T 22 VV362 flown by Sergeant Emmett. During the day, each was to be airborne twice on local flights of approximately ninety minutes duration with four apprentices sitting at their cabin radio stations. At 2.22 p.m., their task completed, led by VV362, at 3-minute intervals they left for home. Meanwhile, at 9.07 a.m., two Anson C19s, TX256 with six passengers, closely followed by TX183 with seven passengers, flown by Flight Sergeant Lapkal and Flight Sergeant Smith respectively, arrived from RAF Ternhill. Both machines dropped off their passengers and then took off for RAF Shawbury. A little later, two other machines also arrived from Ternhill, at 10 a.m. Percival Provost WV601, flown by Group Captain Burns and at 12.48 p.m., Provost WV555, flown by Squadron Leader Taylor. Later in the day the two Anson C19s returned to pick up their passengers, but this time TX256 was piloted by Flight Sergeant Wall and TX183 by Sergeant Cooper. At about 5.30 p.m. both machines took off for Shawbury and the Provosts for Ternhill.

Across at the Hutton Moor Flight Shed it was also going to be a fairly active day for the ATDU. At 10.24 a.m., Avro Lincoln RE231, piloted by Flying Officer Burnett-Smith with a crew of four, took off for a 39-minute visit to the local range, on return making a touch-and-go then a circuit and landing. Four minutes after the Lincoln became airborne, DH Chipmunk WB721, piloted by Flight Lieutenant Thomas took off for a 43-minute solo flight. Later he would make two shorter flights, the last a 4-minute circuit, and return to the hangar. At 1 p.m. Bristol Brigand RH749, flown by Pilot Officer Frazer arrived from Gosport, and, just over an hour later, took-off for the 25-minute return. Meanwhile, Westland Wyvern F4 VZ760, which had arrived from Gosport two days before, at 1.03 p.m., piloted by Lieutenant Marshall, took off for the range with a parachute mine clutched beneath its fuselage and landed back seventeen minutes later. The Lincoln had followed the Wyvern down the perimeter road and took off 5 minutes after it, this time with a crew of three for a final visit to the range, landing back at 3.21 p.m. Westland Dragonfly WP503 with Lieutenant Chaplin at the controls had lifted off and departed for the range at 2.17 p.m. and would be away until 4.50 p.m., assisting in stores recovery. During the rest of the afternoon the Wyvern completed five further flights, its final landing being at 4.27 p.m.

Over at Western Airways, things had been quiet for several weeks, and the next Bristol Freighter to be completed, VR-NAA, that had arrived for repair on 6 May, and due to have its first post-repair flight in a few days, was undergoing final checks in the large hangar. Mixed in with the military activity was the arrival at 11.31 a.m. of Mr Lazenby in Auster J/1 Autocrat G-AHSW from Pengam Moors. At midday, he returned and later would do a similar out-and-return exercise. There was also the pleasure-flight Gemini G-AKHW, flown by Mr S. Smith, which in twelve flights carried twenty-five passengers, and later in a 45-minute flight, was returned to its base at Roborough.

Achilles personnel in front of Cherokee G-AVGH in 1971: Left to right Secretary Pauline James, Instructor Brian Middleton, Instructor/Manager Pete Turner and CFI Stan Sharp (West Air Photography via P. Turner)

The Achilles School of Flying

In 1966, the huts that had been occupied at Weston Airport by RAF Locking's Varsity Flight became vacant, and this coincided with the aspirations of one Norman S. Guy, an ex-flight engineer who in 1962 had been instrumental in forming the Shaftesbury Flying Club at nearby Compton Abbas. By 1963, he had learnt to fly and had soon amassed sufficient hours and experience to become an instructor, and, by 1965, was on the staff of the Bristol and Wessex Aeroplane Club at Lulsgate Airport. Like Norman Edgar some years before, he also saw the potential that Weston presented and with two associates, Malcolm Cockburn and Derek Woodford, set about forming a flying club. Named the 'Achilles School of Flying Ltd', the club was established in May 1967, which coincided with the Western Airways lease of Weston Airport being extended by its owners, the Ministry of Technology, to run until 1979. Officially opened on Saturday 27 May 1967 by Squadron Leader G. C. Webb AFC in the presence of Weston's mayor, C. D. Curtis OBE, MA, the day's celebrations were somewhat inhibited by poor weather, although the many spectators saw a variety of flying events put on by owners of locally-based aircraft. The next day, flying training officially started.

Norman, as chief flying instructor, had taken on two part-time instructors, Stan Sharp, a very experienced wartime instructor with over 3,000 hours flying

In front of the pre-war Terminal Building: Achilles school's Cherokee G-AVWL, Beagle Pup G-AXOZ and Piper Arrow G-AWFB (West Air Photography via P. Turner)

experience, and John White, a local businessman. Operations commenced using a purchased Piper Cherokee 140 G-AVGH and a leased Piper Tri-Pacer G-ATWF, and these were joined by Piper Colt G-ARNH later in the year. Two further Cherokees, G-AVWL and G-ATVL, and a Piper Twin Comanche G-ASRO were to join the fleet in the following year. The school's very first member was Peter Turner who, having started flying in 1961 at 621 Gliding School, was intent on accumulating sufficient hours to become a fully rated instructor and commercial pilot. Pete was to figure in organising many events held at the airport's over the following years and is still very active as a director and trustee of Weston's helicopter museum.

Having the runway lights together with an airport identification beacon and an NDB installed at the end of 1968 for Imperial Tobacco's night-time flights allowed the club to include night-flying training in its syllabus, and with Tom Carpenter who, in due course, was brought in from Oxford Air Training School to take over from Norman Guy, the school had a commercially licensed instrument-rated CFI. Soon Paul Deegan was also brought in as a full-time assistant flying instructor and Norman then became deputy CFI, allowing more time to be given to management of the school. Achilles now also took over the pleasure flying franchise, mainly around Weston Bay but also up to the Severn Bridge and down to Cheddar Gorge. Social activities also took on a certain prominence, with the school becoming well known for its open days. Links were also established with the Aero Club de Granville 50 miles (85 km) south of Cherbourg and regular duty-free trips were made in both directions

G-ASVM, John White's pleasure flying Cessna 172 (West Air Photography via P. Turner)

by members of each club. Benefiting from having the school close at hand, the adjacent coastguard station took the opportunity to co-opt the school's instructors as auxiliary coastguards and thereafter, during daylight hours in all but the worst weather, aircraft could be launched to assist the crew of Weston's lifeboat in rescue operations.

In 1969, Norman Guy, now managing director, and Tom Carpenter departed the school and John White became CFI with Pete Turner manager and newly-qualified assistant flying instructor. Meanwhile, school equipment was constantly being upgraded, and when training for twin-engine 'B' ratings was introduced, it was on Twin Comanche G-ASRO. A Link Trainer had also been purchased and was being used for instrument flying training. Around 1970, the fleet comprised two Cherokee 140s G-AVGH and G-AVWL, Cherokee Arrow G-AWFB, Cessna 172 G-ASPI, Cessna 150 G-ATLS and Beagle Pup G-AXOZ, and it was at this time that both Paul Deegan and Peter Turner became fully qualified flying instructors. In 1971, John White left to concentrate on his aerial photography business and Stan Sharp became CFI with Peter taking over as deputy CFI and manager, with Brian Middleton joining as a full-time assistant instructor.

By 1972/73, the fleet had changed further with two new Glos Airtourer 115s, G-AZTM and G-AZTN, now the main training aircraft, and Cherokee 140 G-AVWL, Cherokee Arrow G-AWFB and Cessna 172 G-BAHT used for self-fly hire. Stampe G-AXME was also in the fleet for aerobatic/tailwheel training and Twin Comanche G-AVGT was being used for twin-ratings. G-

AVWL and G-BAHT were also used for pleasure flying being mainly flown by Peter, who by this time had gained his Commercial Pilot's Licence. Ashley Flynn had taken over as full-time instructor from Brian, and he was succeeded by Mike Waters. In late 1973, Pete gained his Instrument Rating and left to join Bristol Air Taxis as a charter pilot on their fleet of Piper Aztecs, although he continued to instruct part time into 1974. His place in the school was taken by Ken Rickards.

In the period from 1974 to 1978, the club's main fleet was Cherokee 140 G-AVWL, Cherokee Arrow G-AWFB, and the Airtourers. Airtourer G-AZTM was replaced in 1975 by G-AWOZ; however, it was unfortunately lost in a crash during a flying demonstration at Chew Magna's Summer Fair on 7 June 1975 when club member Jim Hamilton and the very experienced Stan Sharp were sadly killed. Ken Rickards then became CFI and remained in this position until the club's demise, and John White took over the pleasure flying franchise using his Cessna 172 G-ASVM.

Mendip and Woodspring Gliding Clubs

In 1964, 621 Gliding School was joined on the airport at weekends by a gliding club run for the benefit of service personnel at Locking Camp. Named 'Mendip', it was a part of the RAF Gliding and Soaring Association (RAFGSA) and was led for a time by the well-known competition pilot John Williamson. Its gliders were kept in the remaining Blister hangar, it having been rebuilt by club members to a very high standard. By mutual agreement with 621, the RAFGSA

Mendip RAFGSA's John Williamson sometime in 1968 takes Lin Turner for an instructional flight (P. Turner)

Some of Woodspring's notable members in front of the club Bocian. Left to right: Pete Turner (CFI), Arthur 'Robbie' Robinson (late CO of 621 Gliding School), David Driver (President) and John Ward (Secretary) (Via P. Turner)

usually operated from the northern side of the airport and flew circuits towards the town, whereas 621 operated on the other side and flew circuits towards the Mendips. The club, which also had the advantage of being able to fly mid-week, with five machines, in an average year was able to achieve some 4,500 to 5,000 winch-launches. Departing in 1975, the RAFGSA club's place at the airport was taken by a new civilian gliding club named 'Woodspring'. Formed on 2 March 1975, its CFI and chairman was Flight Lieutenant Jim Martin and it was equipped with a Slingsby T21 2-seater, a syndicate-owned ASK 7 single-seater and a double-decker bus which acted as canteen and control-vehicle. During its first year of operation, 120 members had joined the club, and it flew Thursday afternoons and at the weekend. Once fully established and with delivery of a new high-performance Bocian 2-seater and a single-seater, the club was able to complete a creditable average 4,000 winch-launches a year. With ATC gliding schools equipped in the late 1980s with Vikings and other high-performance soaring machines, Halesland became redundant and, in 1988, was handed over to the Woodspring Gliding Club, which like 621 had been forced into leaving Weston due to the airport's change in ownership. The club then aptly altered its name to 'Mendip'. Over the following years, Halesland was improved, with the old hut made into an excellent clubroom, parts of the boundary wall were removed to enlarge the aircraft movement area and a strip of gravelled track laid diagonally from the hangar to the field's far end.

The Rundown of Weston Airport and Airways Union

It had always been understood that the Achilles School of Flying was operating on borrowed time, and it was of no great surprise when, in 1978, a notice to quit was received from Airways Union Ltd, with the added news that the airport operating licence was to be relinquished at the end of the year. Retention of the licence was essential for the school, and indeed the airport's survival, for without it there would be an end to all commercial flying and a withdrawal of air traffic control and the fire-fighting facilities. During the preceding ten years there had been a dramatic slump in light-aircraft maintenance and repair work at Western Airways that had cost an estimated £150,000, and to cap it all the Civil Aviation Authority had recently informed the company that the runway, which over the previous three years had taken approaching 27,000 movements, most by Achilles aircraft, would need to be resurfaced at a cost of £150,000. In the circumstances, closure of Achilles was inevitable, and the majority of members moved the short distance away and joined the Bristol and Wessex Aero Club at Lulsgate.

The decline continued, with the last ten aircraft maintenance and repair workers still at Western Airways receiving redundancy notices to take effect in December 1978. Whitney Straight died the following year, and, in 1980, the Arran Trust Ltd shares were purchased from Lady Daphne by Reginald Price, and his trading part of the company, Barber (Weston) Ltd, was then renamed 'RJ Products (Weston) Ltd' with the new owner being chairman and managing director. In this form the company continued in being until 1989, when RJ Products (Weston) Ltd and Arran Trust Ltd went into receivership. In May 1989, Boxford Holdings, an engineering company based in Halifax, West Yorkshire, acquired RJ Products (Weston) Ltd out of receivership and, under the name of RJ Mobility, continued to manufacture wheelchairs of a unique design for the National Health Service until May 1990 when the 11-acre (4.5-hectare) site was acquired by local businessman entrepreneur John Wall, who planned to develop it using the existing buildings as a business park. Trading under the name of Moor Park, Weston Business Park, many of the buildings were renovated and parking areas laid out for the storage and distribution of goods and a number of small industrial units were formed. Planning permission was also obtained to hold exhibitions, antique fairs, conferences, etc., and John's extensive collection of historic retail memorabilia was displayed (now to be seen at Oakham Treasures, Portbury, near Bristol). However, some of the structures, one being the timber Terminal Building, had become vandalised and dilapidated through neglect, and unfortunately in due course, had to be demolished, but the original 1936 hangar, together with its larger partner and the building that joined them together, were still in existence in 2010. RJ Mobility meanwhile had relocated to modern single-storey premises on the Oldmixon Industrial Estate where manufacturing and design work continued until May 2000, when the business was relocated to the Halifax headquarters.

Visitors to Weston's Airspace

In the mid-1950s, one could often see over Weston at contrail height Boeing B-47 Stratojet and B-52 Stratofortress bombers and Douglas Globemaster transports of the USAF, the latter with day-glo extremities, droning their way from the Azores to bases in the east of England. Before the arrival of the American jet-propelled bombers, on the afternoon of 16 January 1951, many of Weston's inhabitants were brought into their gardens by the noise and vibration from eighteen unsilenced 4-row radial piston engines and twelve jet engines. The like of this aerial onslaught on the town, not seen since the war, belonged to three giant Convair B-36F 10-engined bombers of the United States Strategic Air Command flying in formation at an altitude of about 1,000 feet (305 metres). Having just made landfall, they were on the last stage of a 5,000 mile (8,047 km), 24-hour long, 2-stage navigation exercise that, with three other machines had taken them from Carswell AFB near Fort Worth in Texas, to Limestone AFB, Maine and was to end up at the US airbase at Lakenheath in Suffolk.

Bristol Brigands and Buckmasters being chased by Boulton Paul Balliols were also a common sight in the mid-1950s. Operating out of Colerne, from June 1952 until January 1957, radar operators in the twin-engined aircraft belonging to No.238 OCU were trained in the skills of AI radar interception. Also from the same air station, there was the occasional glimpse of Handley Page Hasting troop transports, one of which, around 1949, would for a time come into Weston Airport on Monday evenings. Also in the same period, from Weston Zoyland and Merryfield there were Gloster Meteor F4 and T7s, DH Vampire TIIs and English Electric Canberras in abundance.

After the war, Weston began to see many aircraft originating from Filton. One, the Brabazon, which first flew in September 1949, in 1951, caused much excitement when Bill Pegg brought this 230-foot (70-metre) wingspan giant over at around 1,000 feet (305 metres) heading in a westerly direction towards the seafront. Only a matter of months later, another British engineering masterpiece appeared. This was the Saunders-Roe Princess flying boat, G-ALUN, which flew over Uphill on its way to be shown off to the makers of its ten Proteus gas-turbine engines at Bristol's Patchway Factory. On occasions, Filton's test-bed aircraft could also be seen, amongst them its Vickers Valiant and Avro Vulcans with large bulges hiding the engines under test. Another memorable visit was in September 1972 when there was a low-level presentation flight over Weston of Concorde 002 following its appearance at the Farnborough Air Show.

Once in service, those living in and around Weston received a daily reminder of the British Airways *Speedbird* Concorde and its Olympus engines, with the late-afternoon contrails and the muffled sonic 'boom boom' that reached far inland, as it came in over the Bristol Channel and then Sand Bay on its return to Heathrow from New York. After its premature retirement from service, the last Concorde to fly, G-BOAF, and in fact the last to come from Filton's

In readiness for the first ever live air-to-ground public TV broadcast, Widgeon G-ALIK and WS-55 G-AOCZ are parked on Birnbeck Pier Saturday 4 August 1956 (Westland)

production line in 1977, on Wednesday 26 November 2003, made a farewell tour flying over Weston at about 1,000 feet (305 metres). Captain Les Brody was at the controls and it was on its way back to Filton for preservation, to be cared for by members of the Bristol Aero Collection.

By mid-1956, the Bristol Aeroplane Company, well underway with transfer of its helicopter work to the Oldmixon Factory, received a reminder that Westland, the opposition, was only just down the road at Yeovil, for on Friday 3 just prior to the 1956 August Bank Holiday, some of its machines arrived at Weston. Reason for the visit was Westland's participation in the first live air-to-ground public TV broadcast from a helicopter. Pioneered by Bristol and Pye several years previously using Bristol Sycamores, the glory of demonstrating this nationally was to go to Westland and the BBC. Having refuelled at the airport, Westland S-55 G-AOCZ and Widgeon G-ALIK, flown by test pilots Roy Bradley and John Fay were flown into the town where they were operated from the lawns of the Royal Hotel and from Birnbeck Pier, where both were parked overnight. On Saturday afternoon, televised search and rescue demonstrations with Weston's lifeboat that had been simulated the previous week by the Westland crews off Chesil Beach using dinghies, were shown live to the nation in the series *Saturday Night Out* with commentaries by those doyens of the BBC, Brian Johnson and Raymond Baxter. Roy Bradley, a rather colourful character who had been educated at Weston's Walliscote Road School and, until joining the Royal Navy in 1941 worked for the Bristol

Aeroplane Company, had many claims to fame, probably his finest being that he had taught King Hussein of Jordan and his brother, the Crown Prince, to fly helicopters. When Bristol Helicopters was taken over by Westland in 1960, visits by Yeovil's Widgeons and WS-55/Whirlwinds were to become commonplace.

In 1960 Weston had found itself on the low-level route of the London — Cardiff Air Race, an event revived from pre-war days, when nearly forty aircraft, ranging from Comper Swift to Spitfire, flying at 500 feet (150 metres), passed over the southern edge of the town. On Tuesday 27 March 1962, there was a reminder of the war when one of the three Boeing B-17 Fortresses, brought to England from the USA for making the film *The War Lovers,* flew over Weston Airport heading due west. There were also the Aer Lingus's DC3s, that, from May 1951, regularly plodded their way to Whitchurch and, when that airport closed, Lulsgate Bottom, that was officially opened 1 May 1957. At an altitude of about 1,000 feet (305 metres), on a course from Dublin or Cardiff's Rhoose Airport, that took the aircraft over the northern edge of town, their large format under-wing registration letters made it easy for 'Regi-spotters' living under their flight path to claim the complete fleet list in their Ian Allan *ABC Civil Aircraft Markings* pocket book without the use of binoculars. DH Dragon Rapides, and, later, Douglas DC3 Dakotas of Cambrian Air Services (renamed 'Cambrian Airways' on 23 May 1955), from early 1953, also flew the Cardiff — Bristol route that passed over the edge of Weston. There were rumours circulating on more than one occasion that a DC3 and, at a later date, a Sud-Est Caravelle jet airliner, had started an approach to Weston's Locking Road, the pilots having mistaken the road's sodium lights for those on the approach to Lulsgate's runway! As air travel became more affordable and Lulsgate was enlarged, a greater number of airlines used the airport and Vickers Viscounts, Fokker Friendships, Handley Page Dart Heralds and sightings of other jet and turboprop airliners associated with business and holiday travel became commonplace. Today it is a very different place and known as 'Bristol International Airport'.

Another aviation event to be staged at Weston was in the 1970s. Avon Air Days, organised by the owners of 'Monty's' Miles Messenger, Jim Buckingham, and Eddie King, were usually held in July/August at the airport, and were a reminder to some of the older inhabitants of the fabulous Cobham Flying Circus displays of the 1930s. Again a great variety of aircraft were to be seen such as the DH Vampire, Gloster Meteor, Beech Staggerwing, Messerschmitt Bf 108, Lockheed C-130 Hercules and even a B-17 Fortress. To round off displays, the Red Arrows and the Battle of Britain Memorial Flight were usually on hand. Closure of the airport brought an end to these events, but in July 1980 the first of the Great Weston Air Days was staged by the District Council and using the length of Weston's Sands and Beach Lawns, gave residents and holidaymakers alike an opportunity to see well-known aircraft making low-level flights at relatively close range. There was often something new such as the James Bond

(007) gyroplane demonstrated by designer Wing Commander Ken Wallis and again the Red Arrows or the Royal Navy Historic Flight would often provide the finale. In 1991, the Great Weston Air Days gave way to Weston Super Heli Days, the Beach Lawns again being the venue, but this time featuring large fly-ins of both civil and military helicopters.

The Helicopter Museum

In 1961, Elfan ap Rees was a young man employed by Westland's Bristol Division at Oldmixon working in the Technical Publications Department. Like one of the authors of this book who also worked in the same department, he had an interest in fixed-wing and rotary-winged aeroplanes and already had a collection of information and photographs relating to these subjects. However, he soon realised that working in an office, rather than being more involved in the sharp operational end of helicopters, was not for him, and he left to pursue his interest in the more glamorous environment that included flying some of the very aircraft that were later to end up in The Helicopter Museum at Weston Airport! Over the next several years he also contributed to various aviation magazines as a freelance journalist, with a special interest in all things rotary-winged. This was to eventually culminate in Elfan setting up his own publishing company to launch the magazines *Helicopter International* and *Helidata News & Classified*. Alongside this bread-and-butter activity, his interest in aviation history also grew and was recognised by Westland Helicopters, where, paid a retainer, he became for a time their official historian, providing information and photographs to those writing into the company with questions on its aircraft.

In 1969, Bristol Sycamore G-ALSX became surplus to the requirements of Westland, and Elfan obtained this, his first piece of hardware, to add to his collection. Initially, this went on loan to the Skyfame Museum at Staverton but, with his appetite whetted, as space and funds permitted other British helicopters and artefacts were accumulated at the speed that others would obtain specialist books! These additions included the rotor-blades, rotor-head and mast, and a large fuselage section of Fairey Rotodyne XE521 and Ultra Light G-AOUJ, Bristol Belvedere HC I XG452 and Sycamore HR 14 XG547, Saunders Roe Skeeter AOP 12 XM556, Westland Widgeon 2 5N-ABW (G-AOZE) and Dragonfly HR5 WG719, and the remains of Cierva C30A G-ACWM. But, as with any collection, it needed to be put on display. Initially the helicopters were stored, the smaller ones in sheds and garages. Elfan even had the Skeeter in his front garden for a time, whilst the larger ones were kept on Westland's premises at Oldmixon, mainly in the open, with most alongside the factory railway siding. With the need to find a permanent home for the collection, in 1974 Elfan formed the British Rotorcraft Museum and made plans to open it to the public. Using voluntary help, this was achieved

Some of the remarkable machines exhibited in The Helicopter Museum (R. Dudley)

in 1976 at that year's Avon Air Day on Weston Airport, and then, on a longer temporary basis, during the summers of 1978 and 1979 on a site provided by Western Airways adjacent to the pre-war Terminal Building. By the time it ended, the display had attracted a rewarding number of visitors, some 19,000 during the second year alone.

By 1980, having concluded that the museum had been developed as far as possible with his limited time and resources, and to put it onto a more secure footing, it was decided to change the museum's status to that of a limited company and form it into a registered charity with a management committee with Elfan, Chairman. Coming into effect on 1 April 1981, the museum was now able to obtain grants and sponsorship from industry, the primary supporters being Westland, Rolls-Royce and Bristow Helicopters. This also led to the first aircraft being donated directly to the museum in its own right, as opposed to being on loan. In the same year, Westland took over most of the airport, thus opening the door for overtures to be made to the company regarding the museum being able to permanently lease a 4.5-acre (1.8-hectare) site. It was eventually agreed that this would be near the control tower and include the post-war airport entrance and the old timber hut formerly occupied by the Achilles School of Flying. It had always been recognised that it would be nice to obtain use of an existing hangar at the airport, but this was discounted as unaffordable and because it was considered essential that the museum should be on a main road with easy public access. Meanwhile, pending the outcome of negotiations with Westland, most of the machines had returned to open storage within the confines of the Oldmixon Factory, where the weather took its toll and the small team of enthusiasts had their time cut out keeping the airframes up-together.

By this time, Elfin had become well known in the helicopter industry and would, on occasions, be seen on local TV as a 'helicopter expert' to give his prognosis on helicopter-related news items, especially during the summer of 1985 when Westland nearly went to the wall. A number of books on helicopters had also been published alongside the still-flourishing *Helicopter International* and its associated newsletters, which by now was the industry's 'Number 1' news magazine. In 1988, a long-term lease was agreed with Westland and planning permission obtained for the museum site, and, by early June, a secure 4.5-acre compound erected, the hut partitioned to have a display area and souvenir shop, and the exhibits brought in from all corners. With the move completed over the weekend of 24/25 June, the embryo museum was able to open on schedule on 24 July for a preview opening period that lasted until the end of August, and during this short season over 4,000 visitors had passed through the gates and £6,000 had been banked. An added bonus was that the museum was also allowed to use the old airport fire station (formerly the ATDU Bomb Shop), control tower and associated building for storage and some limited restoration work, with Dragonfly WG719 being the first tackled. Although helicopters in the collection now totalled thirty-eight, seven of them Westland Wessex, only eleven (four Wessex, a Sycamore, the Belvedere, a Westland Wasp, Dragonfly, Widgeon and Whirlwind, and a Skeeter) were to be initially put on display, together with a small exhibition of rotor-heads and gearboxes. This, with the addition during the following winter of a further temporary building, the former timber Westland Apprentice Training School in the Oldmixon Factory, represented what was known as the 'Phase One' development and, together with road-widening outside the museum's entrance, was to cost an estimated £57,000. A pump-priming grant from the Woodspring District Council provided £19,000 of this, but it had to be promptly handed to Avon County Council for the road improvements, and the remaining funds came from other organisations and the museum's own fund-raising.

To make the museum of greater appeal to the general public, in 1989, it was renamed the 'International Helicopter Museum'. The net was now spread further afield and, using Elfan's many contacts, machines started to turn up from all over the world. The change in name also coincided with the first full season of opening between Easter and October. With the museum now firmly established, events could be held within its grounds and there began a very popular monthly event, usually on 'Open Cockpit' Sundays – 'Helicopter Air Experience Flights' from the museum's heliport. The new museum was officially opened on 3 November 1989 by HRH Prince Andrew, the Duke of York, who piloted a Wessex HCC 4 of the Queen's Flight into the museum. Also gathered together for the celebrations were local dignitaries, company test pilots and the surviving British helicopter pioneers that before and after the war had been associated with Bristol, Fairey, Cierva, Saunders Roe, Weir, Westland and BEA Helicopters.

In the following January, winds of over 100 mph (161 kph) caused damage to several of the helicopters which, although tethered, were overturned or blown into each other. Meanwhile, on 27/28 July 1991, the Beach Lawns was the venue for the first 'Weston Super Heli Days', a helicopter fly-in event organised entirely separately from the museum by Elfan, daughter Claire and a group of volunteers dedicated to raising capital funding for the museum and other local charities. This quickly became an annual event, which by the end of 2008, had raised more than £500,000 for good causes. Some of the fruits of the first two Heli Days events were put into funding a hangar that was entirely financed by funds raised, and built on the old taxi track. A structure of 4,800 sq. feet (446 sq. metres), it was opened by Lord Glenarthur, Chairman of the British Helicopter Advisory Board, and aptly named 'The Raoul Hafner Memorial Building' after Bristol's chief helicopter designer, and was to be used as a dedicated restoration workshop with public access. When further funds became available, a second hangar of similar dimensions was built in the winter of 1995, which, when completed early the following year, was named 'The Cierva Memorial Building', after the world-famous rotary-wing pioneer.

September 1993 saw the initial launch of the museum's appeal for £300,000 to provide a permanent display hangar which would form the centrepiece of the 'Phase 2' building programme. Towards the end of 1998, the trustees heard that they had been successful in attracting a lottery windfall of £334,500 from the Heritage Fund which, together with the museum's own funds and sponsorship from Rolls-Royce and GKN Westland, would allow the site to be bought outright and work to start on creating the undercover display, costing in total £500,000, for what now amounted to some eighty rotary-wing machines, 100 engines and a variety of components and models. The new building was opened by HRH Prince Andrew, the Duke of York, during a return visit in 2002, and named in his honour 'The Duke of York Hangar'. By now there were many exhibits on display, one of special interest to the Prince being the Queen's Flight Wessex in which he had flown into the museum back in 1989. After further intensive fund-raising, £150,000 was allocated to build a new conservation and engineering hangar. This was opened on Friday 20 July 2007 by HRH the Duke of Edinburgh KC, accompanied by Her Majesty Queen Elizabeth II during an official visit to Weston, and to commemorate the occasion, this extension was named 'The Duke of Edinburgh Hangar'. A short time later there was further good news when a grant by the Heritage Lottery Fund was awarded towards equipping the museum with a new education/training building that incorporated library, archive, classroom and theatre facilities. This was accompanied by funding totalling £400,000 to complete the insulation of the main hangar and to begin upgrading the display.

Meanwhile, the museum, these days know as 'The Helicopter Musuem', continues to grow, and the dedicated band of engineers is kept busy conserving and refurbishing both the existing and new exhibits. In 2009, much of the work was still concentrated on restoring some of the early acquisitions which had spent the best part of thirty to forty years outdoors exposed to the harsh coastal environment. As a consequence, some are in need of a major rebuild. Less needy aircraft are surveyed and allocated a maintenance slot to ensure their long-term conservation.

Epilogue

In retrospect, there were many people who played a significant part in the development of Weston Airport, but there were two individuals who had been the prime movers, and probably few would argue that it was Norman Edgar, who, in 1933, started the ball rolling and Whitney Straight, who, from 1938, turned Western Airways into one of the country's leading municipal airlines, and the airport a significant site for the repair, maintenance and even manufacture

On the occasion of the retirement of Bill Parkhouse as Exeter Airport's Manager in 1956, Whitney Straight with other directors flew in BOAC's Dove to Exeter Airport for a presentation ceremony. Left to right: Stanley Cox, Roland King-Farlow, Freddie Jeans, Bill Parkhouse and wife Vera, Whitney Straight, Frank Allen and Jack Pearse (Parkhouse Family via K. Saunders)

With Weston's fixed-wing visitors long-gone, the old pre-war and wartime buildings gently decay (R. Dudley)

of aircraft and components. However, it would not be right to exclude from recognition the foresight of Weston Town Council and give credit to the man who had provided inspiration in the first place; Sir Alan Cobham, who died on 21 October 1973.

Whitney Straight, who had contributed so much to both civil and military aviation, achieving honour and high-rank whilst serving in the Royal Air Force and high office in British European Airways, and then becoming Managing Director of British Overseas Airways Corporation and later its Deputy Chairman, died in a London hospital 5 April 1979. Amongst his other aviation achievements, in 1955, he joined the board of Rolls-Royce Ltd and the following year become its Executive Vice-Chairman, and in due course Chairman. Early in 1956, he was also appointed to the board of Bristol's associated company Rotol Ltd and in 1964 would be appointed Chairman of the Arran Trust Ltd, the last of his many 'Limited' financial facilities which, in December 1978, would swallow up the remnants of his once-famous aviation empire that before the war had controlled twenty-one associated companies.

And what of Norman Edgar? After leaving Western Airways, following its take over by Whitney Straight, he become a captain in the Air Transport Auxiliary's No.2 Ferry Pool at Whitchurch Airport, and in January 1942 was heavily involved in recruitment in the USA of women pilots for that service. Moving to the USA after the war, in 1946 he became executive vice president of Helicopter Air Transport Inc. (HAT), the world's first company to run helicopter services on a commercial basis. After a long illness, early in 1983 he died in Nova Scotia, Canada.

The need for the town of Weston-super-Mare to develop evenly outwards was often used by the Weston Council as a reason for the closure of the airport, and of course complaints of aircraft noise from the residents living in housing developments to the west of the airport was an added reason. Considerable investment would also have been needed to extend the runway and improve facilities to bring the airport into the jet-age. The deciding factor, however, was the closure of Bristol's Whitchurch Airport in the early 1950s, and the development of Lulsgate Bottom into a new Bristol Airport and latterly the regional airport. This was somewhat ironic, since it was from the small number of fields at Lulsgate Bottom that in 1940 had been opened up as the Relief Landing Ground for the DH Tiger Moths of 10 EFTS at Weston that would ultimately seal its fate.

To mark the seventieth anniversary of the opening of Weston Airport, at mid-day on 25 June 2006, the Deputy Lord Mayor of Cardiff and other VIPs landed at Weston Airport, albeit in the Helicopter Museum, to replicate the event. Received by the Mayor of Weston in the museum, the party was able to see an exhibition showing development of the airport and local aviation from 1936 to 2006. Strangely, in 2010 some thirty years after the airport that had contributed so much to the growth and prosperity of Weston was effectively closed to the aeroplane, it still remained undeveloped and remarkably was very much as it had been in the dark days of 1940.

5

INCIDENTS AND ACCIDENTS

The following incidents and accidents, some of which are unsubstantiated but included for interest, occurred within approximately 12 miles (19 km) of Weston, and did not necessarily fit into the narrative within the other chapters.

1933

21 June. Jall Sorabjee, a barrister of Nairobi, Kenya, on an extended holiday of Britain joined the Bristol and Wessex Aero Club as a temporary member so that the surrounding countryside could be explored by air. Hiring the club's DH Gipsy Moth G-ABWM with the intention of flying to Wells, after circling the city he headed back in the general direction of Whitchurch as the weather was deteriorating. Over Yatton, with little fuel remaining, he made a precautionary landing in a field at Horsecastle, but the landing area which adjoined the town's High Street was on the small side, and by the end of its run the machine had reached the street where it tipped onto its nose and hit a passing cyclist. Luckily, neither the cyclist nor the pilot were injured.

1935

24 June. A Hawker Audax, piloted by Lieutenant Weldon of the Sherwood Foresters and crewed by Corporal Brooks of the RAF was being flown from RAE Farnborough to Swansea using the short Channel crossing between Weston and Barry. But soon after the coast was crossed, the machine's engine started to misfire necessitating an about turn, and after a total failure, the aircraft was safely put down at Yatton coincidently, in a field that also belonged to the same farmer as in above incident!

1938

22 November. Lockheed Model 14 Super Electra G-AFGO, belonging to British Airways Ltd, during a test flight crashed into the rocky shore of Walton Bay, between Clevedon and Portishead. The aircraft burnt out and the pilot Captain Robinson was killed. This machine was one of four imported through Southampton Docks, and erected and test flown at Southampton's Eastleigh Airport.

1939

10 September. Bristol Blenheim IV P4853 of 82 Squadron, after take-off from Netheravon had an engine fail, and on the approach to a field near Cleeve, 5 miles (8 km) south-east of Clevedon, hit wires and cartwheeled. Two of the crew were killed and two survived.

28 October. Following a cross-country flight, probably from Yatesbury, DH Tiger Moth K4256 of 10 EFTS undershot on the approach to Weston Airport, hit a mound, and its undercarriage was ripped off.

18 December. Due to bad weather, the pilot of Hawker Hind K4641 of 19 MU on a mail flight, made a precautionary landing 2 miles (3 km) south of Cheddar; the selected field was overshot and the machine overturned on hitting a hedge. Pilot safe.

1940

27 August. A Hawker Hurricane crashed at Chelvey, near Brockley. Polish pilot safe.

18 September. Westland Lysander P1687 of 16 Squadron, Westland Zoyland, was damaged in a forced-landing in a field near Banwell. Pilot safe.

23 September. A DH Tiger Moth force-landed at Chew Stoke. Crew safe.

27 September. During a night navigation exercise in Handley Page Hampden I X2914 of 106 Squadron, Cottesmore, the pilot became lost and when an engine failed the machine was abandoned, it crashing on West House Farm, Chilton Polden. Pilot injured, three killed.

30 September. Hawker Hurricane I P3021 of 504 (County of Nottingham) Squadron, whilst on detachment to Filton to help defend the Bristol Factory against a possible follow-up attack to the one on the 25th, and believed to have been piloted by Sergeant Mike Bush, crashed 1½ miles (2.4 km) south of Priddy Church. Pilot unhurt.

1 October. Hawker Hurricane P1653 of 5 OTU, Aston Down, crashed in Bennet's Field 2 miles (3.2 km) west of Congresbury. Pilot safe.

16 October. Hawker Hurricane I N2603 of 55 OTU, forced-landed at Chewton Mendip. Polish pilot injured.

2/3 December. An aircraft was reported to have crashed near Redhill.

9 December. During a cross-country flight from Weston, DH Tiger Moth K4265 of 10 EFTS flew into the ground at Creech St Michael.

12 December. Whilst low-flying approx a mile (1.6 km) south of Brean Down, DH Tiger Moth T5422 of 10 EFTS was seen to make several rapid descents as though the pilot was practicing dive-bombing. During these procedures the wheels touched the water twice, the machine crashed into the sea and the crew was drowned.

24 December. Whilst flying in cloud during a ferry flight, Hawker Hurricane I P3083 of 247 Squadron, Roborough, crashed into Bristol Plain Farm, near Priddy. Pilot killed.

31 December. A Hawker Hurricane crashed in a field 300 yards (274 metres) south of Sidcot School. Pilot safe.

1941

1 January. During a cross-country flight from Weston to Yatesbury, DH Tiger Moth N6469 of 10 EFTS crashed during an overshoot.

16 January. DH Tiger Moth R5120 of 10 EFTS force-landed at Higher Pipps, Priddy.

17 January. Whilst low-flying, DH Tiger Moth T7047 of 10 EFTS flew into the ground at Bleadon Wharf, near Lympsham.

25 January. Fairey Battle I P6764 from 1 FTS Netheravon, after dropping off a passenger at St Athan, South Wales, on return to base and whilst flying in low cloud, flew into the steep rock face of Weston Town Quarry at Cecil Road. The aircraft dropped onto tar barrels and blew up. Pilot killed.

4 February. A North American Harvard force-landed 200 yards (183 metres) north-east of Rode Church. Crew safe.

11 February. During a ferry flight to St Athan, Westland Wallace II K8701 of 1 SS overturned whilst carrying out a forced landing ½ mile (.75 km) south of Walton, Sedgemoor.

15 February. During an overshoot at Lulsgate Bottom, DH Tiger Moth N9464 of 10 EFTS stalled at 30 feet (9 metres) and on contact with the ground overturned.

3 March. An unidentified aircraft forced-landed at Berrow.

7 March. A Fairey Battle force-landed near Red Road, Berrow. One injured, one safe.

20 March. A DH Gipsy Moth force-landed near Weston Gasworks. Pilot safe.

28 March. DH Tiger Moth R5127 of 10 EFTS spun-in at West Broadstone Halt, a mile (1.6 km) west of Kingston Seymour. Pilot seriously injured.

6 April. Whilst landing on soft ground at Weston Airport, the undercarriage of Bristol Blenheim IV L9252 of 272 Squadron, Chivenor collapsed and the aircraft was damaged beyond repair.

2 May. Hawker Audax I K3103 of 1 FTS Netheravon was damaged during a forced landing at Milton Hill Farm, Weston. Crew safe.

20 May. Whilst performing an attempted over-shoot at Weston Airport, DH Tiger Moth N9274 of 10 EFTS hit a vehicle and was damaged beyond repair.

1 June. An FAA Percival Proctor crashed ½ mile (.75 km) west of Churchill Church. Two injured, one safe.

10 June. Weston's barrage balloons, in addition to keeping the enemy at bay, were responsible for causing a certain amount of friendly damage. The worst case was the unfortunate downing of Supermarine Spitfire IIA P8143 of 501 Squadron, Colerne. One of a pair on convoy patrol, it caught the cable of a balloon at 19 Site, and crashed on Shiplate Court Farm, Bleadon. Pilot killed and aircraft burnt out.

12 June. Handley Page Hampden I P2111 belonging to 25 OTU, Coningsby, took off with a crew of four from Finningley for a combined navigation, air-firing and practice bombing exercise, the latter over the Bristol Channel. It was presumed that the aircraft came down in the range area, as bodies of two of the crew were washed ashore at Burnham-on-Sea on 28 June.

17 June. A Fairey Albacore force-landed on Cars Cliff Farm, Cheddar Gorge. Crew of three injured.

20 June. Whilst flying at low altitude near Brean Down, DH Tiger Moth R5122 of 10 EFTS stalled and came down in a field. One killed, one injured.

28 June. A barrage balloon at Devil's Bridge broke away and fouled the electricity grid.

20 July. During a thunder storm, a number of barrage balloons were struck by lightning, with one landing on the Borough Arms Hotel causing a certain amount of damage.

9 August. DH Tiger Moth R4783 of 10 EFTS force-landed in a field near Hutton.

10 August. A Bristol Beaufort force-landed a mile (1.6 km) south of Mark Church. Crew safe.

14 August. A DH Tiger Moth force-landed at Brent Knoll. Crew safe.

10 September. Bristol Beaufort I L9806, crewed by members of the No.2 FPP, on the first stage of a delivery flight to Australia, had an engine cut, and not being able to maintain height, it was belly-landed at West Ham, Wedmore.

25 September. DH Tiger Moth T6617 of 10 EFTS, after touching-down at Weston Airport swung and overturned.

3 October. An unidentified aircraft crashed ½ mile (.75 km) south-east of Paulton Church.

13 November. A Miles Magister crashed at Weston. Crew safe.

20 November. Miles Hawk Major DP848 from 39 MU, Colerne, crashed during a forced-landing on Bristol Plain, 1½ miles (2.4 km) west of Priddy Church. Pilot killed and aircraft burnt-out.

23 November. An unidentified aircraft crashed on Berrow Sands.

23 *November.* Supermarine Spitfire I R6921 of 52 OTU crashed during a forced-landing on Cheddar Head Farm.

1942

5 *January.* Armstrong Whitworth Whitley Z6979 of 10 OTU, Abingdon, force-landed on Stert Flats. Crew safe.

16 *January.* An unidentified aircraft forced-landed at Chew Magna. One safe.

8 *February.* Hawker Hurricane II BD941 of 87 Squadron Charmy Down crashed on Naish Farm, Clapton-in-Gordano. Pilot killed.

12 *February.* Avro Anson I W2641 from 32 MU force-landed near the Full Quart Inn, Hewish. Crew safe.

24 *March.* For a series of trials associated with aircraft parting barrage-balloon cables with wing-mounted cutters, Vickers Wellington IA P9210 of RAE Farnborough had been detached to Churchstanton. Over Pawlett Hams, where the trials were taking place, the aircraft was deliberately flown into a cable beneath a balloon, but the machine rapidly became uncontrollable and started to break up. The pilot, who was the sole occupant of the aircraft, successfully bailed out, and the aircraft came down on Rowlett Farm, a mile (1.6 km) west of Pawlett Church. The large balloon shed built at the beginning of the war on the western edge of Pawlett Hill for the experiments, although now rather dilapidated, can still be seen jutting up high above the surrounding fields.

25 *March.* Whilst returning to Wigsley on a transit flight, the starboard airscrew of Handley Page Hampden I P5329 of 455 Squadron became detached and the aircraft crashed onto Sparks Farm, Watchfield, 2 miles (3.2 km) east of Highbridge. Crew killed and the aircraft burnt-out.

6 *April.* Carrying four live 250 lb (113.5 kg) bombs, Handley Page Hampden I P1299 from 16 OTU, Upper Heyford, flying towards Banwell across Locking Village at about 1,000 feet (305 metres), pitched-up, turned towards RAF Locking, stalled and entered a spin from which it didn't recover. It impacted close to the camp's boiler house and the crew of four was killed.

22 *April.* A Vickers Wellington landed at Weston with an engine on fire.

25 *April.* Hawker Hurricane Z2461 of 87 Squadron, Charmy Down, force-landed at Kewstoke. Pilot safe.

27 *April.* Supermarine Spitfire Vb AD553 from 312 Squadron, Fairwood Common, crashed 658 yards (200 metres) from Axbridge Railway Station. Czech pilot killed.

3 *May.* Vickers Wellington III X3756 of 57 Squadron, Methwold, on a night-time cross-country training exercise ran short of fuel and the crew safely bailed out. The aircraft flew on and eventually crashed in Sand Bay some 200 yards (183 metres) west of the Sand Point car park.

29 *June.* A North American Mustang of 16 Squadron, Weston Zoyland, crashed at Pawlett Hams. Pilot safe.

5 July. Bristol Blenheim IV R3912 of 13 OTU, took off from Bicester with a crew of three on a cross-country navigation exercise, culminating in a medium-level bombing practice run at Pawlett Hams Bombing Range. When over the range, the machine was seen in a steep dive entering a large cloud. On emerging it appeared to level out, whereupon it started another dive from which it didn't recover. The Blenheim crashed on the edge of the range on the east bank of the River Parrett and the crew was killed.

12 July. Two Supermarine Spitfire IIs P8148 and P8278 from 52 OTU, Aston Down, during a training sortie collided over Weston. P8278 was relatively undamaged and returned to base, but the pilot of P8148 had to bail out and the machine crashed at Draycott.

18 August. A barrage balloon was seen adrift at high-altitude over the Milton area of Weston.

15 October. Fairey Fulmars N4079 and N4008 from 761 Squadron, Yeovilton, collided over Lulsgate Bottom. The former crashed on top of Cheddar Gorge killing the pilot, whilst the pilot of the other machine bailed out and was unhurt.

17 December. Airspeed Oxford I L9695 of 8 AACU, whilst low-flying hit HT cables and crashed on Durbin's Farm, Nailsea. Crew killed.

1943

11 January. Whilst operating from Weston, Boulton Paul Defiant AA443 of 286 Squadron force-landed near Bleadon Church.

26 January. Supermarine Spitfire IIbs P8207 and P8208 of 52 OTU, Aston Down, collided during gunnery practice over the Bristol Channel. The former managed to return to base but the other had to be ditched off Portishead. Pilot safe.

12 February. Shortly after taking off from Weston Airport, both engines of Airspeed Oxford I DF252 of 286 Squadron cut, and in the ensuing forced-landing the sea wall on Bowley Farm, Brean Down, was hit. Luckily, Mr C. T. H. Howe of the St Johns Corps and incidentally No.3 Civil Defence Area transport officer was nearby, and with two others helped extract the crew from the wreck which had fuel pouring from ruptured tanks. For the officer's valiant rescue efforts, the St John Bronze Life Saving Medal was awarded. One killed, one injured.

3 April. Boulton Paul Defiant I DR979 of 286 Squadron belly-landed at Weston.

4 April. Armstrong Whitworth Whitley EB285 of 42 OTU crashed a mile (1.6 km) east of Highbridge. Two injured, the others safe.

5 April. A Hawker Hurricane crashed at South Berrow. Pilot injured.

13 April. DH Tiger Moth DE672 from 10 GP Communications Flight, force-landed at Kewstoke. Crew safe.

8 May. North American Mustang AG519 of 4 Squadron, Odiham force-landed at Stockland Bristol, Somerset. Pilot safe.

18 May. Hawker Typhoon I B EK171 of 175 Squadron, Colerne, following engine failure, overshoot whilst attempting a forced-landing at Weston Airport.

29 June. Vickers Wellington III X3888 from 22 OTU Wellesbourne Mountford, whilst engaged in air-to-sea firing practice over the Bristol Channel, during a low turn a mile (1.6 km) west of Flat Holm, a wing struck the sea and the aircraft broke up. The crew, except for the bomb aimer, was saved by ASR launches.

25 July. Supermarine Spitfire Vb BL291 from 504 Squadron, Ibsley, force-landed at Yatton. Pilot safe.

28 July. A Vickers Wellington crashed into the sea off Brean Sands.

2 August. During a night-flying exercise from Lulsgate Bottom, Airspeed Oxford I LX218 of 3(P) AFU had an engine cut, the aircraft stalled and it crashed on Quarry Farm, Wrington. Pilot killed.

5 August. An Airspeed Oxford of 3(P)AFU, Lulsgate Bottom crashed at Backwell, Brockley. Crew killed.

6 September. A Miles Martinet crashed at Brent Knoll. One injured, one safe.

16 September. A Miles Martinet crashed on Brean Down Marshes. One injured, one safe.

2 December. A Miles Martinet crashed onto Mendip View Farm, Kingston Seymour. Crew killed.

5 December. A Supermarine Seafire force-landed at Shipham. Pilot safe.

14 December. Miles Martinet I EM411of 587 Squadron, Weston Zoyland, crashed during low-level flying a mile (1.6 km) north of Woolavington. Crew killed.

16 December. In poor weather, Supermarine Spitfire IV BS491 of 541 Squadron, Benson, crashed on Chelvey Farm, Backwell, and burnt out. Pilot killed.

20 December. A Miles Martinet from Weston Zoyland force-landed at Wedmore. Crew safe.

24 December. A Hawker Hurricane crashed at Draycott. Pilot killed.

28 December. Hawker Hurricane IV KX539 of the No.2 FPP at Whitchurch, whilst taxiing on soft ground at Weston Airport, tipped onto its nose.

31 December. Boeing B-17F Fortress 42-3093 *Nobody's Darling* of the 351 Bomb Group, Polebrook, with a crew of eleven returning from a raid on Cognac and Chateaubernard airfields, force-landed at Burnham-on-Sea on the mudflats close to the lighthouse. Crew safe.

Sometime in 1943/44. When the starboard engine of one of the Airspeed Oxfords of 116 Squadron was being started on a concrete hard-standing at Weston Airport, due to the undercarriage retraction lever having been inadvertently left in the 'up' position, as hydraulic pressure became available, the undercarriage retracted. The aircraft was extensively damaged and an airman on the wing was violently thrown around but luckily escaped injury.

1944

14 January. Whilst on a Searchlight Co-operation Exercise, the pilot of Airspeed Oxford I LX480 of 286 Squadron lost control after being dazzled by a light and the aircraft crashed at West Harptree. Pilot killed.

8 May. Miles Master II EM355 of 3 FIS, Lulsgate Bottom, following engine failure force-landed ½ mile (.75 km) west of Uphill Railway Station. Crew injured.

15 May. A Stinson reported to be missing from Weston was believed to have ditched in the sea off Porlock/Lynton.

8 July. Due to a misjudged landing, an undercarriage leg of DH Mosquito XVI MM129 of 692 Squadron, Graveley collapsed, and the machine slid off the runway into the rhyne that bordered the east end of the airport where it suffered a smashed nose.

17 July. A troop-carrying glider, believed to have been from Weston Zoyland, landed at Wedmore.

21 August. During a daytime exercise, Miles Master II AZ605 of 3 FIS, Lulsgate Bottom, crashed into the sea to the west of Clevedon at Langford Grounds. Crew killed.

1945

26 April. Airspeed Oxford II BM777 of 1335 CU, Colerne, caught fire on the approach to Weston Airport, but although landing safely was damaged beyond repair. The same day a Gloster Meteor, probably the first jet to call in at Weston, also landed after a mock dogfight over the town with a Hawker Tempest.

3 July. Avro Lancaster B I SW278 of 166 Squadron, Kirmington, crashed vertically into the sea 5 miles (8 km) north-west of Kewstoke Church. The crew of seven was killed. Rescue services were alerted by a telephone call from a lady who saw the accident from Worlebury Hill and Weston's lifeboat was speedily launched, but first on the scene was a powered dinghy belonging to the Royal Navy and one body was recovered. Initially it was considered that he was the pilot and sole occupant of the aircraft, which at that time was not known to be a Lancaster. It was only later that it was realised that the aircraft had a crew of seven, and during the next few days a further four of the crew were washed-up between Brean Down and Clevedon.

7 July. Chance Vought Corsair II JS745 of 759 Squadron FAA, Yeovilton, piloted by Sub Lieutenant John Alistair Clemance was at 9,000 feet (2743 metres) several miles off Burnham-on-Sea practicing aerobatics. An inverted spin was inadvertently entered and, unable to recover, at 5,000 feet (1524 metres) in front of hundreds of holidaymakers he bailed out and, after three hours in the choppy sea, reached Stert Island. Although a Supermarine Sea Otter from Yeovilton and Weston's lifeboat were launched to search for the downed airman, it was a resident of Burnham who reported someone on the island, and a rowing boat sent out recovered the very cold and bedraggled airman.

23 August. Gloster Meteor F3s EE280 and EE283 from 245 Squadron, Bentwater, during an exercise over the Bristol Channel, collided and EE280, losing its tail, crashed 3 miles (4.8 km) west of Weston.

1946

9 December. Hedge-hopping a Supermarine Spitfire over the flat area around Brent Knoll, Pilot Officer Hodgeson flew into HT cables near the Bristol — Bridgwater road at Rooksbridge and an explosion scattered bits of aircraft over the road and adjacent field. Although control was maintained for several minutes, the aircraft had to be belly-landed in a field 3 miles (5 km) east of Axbridge. Pilot safe.

1947

4 March. Early in 1947 four Supermarine Sea Otters belonging to the FAA Station Flight, Belfast, were detached to Weston Airport and for a time ranged in line on the grass in front of the tower. On the afternoon of Tuesday 4 March, JM874, whilst being flown solo by Sub-Lieutenant N. E. Peniston-Bird, who was returning from RAF Valley in Wales in a sleet and hail storm became lost. In the severe weather the machine's radio and some of the instruments failed, and after an hour of searching for the airport, the pilot spotted Weston Beach and successfully put down the amphibian in the bay. Coming in low over the Beach Lawns, it splashed-down near the Grand Pier and taxied to Knightstone Slipway where it was beached. (Via G. Bell)

Supermarine Sea Otter JM 874, 4 March 1947

Avro Anson NK734,
27 July 1949

1949

2 July. Miles Hawk Trainer III G-A KMU was written off whilst landing at Weston Airport.

27 July. NK734, an Avro Anson I from 66 GCF RAF Turnhouse, bringing visitors to the ATDU at Weston, at the end of its easterly landing run ground-looped onto the taxi-track. Its starboard tyre burst, the undercarriage radius-rod and wheel broke free, and on contacting the ground the starboard wing fractured just outboard of the engine nacelle (R. Vallan).

20 August. In 1949, DH Tiger Moth G-AHWE was still available to members of the Weston Aero Club and, during an expedition to Exeter and Plymouth, due to fuel running low, its pilot was forced into carrying out a precautionary landing in a small cornfield at Sampford Brett, Williton, near Watchet. The machine was recovered to Weston the following day by Lew Lisle.

31 August. During a take-off run with two passengers on board, one of the last of Weston Aero Club's Fairchild Argus escaped serious damage when a part of the undercarriage failed and the aircraft nosed-over.

1950

25 October. The pilot of a Gloster Meteor gave what initially appeared to be an impromptu low-level display of aerobatics at lunchtime over Weston Beach, but it had obviously been pre-planned for when heading off towards Bristol at full throttle, sufficient flap was lowered to allow two toilet rolls that had been carefully positioned in the wing to deploy and flutter down to the sands.

1951

Mid-April. Partway through a cross-country training exercise, a Percival Proctor (either G-AHTV or G-AKZN) belonging to Air Service Training piloted by Mr O. Salhihi of Southampton, was damaged when it tipped onto its nose whilst taking-off from Weston Airport.

1952

23 February. Westland Wyvern S 4 VW880, piloted by Harald J. Penrose, chief test pilot of Westland Aircraft, had taken off from Westland's satellite base at Merryfield to carry out a number of high-speed runs at altitude over Berrow Flats, the area favoured by Westland for much of its test work. During one run, there was a loss of oil pressure in the contra-rotating airscrew's troublesome gearbox. Weston Airport was chosen for an emergency landing, but when almost lined-up on the runway, the gearbox unit with its eight large blades ground to a halt. In the ensuing 100 mph (161 kph) dead-stick belly-landing parallel to Moor (Windmill) Lane Drove, the 10 ton (10,160 kg) projectile crossed two fields and rhynes, stopping in a cloud of dust on Moorlands Farm, 360 yards (329 metres) short of the runway threshold. The aircraft appeared to be not seriously damaged and after several days was dismantled and taken back to Yeovil, but due to it having sustained a twisted structure it was never to fly again. Such were the problems with the Wyvern that six test pilots were killed during the type's protracted development programme (Westland).

6 August. Three DH Vampire F Is of 208 AFS, Merryfield, had taken off for formation flying practice over the Bristol Channel when TG305, flown by Pilot Officer D. J. Atkins, whilst at 10,000 feet (3048 metres) and carrying out a tail-chase, lost sight of the others. During a descent in hazy conditions he flew into the sea just to the west of Steep Holm, and it was to be some hours before the pilot's body was recovered from near Barry Docks.

Westland Wyvern
VW880, 23
February 1952

11 October. There were also DH Vampire FB 5s occasionally seen around Weston that belonged to Filton's 501 (County of Gloucester) and Rhoose's 614 (County of Glamorgan) R Aux. AF Squadrons. Shortly after take-off from Filton, VV698, one of 614 Squadron's machines flown by Squadron Leader H. Ambrose was to suffer an engine malfunction, and with Weston Airport enveloped in mist the only area suitable for a forced-landing was Berrow Beach. Escorted down by another Vampire, the aircraft was belly-landed on the sands near Berrow Church. Luckily it was low tide and there then started a rush against time to recover the machine, with first a water tender then a fire service breakdown truck from Yeovil becoming stuck in the mud. It was eventually five tractors with crews working by the light of oil lanterns that succeeded in recovering the aircraft and the other vehicles to the top of the beach in an 8-hour long rescue operation.

1953

Early June. During a cross-country flight in a DH Chipmunk from Southampton's Eastleigh Airport to Weston Airport, Denis Todd, a Burmese pilot training for a commercial licence, because of deteriorating weather conditions decided to carry out a precautionary landing near Mark. The field alongside Vole Road belonging to farmer Edward Tucker was full of cows, and because of this the landing was exceptionally difficult. The next morning a further Chipmunk with two instructors landed, and after a daily inspection, both machines took off for Eastleigh Airport with the trainee who had spent the night in the local police station.

11 June. At high altitude, Javelins under test from Gloster Aircraft's Moreton Valence airfield were over Weston most days and, even without being seen, their howl was an unmistakable recognition feature. Only two weeks after making its first flight, on 11 June 1953 prototype WD808, flown by test pilot Peter Lawrence, during aft CG stalling-trials, at about 11,000 feet (3353 metres) with flaps lowered got into the little-known 'deep stall' condition. Coming down almost vertically in a horizontal, nil airspeed, state, it crashed in a field near Flax Bourton and the pilot, ejecting at too low an altitude, was killed when his parachute failed to deploy fully.

Mid-July. During a cross-country flight from RAF Chivenor, Devon, the pilot of an Auster low on fuel had to carry out a precautionary landing on Six Acres field, Manor Farm, Edingworth, near Lympsham. Although not damaged in the landing, the machine was dismantled the following day and returned to base by road.

3 August. Auster J/1N Alpha G-AIFZ was damaged when force-landing at Portishead.

1954

21 October. Flight Lieutenant R. J. Ross on detachment to Gloster Aircraft from RAE Farnborough to assist with the protracted Gloster Javelin stall/spin-recovery trials programme, whilst piloting FAW I XA546 between Weston and Portishead, entered a spin from which he was unable to recover, the machine coming down in the sea somewhere off the end of Sand Point. First on the crash scene were lifeboats from Weston and Barry, an RAF ASR launch from Porthcawl and a Bristol Sycamore from Filton flown by Sox Hosegood with Walter Gibb as observer; then the sky became full of aircraft searching for this early production top secret machine. Two Avro Shackletons, one from RAF St Eval and the other from RAF Llandow were joined by a Short Sunderland from RAF Pembroke Dock, a DH Vampire from Filton and a Supermarine Seafire from Yeovilton, but except for a patch of oil off Sand Point there was nothing to be seen.

Attempts to locate and recover the Javelin, which by now would have sunk into deep mud, went on for some months. Initially seaward defence vessels *Shalford*, *Aberford* and *Camberford* combed the area and then, following little success, they were joined by frigate *Venus* and boom defence vessel *Barrage*, mine-sweeper trawler *Flatholm*, mine-sweepers *Chillingham* and *Asheldham*, a tug, a motor-ferry and the ATDU's landing craft. The wreck was considered to be in water between four and ten fathoms deep where there were strong currents and underwater visibility was zero. Divers sent down to examine the only Asdic contacts by feel found them to be only an old anchor and a rock. Following completion of the official search at the end of November, Gloster Aircraft, having privately commissioned three local sprat fishermen to continue the quest had success, when on 21 January of the following year, a diver from one of the boats confirmed that a contact was in fact the Javelin. Buoys were placed over the wreck but by the following day, when recovery vessels returned, the markers had disappeared! During the months of searching, only the nose radome, a wing-tip and the pilot's bone-dome had been recovered. As late as the middle of the following March a further attempt was made to locate the Javelin, when a Shackleton reported to be equipped with a 'secret apparatus', no doubt a Mk 2 with the new magnetic anomaly detection equipment in the tail, was brought in for low-runs over the area.

1955

15 February. It was not unusual in the 1950s, when walking on the Mendips near Crook Peak, to look down onto Gloster Meteors from Weston Zoyland flying at low-level in formation. These pilot-training activities were highlighted by quite frequent reports in the local newspapers of smoking craters appearing in fields on the far side of the Mendips. The closest one came to Weston, was when during aerobatic practice, Meteor T 7 WH194 of 12 FTS, Weston Zoyland, had to be abandoned and the resulting crash made a 15 foot (4.6 metre) deep crater near Brean Halt with wreckage scattered over a wide area. The instructor Flight Lieutenant D. A. Cooper with Salah Balhowan, a foreign student, both managed to successfully bail out (no ejection seats), with the trainee landing on Rhynemoor Farm near Bleadon.

22 April. Whilst *en route* to Weston from RAF Ternhill, the port engine of Avro Anson T21 WD410 failed, but luckily Master Pilot Brown was close enough to carry out a safe emergency landing at the airport.

1958

6 October. Auster J/1 Autocrat G-AJUM, at that time being operated by the Plymouth Aero Club, took off in good conditions for a cross-country to Weston Airport. Its pilot, Geoffrey Francis Windsor Parker, a manager with BOAC, home on holiday from the Middle East, had with him a friend who farmed at Kingsbury Episcopi. A detour was made to the village and the machine made several low-level circuits of the farm. On the fourth it stalled, entered an incipient spin and crashed in an adjacent orchard. Both men trapped in the wreckage were released by firemen from Martock but they died soon after. The aircraft was in due course recovered to Western Airways for a detailed inspection.

1960

14 July. Whilst on a cross-country exercise in the vicinity of Weston, the engine of DH Vampire T II XE827 of 8 FTS, RAF Swinderby, blew up. With flying controls partially disabled, a successfull forced-landing was carried-out at Weston Airport. Extensively damaged, the machine was not repaired.

9 November. Sudanese student pilot Omar Ibrahim Eisa had been tasked to do an out-and-return solo cross-country from Exeter in Exeter & Plymouth's Aero Club's Chipmunk G-AORV, with landings at Lulsgate Bottom and Weston Airports. After taking-off from Weston on the final leg of the flight back to Exeter, weather conditions deteriorated with low cloud and intermittent rain reducing horizontal visibility to approximately 3 miles (5 km). Approaching the Quantocks, the pilot was 2 miles (3 km) off course, and in the poor visibility wasn't aware of rising ground. About 2 miles (3 km) east-south-east of Crowcombe at The Slades, trees were hit and such was the impact that the aircraft was destroyed and the pilot killed.

1962

15 May. During flight trials from Westland's Oldmixon Factory, a Westland Whirlwind HAR 10 suffered engine failure and was successfully auto-rotated down into a field.

24 July. Only one week to the day after its ailing starboard motor caused the crash of 3/4 CAACU's DH Mosquito at Weston Airport, another aircraft met its end near the Oldmixon Factory, but in rather unusual circumstances. This was all-black Armstrong Whitworth Sea Hawk FGA 4 WV919 from the Fleet Requirements Unit at Hurn Airport. Operated by Airwork Services Ltd with fourteen Sea Hawks and a variety of other aircraft, the unit under contract to the Admiralty provided radar collaboration and target-towing facilities to warships in home waters. Its pilot, Alfred 'Dusty' Rhodes, who some years before had flown a Vickers Valetta for Airwork/EMI from the Hutton Moor Flight Shed, saluting his mother who lived in Hutton in the usual aviator fashion, commenced a roll over the Oldmixon Factory at about 1,500 feet (457 metres). Whilst inverted, the pilot strapped in an unsecured ejector seat, smashed through the cockpit canopy, a dirty yellow parachute deployed and the combination came down between the factory and the Mendips. The unmanned Sea Hawk remained inverted and crashed to the south of the Mendips, impacting on the former course of the River Axe a few hundred yards from White Gates Farm, Bleadon. Shortly afterwards a pall of black smoke rose above to mark the position of a large crater. Within a few minutes, a Whirlwind HAR 10 that had been outside Shop 3 at the Oldmixon Factory ready for a test flight was scrambled by Bob Smith and was on its way to assist the aviator. However, on arrival it was discovered that the pilot had neck injuries and had probably fractured both legs, and the Whirlwind had to await arrival of the emergency services. After being hospitalised at Christchurch, Dusty returned to flying with Airwork, but soon after was lost without trace in another accident, this time over the English Channel.

1963

28 April. With the slackening of post-war import restrictions in the late 1950s, American light aircraft started to be imported into the UK. A fairly early arrival was Piper Aztec 250 G-ASCR and it could be viewed for a couple of days from close quarters on top of Worlebury Hill, albeit in a rather sorry state. During a flight from Halfpenny Green to Weston Airport, in low cloud that shrouded the high ground around the town, Worlebury Hill was clipped at a point just below the Observatory. Although inverted with a smashed nose and the starboard wing severed, the pilot Captain Peter Beechey and two passengers were not seriously injured, and with the help of four golfers managed to extract themselves from the wreck. It was probably the fog's muffling effect that prevented Mrs Audrey Thornton hearing the aircraft arrive at the bottom of her garden!

1967

12 September. Chipmunk WK610 of Bristol UAS, flying in formation with WP838, was abandoned 2 miles (3.2 km) south-west of Portishead.

1969

During a practice forced-landing in an area to the west of Bleadon/Lympsham, the engine of Achilles School of Flying Cherokee 140 G-AVWL failed to respond to the throttle, probably due to carburettor icing, and the machine was put down by instructor John White in a rough field that caused the nose-leg to collapse. (Via P. Turner).

Cherokee 140 G-AVWL, 1969

1970

26 August. DH Sea Vixen FAW I XN686, on a test flight from A&AEE Boscombe Down, whilst flying off Burnham-on-Sea experienced trouble and the pilot Flight Lieutenant Richard Statham and Observer Flight Lieutenant David Allerdyce ejected only seconds before it ploughed into Kings Farm, East Huntspill, near Highbridge. The pilot, uninjured, was flown back to base by helicopter, but the Observer, who had a suspected fractured leg, was taken to Weston General Hospital for treatment.

1972

25 March. Jodel DR1050 Ambassadeur G-AYEA had been flown by Mr C. Roberts, accompanied by his three small sons and an adult from Elstree to Winkleigh in Devon. After lunch and with the aircraft refuelled, it took off for the return trip to Elstree leaving the adult at Winkleigh. Cloud-base was between 700 feet (213 metres) and 1,000 feet (3048 metres), meaning that the high ground over Exmoor was shrouded in cloud. A direct course back would take the machine close to Wells but, except for a reported sighting of the machine flying northward over Exmoor, no trace of the aircraft was seen until the 27th when aircraft wreckage, which included one wing, was washed-up on Berrow Beach. Three of the four on board were also found washed up on various parts of the coast during the following few days.

30 July. During the first of Weston's Avon Air Days, DH Tiger Moth G-ANMO of the Barnstormers and Stampe G-AYGR belonging to the Rothmans Aerobatic Team, during a flour-bombing event collided in mid-air at an altitude of about 100 feet (30.5 metres). It is believed that the crews, although injured, made a full recovery. (E. ap Rees)

DH Tigermoth G-ANMO and Stampe G-AYGR, 30 July 1972

1975

22 June. The remains of Woodspring Gliding Club's ASK 7, following a too slow recovery from a cable break at around 250 feet (76 metres). Luckily the pilot Susan Dixon, only sustained only a broken leg and fractured chest bones. (West Air Photography)

ASK 7, 22 June 1975

1976

10 August. Airtourer G-AZTM of the Achilles School of Flying, on touch-down bounced, stalled and arrived heavily damaging its nose, engine, airscrew and undercarriage. (West Air Photography)

26 August. During a preview to advertise the Avon Air Day, there was an interesting and potentially serious incident that occurred to Richard Wyatt, Harlech TV's reporter/newscaster. A Westonian, who's dad Bob worked for Westland at Oldmixon in its Shop 7 Tool Stores, was being filmed commentating on a slow, low and very close fly-by of Piper Cub 329417 flown by Ken Rickards. However, the fly-by was closer than anticipated, for the machine's starboard wing-tip actually hit Richard, leaving the shape of his scull in the light alloy leading edge. Badly shaken, Richard was soon on his feet and Gerry Mallett, the Western Airway's employee tasked with carrying out repairs, was several weeks later able to present Richard with the tip section, suitably mounted as a memento. (E. ap Rees)

1977

3 July. Taylor JT-1 Monoplane G-AWGZ, built and owned by John Morris of Weston, following engine failure lost its undercarriage in the ensuing landing near Cheddar.

Airtourer G-AZTM, 10 August 1976

Piper Cub 329417, 26 August 1976

1978

14 February. Orlicon L-40 Meta-Sokol G-APVU landed heavily and its undercarriage collapsed causing extensive damage to its underside.

1980

18 May. Tempete G-ASUS owned by Mr D. G. Jones stalled and crashed onto the airport perimeter resulting in extensive damage to the machine's undercarriage and airscrew.

1982

March/April. During a long cross-country flight from Plymouth to Arbroath in Scotland, four Westland Gazelles of the Plymouth-based Royal Marine 3rd Commando Brigade encountered early morning mist that enveloped the Mendip Hills. Unable to reach Weston Airport, a precautionary landing was carried out in a field at Purn Farm, Bleadon. With poor conditions persisting, a guard was mounted on the helicopters and the crews stayed overnight at RAF Locking. The following morning conditions had improved and the flight continued to Arbroath where the machines would continue to Norway for a mountain flying exercise.

1991

12 September. Panavia Tornado GR I ZA540 of 27 Squadron, Marham, on a weapon-training sortie, was flying low over the Bristol Channel when there was a bang and the aircraft shuddered. The Central Warning Panel (CWP) indicated a fault in the machine's fly-by-wire flight-control system, and shortly afterwards the flying controls reverted to manual. A climb was instigated, during which the machine started to pitch and roll and the CWP gave indication that the port engine bay was on fire. Reheat was selected on the starboard engine, but by the time 5,000 feet (1524 metres) was reached, the machine, out of control, commenced a dive to port. At this point the crew ejected, and they, together with the aircraft, came down in the sea just to the south of Steep Holm. Forty minutes after ejection, a Westland Sea King HAR 3 from Chivenor recovered the crew. Although a major salvage operation was launched, as with other aircraft recovery operations in the Bristol Channel, no trace of the aircraft was found.

APPENDIX 1

Aircraft Associated with Norman Edgar (Western Airways) Ltd and Straight Corporation Ltd – 1936 to 1967

Note: Where there was conflicting source information, common sense prevailed

NE (WA) L: Norman Edgar (Western Airways) Ltd
C of A: Certificate of Airworthiness
CTL: Channel Trust Ltd
EACL: Exeter Aero Club Ltd
E&PACL: Exeter & Plymouth Aero Club Ltd
HCACL: Home Counties Aero Club Ltd
IACL: Ipswich Aero Club Ltd
I/TACL: Ipswich/Thanet Aero Clubs Ltd
INACL: Inverness Aero Club Ltd
PAL: Plymouth Airport Ltd
PACL: Plymouth Aero Club Ltd
P&DACL: Plymouth & District Aero Club Ltd
P&EAL : Plymouth & Exeter Airports Ltd
RAL: Ramsgate Airport Ltd
SAC: Straight Aero Clubs
SATL: Straight Aviation Training Ltd
SAL: Southern Airways Ltd
SCL: Straight Corporation Ltd
TACL: Thanet Aero Club Ltd
WACL: Weston Aero Club Ltd
W&HCACL: Weston & Home Counties Aero Clubs Ltd
WAL: Western Airways Ltd
WSL: Whitney Straight Ltd
wfu: Withdrawn from use

Pre-Second World War

G-AAVR, DH60M Gipsy Moth 1, NE(WA)L, sold 1936

G-ABFV, DH80A Puss Moth, NE(WA)L 1932, P&DACL, impressed 24/1/40 to 41 Group and as 2067M 7/7/40 probably to RAF Locking

G-ABWZ, DH80A Puss Moth, NE(WA)L -/7/32, written off near Chipping Norton 19/12/38 whilst registered to the P&DACL

G-ACAO, DH84 Dragon I, NE(WA)L (the Lady Apsley nominee 15/10/35), WAL 18/10/38, impressed 2/4/40 as X9398

G-ACJT, DH84 Dragon I, NE(WA)L 26/8/33, WAL 18/10/38, SAL 14/2/39, loaned to 24 Sqn Hendon 7/10/39 to 11/11/39, crashed Weston Airport 20/12/39

G-ACLE, DH84 Dragon I, WAL 18/5/39, impressed 2/4/40 as X9397

G-ACMJ, DH84 Dragon I, NE(WA)L (K. Machonochie nominee 22/7/36), WAL 18/10/38, impressed 2/4/40 as X9396 to 24 Sqn

G-ACPX, DH84 Dragon II, NE(WA)L (H. Crook nominee 8/9/36), WAL 18/7/38, impressed 2/4/40 as X9399 to 6 AACU

G-ACRD, British Klemm L-25C 1A Swallow, IACL -/12/38 (used by WACL June to September 1938), impressed 9/4/40 minus engine as X5011

G-ACTU, DH89 Dragon Rapide, NE(WA)L (CTL nominee 14/7/37), WAL 9/11/38, 30/9/39 to 24 Sqn Hendon, WAL -/5/40, impressed 8/6/40 as AW115 (initially as G-ACTU) to 8 AACU

G-ADBV, DH89 Dragon Rapide, NE(WA)L (J. Dade nominee 31/5/37), WAL 1/11/38, to 24 Sqn 30/9/39, impressed 2/3/40 as X8511 -/2/41

G-ADDD, DH89 Dragon Rapide, NE(WA)L (CTL nominee 8/5/37), WAL 9/11/38, impressed 4/6/40 and became AW116 in 8 AACU

G-ADDV, Short S.16 Scion 2, 22/5/36 RAL/SAL, impressed -/4/40 as X9456

G-ADDX, Short S.16 Scion 2, 15/5/36 PAL/SAL, impressed -/4/40 as X9430

G-ADKM DH 87B Hornet Moth, EACL 12/11/35, impressed 25/1/40 as W5751

G-ADNA, DH90 Dragonfly, SAL 27/1/39, impressed 17/4/40 as X9452

G-AEAU, BA Swallow II, WACL 1/7/39, wfu Exeter 13/6/40

G-AECZ, DH84 Dragon II, SCL (Ramsgate) 1/2/37 (RAL 15/11/37), operated by NE(WA)L in 1938, WAL -/10/38, SAL (Ramsgate) 14/2/39, taken over by NAC and used by 24 Sqn from 11/10/39, returned to WAL and impressed 8/5/40 as AV982, to 110 (AAC) Wing, Filton

G-AEDH, DH90 Dragonfly, PAL 25/9/37, WAL 15/2/39, impressed 10/5/40 as AV987 to 110 (AAC) Wing

*G-AEMV, BA Swallow II, SC 10/9/36, wfu 6/2/40, WSL -/11/46, registration cancelled /10/47

G-AERC, Miles MIIA Whitney Straight, IACL -/5/38, impressed -/4/40 as AV971

G-AERK, BA Swallow II, SC 1938/WACL -/1/39, dismantled Weston -/3/40

G-AETM, DH86b Express, WAL 18/4/39, sold to Finland -/12/39 as OH-SLA but not taken up

G-AEUP, Hillson Praga, IACL -/12/38

G-AEUT, Hillson Praga, IACL -/11/38

G-AEUU, Hillson Praga, WACL 16/3/38, scrapped during war

G-AEYL, Hillson Praga, IACL 19/1/38

G-AEYM, Hillson Praga, IACL 19/1/38, crashed Weston 1/9/39

G-AFBV, Miles MIIA Whitney Straight, I/TACL, collided with windsock
Ipswich Airport 15/6/39

*G-AFDT, DH 87B Hornet Moth, TACL, impressed 22/1/40 as W5779, WAL
20/5/46, sold 1948

G-AFDY, DH 87B Hornet Moth, WACL 5/12/38, impressed 13/1/40 as
W5780 to 5 Coastal Patrol Flight

G-AFEE, DH 87B Hornet Moth, TACL 20/6/38, used by WACL -/7/39,
impressed -/1/40 as W5781

G-AFET, Miles M.14A Hawk Trainer Mk III, WACL 3/2/38, impressed -/5/40

G-AFEU, Miles M.14A Hawk Trainer Mk III, TACL 5/2/38, crashed in sea
off Cliftonville 17/7/38

G-AFEV, Miles M.14A Hawk Trainer Mk III, WACL 5/2/38, crashed Lyme
Regis 30/8/39

G-AFEW, Miles M.14A Hawk Trainer Mk III, PACL 5/2/38, written-off
Roborough 1938

G-AFIX, Percival P.16A Q6, SCL -/4/39, impressed 2/4/40 as X9406

G-AFMP, DH 87B Hornet Moth, NE(WA)L 21/4/37, SCL 1938, impressed
22/1/40 as W5782 to 6 CPF

G-AFSO, DH89A Dragon Rapide, WAL 21/5/39, from 10/10/39 used by 24
Sqn, impressed 23/1/40 as W6457

G-AFSP, DH82A Tiger Moth, SAC 22/4/39 (TACL), to 20 MU 13/1/40,
impressed 15/1/40 as W7951

G-AFSR, DH82A Tiger Moth, SAC 22/4/39, impressed -/2/40 as W7953

G-AFSS, DH82A Tiger Moth, SAC 22/4/39, impressed -/3/40 as X9318

G-AFST, DH82A Tiger Moth, SAC 22/4/39, impressed -/2/40 as W7956

G-AFSU, DH82A Tiger Moth, SAC 22/4/39, impressed -/2/40 as W7970

G-AFTB, Piper Cub-Coupé J-4A, SCL -/6/39, used by IACL, still flying at
WAL 15/12/40, impressed -/12/40 as BV989

*G-AFTC, Piper Cub-Coupé J-4B, SCL 31/5/39, impressed 1/12/40 as
BV990, SCL -/1/46, sold -/7/46

G-AFVC, Percival P.16A Q6, SCL 30/6/39, impressed 10/5/40 as AX860

G-AFVF, Piper Cub Coupé J-4A, SCL -/7/39, used by WACL, impressed
-/1/41 as BV991

G-AFVG, Piper Cub-Coupé J-4A, SCL -/7/39, used by IACL, impressed
-/12/40 as BV987

G-AFVM, Piper Cub-Coupé J-4A, SCL -/6/39, used by IACL, impressed
-/12/40 as BV988

G-AFWA, Piper Cub-Coupé J-4A, SCL -/7/39, used by INACL, impressed
-/3/41 as BV980

G-AFWB, Piper Cub-Coupé J-4A, SCL 4/7/39, impressed -/3/41 as BV181

*G-AFWS Piper Cub-Coupé J-4A, SCL 2/8/39, used by WACL, impressed -/5/40 as ES923, SC -/1/46, sold -/6/46

G-AFWU, Piper Cub-Coupé J-4A, SCL -/8/39, used by P&DACL, scrapped during war

G-AFWV, Piper Cub-Coupé J-4A, SCL -/8/39, used by P&DACL, sold to RAF for spares -/5/41

G-AFWW, Piper Cub-Coupé J-4A, SCL -/8/39, used by P&DACL, sold to RAF for spares -/5/41

*G-AFXS, Piper Cub-Coupé J-4A, WAL 22/8/39, impressed -/2/40 as DG667, flying with WAL 29/1/43, SC -/1/46, sold -/6/46

Post Second World War

Also see DH Hornet Moth, BA Swallow and Piper Cubs listed * Pre Second World War

G-ADOT (ex X9326), DH 87B Hornet Moth, WAL 20/5/46, sold

G-ADKL (ex W5750), DH 87B Hornet Moth, WAL -/5/46, sold -/4/47

G-ADLY (ex W9388), DH 87B Hornet Moth, WAL -/5/46, sold

G-ADSK (ex AV952), DH 87B Hornet Moth, WAL -/5/46, sold

G-AGVF, Auster J/1N Alpha, E&PACL 1959, still with club 1969

G-AGWV (ex P6197), Percival P.28B Proctor 1, WAL -/1/46, sold -/6/46

G-AHBH, Percival P.44 Proctor V, WAL -/3/49, sold -/7/54

G-AHOM (ex Petrel I P5637), Percival P.16E Q6 Mk V, WAL 21/5/46, sold late 1946

G-AHUJ (ex Magister R1914), Miles M-14A Hawk Trainer Mk 3, W&HCACL (Weston or Radlett) 29/6/46, sold late 1946 to Loch Leven Aero Club

G-AHUK (ex Magister T9672), Miles M-14A Hawk Trainer Mk 3, W&HCACL (Weston or Radlett) 29/6/46, sold -/8/49

G-AHUL (ex Magister L8210), Miles M-14A Hawk Trainer 3, W&HCACL (Weston or Radlett) 29/6/46, not converted, broken up Weston -/2/47

G-AHUM (ex Auster I LB286), Taylorcraft Plus Model D, W&HCACL (Weston or Radlett) 11/6/46, sold 1950

G-AHSA (ex K3215), Avro 621 Tutor, WAL 20/7/47, sold

G-AHTA (ex P5640), Percival P16A Q6, WAL 31/5/46, sold -/11/46

G-AHTB (ex P5634), Percival P16A Q6, WAL 31/5/46, sold -/7/47

G-AHTF, Percival P.44 Proctor V, WAL -/10/49, sold -/12/53

G-AHWE (ex NL995), DH82A Tiger Moth II, WACL 13/7/46, with EACL 1954 to 1955. Crashed into radio mast Exeter 17/8/55

G-AHVV (ex EM929), DH82A Tiger Moth II, HCACL 24/6/46, WACL early 1948, PACL 1950 to 1960, sold 1963

LF863 DH 82B Queen Bee 6/12/46, not converted

G-AIDD (T5491), DH 82A Tiger Moth, P&DACL 1954, current with PACL until 18/9/57 when damaged beyond repair after striking boundary wall on take-off from Roborough

G-AIEJ (ex HD903), Supermarine Walrus II, WAL 24/8/46, broken up Renfrew -/12/48

G-AIEZ (probably ex NK728), Avro 652A Anson I, SATL 3/7/46. WAL, sold 9/1/48

G-AIFA (probably ex EF928), Avro 652A Anson I, SATL 3/7/46. WAL, sold 16/9/47

G-AIFB (probably ex EG593), Avro 652A Anson I, SATL 3/7/46. WAL, sold 9/1/48

G-AIFC (probably ex EG391), Avro 652A Anson I, SATL 3/7/46. WAL, sold 9/1/48

G-AIFD (probably ex DJ492), Avro 652A Anson I, SATL 3/7/46. WAL, sold 21/6/48

G-AIKL (ex HD915), Supermarine Walrus II, WAL 23/9/46, C of A not issued, scrapped Weston -/10/47

G-AINZ (ex MG218), Avro 652A Anson I, SATL/WAL 7/10/46, broken up Weston 19/2/52

G-AIOA (ex NK601), Avro 652A Anson I, SATL/WAL 7/10/46, broken up Weston 19/2/52

G-AIOB (ex NK843), Avro 652A Anson I, SATL/WAL 7/10/46, sold -/5/50

G-AITJ (ex MG874), Avro 652A Anson I, WAL -/10/46, sold 16/12/50

G-AITK (ex W2628), Avro 652A Anson I, WAL -/10/46, sold 3/4/50

G-AITM (ex G-AETS/DR611 (incorrectly applied as DR617)), Miles MIIA W Straight, WSL 11/11/46, broken up Weston -/3/48

G-AJIP, Auster J/1N Autocrat, EACL 1954, with E&PACL 1966

G-AJIR, Auster J/1 Autocrat, WACL early 1948, sold 1950

G-AJIT, Auster J/1 Autocrat, HCACL 22/5/47, WACL early 1948 to 1949, sold 1952

G-AJIW, Auster J/1N Alpha, E&PACL 1960, still with club early 1967

G-AJOW (ex EV790), Fairchild 24W-41A Argus I, HCACL 21/4/47, WACL early 1948, sold 1950

G-AJOX (ex FK352), Fairchild 24W-41A Argus I, HCACL 21/4/47, WACL early 1948, sold -/5/51

G-AJOY (ex FK358), Fairchild 24W-41A Argus I, HCACL (Radlett) 21/4/47, WACL early 1948, written off during forced landing Colebrook, Devon 20/12/49

G-AJOZ (ex FK338), Fairchild 24W-41A Argus I, HCACL 21/4/47, WACL early 1948, sold 1950

G-AJPA (ex FK343), Fairchild 24W-41A Argus I, HCACL 21/4/47, WACL early 1948, sold -/7/50

G-AJPB (ex EV782), Fairchild 24W-41A Argus I, HCACL (Radlett) 21/4/47, WACL early 1948, sold -/5/50

G-AJPC (ex FK315), Fairchild 24W-41A Argus I, HCACL 21/4/47, WACL
    early 1948, sold -/3/50

G-AJPD (ex FK357), Fairchild 24W-41A Argus I, HCACL (Radlett) 21/4/47,
    WACL early 1948, sold -/4/50

G-AJSA (ex HM174), Fairchild 24W-41A Argus I, HCACL 5/5/47, WACL
    early 1948, written off 1949

G-AJSB (ex EV803), Fairchild 24W-41A Argus I, HCACL (Radlett) 5/5/47,
    WACL early 1948, written off on Dartmoor, Devon 20/3/48

G-AJUJ, Auster J/1 Autocrat, WACL 5-6-47, still with club 1949

G-AJUL, Auster J/1N Alpha, E&PACL 1958, still with club early 1966

G-AJUM, Auster J/1 Autocrat, WACL 22-6-47, P&DACL 1954 to 1957,
    registered to WACL but in markings of PACL when it crashed Kingsbury
    Episcopi, Somerset 6/10/58

G-AJUO, Auster J/1 Autocrat, WACL 18/6/47, EACL 1954, E&PACL 1963,
    sold 1971

G-AKBM, Miles Messenger 2A, PACL 15/7/47 and current with E&PACL
    when wfu Weston 22/5/61 and dismantled

G-AKHW, Miles Gemini 1A, PAL 21/10/47, with E&PAL 1960, sold 1961

G-ANJD (ex T6226), DH82A Tiger Moth II, EACL 8/12/53, with E&PACL
    1967

G-ANJE (ex N6736), DH82A Tiger Moth II, E&PACL 8/12/53, still with
    club when it crashed at Roborough 27/2/60

G-ANOS (ex DE465), DH82A Tiger Moth II, PACL 4/3/54, with E&PACL
    early 1967

G-ANOR (ex DE694), DH82A Tiger Moth II, WACL 4/3/54, with E&PACL
    1963 to 1967, wfu -/12/68, sold 1971

G-AOFI, DH 104 Dove 6, EACL 1964

G-AOIN, (ex N6660), DH82A Tiger Moth II, PACL 1962, still with club
    1964

G-AORE (ex WB757), DH C.1 Chipmunk 22, E&PACL 24/4/56, still with
    club late 1968

G-AORV (ex WB725), DH C.1 Chipmunk 22, E&PACL 15/5/56, still with
    club when it crashed Crowcombe, Somerset 9/11/60

G-ARDF (ex WD375), DH C.1 Chipmunk 22, E&PACL 1960, still with club
    early 1967

G-ARMK, Cessna 310F, WAL 6/7/61, still with company 1968

G-AROM, Piper PA-22 Colt 108, E&PAL 1962, still with club 1964

G-ARRF, Cessna 150A, PACL 1967, still with club 1971

G-ARTX, Cessna 150B, PACL 1972, still with club 1972

G-AVER, Cessna 150G, PACL 1968, still with club 1972

APPENDIX 2

Aircraft Built by Western Airways

Construction no.	Registration no.	Remarks/Location Survivors
Bristol Freighter Mk 31		
13140	G-18-142, F-VNAR	Cie Air Vietnam (delivered 8/10/53)
13250	G-18-197, G-APLH	Dan Air (delivered 25/3/58)
13255	G-18-202, ZK-BVM	Safe Air (delivered 20/2/58)
Total: 3		
Bristol Freighter Mk 31M		
13161	G-18-153, S4408	Royal Pakistan Air Force (delivered 30/3/54)
13163	G-18-155, S4410	Royal Pakistan Air Force (delivered 29/3/54)
13164	G-18-156, S4413	Royal Pakistan Air Force (delivered 1/6/54)
13166	G-18-158, S4415	Royal Pakistan Air Force (delivered 29/6/54)
13167	G-18-159, S4417	Royal Pakistan Air Force (delivered 29/6/54)
13168	G-18-160, S4419	Royal Pakistan Air Force (delivered 25/6/54)
13170	G-18-162, S4421	Royal Pakistan Air Force (delivered 18/9/54)
13172	G-18-164, S4422	Royal Pakistan Air Force (delivered 18/9/54)
13173	G-18-165, S4424	Royal Pakistan Air Force (delivered 25/10/54)
13174	G-18-166, S4426	Royal Pakistan Air Force (delivered 11/2/55)
13176	G-18-168, S4427	Royal Pakistan Air Force (delivered 11/2/55)
13178	G-18-170, S4429	Royal Pakistan Air Force (delivered 22/3/55)
13182	G-18-174, S4430	Royal Pakistan Air Force (delivered 23/3/55)
13187	G-18-179, S4432	Royal Pakistan Air Force (delivered 1/3/55)
13189	G-18-181, S4433	Royal Pakistan Air Force (delivered 1/3/55)
13190	G-18-182, S4435	Royal Pakistan Air Force (delivered 2/4/55)
13191	G-18-183, S4437	Royal Pakistan Air Force (delivered 2/4/55)

13193	G-18-185, S4438	Royal Pakistan Air Force (delivered 2/4/55) In its later life it became AP-ADM, then exported to Australia as VH-ADL in 1962, was used extensively by Air Express until 1979. Now in the Australian National Aviation Museum, Melbourne.
13253	G-18-200, RCAF 9850	Royal Canadian Air Force (delivered 1/11/57)
Total: 19		

Bristol (Super) Freighter Mk 32

13254	G-ANWJ	Silver City (delivered 1/6/56)
13256	G-18-203, G-APAU	Air Charter (delivered 6/6/57)
13257	G-18-204, G-AOUU	Air Charter (delivered 12/12/56)
13258	G-18-205, G-AOUV	Air Charter (delivered 27/12/56)
13259	G-ANWK	Silver City (delivered 19/6/56)
13260	G-ANWL	Silver City (delivered 6/7/56)
13261	G-ANWM	Silver City (delivered 19/7/56)
13262	G-ANWN	Silver City (delivered 26/7/56)
13263	G-18-210, G-APAV	Air Charter (delivered 18/4/57)
Total: 9		

Campbell Cougar

| CA/6000 | G-BAPS | Built 1972/3; The Helicopter Museum |

APPENDIX 3

Aircraft Built During the Second World War at the Oldmixon and Banwell Factories

Bristol Beaufighter
Mk IF: X7540 - 7541, **Mk VIF Prototype:** X7542, **Mk VIC Prototype:** X7543, **Mk IF:** X7544 - 7589, X7610 - 7649, X7670 - 7719, X7740 - 7779, X7800 - 7850, X7871 - 7879. *Total:* 239 delivered between February 1941 and February 1942.
Mk VIF: X7880 - 7899, X7920 - 7924, **Mk VIC:** X7925, **Mk VIF:** X7926 - 7936, **Mk VIC:** X7937 - 7939, **Mk VIF:** X7940 - 7969, X8000 - 8029, **Mk VIC:** X8030 - 8039, X8060 - 8099, **Mk VIF:** X8100 - 8109, X8130 - 8169, X8190 - 8229, X8250 - 8269. *Total:* 261 delivered between October 1941 and July 1942.
Mk VIF: EL145 - 192, EL213 - 218, **Mk VIC:** EL219 - 246, EL259 - 305, EL321 - 370, EL385 - 418, EL431 - 479, EL497 - 534. *Total:* 300 delivered between July and October 1942.
Mk VIC: JL421 - 454, JL502 - 549, JL565 - 582, **Mk VI ITF:** JL583, **Mk VIC:** JL584 - 592, **Mk VI ITF:** JL593, JL610 - 618, **Mk VIC:** JL619 - 628, **Mk VI ITF:** JL629 - 638, **Mk VIC:** JL639 - 648, **Mk VI ITF:** JL649 - 658, **Mk VIC:** JL659, JL704 - 712, **Mk VI ITF:** JL713 - 722, **Mk VIC:** JL723 - 735, JL756 - 779, JL812 - 826, **Mk VI ITF:** JL827 - 835, **Mk VIC:** JL836 - 855, JL869 - 875. *Total:* 269 delivered between October 1942 and February 1943.
Mk XI: JL876 - 915, JL937 - 948, **Mk VI ITF:** JL949 - 957, JM104, **Mk XI:** JM105 - 136, JM158 - 185, JM206 - 250, JM262 - 267, **TF Mk X:** JM268 - 291, JM315 - 356, JM379 - 417. *Total:* 277 delivered between February and May 1943.
TF Mk X: LX779 - 827, LX845 - 886, LX898 - 914, LX926 - 959, LX972 - 999, LZ113 - 158, LZ172 - 201, LZ215 - 247, LZ260 - 297, LZ314 - 346, LZ359 - 384, LZ397 - 419, LZ432 - 465, LZ479 - 495, LZ515 - 544. *Total:* 480 delivered between May and November 1943.
TF Mk X: NE193 - 232, NE245 - 260, NE282 - 326, NE339 - 386, NE398 - 446, NE459 - 502, NE515 - 559, NE572- -615, NE627 - 669, NE682 - 724,

NE738 - 779, NE792 - 832. *Total:* 500 delivered between November 1943 and April 1944.

TF Mk X: NT888 - 929, NT942 - 971, NT983 - 999, NV113 - 158, NV171 - 218, NV233 - 276, NV289 - 333, NV347 - 390, NV413 - 457, NV470 - 513, NV526 - 572, NV585 - 632. *Total:* 500 delivered between April and September 1944.

TF Mk X: RD130 - 176, RD189 - 225, RD239 - 285, RD298 - 335, RD348 - 396, RD420 - 468, RD483 - 525, RD538 - 580, RD685 - 728, RD742 - 789, RD801 - 836, RD849 - 867. *Total:* 500 delivered between September 1944 and August 1945.

TF Mk X: SR910 - 919. *Total:* Ten delivered between August and September 1945.

Grand total: 3,336.

Weston Beaufighters used for Trial Installations/Trials
X7540 Airspeed measurements
X7542 Beaufighter VIF prototype maximum still-air range
X7543 Beaufighter VIC prototype
X7574 Target towing
X7579 AI Mk VIII installation
X7624 AI development at TRE
X7712 AI development at TRE
 X7880 Individual engine exhaust pipes
X7881 Engine oil cooler
X7882 Engine oil cooling system & airscrew surging
X7883 Non-magnetic blast tubes
X8065 Torpedo
X8209 Handling
EL151 Fairey-Youngman dive-brakes
EL161 Handling at RAE Farnborough
EL223 Handling at AUW
EL290 Engine cooling
EL292 Gunnery, including B20 dorsal blister mounting and bomb-carrier
EL329 Rocket projectile (RP)
EL343 Non-magnetic blast tubes
EL393 RP Mk III Installation
JL871 Cannon ammunition feed mechanism
JL876 Single-engine performance and escape hatch operation in flight
JL948 Navigation and compass
JM119 Navigation and compass
JM444 Torpedo delivery performance
LZ293 Handling at AUW 25,500 lb (11,591 kg)
LZ437 Smoke-handling trials at Porton Down
NE343 Performance with 200 gallon (909 litre) drop-tank

NE352 Windscreen wiper and RP Mk III
NT913 Prototype Beaufighter TT 10
NT921 Under-wing and under-fuselage bomb carriers
NV246 RP accuracy and jettison
NV 451 Modified fin and tailplane
NV535 1,000 lb (453.5 kg) bomb
NV612 Performance with 200 gallon (909 litre) drop-tank and ATDU
Many other aircraft were used for tests at the Experimental Units and
Establishments including Boscombe Down, Farnborough, Gosport and
Defford, some of those aircraft are listed below:
A&AEE/RAE: X7672, X7710, X7821, X7884, X8095, X8204, X8218,
EL170, EL285, EL285, JL949, JL955, LX880, LZ184, NE444, NV290,
NV303, RD388, RD810, RD834
TDU/ATDU: JM207, LX856, LZ411, NE463, NV186, NV316, NV 441,
RD750, NV612, NV290
RRE/TFU: X7562, X7565, X7613, X7618, X7630, X7802, X7813, X7816,
X7826, X7832, X7836, X7840, X7926, X8204, EL156, EL160, EL167,
EL180, EL181, EL182, EL183, RD255, RD326, RD835
ASWD: NV502, NV546, RD389, RD466, RD484
Survivors: **Mk IF** X7688, Skyport Engineering, Biggleswade, UK; **Mk XI**
JM135 (A19-144), being rebuilt with parts from **Mk 21s**, The Fighter
Collection, Duxford, UK; **TF Mk X** RD220, Museum of Flight, East
Fortune, UK; **TF Mk X** RD253, RAF Museum, Hendon, UK; **TT 10** RD867,
Canadian National Aeronautical Collection, Ontario.

Bristol Beaufort IIA (Banwell)

LS129 - 149. *Total*: Eight delivered between August and November 1943.
ML430 - 476, ML489 - 524, ML540 - 586, ML599 - 635, ML649 - 692,
ML705 - 722. *Total*: 242 delivered between November 1943 and April 1944.
Grand total: 250; LS130 and ML556 - 564, and ML565 onwards, were
converted during build to dual-control trainers with turret faired-over. Twelve
of the 250 went to Turkey.
Survivors: Nil.

Hawker Tempest II (Banwell)

MW375 - 423 and MW435. *Total*: 50 delivered between February and
August 1945. Forty of the 50 went to the Royal Indian Air Force (RIAF).
Survivors: MW376 (RIAF HA564) being restored in France; MW401 (RIAF
HA604) stored at Hemswell, UK, and MW404 (RIAF HA557) stored in
Sussex, UK.

APPENDIX 4

Helicopters Built at the Oldmixon Factory

Construction no.	Serial/Registration no.	Remarks/Location Survivors
Bristol Type 171 Sycamore HR 14s for the Royal Air Force		
13385	XG545	
13386	XG546	
13387	XG547	Royal Army Museum, Belgium.
13388	XG548	
13389	XG549	
13242	XJ380	Boscombe Down Aviation Collection, UK.
13244	XJ382	
13390	XJ383	
13391	XJ384	
13392	XJ385	
13404	XJ895	
13405	XJ896	
13406	XJ897	
13408	XJ898	
13409	XJ915	
13410	XJ916	
13412	XJ917	Bristol Aero Collection, Kemble, UK.
13413	XJ918	RAF Museum, Cosford, UK.
13414	XJ919	
13460	XL820	
13415	XL821	
13468	XL822	
13417	XL823	

13438	XL824	Museum of Science and Industry, Manchester, UK.
13471	XL825	
13474	XL826	
13441	XL827	
13444	XL828	
13447	XL829	The Helicopter Museum, Weston-super-Mare, UK.
Total: 29		

Bristol Type 171 Sycamore HR 51s for the Royal Australian Navy

13504	G-18-177/XN449	
13505	G-18-178/XN450	Last Type 171 built. Aviation and Military Museum, Mareeba, Australia.
Total: 3		

Bristol Type 171 Sycamore Mk 52s for the West German Army, Navy and Air Force

13411	G-18-117/AS+321	
13439	G-18-122/AS+322	
13416	G-18-119/AS+323	
13440	G-18-123/AS+324	
13464	AS+325	
13465	AS+326	
13469	AS+327	
13470	AS+328	
13472	AS+329	
13473	AS+330	D-HALC, Focke Museum, Bremen, Germany.
13442	BA+176	Luftwaffe Museum, Berlin, Germany.
13443	BA+177	
13445	BA+178	D-HAHN Motortechnica, Bad Oeynhausen, Germany.
13466	G-18-130, BB+176	Cockpit, Flugausstellung L und P Junior, Hermeskel, Germany.
13467	BB+177	
13476	G-18-149/BB+178	D-HELM, Fahrzeug Museum, Marxzell, Germany.
13477	G-18-150/BD+176	
13482	G-18-155/BD+177	
13483	G-18-156/BP+178	HB-RXA, Flieger Museum, Switzerland.
13463	G-18-147/CA+327	

13475	G-18-148/CA+328	HB-RXB operated as XG544, Altenrhein, Switzerland.
13486	G-18-159/CB+011	
13487	G-18-160/CB+012	
13492	CB+013	
13493	CB+014	D-HFUM, Flugausstellung L und P Junior, Hermeskeil, Germany.
13496	CB+015	
13497	CB+016	
13499	CB+017	
13500	CB+018	
13503	CB+019	LB+105, Luftwaffe Base, Landsberg, Germany.
13488	G-18-161/CC+061	
13489	G-18-162/CC+062	
13490	G-18-163/CC+063	
13491	CC+064	
13494	CC+065	
13495	G-18-168/CC+066	
13498	CC+067	
13501	CC+068	
13502	CC+069	
13461	DA+391	Flugzeug-Oldies, Schwechat, Wien, Austria.
13462	DA+392	
13484	G-18-157/DB+391	
13485	G-18-158/DB+392	
13446	GA+119	D-HEMD, stored Altenrhein, Switzerland.
13459	G-18-132/GA+247	
13458	G-18-131/GB+117	
13478	G-18-151/SC+201	Hubschrauber Museum, Buckeburg, Germany.
13479	G-18-152/SC+202	D-HFUM, stored Altenrhien, Switzerland.
13480	SC+203	
13481	SC+204	Luftwaffe, Ahlhorn, Germany.
Total: 50		
13506	N/A	Components used for spares.
13507	N/A	Components used for Bristol Type 203 Prototype.

Bristol Type 191 (Series 1) for the Royal Navy		
13274	XG354	Modified to Series 2 standard, it becoming Rig No.1 (No cockpit).
13275	XG355	Modified to Series 2 standard, it becoming Rig No.2.
13276	XG356	Rig No.3 used for flying-control trials.
Total: 3		

Bristol Type 192 (Series 2) Belvedere HC I for the Royal Air Force		
13342	XG447	MoA aircraft. F/F 5/7/58. 1st development aircraft.
13343	XG448	F/F 11/4/59. 2nd development aircraft. To pre-production standard. To production standard.
13344	XG449	Initially a strain-gauged non-flying control rig, but when decided to put it into service, was rebuilt. F/F 16 August 1963.
13345	XG450	F/F 16/11/59. 3rd development aircraft. To pre-production standard. To production standard. Suffered from incurable vibration and not delivered.
13346	XG451	F/F 10/7/59. 4th development aircraft. To pre-production standard. To production standard.
13347	XG452	MoA aircraft. F/F -/2/60. 5th development aircraft. To pre-production standard. To production standard. Not delivered. The Helicopter Museum, Weston-super-Mare, UK.
13348	XG453	F/F 21/5/60. 1st pre-production. BTU/66 Squadron. To production standard.
13349	XG454	F/F 18/6/60. 2nd pre-production. To BTU, but crashed at Farnborough during Air Show rehearsal 30/8/61. To production standard for Min Tech. Museum of Science and Industry, Manchester, UK.
13350	XG455	Initially a strain-gauged non-flying test airframe, but when decided to put it into service, a new fuselage built. F/F 10/1/63.
13351	XG456	F/F 18/9/60. 3rd pre-production. BTU/66 Squadron. To production standard.
13352	XG457	F/F 10/2/61. 1st production.
13353	XG458	F/F 15/3/61. 2nd production.
13354	XG459	F/F 23/4/61. 3rd production.
13355	XG460	F/F 5/5/61. 4th production.
13356	XG461	F/F 11/5/61. 5th production.
13357	XG462	F/F 31/8/61. 6th production. Cockpit in The Helicopter Museum, Weston-super-Mare, UK.

13358	XG463	F/F 10/10/61. 7th production.
13359	XG464	F/F 18/10/61. 8th production.
13360	XG465	F/F 16/11/61. 9th production.
13361	XG466	F/F 9/12/61. 10th production.
13362	XG467	F/F 7/1/62. 11th production.
13363	XG468	F/F 24/1/62. 12th production. Modified for Cold Weather Trials in Canada. De-modified.
13364	XG473	F/F 21/2/62. 13th production.
13365	XG474	F/F 2/3/62. 14th production. RAF Museum, Hendon, UK.
13366	XG475	F/F 7/5/62. 15th production.
13367	XG476	F/F 18/6/62. 16th production.
Total: 26		

APPENDIX 5

Bibliography/Sources/Credits

ABC Civil Aircraft Markings Taylor J., Ian Allan

Achilles School of Flying — Official Handbook

Action Stations 5. Military Airfields of the South-West Ashworth C. and Stephens P.

Adolf Hitler's Holiday Snaps Clarke N., N. Clarke Publications

Aeromilitaria & Archive Air-Britain

Aeronautical Engineering Beaumont R., Odhams Press

Aeroplane Monthly IPC Business Press

Aero Modeller Model Aeronautical Press

A History of British Rotorcraft 1866 — 1966 Brie R., Westland Helicopters

Aircraft Illustrated Ian Allan

Air Pictorial Air League, Seymour Press

A Span of Wings Russell Sir A., Airlife

As We Were — Air Cadet Gliding Schools from 1939 — 1988 Headquarters Air Cadets

Atlantic Bridge Ministry of Information, HMSO

Aviation News Hall A.

Aviation in Birmingham Negus G. and Staddon T., Midland Counties

Avro Manchester Kirby R., Midland Counties

Bristol Beaufighter Bingham V., Airlife

Beaufighter Bowyer C., William Kimber

Beaufighter at War Bowyer Chaz, Ian Allan

Beaufort Special Robertson B., Ian Allan

Birnbeck Pier Terrell S., North Somerset Museum Services

BMFA News British Model Flying Association

Brean Down Fort van der Bijl, N., BEM Hawk Editions

Bristol Aero Collection Team Newsletters

Bristol Aircraft Since 1910 Barnes C., Putnam

Bristol Beaufighter Scutts J., Crowood Aviation

Bristol Review Bristol Aeroplane Company

British Aviation The Pioneer Years 1903 — 1914 Penrose H., Putnam
British Aviation Widening Horizons 1930 — 1934 Penrose H., RAF Museum
British Civil Aircraft Jackson A., Putnam
British Civil Aircraft Registers 1919 — 1999 Austin M. with Evans K. & Fillmore M.
Cambrian — History of Cambrian Airways Staddon T., Airline
Canberra The Operational Record Jackson R., Airlife
Cardiff Airfields Jones I., Aureus
Challenge in the Air-Story of the ATC Bryan Philpott, Model & Allied Publications
Civil Defence No.3 (Weston-super-Mare) Area Bingham-Hall D., Lawrence
Coastal Support and Special Squadrons of the RAF and their Aircraft Rawlings J., Janes
Cornwall Aviation Company Chapman E., Glasney Press
De Havilland Mosquito Smith D., Crash Log Midland Counties
Dorset Flight Legg R., Dorset Publishing
Diary of Events in the UK with the USAAF from mid-1942 Cleland B., Unpublished
Flight Dorset House
Flight International IPC Transport Press
Flight Path Masefield Sir P. and Gunston B., Airlife
Fly Me I'm Freddie Eglin R. and Ritchie B., Futura
Fly Past Key Publishing
Flying Training and Support Units since 1912 Sturtivant R. with Hamlin J., Air-Britain
Front Line Ministry of Information, HMSO
Gloster Javelin Allward M., Ian Allan
Handley Page Victor Brookes A., Ian Allan
High Calling Straight Aviation Training Ltd
Intercom British European Airways
Jane's All the Worlds Aircraft Janes
Lest Banwell Forgets Rice, Lynette, Banwell Society of Archaeology
Luftwaffe Encore Wakefield K., William Kimber
Man Power Ministry of Information, HMSO
Men of the Battle of Britain Wynn K. G., Gliddon Books
Minutes of the Bristol Aeroplane Company Ltd Weston Aircraft Factory Management Committee 1939 — 1945 & 1950 — 1954 BAC
Over & Out — History of RAF Locking Tillbrook Squadron Leader R., Forces & Corporate
RAF Flying Training & Support Units Since 1912 Sturtivant R. with Hamlin J., Air-Britain
Recollections of an Airman Strange L., J. Hamilton
Roof Over Britain Ministry of Information,HMSO
Royal Air Force Bomber Command Losses of the Second World War Chorley

W., Alden Press

Royal Air Force 1939 — 45 Vol. 1 The Fight At Odds Richards D., HMSO

Royal Air Force Register Series Hamlin J., Air-Britain

Sent Flying Pegg B., Macdonald

Shadow to Shadow-History of the BAC Banwell Factory & BAJ 1941 — 1991 BAJ Coatings

Slide Rule Shute Nevil, Pan

Somerset at War 1939 — 1945 Mac Hawkins, Dovecote Press

Somerset v Hitler Brown D., Countryside Books

Somewhere in the West Country Wakefield K., Crecy

South West Wings Sutton M., ALD

Straightaway Review for 1938 Straight Corporation

Straight Up The Helicopter Museum

Target Filton Wakefield K., Redcliffe

Teignmouth's Haldon Aerodrome Saunders K., Teignmouth Museum and Historic Society

The Aeroplane Temple Press

The Aeroplane Spotter Temple Press

The Anson File Sturtivant R., Air-Britain

The Beaufort, Beaufighter & Mosquito in Australian Service Wilson S., Aerospace Publications

The Bombing of Weston-super-Mare 1940 — 1944 Penny J.

The de Havilland Dragon/Rapide Family Hamlin J., Air-Britain

The Elmhirsts of Dartington Young M., Dartington Hall Press

The Father of British Airships Mc Kinty A., William Kimber

The Hampden File Moyale H., Air-Britain

The Hornet File Cooper L., Air-Britain

The Lonely Sea and the Sky Chichester F., Readers Union/Hodder & Stoughton

The Luftwaffe over the Bristol area 1940 — 1944 Fishponds Local History Society

The Mighty Eighth Freeman R., Macdonald

The Oxford, Consul & Envoy File Hamlin J., Air-Britain

The Queen's Flight Burns M., Blandford Press

The Story of RAF Lulsgate Bottom James I., Redcliffe

The Typhoon Story Thomas C. & Shores C., Arms & Armour Press

The Westonian County School for Boys, Weston-super-Mare

Those Fabulous Flying Years Cruddas C., Air-Britain

UK Flight Testing Accidents 1940 — '71 Webb D., Air-Britain

Venom Watkins D., Sutton

Wartime Britain 1939 — 1945 Gardiner J., Review

West at War Belsey J.and Reid H., Redcliffe

Westland Group News Westland

Weston Airport Log April 1954 — September 1955

Weston Clevedon & Portishead Railway Maggs C., Oakwood Press
Weston-super-Mare Tramways Maggs C., Oakwood Press
Weston Mercury & Somersetshire Herald/Weston & Somerset Mercury
Weston Gazette & Somerset Advertiser
Western Airways the West Country Airline Simons G., Redcliffe
Weston at War 1939 — 1945 Woodspring Museum
Woman Pilot Moggridge J., Pan
Wrecks & Relics Ellis K., Midland Publishing
Yer tiz... Bournville Memories Galloway H.

The authors are indebted to: Sarah Bowen of Weston Library, Nick Goff of North Somerset Museum, Simon Angear of the *Weston & Somerset Mercury*, Weston Town Council, John Baker of the British Motor Heritage Trust, John Crockford-Hawley, D. S. Brown, John Bright, Derek Chapman, Agusta Westland, Oliver Dearden and John Battersby of the Bristol Aero Collection, Richard Riding who founded *Aeroplane Monthly,* and Nick Stroud the Deputy Editor of what is now *Aeroplane,* Alan Baxter of the Rolls-Royce Heritage Trust, Soph Moeng of Midsummer Books, Ian Tasker of Tasker Printers, Dean Harvey and Danny Hodgetts of Scootopia, Nick Grant of Ian Allan, and Chris Small of Airbus. The following people, some of whom are no longer with us, also provided valuable help with this book: Lew Lisle, Steve Stevenson, Alan Wilks, Ron Acock, Phillip Robinson, T. F. Allen, G. R. Manning, Ernie Gunton, Frank Mudge, Bob and Bill Cooke, Derek and Raymond 'Tommy' Stabbins, Mrs Archer, Mrs Passmore, Rod Salchwell, Bernard Miers, Alec Kingsmill, John Hopworth, Betty Abraham, Grace Hawkins, Tony Shallish, Maurice Pitman, Ron Waite, John Down, Ray Teague, Alfie Smith, Norman Perriman, Cecil Dudley, Brian and Norman House, John Westlake, Daryl and Maurice Mansbridge, Fern and Tony Britton, Mike Davis, Ray Caple, Brian Patch, Colin Parish, Simon White, Ken Crane, Rae Vallan, Ben Brooks, Ian Davis, Pete Noyle, Chris Hallewell, Lee Mills, Harald Penrose, Sox Hosegood, Peter Wilson, Don Farquharson, Bob Smith, Jerry Tracey, Peter Garrod, Francis Boreham, Bill Yeadon, Reg Cook, John Jupe, Reg Austin, Paul Whitney, Keith Pardoe, Idris Gane, Roy Rice, Christopher Butt, Mike May, Stan Terrell, Derek Croker, Clive Cooper, Miss P. Press, Peter Adams, Sandy Sproule, Dave Cuff, Gordon Libby, Fred Ballam, Tony Ives, Tom Kennedy, W. F. Smart, Ken R. Turner, W. Maulds, Dan Godden, Steve D. Willis, Derek King, Mick Burrow, J. N. Pratlett, P. Warrilow, John and Jill Bailey, Laurie Barr, Ron Moulton, Philip Jarrett, John Greenland, Pat Dobbs, Ron Regan, Pat and John Stride, Geoff Bell, Chris Unitt, Kenneth Wakefield, Keith Saunders, Bob Kirby, Mac Hawkins, John Strickland, John Chapman, John and Zoe Wall, Mrs Chapman and Ruth Mackintosh. We are also especially indebted to: Elfan ap Rees, Peter Turner, Brian Kick and Stephen Parsons for their assistance in editing those areas where their expertise is well known (i.e. The Helicopter Museum/Helicopters in general; Achilles School of Flying/Bristol Air Taxis; Western Airways/Barber; Bristol Aerojet respectively).

The tattered remains of Weston Airport's last windsock lift in a light south-westerly breeze (R. Dudley)